Isobel Charman graduated from Bristol University in 2003 with a first-class degree and the George Hare Leonard prize in history. Since then she has worked in factual TV production in Berlin, Cornwall and London. She specialises in historical subjects, and has worked as a researcher, producer and director on award-winning films for TV and cinema. She did all the original research for *The Great War: The People's Story* with support from the historians of Imperial War Museums, and from numerous librarians, archivists and families up and down the country. She also produced the series. *The Great War* is her first book.

Praise for *The Great War*

'Deeply moving, fascinating and powerful.'

Sunday Mirror

'A handful of people dominate this wonderful book. They are not special or famous but their stories will haunt you for a very long time ... Charman's great achievement is to let the people who lived through all this speak for themselves. You will be torn between admiration, pity and anger.'

Herald

'This tome lets those who lived through these terrible times tell you how it *really* was in their own words. From the gung-ho to the fearful, the petty to the practical, the sorrows and the shocks, the pitiful, the heroic, the angry ... they put it all down on paper in a way that lets you gauge whether *you* could have lived through the terror – and be in awe of those who did.'

Sunday Sport

'This is a deeply sobering, essential read.'

Bookbag

The Great War

A Nation's Story

ISOBEL CHARMAN

arrow books

1 3 5 7 9 10 8 6 4 2

Arrow Books
20 Vauxhall Bridge Road
London SW1V 2SA

Arrow Books is part of the Penguin Random House group of companies
whose addresses can be found at global.penguinrandomhouse.com.

Penguin
Random House
UK

First published by Random House Books in 2014
First published in paperback by Arrow Books in 2015

www.randomhouse.co.uk

A CIP catalogue record for this book is available from the British Library.

ISBN 9780099591252

Typeset by Palimpsest Book Production Limited,
Falkirk, Stirlingshire
Printed and bound by CPI Group (UK) Ltd, Croydon, CR0 4YY

Penguin Random House is committed to a sustainable future for our business, our readers
and our planet. This book is made from Forest Stewardship Council® certified paper.

MIX
Paper from
responsible sources
FSC
www.fsc.org
FSC® C018179

For Reg, Alan, Dorothy, Helen, Kate, Duff, Diana,
Andrew, Hallie, James, Will, Emily, Arthur, and Ted:
I hope you would have approved.

Contents

TOTAL WAR

DARKEST DAYS

THE LAST PUSH

Acknowledgements

Firstly I want to thank all those who have allowed me the huge privilege of telling their loved ones' stories: Pamela and Peter Campbell, Vivien Cockcroft, Alan and Judy Lloyd, Jenifer Glynn, Colin Franklin, Elizabeth Crawford, John Julius Norwich, Colin and Helen Oberlin-Harris, Alison Mackenzie, Andrew Hamilton, Richard and David Walters, Robert Butlin, Morag Miller, Roy Laycock, Joanna Vernon and Lynne Harrison. I could not have done this without your support, help and hospitality and it has been a pleasure to get to know many of you.

This book would obviously never have happened if it hadn't been for the TV series, and for that I must thank its creators Paul Copeland and Ollie Tait: collaborators and friends. Thanks for pushing for me to write this, and to Paul for your good company and support along the way. Thanks to Clare Hix and Ziyaad Desai for your brilliant research skills, sense of humour and patience. Thanks to Steve Standen for freezing on the Somme with me, and to Rebecca Keating and everyone else who made *The People's Story* such fun to work on and gave me such enthusiasm for carrying on.

Thanks to Nigel Steel, Anthony Richards, Victoria Kingston and Bryn Hammond of the Imperial War Museum for introducing me to Alan and Dorothy, James, Will and Emily, and Ted. Thanks to the staff of the department of documents for putting up with me for so long. Thanks too to the Women's Library, the Liddle Collection, the British Library and all the other archives and libraries that I spent so many wonderful weeks in. It is amazing that such resources exist.

Thanks to Shirley Patton at ITV Publishing and to Nigel Wilcockson at Random House for making this happen. And to my editor Harry

Scoble, for being so supportive of me on my first foray into the publishing world – and for dealing with a hugely long manuscript with such sympathy and skill.

Last but by no means least my love and gratitude are due, as ever, to the Charmans, Christies and Bennetts. Thank you for your unfailing interest, support and encouragement, spare rooms and seafood platters.

Introduction

The accounts featured in this book were uncovered during the many months of research I did for the TV series. In archives, libraries and living rooms up and down the country I read hundreds of letters and diaries written by ordinary Britons during the extraordinary years of the First World War. Each was remarkable in its own way, but inevitably and unfortunately we could only include a tiny selection. These accounts were chosen for a very simple reason: between them, we believe they give the fullest account of the experience of these years, told in the most engaging way.

I have lived with Reg, Alan, Dorothy, Helen, Kate, Duff, Diana, Andrew, Hallie, James, Will, Emily, Arthur, and Ted for almost two years now, and I admire each and every one of them. I cannot imagine what I would have done in any of their shoes. I felt an enormous responsibility to represent them faithfully and have tried my very best to do so. Wherever possible their journeys are based on the records that they themselves left behind, and I have kept any supposition beyond that to a bare minimum.

I have sometimes combined extracts from letters or edited them down, and occasionally I have corrected spellings and grammar to make extracts easier to read. But I have tried as far as possible to leave these people to tell their own remarkable stories in their own words, and to allow the reader the privilege of sharing their feelings, fears and adventures, one hundred years later.

– Isobel Charman, 2014

THE CALL TO ARMS

I

THE OLD ORDER

Spring and Summer 1914

They know we have got to have 'Votes' – and to think they have got us to
this state. Oh what a fuss to cause – and in a so called civilized country!
                                                    Kate Parry Frye's diary, May 1914

The year 1914 began pretty miserably for Britain, certainly in terms of
the weather. Floods ravaged East Anglia, gales battered Cornwall and
Wales, and London experienced the wettest March on record.[1] But as
that month drew to a close, things started to look up. The sun came
out; and Britons, as they always do, dared to hope that they might be
in for a nice summer.

On the last Saturday in March, the well-to-do of Edwardian society
gathered along the banks of the River Thames for the first society
sporting event of the season: the University Boat Race. The press had
been hyping it up for weeks. The Oxford team, which had generally
been considered the poorer, had been performing exceptionally well
in training and suddenly the stage seemed set for a great contest.[2]
Crowds flooded in to West London to witness the spectacle. Ladies
donned hats laden with flowers and feathers; gentlemen wore frock
coats and silk hats, the more daring also sporting brightly coloured
gloves. Everyone marvelled at their luck that the day had turned out
so fine.

One young man who had not made the pilgrimage to the riverside
that year was 25-year-old **Alan Lloyd**. A former Cambridge student,
he was a devoted follower of rowing in general and the Boat Race in
particular, and was a member of the exclusive Leander Club at Henley.
He'd rowed for Trinity College during his time there, though – much
to his annoyance – he hadn't himself secured the privilege of rowing

for the University.[3] But this year Alan had other things on his mind: he was in love.

A handsome, confident man, who stood six foot three inches tall, Alan was every bit the dashing Edwardian gentleman – if a somewhat unconventional one.[4] The son of a Quaker businessman of the Lloyds banking family, he'd lived a privileged life centred on boarding school, Cambridge University and his family home in Birmingham with its team of servants.[5] However, since graduating, he'd sought to experience more of the world than the elite English bubble in which he'd grown up. He had set off in search of adventure, travelling around South America and Southern Africa before buying some land in Nyasaland (now Malawi). Having studied agriculture and economics at Cambridge, he felt he had a reasonable grasp of how to manage such an estate – his plan was to grow cotton and, so he bragged, turn himself into 'a cotton king'.[6]

But these plans were sent awry by **Dorothy Hewetson**, the beautiful woman from Boston Spa with whom Alan had fallen in love. She was tall with blue eyes and golden hair; she and Alan made a handsome couple. The two had courted for some years and Dorothy had waited as Alan explored the world. On his return from Africa in January 1914, they had decided to marry. But her parents disapproved of what they saw as his restlessness and unreliability, and months of wrangling followed. Alan's dreams of disappearing to Africa were put on ice, while he tried to prove to his prospective in-laws that he would make a good and dependable husband. By March 1914, he was looking for a farm in Britain where he and Dorothy would be able to begin married life in a more conventional manner than in the heat of an African plain.[7]

On the weekend of the Boat Race, Alan was driving his motorcar (nicknamed Belinda) along the Welsh borders, viewing farms and houses for sale. Stopping off at inns along the way, he would sit down at the bar in the evenings with a drink at hand to write to his beloved and tell her (and by extension her parents) of his endeavours to secure their future. On the eve of the University Boat Race, Alan wrote to 'his little belovedest' from the Star Inn, Worcester. The letter was delivered to Dorothy at home in Yorkshire on the sunny Saturday of the race itself:

My little belovedest, I do wish I had you here now.

I have got here after touring half over West of England in Belinda, who has gone splendidly. I found one beautiful old house near Melksham in Wiltshire, oak-panelled throughout but very near Melksham which has factories, and I will not live within sight of a factory!

I'd have liked to see the boat race but there's something – some little tiny darling of a something, which I want to see more than a million boat races and so I shall come to Brum to get it or take it with me. You darlingest of all girls, how I long to see you. Till tomorrow.

Your ownest

Allie[8]

That day, Alan made the drive from Worcester back to his family home in Edgbaston, a suburb of Birmingham. Dorothy, on getting word from her 'Allie', was soon Birmingham-bound too, on a steam train from Boston Spa. As the two lovers travelled towards each other across the English countryside, in London the race had started. Cheering voices rippled upriver as the two teams set off. Cambridge had something to prove: Oxford had won the previous five years running. And prove it they did – they won by four and a half lengths, in what was later described as 'one of the most uninteresting races of the series'.[9]

While Alan had not missed an exciting contest, he certainly missed out on the raucous celebrations of the long-awaited Cambridge victory. One young gentleman was arrested for riding on the roofs of motorcars in Piccadilly – his escapades only halted by a lady passenger pushing him off the footboard as he tried to clamber up on top of the cab she was riding in.[10]

Oxford would have to wait to take their revenge. The following year, for the first time in its history, the University Boat Race would not take place.

Thirty miles from the finishing line, **Reg Evans** spent that Saturday at work in the carpentry workshop of Kent's Brush Factory in Hemel Hempstead. A year older than Alan at twenty-six, but almost a foot shorter, Reg was a wood-borer who had been apprenticed to Kent's almost a decade earlier. A slight, energetic and hard-working man, he was popular at the company, and was settled in the town, living with his mother in her guesthouse just off the High Street.

Reg's life hadn't always been so straightforward. Two weeks before his birth in 1888, his father, a clerk working at an engineering firm in Southwark, had died. The family story was that he was trampled to

Reg Evans in the workshop at Kent's Brush Factory.

death in a riot. Reg's mum, **Frances Evans**, a widow at thirty-five with four children to look after, was unable to cope with a new baby as well, and Reginald was put into the care of an orphanage. For fifteen years he was educated at Spurgeon's Infant Asylum in Wanstead, Essex. Reg and his family remained in contact, and when he secured a five-year apprenticeship at Kent's Brush Factory in 1905, he was finally reunited with them.[11]

Reg probably wasn't all that interested in the Boat Race – as a working-class boy it's unlikely he'd had the chance to get into rowing himself, which was a gentleman's sport. He had, however, received a rigorous, traditional Victorian education through the orphanage, and his interests as a youngster had been focused on the science and history he'd been taught there. He kept up his rather serious hobbies, and as a young man he'd joined both the Junior Conservative Association and the Junior Imperial and Constitutional League in Hemel Hempstead, and held committee positions in each of them.

Unlike Alan Lloyd, Reg had never seen anything of the British Empire. In fact, he had never left England, and probably never expected to. But in the cold classrooms of the Infant Asylum he had learnt all about the Empire on which the sun never set. It meant something to Reg, as it meant something to Alan – both had been born into the age when British imperialism was at its peak. Recent years had shaken the foundations of the British establishment: the early 1910s were a turbulent time, with declining real wages adding to a mounting sense of dissatisfaction amongst the working class. The young Labour Party was finding its voice; the trade-union movement was growing; political tensions ran high. Reg Evans, though a working man himself, did not approve of these new forces rocking the British boat.

Reg passed his working days peacefully in an old-fashioned, family-run factory, overseen by the paternalistic Mr Kent. Strikes were not something he'd experienced first-hand. But being a highly literate young man, he would have read of the industrial unrest that had gathered steam from 1910 onwards: the summer of near-revolution in Liverpool in 1911, the miners' strike of 1912, the Dublin lock-out in 1913. Such things worried him. Perhaps he connected radicalism with the tragedy of his father's death, or perhaps he simply ascribed to the popular nationalism and conservatism pedalled by the elite.

In 1912, Reg had even been moved to pen a patriotic call to arms. He was proud to see it published in the West Herts Conservative and Unionist Association newsletter that April:

> *The country is writhing in agonised turmoil*
> *Black clouds are gathering, the storm mutters near,*
> *Downhill to destruction our Empire is gliding*
> *Where is the man who will stop her career?*
> *Midst socialist curses and radical weeping*
> *We'll handle with firmness the great ship of state;*
> *Lay hold of her rudder – whilst elders are sleeping*
> *We'll guide her to safety before it's too late.*[12]

Industrial unrest was one cause for concern for Reg and his fellow conservatives; Ireland was another. Ireland had been united with Britain for over a century, but now there was renewed pressure for Home Rule, and this was a cause of fierce political tension. Conservatives like Reg saw an independent Ireland as a huge blow to the stability of the Empire – and the enthusiastic young patriot wasn't going to let it happen without a fight. At the beginning of April 1914, the weekend following the Boat Race, Reg got up at the crack of dawn, put on his best Sunday suit and headed out down the High Street bound for the station.

A massive rally had been organised in Hyde Park by the British

League for the Support of Ulster and the Union, in response to the
latest proposals of the Liberal Government for Home Rule. Hundreds
of thousands of people gathered in the park, waiting eagerly for the
speakers who would prophesy terrible danger to Britain. Reg had led
a delegation of men from Hemel Hempstead, and when the leading
unionist of the day, Edward Carson, took to the stage, they strained
with the rest to hear the impassioned sermon floating over the jostling
crowds.

Suddenly, a commotion broke out near the front. A band of women
was trying to drown out the speaker, shouting and clamouring. One
woman was raised on another's shoulders and was yelling at the top of
her voice. These intruders were quickly pulled away by the police, but
the scene added fuel to the fears of all those assembled. The preceding
years had witnessed the blossoming of many new political movements
which were now tugging at the fabric of established British life, and
nowhere was this more dramatically apparent than in the giddying
escalation of the campaign by the 'suffragettes'. Only a few weeks earlier,
Mary Richardson had taken a cleaver to one of the most famous paintings on the walls of the National Gallery, a Velázquez, in order to draw
attention to the cause of 'votes for women'.[13]

The unionist leader Sir Edward Carson addressing a rally in Hyde Park, London.

The following month, on Thursday 21 May, the suffragettes organised a mass rally of their own. After repeated failed attempts to win women the right to vote through Parliament, the Women's Social and Political Union yet again turned to more direct action. This time their leader, Emmeline Pankhurst, led a delegation to the gates of Buckingham Palace to demand an audience with King George V. Two hundred women made their way up the Mall. Some were clothed in the elegant attire of the upper class, some in simple working dresses; many were secretly armed with means of sabotage, from coloured paints to scissors and clubs. Over a thousand police officers awaited them.[14]

Kate Parry Frye was amongst the hundreds of spectators who had massed outside the palace that day. Kate was depressed, and tired. Aged 32 and unmarried, life had become a lot harder for her of late. Her father was a self-made man, a grocer who'd worked his way up to owning a chain of shops in London. In her youth Kate had become accustomed if not to luxury, then certainly to comfort. But the business had recently gone bankrupt and her family had plummeted back down the social ladder. For the extrovert Kate, a failed actress and aspiring writer, the drudgery of poverty was proving hard to swallow.

For the past few years, Kate had worked as a paid organiser for a small suffrage organisation, The New Constitutional Society for Women's Suffrage. The society used more conventional methods than slashing paintings and fighting police officers to publicise the cause of votes for women. Kate's job mainly involved giving out leaflets and arranging meetings. Kate had been glad of an independent income but, more than that, she had relished the controversy of her role. Until recently she had continued to live at the family home when she wasn't travelling for work. However, when they were forced to give up their Buckinghamshire house, Kate had taken dingy rented rooms in Pimlico, which was then rather down at heel. Suddenly her job was a necessity rather than a luxury.

Kate wasn't married, but she did have a long-term boyfriend, **John Collins**, an actor whom she'd met when they were in a theatre company together. They'd been a couple for over a decade, and unofficially engaged for years, but Kate had always refused to marry him as she felt he didn't have the means to keep her in the manner she thought appropriate. She also liked having her independence and, despite the recent reduction in her circumstances, she still was not prepared to become a wife. This didn't seem to dampen John's ardour for her, as she later confided to her diary,

with typical immodesty: 'John is absolutely devoted as ever – seems to
care for nothing or nobody but me – it's extraordinary and has now been
going on eleven years with undiminished fervour. Poor dear, I wish I
could make him happy.'[15]

As someone used to the more sedate side of suffrage campaigning,
Kate was both shocked and a little elated by the violent conflict that
she witnessed that morning when the suffragettes and the police collided
at the palace gates:

> It was simply awful – oh! Those poor pathetic women – dresses half
> torn off – hair down, hats off, covered in mud. And some dragged away
> looking in the greatest agony. But the wonderful courage of it all. One
> man led away – collar torn off – face streaming with blood – he had
> gone to protect them. Fancy not arresting them until they got to that
> state. It is the most futile precaution because they know we have got to
> have 'Votes' – and to think they have got us to this state – some women
> thinking it necessary and right to do the most awful burnings etc. in
> order to bring the question forward. [16]

Over sixty women were arrested that afternoon, though this was nothing
new in the context of the militant suffrage campaign that had shocked
Edwardian society for years.[17] The established model of femininity
prescribed that women should be wives and mothers, and that their
domain ought to be the comfort and simplicity of the home. The violent
political struggles of the WSPU were, therefore, nothing short of
heretical, even if they were increasingly common.

Kate did not engage in street battles – not that day or ever – but
she was nonetheless subverting the norms of Edwardian society by
remaining independent and childless, by choice. She stood in the crowd
watching as protestors cut police horse bridles and officers dragged
women down by their skirts as they clambered up the palace railings.
This was to be the final major entry in the history of the militant
suffrage campaign.

Someone who knew all about the conventional Edwardian model of
femininity was the writer **Hallie Miles**. The wife of a famous former
Olympian, Eustace Miles, she had made a living preaching the virtues
of traditional womanhood to her readers.

The leader of the Women's Suffragette movement, Mrs Emmeline Pankhurst, is arrested outside Buckingham Palace, London, 21 May 1914.

Hallie had been born Harriet Killick, the youngest daughter of a country vicar. As a girl she was denied formal education and was destined, like so many middle-class women of her generation, for a life of comfortable obscurity. However, after the death of her father, she started writing – strange little books and articles about life's emotions and aesthetics, inspired by the work of Eustace Miles, a Real Tennis champion who had transformed himself into a health guru and pioneer of vegetarianism. Eventually the two had met, and when Hallie was in her early thirties they were married. The local paper celebrated it as 'a vegetarian romance'.[18]

In summer 1914, Hallie was forty. She and Eustace lived in a smart flat in central London, and, as was the norm, their servants lived with them: a housekeeper, Charlotte, and a general servant, Joanna.[19] One can presume the flat was immaculately decorated – Hallie had written in her first bestseller, *Life's Orchestra*, that 'every house is a mirror, or a photograph, of the builder, and of those who live in it. Therefore let our houses and "home scenery" be worthy reflections of those who dwell within.'[20] Sitting at her bureau, working on her latest tome,

Hallie herself was no doubt immaculately turned out in the fashion of the day – a floor-length dress with an unforgiving corset underneath to achieve a slim silhouette. Her own advice demanded that women were 'restful to look at, that our style is unobtrusive and in good taste, and that we bring a sense of rest and harmony to those who look upon us.'

Hallie had managed to forge quite a name for herself with her advice on relationships, lifestyle, home decor and household management. Her most recent success had been *The Ideal Home*, published a few years earlier. It was achingly traditional – Kate Parry Frye would have been appalled:

> Most women could write at least one good book on home, for it would call out their individuality as no other topic could. On other topics perhaps we tend to be unbalanced or neurotic; for instance, when we discuss sex, or the suffrage question.
>
> There is no doubt that woman will eventually lead a more outside and active public life, but at present it is not all women who are ready for the public life that a man now lives; no woman is ready for the outside work of the world until she has first been through the inside work of the home: that work which so many modern writers call 'domestic drudgery'. I have myself been through the inner workings of family home life and I say with all my heart 'Blessed be drudgery'.[21]

Paradoxically, Hallie was in reality a pioneering woman. It's true that she made money from espousing the virtues of a womanhood limited to the world of servants and soft furnishings. Yet her own life contravened what she preached: she was a very public figure; and she was a partner with her husband in a very modern business. The Eustace Miles Restaurant, which they had set up together, was London's premier vegetarian restaurant, situated in the heart of the West End. It also served as a shop, selling Eustace's own brand of health-food products, such as 'Emprote' (an early protein supplement) and his monthly magazine, *Healthward Ho!* – and functioned as the base for courses on fitness and vegetarian cookery.[22]

Vegetarianism, then known as 'food reform', was – in contrast to Hallie's writings – fantastically *avant-garde*. Shunning the usual decadence of Edwardian society (endless courses of heavy, rich foods were the norm for anyone who could afford them), it was associated with the new political causes gathering pace in Britain, from socialism to women's suffrage. In fact, the Eustace Miles Restaurant was a favourite haunt of the suffragettes, and Kate Parry Frye also went there on occasion.

On the morning of the Buckingham Palace protest, it is entirely possible that some of the women destined to end up in Holloway Prison later that day made their way along the Strand and up to Chandos Place. At number 40, they might have stopped briefly to look at the day's menu in a glass case – 'egg and mushroom fillets and duxelles sauce' or 'hazelnut sausages', perhaps – and passed through the door into the buzz of the Eustace Miles Restaurant. [23]

Spring rolled into summer and **Alan Lloyd**'s mood was sunny. In the middle of June, his friends were at Royal Ascot, another major event in the society calendar, but Allie had once again forgone its pleasures to continue house-hunting. He wrote to his bride to be, 'Dodums', as he called her, with good news – he'd found the perfect home for them, with not a factory in sight:

> I've found a topping little farm near Wiveliscombe in Somerset, 14 miles west of Taunton. Ripping old house formerly Manor House with grand old oak staircase. About 1670 the house. 3 reception rooms and 6 or 7 good bedrooms. Grand views in priceless country, hills and dales and woods. Awfully sporting district. Possession I think could be had fairly soon. It is really a spiffing spot, best I've seen yet, 550 feet up get good land, no heather grouse or bracken! The house we could make spiffing for Dodums and Allie. I'm really keen about it, I'm sure you'd love it beloved. [24]

Alan had also been busy finalising their wedding plans, having won over her parents with his efforts at long last. 'I have written to your mama to fix the wedding glide for Sept 1st. So don't forget to be there you little beloved, I believe you'll look forward to it!' [25] Everything was set. Alan could afford to relax a little, so in mid-July he went on a cricket tour with the Old Leightonians, his old school team, as he had done for the past few summers.

*

On Saturday 18 July, **Reg Evans** was also at a cricket match. He was at Kent and Co's summer 'beanfeast'. Like many factory bosses at the time, Mr Kent treated his employees to an annual day out. In previous years, Reg and his fellow workers had gone to Southend-on-Sea and Brighton; this year they travelled to Windsor. The weather was warm though a little unsettled, but this was the highlight of the workers' year and, rain or shine, spirits could not be dampened.

In Windsor, an extravagant lunch at The White Hart Hotel awaited the workers; the finest meal most of them would eat all year: consommé aux pâtes d'Italie, boiled turbot with hollandaise, roast mutton and mint sauce, fruit tarts and wine jellies. All washed down with an abundance of wine and beer – a necessity, given the long list of toasts that had to be made. After lunch, the men decamped to the local cricket ground to watch the company's best players take each other on before tea. Reg Evans wasn't amongst the players, but no doubt he would have cheered on his boss and colleagues with his characteristic enthusiasm, aided by a pint or two.

Kate Parry Frye's July was not quite so much fun. She was still adjusting to the much-reduced circumstances she found herself in, and each time she returned to the rundown house on Claverton Street where she was staying, she couldn't quite believe where she'd ended up: 'Oh what a dismal room. How can one bear this sort of thing?'[26]

It didn't help that she was working very hard that summer, at the height of the suffrage campaign. A typical day included hours of leaf-leting and meetings, well into the evening. However, her load was partially lightened by the ever-faithful John, who would often accompany her on her rounds:

[With John] to Office for the Banners and Leaflets. By bus to Hammersmith and train to Hounslow, where we got rid of the rest of the thousand handbills. To Broadway at 7.15 and the Lorry arrived at 7.30 and we decorated it, getting an enormous crowd of children round. Then the speakers arrived. We had a huge crowd, and ours was the first open-air meeting ever held in Hounslow. The people were a bit trouble-some at first but came round wonderfully. We had a little passing trouble with the trumpets and a gramophone but I managed to quell it and we really had a magnificent meeting.[27]

Kate also had a short summer break to look forward to. On 23 July, she met with her colleagues for their last meeting before the bank holiday. Afterwards she treated herself to lunch in Harrods. As she travelled up to the café on what had been the country's first-ever escalator, Reg Evans was at his workbench in Kent's factory, where the buzz of the weekend's outing was still in the air; Alan was in Yorkshire on his cricket tour; and Hallie was busy with the lunchtime rush in her restaurant.

Up and down the country, Britons were huddled over ledgers in dingy offices; playing croquet on perfect lawns; doing their mistress's washing; out in the fields making hay. They had their minds on many things. But the vast majority did not give a moment's thought to the events unfolding on the Continent that day.

Three weeks earlier, the Archduke Franz Ferdinand, heir to the Austro-Hungarian throne, had been assassinated in Sarajevo by Serbian nationalists, angry at Austro-Hungary's annexation of Bosnia in 1908. The Austro-Hungarian government had taken its time to devise its response, in consultation with its German allies. But at 6 p.m. that day, 23 July 1914, an ultimatum was delivered to the Serbian foreign ministry. Austro-Hungary had long been looking for an excuse to strike at Serbia, and, knowing that they had German support, the ultimatum was designed to be near impossible to comply with. The countdown to war had begun.

But for now, the bank holiday weekend was approaching, and everyone was so looking forward to it.

2

BANK HOLIDAY WEEKEND

30 July–3 August 1914

There seems nothing wrong (outwardly) with the world in general, yet the air is full of whispers and coming trouble.

Hallie Miles's diary, 1 August 1914

It was the last week of July, 1914. Lady's maids in houses across the country were packing trunks with their mistresses' silk parasols, whilst outside peak-capped chauffeurs readied their masters' cars for the holiday excursions. In the cities, working men looked forward to an annual day trip to the coast, and imagined the boisterous variety shows they'd enjoy with wives and girlfriends. Children in quiet schoolrooms and deafening mills alike fidgeted with excitement at the thought of Punch and Judy tents and ice-cream carts on the promenade.

On the other side of the Channel, a chain of events that would claim sixteen million lives had already been set in motion. Archduke Franz Ferdinand, heir to the Austro-Hungarian throne, had been dead almost a month. As Britons prepared for their seaside exodus, in Sarajevo, the Serbian Foreign Ministry – despairing over the aggressive Austro-Hungarian ultimatum – had asked their Russian allies for support.

But for most Britons the weather was of greater immediate concern; it was refusing, as ever, to cooperate with their plans. From Blackpool to Brighton, Great Yarmouth to Llandudno, the final days of July were miserable. Rain and wind buffeted the piers and promenades awaiting the holidaymakers. Discussions about the weather dominated parlours, teashops and doorsteps everywhere, as the much-anticipated long weekend threatened to be a total washout.

No one could then conceive that it would be the last weekend of peace for over four years. A few precious days of blissful ignorance lay ahead, whatever the weather.

Kate Parry Frye, like many Britons who followed politics, was at that moment much more preoccupied with tensions in Ireland than with what was happening in Europe. The Liberal government had finally succeeded in passing the highly controversial Home Rule Bill granting self-government for Ireland. It threatened to tear Ireland – and the current British Parliament – apart. George V had invited Irish leaders to Buckingham Palace, to try to work out a deal. But on 24 July this conference had ended in failure. It was this story that dominated the newspapers. The Austro-Hungarian ultimatum did get some mention, but Kate's primary concern was that Ireland would precipitate another election and distract from the suffrage cause – which would ruin her bank holiday. If anything, the European troubles were for her a welcome diversion:

> I suppose if an election comes I shall go through with it (my holiday) but I shall much fear a collapse – and, fought on the Irish question, we shan't get a look in – shan't be listened to. Now there seem such European complications – Austria and Serbia – perhaps our domestic parliamentary quarrels will have to take a second place.[1]

Alan Lloyd had been busy with the important business of buying a new car. On 28 July, a few days before the long weekend, he was at home in Edgbaston Grove, Birmingham, and wrote to tell Dorothy all about his latest toy, a Doriot, Flandrin and Parant car – or, as he preferred to joke, a 'Damn Fool Purchase'. Speedy and sleek, it was the perfect car for a handsome man to whisk his new wife away in on their honeymoon. The wedding was fast approaching:

> I have fixed up the DFP car and it is a beauty. I shall set the chassis in two or three days and shall probably pop up to show it to you, if I can. The body will take three weeks to a month and should be ready alright for honeymoon. I think it shall be a real ripping little car. It's like a miniature Rolls-Royce. You'll love it. I'm having the banns published – what a lot of fuss.

> You little darling, I just long for you, I could eat you! Have got one
> or two nice presents, spiffing old table, claret jug, Sheffield plate box for
> bon-bons, entrée dish, set of dessert knives and forks.[2]

The day that Alan penned these words, having received no satisfactory
response to their ultimatum, Austria declared war on Serbia.

Kate Parry Frye didn't have to cancel her holiday. But by the time she
went to Worthing, to stay with her mother and sister (who had taken
cheap rooms there for the summer), Austria-Hungary and Serbia were
at war and Russia – bound by treaty to support Serbia in the event of
an attack – was mobilising its forces too. Kate left London on the
Thursday evening and she now began to realise that something very
serious was happening in Europe:

> At Victoria it was a pandemonium. I don't know what was the matter
> with the station – it couldn't be all the holiday traffic, but I had to fight
> to get a porter and to get my luggage put in the train. The journey
> seemed short as I had bought no end of papers to read of the crises – it
> is becoming too awfully serious for words. Home politics are clean out
> of it at this moment – everyone's interest is fixed further afield. Fancy
> a European War at this period of our so-called civilisation.[3]

In Worthing the fun limped on, as it did in other resorts dotted along
the shorelines of the British Isles. As Kate wandered around the town,
she would have seen posters advertising all the delights of a typical
bank holiday weekend: Shanley's Cinema at the Winter Hall; the daily
performance by the orchestra on the pier; *The Girl on Film* musical play
at Worthing Theatre; roller skating at the Kursaal; the Worthing
Whimsies performing in the Kursaal gardens.[4]

But Kate could not be distracted. By the following day, the Saturday,
she was really worried. During a warm sunny spell she went to the beach,
but it wasn't long before the heavens opened once again. She sought solace
in books, but it was no use: 'I went out by myself to the library. But I
can't read – there is too much in the papers, and all this uncertainty makes
one nervous.'[5] The numerous treaties binding the European powers into
complex alliances were rapidly escalating the conflict from a dispute
between Austro-Hungary and Serbia into one that threatened to tear

Europe in two. On 1 August, after Russia had refused an ultimatum to halt mobilisation, Germany declared war on Russia.

Hallie Miles was also spending her bank holiday weekend at the seaside. She and Eustace regularly escaped the bustle of the city and the demands of their business to Westgate-on-Sea, a small resort town in Essex. They were lucky this time – the weather was much better there than it was on the south coast.

Hallie and Eustace no doubt made the most of it. According to Hallie's lifestyle books, 'holidays give [husbands and wives] leisure to talk to and understand each other better, perhaps, than they have done hitherto in their busy everyday lives. But they should not carry the old home topics with them: they must have new subjects to discuss.'[6]

That weekend Hallie and Eustace did indeed have new subjects to discuss. As someone who considered herself a journalist, Hallie liked to keep abreast of the latest topics and trends, and no doubt devoured the news of Europe filling the papers. It was already affecting the mood in the town: many French and Belgian people had left the resort to try to get home, leaving numerous hotels and restaurants noticeably understaffed on the busiest weekend of the year.[7]

On Saturday 1 August, the day Germany declared war on Russia, and the day that Kate sat in Worthing Library sick with worry, Hallie was also pondering what war might mean. She sat down at the desk in her suite and took out a new notebook, having decided that she should keep a diary of these important events. She began the first entry:

> We are having a quiet weekend at Westgate-on-Sea. The weather is glorious. There seems nothing wrong (outwardly) with the world in general, yet the air is full of whispers and coming trouble: and the rumours of War are becoming more and more persistent; it is even said that War has already been declared. I am going to keep a daily record (as far as possible) of all that happens at this 'time of trouble'. If there is a War, we know that it will reach each one of us; we know that in some way or other we shall each of us have to take our share.[8]

Reg Evans was ready to take his share, whatever it might be. He too was away for the weekend, but he had more serious things on his mind than seaside diversions. He had joined the 1st Battalion, Hertfordshire Regiment of the Territorial Force a year earlier, and he was at their annual training camp. The Territorial Force had been in existence for only six years, giving men the opportunity to join the army on a part-time basis. For Reg, it was a more direct means of stepping up to the defence of his beloved Britain, and a welcome addition to his wages too.

During the week, Reg and his battalion had joined the men of the Cambridgeshire, Northamptonshire and Bedfordshire territorial battalions already encamped in a canvas town that had sprung up on the Brownlow estate in Hertfordshire. The weather had been fine, and the 4,000 territorials had passed the week in drills and war games.

By the bank holiday weekend their training had taken on new meaning. Britain was not exempt from the complex system of alliances that had caused the conflict to escalate so rapidly already. She was sworn to protect Belgium, now looking increasingly vulnerable as the nations of Europe armed themselves. Reg and his fellow 'Saturday night soldiers' (as the territorials were nicknamed) had been made very aware of their commitment to serve full time in the event of a war. Notices had already been served to special service men of the Cambridgeshire battalion to proceed to various destinations with a view to carrying out 'precautionary duties' and within an hour they'd left the camp.[9] Reg knew that very soon he might be a full-time soldier himself. With a greater sense of purpose, he got stuck back in to the weekend's programme of sports and skirmishes.

Alan Lloyd had gone away for the long weekend as well, having motored all the way from Birmingham to Devon in his new sports car. His bank holiday fun was also marred by anxiety, but not because of ultimatums and alliances and armies marching. He was cross that his long-anticipated and carefully laid plans for married life were being trampled on by his prospective father-in-law.

From the letter he sat down to write to Dorothy on the bank holiday Sunday, it seems that he'd had a run-in with her father. The man who'd been so unenthusiastic about their wedding happening at all was now trying to meddle with the future that Alan and Dorothy were planning together. Alan wrote furiously to Dorothy that he wasn't having any of it, but did seem rattled:

You darling, I do want to have a house of our own where we shall be independent and where no one can tell me to quit. I've stood a lot from your Guv'nor and I'm not sure it's altogether wise to knuckle under to him as I've done in the past by great effort because I've wanted to be with you. He's apt to think I can be pushed about anyhow. He'll find it awkward to deal with me when we're married!

I oughtn't to say all this, it's a bit caddish, but I will not come where I'm kicked out without a bare apology. You can tell him this if you like and let him fume! Don't worry your beloved little self, you can last out til September 1st, ownest. Oh you little angel. I do long for you,[10]

It seems unlikely that he hadn't read in the papers of the rapidly worsening situation overseas. *The Times* reported runs on food shops in the capital, as people began to fear that war must come to them too.[11] But it certainly didn't seem to be of much concern to him. Only his marriage mattered; he'd waited so long for it and now it was only a month away, and he was damned if he was going to let anyone mess things up for him.

Kate Parry Frye was more aware of the life-shattering nature of events. She understood what Alan seemed not to: that lovers would be torn apart if Britain were drawn into the war. John, her boyfriend of eleven years, was an ex-soldier who had fought in the Boer War and had been a member of the Territorial Army for some years. Men like him would be among the first to be called up, should the country get sucked into the turmoil sweeping Europe:

Not out all day – a furious wind, everything jangling and banging. Read and dozed in the afternoon and did some writing in the evening. Germany has declared war against Russia for interfering against Austria and Serbia – and against France. Goodness alone knows why unless this is what she has been preparing for and planning for years. England must be drawn in. I don't see what else we can do. John may be called to a port at any minute. Oh the whole idea frightens me.[12]

On Sunday 2 August, the news that Russia and Germany were at war was spreading like wildfire across Britain. That day, **Andrew Clark** was in Oxford. A 58-year-old Scottish Church of England Minister, he had served as the vicar of the small Essex village of Great Leighs for twenty years. His parish came under the patronage of Lincoln College in Oxford where, thirty-five years earlier, Andrew had studied for a double-first in Greats. He'd spent many years as both a priest and a scholar in the city, before moving on to a quieter life in Great Leighs.[13] He went back whenever he could, and so Oxford was where he found himself on the bank holiday Sunday.

That morning Andrew got up early and walked through the city he loved. He had offered to take the morning service at Hagbourne Church in Berkshire and was headed for the station to catch his train. His head had been full of his morning sermon, but all that was suddenly pushed out when he 'looked in at the Oxford Union Society rooms and found the Steward posting on the entrance door a telegram that Germany had declared war on Russia.'[14] Like Hallie and hundreds of

The Reverend Andrew Clark as a young man at Oxford, 1886.

other ordinary people who recognised the gravity of the situation, he was moved to start a diary that evening:

> In Hagbourne Church, instead of the sermon I had intended, I mentioned the grave news and spoke for a little on the impending war, and the sacrifices it would call for. The churchwarden thanked me for doing this. Several parishioners had sons in the Services and all would count it a kindness to have received such early intimation that the critical moment had come.[15]

Andrew might have been a little pre-emptive. The critical moment for Britons had not quite arrived, but they were inching ever closer to the precipice. On Sunday night, Germany was gearing up for a war with France and issued an ultimatum to Belgium: if German troops were allowed to operate freely in Belgian territory, Germany would maintain Belgian independence on the conclusion of peace. The Belgians had twelve hours to reply.

This was the tipping point for Britain, sworn as it was to defend Belgian neutrality. *The Times* reported that: 'Europe is in arms, and the greatest war of modern times is upon us.'[16]

The following day, Monday 3 August, was Bank Holiday Monday. At 7 a.m., the German ultimatum to Belgium expired. Belgium had already declared their answer: to accept the German proposal would be a complete sacrifice of Belgian honour. That afternoon, Germany declared war on France. British ministers rushed back from their seaside holidays and country houses to the House of Commons to discuss what should be done.[17] The fleet had already been mobilised on Saturday; now a general mobilisation of the armed forces was ordered.

That day **Reg Evans** and the thousands of other men camped with him at Ashridge received the news they'd been half expecting: they were to strike camp and return home to await further instructions. The same orders reached territorial soldiers in summer camps up and down the country. One can only speculate as to Reg's thoughts as he hurriedly packed up his gear and marched back to the station, to catch the train home to his mother in Hemel Hempstead.

*

Kate Parry Frye was feeling patriotic at this dramatic moment in her country's history, even as she grappled with the realisation of what lay in store for ordinary people like her:

> I should think the Blackest Bank Holiday that the world has ever known. What an appalling day – the most dire and awful depression over everyone – like a pall shutting out the idea of holiday – jollity, sunshine and air – everything dead and dumb and yet one's nerves turned up to a frightful pitch. A European War and England must be drawn in.
>
> It is all rushing upon us now – a huge welter of realisation of what we are in for – what our navy means to us, and what the machines of death will bring to innocent men and their wives and families. I am for peace – always for peace, war is too repulsive, but I am for the honour of England too – and come what may we must link ourselves with France and help keep off the aggressive – brutal – nation that is at her doors. What an awful day. Not a smile on the face of anyone one met – simply a grim, hard and quiet manner, but terror at our hearts.[18]

Kate instinctively recognised the gravity of the situation. The other holidaymakers in Worthing, however, were perhaps not quite as miserable as she made out: on Bank Holiday Monday, no fewer than 4,800 of them passed through the turnstiles of Worthing Pier.[19] Kate wasn't one of them, busy as she was keeping track of the signs of war that were already beginning to appear around her. The government extended the bank holiday until Friday to prevent a run on the banks, took control of the railways and attempted to quell the panic buying of supplies that was beginning up and down the country:

> Read the paper all the afternoon. The Bank Holidays are to continue for 3 more days to let the staff get things into order and issue £1 and 10/- notes to make up for the shortage of gold. Some people are getting panic stricken – taking out their money. Then some people are buying up huge quantities of food stuffs and stocking the houses as for a siege. How mean and beastly of them . . . creating an artificial demand and raising prices needlessly. One lady bought 18 hams – besides a huge amount of other goods – some people giving orders of £75. Oh dear – oh dear. It's awful.[20]

The next morning in the House of Commons the Prime Minister, Herbert Asquith, announced that the British cabinet had issued an ultimatum to Germany: that they must promise to respect Belgium neutrality or face the consequences. The ultimatum would expire at midnight German time – 11 p.m. in Britain.

German troops were already moving into Belgium.

Reg Evans was now home in Hemel Hempstead, awaiting further news. Early in the evening, a notice was posted outside the post office, not far from his mother's guesthouse on Broad Street. The same notice was appearing on church doors and town hall notice boards all over Britain. It was a mobilisation order issued by the War Office. Germany had not yet replied to the ultimatum, nor removed her forces from Belgium. Reservists and territorials were instructed to report to their headquarters.

Reg started his war as he meant to go on: having hastily thrown together his kit, he kissed his mother goodbye and rushed off. He was the first man in Hemel Hempstead to report for duty at the drill hall. Others quickly followed and according to the local paper, 'soon the hall was filled with members of the local company, all highly delighted at the prospect of being able to serve their country.'[21]

Similar scenes were repeated up and down the country. That evening in Worthing, the local company assembled in the drill hall and prepared to spend the night there. **Kate Parry Frye** must have been thinking of her boyfriend John, then on holiday in Exeter. She'd got a letter from him earlier that day 'in very low spirits', explaining that he was expecting instructions to join his unit at any minute. Unlike Reg, he'd experienced war before and dreaded the prospect.[22]

There were only a few hours left for Germany to answer Britain's demands. People sought places to await the outcome together. In Worthing the offices of the *Worthing Gazette* seemed the logical spot to congregate, and as the light drained from the sky, a trickle of holidaymakers and locals started heading for the newspaper's building on Chapel Street. Someone hung a Union Jack on the notice board, and the notes of popular patriotic songs floated up from the bandstand a few hundred yards away on the seafront, the instruments accompanied by hundreds of enthusiastic voices.[23]

*

In London, crowds jammed the streets, filling Trafalgar Square and Downing Street, and swelled into the thousands outside Buckingham Palace. The atmosphere was boisterous; the skies above the capital had been filled with cheering and singing for hours. Scores of motorcars carrying men and women in evening dress crowded the streets of Whitehall and The Mall. Union Jacks were waved, hung from windows and draped over lampposts. But as the hands of Big Ben neared 11 p.m., the noise at last started to die down.[24] The nation held its breath.

Inside Whitehall, Herbert Asquith and his government lingered in corridors or at their desks letting the final moments tick by. There was nothing more they could do now. Minutes earlier, they had received Germany's reply: that the British demands had been summarily rejected.[25]

The First Lord of the Admiralty at the time was 39-year-old Winston Churchill. He passed the final minutes of peace in his office in the Admiralty on Horse Guards Parade:

> It was 11 o'clock at night – 12 by German time – when the ultimatum expired. The windows of the Admiralty were thrown wide open in the warm night air. Under the roof from which Nelson had received his orders were gathered a small group of Admirals and Captains and a cluster of clerks, pencil in hand, waiting. Along the Mall from the direction of the Palace the sound of an immense concourse singing 'God save the King' floated in.
>
> On this deep wave there broke the chimes of Big Ben; and, as the first stroke of the hour boomed out, a rustle of movement swept across the room. The war telegram, which meant 'Commence hostilities against Germany', was flashed to the ships and establishments under the White Ensign all over the world.
>
> I walked across the Horse Guards Parade to the Cabinet room and reported to the Prime Minister and the Ministers who were assembled there that the deed was done.[26]

The deed was done: Britain was at war.

As Churchill records, astonishingly, a wave of jubilation swept through central London as the chimes of Big Ben broke the silence. A vast cheer that lasted twenty minutes erupted along Whitehall and the Mall and, outside the Palace, a spirited rendition of the national anthem began.[27]

The Times announces Britain's declaration of war on Germany, 5 August 1914.

In Worthing, following the initial announcement, the crowd hung around the *Gazette* offices for further news, until they were told there would be no more that night. The people drifted onto the seafront to look at the searchlights that were now visible further down the coast at Beachy Head.[28] **Kate Parry Frye** might have been amongst them – certainly she found out the news that night. Despite her days of agonising as the situation had escalated, she shared the general feeling of righteousness and patriotic enthusiasm now that war was certain:

> Well it is settled England is to go in with France to protect her and Belgium. What a slap in the face for Germany!!! Germany expects to be allowed to walk over anywhere just as she pleases. What a brutal country – and what a Kaiser!!![29]

*

Hallie Miles and Eustace were still in Westgate-on-Sea. The small resort took the news of war more quietly than elsewhere. Hallie's reaction to events seems sadder and more reflective than most:

> We already seem to be in a new world. The awful declaration of War has been made, and everything is plunged into chaos. At first one feels paralysed; as if time itself were standing still. We are at once leaving these quiet scenes, for we feel we want to be in the midst of things in London.[30]

The darkness of the ocean could be glimpsed from their bedroom window. Out on the seas, the British fleet was already on a war footing. On this momentous night, as Hallie looked out on 'the new world' beyond her window, she might have thought back to something she'd penned a decade earlier which now seemed startlingly prescient:

> We never know our capabilities until they are proved by emergencies. How often new powers are developed in people by a sudden calamity, shock, or sorrow! We do not know who the heroes are until there is a war.
>
> Perhaps it is only in the dark and silent days that we learn what our mission is.[31]

3

YOUR KING AND COUNTRY NEED YOU

August–September 1914

I don't want to fight a bit, now I've got you, but a man must try and be a man in these times.

Alan Lloyd, letter to his fiancée, 11 August 1914

On Wednesday 5 August, Britain awoke as a nation at war. In the isolated village of Great Leighs, this was a fact the residents discovered only when the morning newspapers arrived at the post office. There had been no late-night vigils there; most of the villagers had farms to look after. **Andrew Clark** probably had his newspaper waiting for him when he came downstairs for breakfast. There, in black and white, he read that Britain was at war with Germany. 'This day will be momentous in the history of all time,' said *The Times*.[1]

Andrew Clark's life was quiet and traditional. Great Leighs was a simple rural community, where suffragette protests and vegetarian restaurants were the stuff of legend only. Andrew lived in the rectory with his wife, his daughter Mary, his daughter Mildred (when she was not at university), two maids and a groom-gardener. It was the second grandest house in the village. The first was Lyons Hall, home to the squire Joseph Herbert Tritton and his family. Vicar and squire kept a watchful eye on the rest of the village: a few dozen farmers, tradesmen and their families – just over 600 people in all. Life in Great Leighs had rolled on unchanged for generations.[2]

However, Andrew sensed that the shockwaves of the momentous happenings that were unfolding abroad must reach even their little

corner of Essex in the end, and – as a scholar and keen local historian
– felt it was his duty to record them in a 'village diary':

> The village of Great Leighs, Essex, although it is within 30 miles by
> road of London, is singularly isolated. It has no resident in the habit of
> going regularly to London. The work of the village is self-centred, on
> the farms, the smithy, the wheelwrights, and carpenter's. It is quite away
> from any railway station.
>
> It seemed, therefore, not out of place to put down from day to day
> such echoes of the war as reached the rectory from outside, giving
> authentic written scraps of genuine village origin.[3]

For some the war seemed at present a distant and rather baffling occurrence, but for others, it was already very real.

Reg Evans had spent the night in the drill hall as a mobilised soldier.
Now, on this Wednesday morning, he was getting ready to depart his
home town, leaving his job in the brush factory behind. As a territorial
soldier, his regiment was embodied for Home Defence only, but rumours
were flying about as to where they might end up. Despite the uncertainty, the mood amongst Reg and his fellow members of the 1st Herts
was one of enthusiasm. All morning, patriotic songs could be heard
billowing out of the drill hall onto Bury Road, where a crowd had
started to gather.

At 11 a.m., Reg and his comrades emerged proudly, lined up outside
the hall and marched to the station. All along the route, the people of
Hemel Hempstead had turned out to see them off, waving handkerchiefs
and cheering. Reg's mother Frances was undoubtedly amongst them.[4]
They travelled by train to Hertford, the HQ of the 1st Hertfordshire
Regiment, where everyone was shown into school buildings on London
Road and subjected to medical examinations. A handful of the men
failed, and found themselves back at home rather sooner than they'd
imagined.[5] Reg Evans was not amongst them. His war was only just
beginning.

At the outbreak of war, the regular British army consisted of about
250,000 troops, stationed all across the globe. Territorial soldiers like
Reg Evans added to their number, along with reservists: former soldiers

and part-time soldiers who had completed a long period of training or experienced real warfare. The total mobilised British army, therefore, including part-time soldiers like Reg with very limited experience, was just over 700,000 men. The German army they would face was considered the most efficient fighting force in the world – and numbered almost 4 million regular troops and reservists. The situation for Britain was grave indeed.

Britain was the only major power fighting this war that did not have a system of compulsory military service. Before 1914, 80 per cent of men of military age in France were conscripted; in Germany it was 56 per cent. In Britain, compulsory military service was seen as contrary to the liberal traditions that were held so dear. And that did not change with the outbreak of war – the government launched a *voluntary* recruiting campaign.[6] A plea was issued to the men of Britain that would go down in history: 'Your King and Country Need You'. From newspapers and hoardings and notice boards everywhere, the stark truth screamed out: 'At this very moment the Empire is on the brink of the greatest war in the history of the world. Will you answer your Country's Call?'

The response was remarkable. Recruiting offices everywhere were inundated with patriotic young men offering their services to the nation. The London recruitment headquarters at Scotland Yard were overwhelmed by thousands of prospective soldiers, and mounted police had to control the crowds who'd come, despite the heavy rain, to watch the young men cramming in to enlist. When the doors closed at 4.30 p.m., there were still hundreds waiting outside.[7] The response was similar across the country. This was day one of what would go down in history as the most successful voluntary recruitment drive ever seen.

Alan Lloyd was at home in Birmingham, having driven back from Devon. The house was quiet; his parents had been on holiday in Switzerland and were now trapped on the Continent.[8] In their absence, and seemingly without consulting Dorothy, Alan made a momentous decision: he offered his services to the War Office. He even volunteered his beloved car. On Thursday 6 August, he received a number of telegrams from Dorothy and from her mother, asking him to come to Yorkshire to see them urgently. His reply probably did not put Dorothy's mind at rest:

I am wondering what all the fuss is about. Surely you are not frightened because I said I might offer my services? Everybody must put their

personal considerations in the background now, and I don't believe you'd
be so selfish as to try and stop me doing my part. Possibly you don't
realize that this is a life and death struggle with Germany. Everybody
who could do something and won't is a beastly, unpatriotic kind of
person.

I'm the last person to be a jingo and hate flag wagging and union
jack hurrahing etc. but I do feel that I might be useful, with my motor
or without it, in case of attack by Germany and so I've offered my
services to the War Office, if they want such a chap as me. There's no
cause at all to be alarmed at this, fellows like me would only be wanted
for defence not for expeditionary force.[9]

Dorothy's heartbreaking reply mirrored the thoughts of thousands of
lovers, wives and mothers across Britain in these early days of war. She
wrote, stoically: 'I think it's splendid of you to want to go – though I
believe it will just about do for me.' However, in the short term, there
was the issue of the wedding that she had planned, which was almost
upon them:

I suppose if you go we couldn't be married first Allie, could we? I can't
realize what it means my darling for everything is ready for the wedding.
Let me know won't you darling for I must see what I can do about all
the things I've got . . . Oh darling I think my heart will break – I can't
write more for I know it's wrong. Oh come and see me first my own
Allie.[10]

Alan set off for Boston Spa to comfort her. But he had made his decision, and Dorothy – whether she tried to or not – would not change
his mind.

On 7 August, the newly appointed Minister for War, Lord Kitchener,
stepped up the recruiting drive. In his call to arms he said he needed
one hundred thousand men to come forward immediately, and five
hundred thousand in the long run. He added that recruits must enlist
for three years, or until the war was over. Most of the people who
rushed to sign up in these early days did not dream it would be for
more than a few months. The majority of people really did think it
would all be 'over by Christmas'. Kitchener already suspected otherwise.

G. R.

YOUR KING & COUNTRY NEED YOU

A CALL TO ARMS

An addition of 100,000 MEN to His Majesty's Regular Army is immediately necessary in the present grave National Emergency.

LORD KITCHENER IS CONFIDENT THAT THIS APPEAL WILL BE AT ONCE RESPONDED TO BY ALL THOSE WHO HAVE THE SAFETY OF OUR EMPIRE AT HEART.

TERMS OF SERVICE

General Service for a period of 3 years or until the war is concluded. Age of Enlistment, between 19 and 30.

HOW TO JOIN

Full information can be obtained at ANY POST OFFICE IN THE KINGDOM or at ANY MILITARY DEPOT.

GOD SAVE THE KING

Lord Kitchener's 'Call to Arms', appealing for 100,000 men to enlist, August 1914.

Regardless of the war's possible duration, for all the people whose husbands, sons, brothers and fathers answered Kitchener's call, it was an emotional time. **Hallie Miles** was now back in London. At forty-five, Eustace was too old to join up (though men with previous soldiering experience were accepted up to that age). But Hallie was no stranger to the poignant goodbyes that were taking place all over the country. She had a ringside seat from her flat in central London – she and Eustace lived next door to a recruiting office:

What sights we see from our windows! We see the women bringing their men to the Recruiting Offices and waiting outside whilst they are being enlisted. Then the men who had entered the building in civilian clothes – working clothes, all sorts of clothes – leave it in spic and span uniform, and the women are handed their men's everyday garments. I have seen them hug these clothes to them as if they were living people, and weep over them, as they turn away, leaving their men behind.[11]

The sad moments that Hallie witnessed from her windows were not, however, sufficient to dent the excitement she felt in these first days of the conflict. After years of political and social strife, Hallie found the explosion of patriotism a welcome change:

> The whole condition of things is so strange to us all; for to have London in a state of war is not within the memory of the present generation. And yet – awful as it is – it is very thrilling! The glorious spirit of loyalty and 'all for England' prevails at every turn. We had been feeling as if that spirit were dead and buried! I notice that people in the streets are now whistling the 'Marseillaise' and 'God Save The King!' and 'Rule Britannia'; the very children are marching instead of walking, and are carrying bits of stick as bayonets and using old pieces of tin pails as drums.[12]

Kate Parry Frye was still in Worthing. Most of the visitors to the town had left after the news of war had broken but Kate's mother and sister had rented rooms for the season and, since she had a few weeks off work, she was staying on with them as planned. It's hard to imagine that they were having much fun in the half-empty, still stubbornly damp town.

On Saturday 8 August, Kate left the bleak seafront behind her and boarded a train back to London. She was only going for the day. It was less than a fortnight since she'd departed from Victoria Station, but upon arrival she sensed immediately that things had changed. The strange scenes she saw as she wandered the streets held a grim fascination for her:

> Pouring when I got to London – so I loitered about the stations and read the unusual notices. Everything seemed strange and all the people subdued with a leaden depression – just like a funeral – the buses and taxis even seemed to glide more softly by.
>
> When the rain stopped a bit I walked up Victoria Street – Whitehall to Trafalgar Square watching everything there was to see – soldiers parading – boy scouts – the recruiting office – Scotland Yard – notices on the walls and hoardings. Went to see the recruits again – fighting to get in – they were holding them back by the police and letting them go through in batches of 15 or 20.[13]

Her impression was very different to Hallie's in those early days. But then Kate was not prone to levity at the best of times, and that day was certainly not the best of times. She had come up to town to meet John, who had been called back from his holiday to rejoin his regiment. He was in a panic about the sudden prospect of having to repeat the experiences he had undergone in the Boer War. Kate went to Paddington to meet his train, the 1.30 from Exeter:

> It was half an hour late. John was wildly looking out of the window. Very excited and feeling very seedy with a cold and internal chill – so in the worst condition for his ordeal. I think myself the strain of the last week has been too much for him, so I was very glad I met him. We drove to his Club in a taxi as it was still pouring and he seemed beyond helping himself.[14]

They spent the afternoon together and it was not a happy one. John was feeling so ill that she took him to see a doctor after lunch, and after that it wasn't long before it was time for her to get back to Worthing:

> John felt so queer I did not want him to see me off but he insisted. We walked to Westminster – then the underground to Victoria and I came by the 8.25 through train. I could see John hated to see me go – he has quite made up his mind that he is going to be done for this time.
>
> Well I have had some miserable journeys to and from Worthing – I don't know that this isn't the worst. I try and take it quietly but it is an awful strain to think of the danger to him and I feel the War may go on for years. Who can foresee the end? Really before another crisis I think I shall have to marry him so that I may have the right to look after him. He is so utterly dependent on me.[15]

This was Kate's first goodbye to John. As her train steamed back to Worthing, John was getting ready for his own journey to join his regiment. He was an officer in the Essex and Suffolk Royal Garrison Artillery, stationed at Shoeburyness and tasked with coastal defence. At least he was not travelling far, not yet.

Reg Evans and his fellow Hemel boys spent several days camping out in requisitioned school buildings. Conditions were basic, and they slept on straw-covered floors without bedding, but Reg took it with typical fortitude. In fact, he was having a pretty good time. Wherever the regiment went they were cheered and welcomed by the locals, and he was thriving on the training and the attention, as he explained to his mother in the first letter he wrote to her as a full-time soldier:[16]

> Here we are for a little while back at school again! I hope you are keeping fit. I have not felt so well for ages. Our blankets have gone astray so we have to curl up in our waterproof sheets at night but I must say it doesn't seem to do us much harm. You won't know me when I get back, everybody says how well I am looking. The public baths are just opposite here and we are allowed the use of them at half price so I had a lovely hot bath last night.[17]

On Saturday 8 August, the day Kate said goodbye to John, the 1st Herts moved from Hertford to Romford. Reg had a far better day than she did, despite the fact that it was raining on him too:

> We left Hertford about 10.30 yesterday morning in pouring rain, by the way it always seems to rain when we are on the move. All the way along at every station and window there seemed to be people cheering and waving but London, well it's got the war fever properly. As we were marching to church this morning motor omnibuses were held up and the passengers leaned over the top singing and cheering. Private motors and taxis are dashing about everywhere with Union Jacks and tricolour flags. When I stood by the railings this morning a lady handed me up a huge bunch of flowers to decorate our room with and said she was just going to church to pray for us all.
>
> Rumours are flying about all the time as to our ultimate destination but we know nothing for sure so don't believe anything you hear for I will write and tell you as soon as ever we know. I hope everyone at No 12 is all right. Give my kind regards to them all.[18]

Reg wrote to his mother again a few days later. Although the territorial forces had initially only been embodied for home service, there were now rumours that they would be asked to volunteer for service abroad to replace regular army troops who were being moved from their overseas garrisons to go to the front. It's hard to imagine that Reg was not excited by the prospect that he, Reg Evans from Hemel Hempstead, might get to see some of the British Empire that had long meant so much to him:

> We are still in Romford and although we are constantly hearing rumours of a move they have not materialised yet and nobody knows where we shall end up. All we are certain of is this. When the troops have to be sent from Egypt, Gibraltar and Malta or India, they will draft some of us out to take their place whilst they are at the front fighting, so don't be surprised any time to get a picture post card from Egypt or some out of the way place. I am beginning to wish they would let us go out to the front but I am afraid they want us for garrison duty only. Anyway, as soon as I know anything certain I will write to you.[19]

On 7 August, the first British soldiers landed in France. The British Expeditionary Force, made up of regular, full-time soldiers, joined with the much larger French army for the initial confrontations with the German enemy. For less experienced soldiers like Reg, the early weeks of war were spent in training in Britain, getting fit and ready for action – wherever that might turn out to be. For brand-new recruits, training at home would last much longer. Suddenly Britain was awash with soldiers in the making. Existing army accommodation was woefully inadequate – hence the requisitioning of public buildings like the school Reg was sleeping in – and many communities suddenly found themselves transformed into garrison towns.

At first, particularly for more out-of-the-way places, the sudden arrival of troops was quite a shock – rather like a circus appearing unannounced. **Andrew Clark** recorded the first time a whole brigade marched through the middle of his village. As he watched hundreds of feet pound the usually quiet path outside his church, he realised he had been correct in his prediction: war really had come to Great Leighs:

> <u>Tuesday 18 August</u>: A brigade of Territorials marched through Great Leighs from Chelmsford. It comprised 6,000 men; hearing that the troops were in movement, I closed the Church School at 9.50 a.m. and sent the children in charge of the two mistresses to see the sight. The children had a good place. Two of the regiments were exceedingly foot-sore. One of the young soldiers explained that the march was an

amusement for him, accustomed daily to tramp miles of ground in ordinary farm work, but it was desperate hard for shop lads and clerks, who for years had never been off pavements, and were in the habit of nothing more than jumping on and off a train.

About 11.30 a.m., a regiment of foot came and halted from the bridge to St Anne's. They were very footsore, dirty and tired and glad to lie down on the grass by the roadside. They bought up all the ginger beer and most of the lemonade at St Anne's and the village shop. The cottagers were delighted to chat with them and brought apples and plums which were much appreciated. Mr John Dean, of St Anne's, put to his horses in his farm wagons and drove relays of the most footsore to their camping ground at Oaklands.

Old Chas. Collins, ex-under-gamekeeper and village patriarch, spent the whole day watching. It took him a long time to get home, because on his way there he stopped every wayfarer, and went into every cottage, to tell his story: 'There's never been a sight like that in Great Leighs!'[20]

The villagers of Great Leighs were not just observing the war, however. They were also leaving to fight in it. A few days earlier, the squire's daughter had given Andrew a list of the men in the parish who had 'gone on service' and for whom the reverend was now to lead the congregation of St Mary's in prayer. This list – by only the second week of war – already numbered thirteen men in total. The squire's son, Alan Tritton was amongst them. Joseph Tritton had instructed that in addition to prayers, the church bells should be rung at one o'clock each day by his own butler, to remind the villagers of the men who had already left them.[21] These were not new recruits and many of them had long been stationed away from home, but it was still a high number for such a small parish – and hinted at the trauma that lay in store for Great Leighs.

The village proved just as susceptible as anywhere else to the patriotic fervour that swept the nation. From the notice boards outside the post office and village hall, Kitchener's call to arms entreated men of the village to enlist. The squire added his own voice to that of the Minister for War; on the first Sunday after the harvest had been brought in, a hot late summer's day, the squire gathered the villagers together in his barn. Andrew was in the wings as Mr Tritton addressed his flock:

Fellow parishioners of Great and Little Leighs, you have been accustomed to assemble in this barn on various occasions – social, philanthropic, religious, but never on a more momentous occasion or to hear of a more righteous cause.

I want to say to the fathers and mothers of these two parishes – do not stand in the way of your sons' going to fight for the country. This I can say as one who has given a beloved son to do the same. Think of what it would mean if we were to have our country overrun as Belgium is, and the scenes of horror there, of daily occurrence here. We have justice on our side and we know it; we have the defence of the country to take on us, and we know it. From the bottom of our hearts we can say: God Save the King and God defend the right![22]

Applause and cheers echoed to the rafters of the barn. A few days later, the village lads began to sign up:

It is reported today that Albert Wright, one of the strongest young farm-hands in the village, is going to volunteer. Jimmy Lewin, the 'boy' who drives Mann's [the baker's] cart is going to do the same; but, as this rests on his own statement, this is not to be believed. Charles Rayner is also to offer himself but the villagers think he will be rejected because of his weak chest.[23]

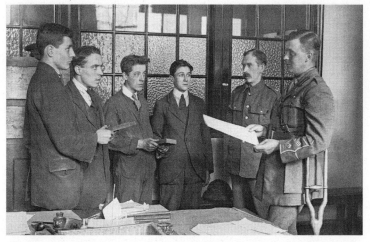

Four young men hold bibles as they take the oath in a recruitment office.

*

Recruitment was, in a certain sense, a leveller in the otherwise rigidly hierarchical society that prevailed in Britain at the time. This was an era when many men from the working class were excluded from political life and did not have the right to vote, but all were welcome in Kitchener's 'new' army, from wealthy, well-to-do men like Alan Lloyd or the squire's son, to the farm hands and bakers' boys of Great Leighs. Once there, however, class divisions remained as rigid as ever. Rich, educated men like Alan could expect a commission as an officer, which meant authority and comfort straight away. Working-class men would come in at the bottom, as privates, and the vast majority of them would stay there.

Alan Lloyd had not queued outside a recruitment office with the masses; he'd written a formal letter to the War Office offering his services. Initially, he heard nothing in response. While they waited, **Dorothy Hewetson** busied herself planning their wedding, still scheduled to go ahead on 1 September. When she wrote to Alan in mid-August, all the anxiety she had expressed on learning of his intentions to sign up had disappeared. Her Allie was still at home in Birmingham, and life went on. Perhaps there was nothing to worry about, after all – other than finalising the arrangements and keeping calm:

> You angel, did you manage to get the banns published? I bet sixpence you forgot? Oh Allie I can't believe even now that I've only that short time to wait, it makes me go nearly mad every time I think about it, and now my things that I've ordered are beginning to come in so it really does seem as if I've only a little time to wait before I belong to you and you only. Oh ownest I shall be happy then and I hardly dare think of what it will be like, for it stirs me up so fearfully and makes it all so hard to wait for you.[24]

Alan replied the same day. He too was hugely excited at the thought of their life together, which he had desired for so long and struggled so hard for. Now, having had some time to mull over his decision to enlist, there was the first hint of worry about what doing his duty might entail:

> Wrong again! I did remember to have the banns put up and I hear they were duly announced in a clear voice and no dissentients! So far so good. Have heard nothing yet from War Office.

I simply long to see your beloved little self, all of you, with no things on! Oh you little angel of mine, I do adore you, though I know you don't think I do because I may soon get grumpy. I just want to have you and I don't want to fight a bit, now I've got you, but a man must try and be a man in these times and not think of his own wants. Oh I do want to hug your beloved little body.[25]

But there was no rowing back now and exactly two weeks after the declaration of war, Alan was in Cambridge, his old university town. He'd finally been called for an interview and a medical. He had not yet been accepted into the army, but as an upper-class man over six foot tall and in rude health, he was justifiably optimistic. He wrote to Dorothy straight away to tell her he'd made his first step to becoming a soldier:

Haven't I got such a big fat catch then! I have seen and impressed the Board and also passed the medical exam. At least the candidate who followed me said he saw the word 'fit' written against my name. Also the Doctor told me I was the record candidate so far for height and weight! So that's something. The board seemed to think I'd got a very good chance of getting a commission in the Cavalry. They told me the War Office would let me know the result. They couldn't say when!! Oh that War Office.

Probably we shall be able to get married before we hear anything. It's been rather good fun, the candidate before me for the medical exam stood 6ft and weighed only 10-9 and had a chest like a shrunken tomato (same colour too) so you can imagine how your Allie pushed his chest out and bent the tape! The old doctor did chortle![26]

On 23 August, British troops were involved in their first battle of the war, at Mons in Belgium. The numerically superior Germans ultimately overwhelmed them, and the Allied troops were forced to retreat. This marked a dramatic psychological turning point for the British public at home. Although recruitment had been going well, the real boom began in the last week of August and peaked in the first week of September.[27] British freedom really did now seem at stake, and the popular opinion was that every man fit to fight must offer his services to the suddenly desperate defence of the nation. **Kate Parry Frye** was more worried than ever:

The news of the appalling losses to the British was so disturbing – I bought a paper and walked on reading it and ended by walking as far as Slaters in Victoria. Then I dined at 7.30 and walked all the way to Claverton St.[28]

Kate's seaside sojourn was now over and she was back living in her own rooms in London. She recorded the details of the recruitment frenzy in London and how it had become part of the fabric of daily life:

Great meetings are being organized to help inspire the men of the country. The Women are being implored to send their men forth. Well, all I possess is doing his duty – if he was sent to the Front – terrible as it would be – I could only say 'go'. How the men can hesitate I don't know.

A walk to the Chapel Royal for service at 6.30. A truly wonderful sermon telling us we must all be prepared to give our only son – and when God asks for him say 'Rather'. The Chapel was packed. I walked up the Strand – a fresh set of Posters and paper boys yelling all different news and no end of people – all very quiet – a hushed feeling everywhere. People just looking into one another's faces anxiously.[29]

One Sunday in early September, Kate got the early morning train out of London towards the Kent coast. She was on her way to visit John for the first time since he'd joined his regiment in Shoeburyness. His earlier soldiering days had predated their acquaintance, so when Kate saw her actor boyfriend turned out as a soldier, it was quite a surprise:

John met me on the Platform – it was exciting. We both gasped. He looks so well and has a most flourishing moustache – some grey twigs in it – and of course he was born to wear khaki. His uniform is a Hills of Bond St – so although old is much nicer than most others. He is as brown as a berry.

He took me through to see his quarters – I don't know if I ought to have gone up but I did. Then to Church and we sat in the married officers' pew. He had got let off parade to go with me – a war service and sermon on 'Abraham' again . . . Afterward for a walk round and for John to leave his sword – and I got introduced to the Major. Then soon after 1 John took me to the Shoebury Hotel where he had engaged a room and we had lunch – I was ever so hungry and ate a lot. Then we went a lazy walk to see barbed wire entanglements – then back to sit by the river – or sea. The tide was up and it was gorgeous – such a nice air.

He saw me off at 7.15 and kissed me at the railway station. John wants to marry me if they are sent off to Malta and take me. But I don't think we could live on his pay. He is applying for a captaincy in Kitchener's Army. If he gets that he will go to the front I suppose. We never seem to get any nearer getting married – and don't suppose we ever shall now.[30]

John Collins in uniform as a captain in the Royal Garrison Artillery.

The war did not stand in the way of **Alan Lloyd**'s wedding after all. On the afternoon of Tuesday 1 September, he married **Dorothy Hewetson** in her home town of Boston Spa. She had looked beautiful in 'a dress of cream charmeuse, trimmed with old lace, the gift of her mother, [with] a train of silver brocade veiled with old lace. She wore too a veil and wreath of orange blossom and carried a sheaf of white madonna lilies.'[31] Though it was a sumptuous wedding, the war did cast a shadow over the proceedings: Alan's first choice of best man couldn't be there because he was in the army, and his parents had only just made it back from the war-torn continent in time.

After the ceremony, the newlyweds had left Boston Spa for Derby, and from there they'd travelled on to Wales for their honeymoon. They spent the first week of September in Barmouth, a little resort town in North Wales with a long sandy beach and a picturesque harbour. **Dorothy Lloyd** wrote to her new mother-in-law from their hotel on the promenade not long after their arrival, bubbling over with happiness:

> Just a line to say we arrived here this evening, we both are <u>frightfully</u> happy, Allie is kindness and goodness itself and is spoiling me dreadfully. We did enjoy the wedding and are both feeling heaps better already for the sea lungs. It was lovely having you all at the wedding. You can't think how happy we are little Mama. Tons of love to all.[32]

Alan was slightly more down to earth in the letter he wrote home the following day – he'd already had enough of the holiday crowds at Barmouth and his mind was wandering back to its usual preoccupations – his car and his application to join the army:

> Do write and tell us if you know of any nice quiet little mountain spot in Wales. There's too many pierrots and people here for us! Up here things don't look like war, it's not like the East Coast.
>
> We got several letters here addressed by you but nothing from War Office. Has a speedometer arrived for me? If any parcel looks likely please see if it's it, and if so have it taken at once to Mulliners in Gas Street, who will fit it to my DFP.[33]

By early September, **Reg Evans** and the 1st Herts had moved on yet again. Accommodation in the schools in Hertford and Romford had been basic enough, but since then they'd been camping, and conditions were worse still. Reg wrote to his mother on 2 September from Bury St Edmunds, where they were living in bivouacs outside the town whilst their training continued:

> We have been out of town here and bivouacked in some meadows and are as comfortable as we can expect. There is one thing that we are very

grateful for, that is we have a running stream close handy in which we can wash and splash to our hearts' content. When I tell you that at our last camping place we had to go 2½ miles for a proper wash, you will understand how much we appreciate this. At Long Melford we used to go into the cottages in the village at first but after a day or two all you met with was, 'for drinking purposes only, we are short of water.'

You would enjoy seeing us here. First thing in a morning we have to sprint round the country lanes here and go in for physical and Swedish drill. After breakfast company drill and handling arms, in the afternoon a lecture. This is of course only a sample day's work, it is varied a little, for instance last night we were out till 11 o'clock on night operations.

T Howe and I are both in the same bivouack so we 'kit in' together. We got up early on Tuesday morning 4.30 and slipped out of camp, up a little lane and cooked the bacon and eggs which he had been sent on a fire by the side of the road and had a rare meal though it was a little smoked. (By the way, if you send to me again don't send eggs, his were in a horrible state.) I am sorry to say that the food here isn't up to much so we have to supplement it by bringing it ourselves and when I tell you we only got 4/- last payday you will understand I am not very flush. But don't you worry, I am in the best of health and spirits and as hard as nails and haven't felt better in my life, so now you know that you needn't have the slightest anxiety on my account.[34]

As well as the source of their next wash or good meal, Reg and his fellow 1st Herts had something else on their minds: their deployment. That day, another Hertfordshire regiment was due to set sail for France, and Reg was thinking about when his moment would come, as it must come soon:

The Herts Yeomanry and Artillery are going out tonight but we don't know where we are going yet.

I don't want to swank, but I thank God every minute very near, that I am some use to our Country even if it isn't much and I know this, we couldn't be in a more honourable war. I am an Englishman and know that whatever happens nobody shall ever say that I failed in my country's crisis and please God I get back safely and shall always have pride in the knowledge that I did my duty.[35]

*

At the end of September, **Alan and Dorothy Lloyd** were coming to the end of their honeymoon. Though Alan had still not heard from the War Office, his new marriage had not quelled his desire to fight for his country. He was as much in love with Dorothy as ever, but was also still the same gung-ho, adventure-seeking young man he'd always been. Finally, on Dorothy's birthday, the telegram he'd been waiting for arrived:

> Temporary Second Lieut – AS Lloyd Edgbaston Grove Birmingham
> A 3772 reference War Office Letter no 112 over Artillery over 1965 of 3rd October Join at once 17th Divisional Artillery – Swanage.[36]

He wrote to his father from London with great excitement:

> War Office discovered I had a commission, asked me why the devil I hadn't obeyed orders and reported to York as ordered, told me to do so at once! I have ordered all my kit – awfully expensive, please note my birthday's very near![37]

At last, Alan was a soldier.

As the days shortened and turned cooler, the excitement of the summer faded. Britain had to adjust to the cold, difficult realities of being a country at war. Alan Lloyd was one of 750,000 men who had enlisted by the end of September, in addition to the existing soldiers who had been called up. That meant thousands of communities diminished; hundreds of thousands of families left without a loved one; hundreds of thousands of jobs left empty.

Hallie Miles had not had to see someone very close to her join up. But she had been forced to adjust to some very inconvenient absences. Her vegetarian restaurant might have been terribly alternative, but its staff and customers were no different from anyone else when it came to the war; all were keen to do their bit. Hallie and Eustace had worked hard for eight years to establish their business; that now became markedly more difficult. The initial patriotic fervour that Hallie had experienced along with everyone else had run its course – now she understood what war would mean for her:

We are paying half wages to the married men who have gone to join the army. We are replacing our men as far as possible by other men on the Staff, so as not to increase the wages, since the paying of half wages to the wives comes heavy.

Then, nearly every day we see more vacant seats at our tables, and we know that more of our old customers have gone to the Front. Sometimes they come and say goodbye to me; that always seems so solemn; a sort of 'rite'. I hardly know which I am feeling most – glad that they are going to fight for their country or sorrow at the thought they may never return![38]

4

THE HOME FRONT:
DEFENDING THE REALM

August–November 1914

One hardly knows London at night now. Scarcely any streetlights are allowed.
We can hardly believe or realise it is the same world as we used to live in.

Hallie Miles's diary, Autumn 1914

A specially onerous, but most important duty, incumbent both on citizens and police, is that of watching 'spies'.

Andrew Clark's diary, September 1914

On 13 August, a special edition of the *London Gazette* was being run off the press at His Majesty's Stationery Office. The official journal of the British government, in wartime it assumed new significance, publishing dispatches from the front.[1] On this afternoon, however, the important information that was being printed on its pages concerned not the soldiers soon to be fighting abroad, but the people staying at home. It set out details of the Defence of the Realm Act, which had been hurried through Parliament the previous week without debate, and which had given the government unprecedented, wide-ranging powers on the home front during wartime.[2]

Few ordinary Britons would have seen the *Gazette* itself, but the story was picked up by the regular press. In black and white, on pages stuffed into the back pockets of flat-capped men on trams and into the briefcases of suited men in motorcars; on papers piled up on the hearthside bookshelf in the rectory of Great Leighs and on the meat-free breakfast table of **Hallie Miles** in London, there was a warning of how gravely this war would affect Britons' lives, even if they weren't going near a battlefield.

The government recognised that the war Britain had embarked on would be different: the first to be fought by industrialised nations. Much more than a meeting of men on foreign fields, it would come down to the ability of the nation to muster its resources and population behind those men; through control of its finance, its industry, its resources, its press at home. The support of the army, the defence of Britain against invasion, keeping morale up on the home front – after recruitment to the army, these were the priorities, and the rights of individual citizens would now come second to the objectives of the government.

At her kitchen table in Hemel Hempstead, **Reg Evans**'s mother was carefully wrapping up the latest edition of the *Hertfordshire Gazette* to put in the post to him. **Frances Evans** knew that Reg liked to keep abreast of the local news and he was constantly reminding her in his letters to send the paper. She herself had skimmed through the article on page seven, 'Warnings to the Public: what you must not do.'[3] However, like most ordinary people, she had probably not taken in all the detail of the government's new powers, which ranged from the right to requisition property and land or to destroy buildings and evacuate neighbourhoods; to censorship of the press, of letters, and even of conversations on military and naval matters; to forbidding trespassing on railways or loitering on bridges and viaducts.

Much of this was old news to Frances anyway, who had already seen with her own eyes how her little slice of England had been changed by the war. The railway had been taken over and, with priority given to the transportation of troops, local rail services had been drastically altered or cancelled altogether. All public buildings in the town had been requisitioned for use by the army, along with practically all open spaces and most of the area's stabling. And while Frances had waved goodbye to her own son, she'd watched the arrival of hundreds of other women's sons in Hemel Hempstead, many of whom had to be accommodated by the townspeople. In all likelihood, Frances had already put up at least one soldier under her own roof, whilst Reg made do in a tent not far away.[4]

Requisitioning was as widespread in London as anywhere else, and institutions from The Royal Opera House to The Landmark Hotel would be seized for war use. It wasn't just buildings that were needed; over the course of the war almost half a million horses were requisitioned by the government, and not just from the countryside. **Hallie Miles** was worried that there would now be problems with the delivery of goods within the capital:

> I saw a sad procession yesterday of the dear horses being marched through the streets – even they have to take their share! I believe that the big stores have had nearly all their van horses commandeered.[5]

And there were further inconveniences to come. After she and Eustace had had their bank holiday break in Westgate-on-Sea cut short by the outbreak of war, they'd made plans for a late summer holiday to Cornwall. But just before they were due to set off, their hopes of a relaxing getaway were scuppered by the war once again. All trains were now for the priority use of the military:

> We were going to lovely Looe in Cornwall, and were actually within two days of starting, but the Great Western Railway will not guarantee our being able to get back, even if we were able to get there. The Railways have all been taken over by the government.[6]

Hallie considered herself a journalist (she had listed that amongst her other professions of author and company secretary in the last census). As she wrote her diary in these early days of war, it is fair to assume that she already intended to later publish this writing, if the war turned into the big event it was shaping up to be.[7] This probably accounts for what appear to be efforts on her part to ensure she didn't appear unpatriotic. She wrote, somewhat over-enthusiastically, of the alternative ways she and Eustace had found to escape from the unrelenting work of the restaurant. Their favourite was the cinema. The films might have been silent, but audiences were not. As Hallie observed, the grainy newsreels conveying the latest developments of the British war effort were hugely popular:

> Another way that we are taking our holiday is by going to the Cinemas. We find it a real help and recreation, and the pictures thrown upon the screen are so loyal and thrilling and realistic. In this way we see everything that is going on. It is splendid that Lord Kitchener is at the head

of the War Office and that Lord Roberts and General French are alive to help us in this great crisis. When their portraits are thrown on the screen the audience nearly burst with enthusiasm and excitement.[8]

The British government had not yet harnessed the power of the cinema for propaganda purposes (though that would come in time), but newsreel content was carefully controlled. The censorship of the press was immediate. No journalists at all were permitted at the front, and all war news came from the War Office's own correspondent, whose reports were personally vetted by Kitchener. The support of the British public was paramount and no inconvenient truths could be allowed to spoil the official narrative of the British struggle.

The day after it published its piece on the Defence of the Realm Act, *The Times* ran an article entitled 'Lord Kitchener's Plan: Preparing to see the struggle through.' Kitchener's message to the public was unequivocal: they must get behind the war effort. In this life and death struggle with Germany, Britain was the underdog: 'What is the situation? We are fighting a nation in arms of 70 million people and we have no good reason to suspect that they have any object in life but to crush us if they can.'[9] *The Times* readership was right on board, it seemed; over August, suggestions poured in from patriotic readers on how ordinary people could help out, which ranged from holidaymakers volunteering to help with the harvest on farms where horses had been commandeered, to turning over greenhouses to food production[10]. Britons, it seemed, had got the message: that this war would involve civilians at home in a way never before seen.

Helen Franklin had been spending the summer in her family's country house, Chartridge Lodge, in a quiet, leafy village in Buckinghamshire. Her father, a banker from a well-known Anglo-Jewish banking family, only read *The Times*, which was therefore the source of most of 22-year-old Helen's war news. In August 1914, Helen had just started what would grow into a lengthy and intimate correspondence with a friend of the family, a successful lawyer based in Cairo called **Norman Bentwich**. She was initially a little overwhelmed that such a grand young man had taken an interest in her, but rose to the challenge. One summer's evening, as her siblings thwacked a croquet ball around the lawn outside, she sat down to compose a response to his long letter to her, which had asked about her thoughts on the outbreak of war. The ideas espoused in *The Times* certainly seem to have found fertile soil in her brain:

> It's good for you to find time to write to me, when you are so busy. You say you wonder what I think of the war; I'm afraid my opinions are very childish, and pure jingo. Because I think that the only thing to do is to concentrate on smashing Germany.
>
> I believe we are fighting for an ethical truth, and that the war is a struggle between civilisation, and all it stands for, on one side, against Germany's barbarism, which seems the result of their extraordinarily rapid and material progress of the last forty years, which isn't based on any solid civilisation.[11]

Helen was exceptionally well educated for a woman of her generation, having recently graduated from Bedford College, the first higher education institution in the country for women only. But now, having completed her studies, a life of leisure was looming ahead of her – the fate of most women of her highly privileged background. Helen was somewhat unconventional and had started doing some social work with poor Jewish girls in the East End, as well as looking after a local troupe of girl guides. But the outbreak of the war highlighted for her the limitations placed on women's lives – and she didn't like it. Helen had to watch her brother Ellis head off on what she saw as an exciting new adventure while she was left behind:

> Ellis has been up to London today, for his first drill, he has joined the old public school boys' force and is going into camp next week. Now he's going, it makes me wilder than ever at being a girl. Of course, I know you're right and that home interests and life must be kept going all the time, but it's like telling the stage carpenter not to be jealous of the actor as he is just as useful a part of the production. I think everybody likes doing the work that shows – and, after all, it seems much finer to be working for the cause than for the effects.
>
> I am just existing as a useless female at present. There's nothing definite for us women to do.[12]

In truth there was something for her to do at home: war or no war, the number one priority for a young woman of Helen's age and class was marriage. With her letters to Norman she was making progress in that, at least.

Kate Parry Frye found herself in an altogether different situation. **John Collins** had left her to join the war effort but, unlike Helen, she was not simply sitting at home feeling left out. She found herself – suddenly and unexpectedly – with her own war work to do. Like most suffrage societies, The New Constitutional Society for Women's Suffrage (where Kate worked) had decided to ditch protest activities and, in the spirit of national unity, turn its energies towards the war effort.

Kate had received a letter from them. The NCS offices in Knightsbridge, formerly the hub of their campaigning activities, would now be turned into a clothing workshop. The society would give gainful employment to young women whose ordinary work had disappeared with the sudden loss of supply sources and export markets in Europe, paying them for the production of clothes for the Red Cross and the army, as well as ordinary civilian clothing:[13]

> The NCSS will take as their special object the care of girls who are thrown out of their ordinary work by the dislocation of trade owing to the war. In connection with this we hope to be able to use our Hall as a workroom for girls, who will receive payment for work done for the benefit of sufferers during the war. Money, materials, sewing machines, etc are needed at once. The office has been reopened. There is much to be done and offers of help are urgently needed.[14]

Kate was to have an early taste of what was in store for so many women in this war: hard work. For many of them, it would be their first experience of it outside the home. On the morning of 28 August, Kate made her way to the NCS offices in Park Mansions Arcade, Knightsbridge:

> To the Office. Miss McGowan and Gladys turned up and later Alexandra turned up and explained the new scheme to us. I am to take Miss McGowan's place and run the Workroom and Miss Simeon is to run the Office. I tried to take it calmly but my brain reeled a bit. There is a splendid forewoman and 11 girls in the Hall hard at work. All have been deserted owing to the War. Miss McGowan showed me the books etc and again I tried to keep calm.[15]

Young women working in the converted NCS offices in Knightsbridge.

In Great Leighs, the Rev. **Andrew Clark** was taking on the important role of channelling the villagers' patriotism to constructive ends. He called a meeting in the Mission Hall, a corrugated iron barn that the squire had built on his land that was generally known by the locals as 'the tin tabernacle'.[16] Andrew had decided that they too should aid in the provision of clothing for the armed forces, and called together the women of the village to tell them this:

> Meeting in the Mission Room Great Leighs, at 7 p.m. to consider whether and in what way the parishes of Great [and Little] Leighs could help in providing garments for the sailors and soldiers in the field, in hospital and in camp. The Rector who had called the meeting, explained its purpose to a large meeting of women and girls of the parishes and then withdrew.[17]

It would not be long before Andrew found war work that he took to more enthusiastically. In rural Essex, as elsewhere in Britain, there was real fear of a possible German invasion during the first months of war, and anxiety that Germany might have undercover agents all around the country, primed to carry out devastating acts of sabotage. Essex was seen as particularly vulnerable, both because of its proximity to the capital and because it was thought that the Germans planned to invade the east coast. Rumours flew around Great Leighs, and Andrew faithfully recorded them in his diary:

> Last night Mrs Earl said that in a letter from her daughter, in domestic service in London, she was told that 'five' foreigners had been seized attempting to poison the great reservoir at Chingford, Essex, the most recent and most important source of supply for London.[18]

In this climate of fear, there was only one task any self-respecting patriot could dedicate himself to: counter-espionage. Andrew and the men of Great Leighs answered the government's call for volunteer policemen, a 'special constabulary' to supplement the work of the ordinary police force. The village had its own regular constable, but in this, the nation's hour of need, that was no longer deemed sufficient. Once more, the people of Great Leighs gathered in the 'tin tabernacle' – though this time, it was the men of the village who crowded in. Andrew recorded these proceedings rather more enthusiastically than the last:

> Meeting to enrol Special Constables: The meeting was held in the Mission Room, Joseph Herbert Tritton in the Chair. There were forty persons present, including all the farmers not too old to serve, and others. The Chairman stated briefly that there was great need of the services of Special Constables throughout the country.
>
> The legislation of last month had laid upon the ordinary police an enormous amount of extra duty. A specially onerous, but most important duty, incumbent both on citizens and police, is that of watching 'spies'. There are at least 50,000 aliens (Germans, Austrians and Hungarians) in this country. Of these a large number come regularly, week by week, to the market at Chelmsford and elsewhere. Special Constables are to arrest all persons speaking to the dishonour of this country.
>
> The main duty will be to protect all roads and especially the abutments of bridges, telegraph posts and the like. The hired agents of the enemy may try to do damage and if our fleet or army suffer any reverse they are sure to be very much bolder and more active.[19]

The two names on the top of the list of volunteers were. A. Clark and J. H. Tritton, the seventy-year-old squire.

In the heart of cosmopolitan London, **Hallie Miles** also noted the angry, anti-German mood and fears of espionage, though in her own, ever-genteel way:

> One hardly ever hears a strain of German music nowadays. I wanted to play some stray bits of Schumann and Schubert the other day but I felt I simply couldn't. Then there is always the spy peril round us. I know I travelled in a bus with two German spies today, and it was such an awful feeling, as if a dark shadow was present.[20]

At least she and Eustace finally managed to have their holiday. At the end of September, they escaped the noisy streets of the capital and returned to Westgate-on-Sea, their favoured seaside haunt:

> We are spending another quiet weekend at Westgate-on-Sea. It is such a relief to be out of the vivid reality of War for a few days. The constant shouting of the paper-boys, the huge posters that one hardly dares to look at, and the stricken faces one meets in the streets, seem tearing at one's heart-strings all day long.[21]

Nevertheless, Hallie might well have been shocked at the changes that had come over the little resort. The scene that met them was a world away from that of the bank holiday weekend only six weeks earlier. Bathing at Westgate had been forbidden; the bandstand had been annexed for military purposes; the grounds of the finest hotel on the front had been commandeered by the authorities for a wireless station; and the navy had established a base for seaplanes on part of the shore, with all public access forbidden.[22]

Furthermore, on the Sunday before their arrival, a minesweeper, HMS *Yarmouth II*, had drifted ashore a few hundred yards up the coast. All attempts to remove the wreck had failed and it languished in the waters for all to see, half sunk.[23] 'The vivid reality of war' had followed them on their holidays again.

*

The men of the Great Leighs' special constabulary were undertaking the physical training and drilling regimes appropriate to their role. **Andrew Clark** recorded the difficulties they'd encountered, which were not for want of effort on the volunteers' part:

Monday 14 September: At 6.30 p.m. the special constables met at the gate of Bishop's Hall for their first drill – 22 present. It was decided that, by reason of the cows which had been at pasture in Mr Brown's field, the drill should be in Mr Jack Stephen's field, next to it.

The drill was carried out vigorously till light failed (7.15 p.m.) It was undertaken under various unusual difficulties: the surface of the field was very uneven; there was blowing a gale and the drill-instructor's voice was mostly inaudible; the instructor is not a tall man and he stood beyond much taller men than himself so that his demonstrations ('You move this way,' 'You wheel that way') were invisible to three-quarters of the company. The right-about movement produced time after time the most ludicrous clumps or dispersed confusions which produced shouts of mirth on the part of the company when they took breath to see the tangle they had got into.[24]

Annoyingly, the competition was doing well. Just down the road from Great Leighs was Little Waltham. Their special constabulary was headed up by a retired Metropolitan Police officer, who was already advertising his own force's successes at spy-catching, whilst the men of Great Leighs were still floundering in basic training:

Sir Richard Pennyfeather plumes himself that he has caught a spy. An elderly woman with a strong German accent, selling lace at Little Waltham, was arrested by his order. She said that her husband was a doctor, in a small way, at one of the East Coast towns, but by Sir Richard's order she was imprisoned for the night. In the morning her account of herself was confirmed but Sir Richard, still suspicious, has ordered her to be kept under public surveillance.[25]

The men of Great Leighs had other things on their mind as well. It was September: harvest time. Once the crop was brought in early in the month, the farmers moved on to the task of ploughing the fields ready for the winter's crop. This year the work was harder than ever: 'The farmers in the district are making special efforts to get the land ready for winter-wheat sowing. There is also a shortage of horses, the most powerful farm horses having been taken for Army purposes.[26]

Kate Parry Frye was struggling to deal with the new hardships the war was heaping onto her daily life. She had been a paid worker for the suffrage society for three years, doing long days on the campaign trail, but in the first weeks of September, the reality of a highly demanding, full-time managerial job had hit her hard.

Five or six days a week, Kate arrived at the Knightsbridge workroom to be greeted by the noisy clatter of sewing machines and the voices of a growing number of workers. Needles were busy stitching Red Cross overalls and aprons, men's shirts and even ladies' dresses. As the orders mounted up and new girls were taken on, Kate – whose only work experience was the acting she'd done in her youth and her more recent suffrage campaigning – couldn't keep up with the paperwork that landed on her desk:

> Monday 31 August: A tremendous day of work at the Office. My hair nearly stood on end. I only dashed out to lunch at 1.30 back at 2. Swallowed a cup of tea and then worked on until 8. If only I were efficient!
>
> Tuesday 1 September: A fearful day in the Office. Hard at it until 7. Miss Simeon stayed on until 6 – I didn't finish my work but I felt tired and it was wisest to stop. It surely can't be like this every day. Not only the office work but the Work Room.
>
> Thursday 10 September: To the Office at 10.30. People waiting to see me then and onwards through the day a tremendous rush. We have taken on more girls – are now 20 in the Workroom and so busy and don't know which way to turn and still orders come.[27]

Kate was now realising how inadequately her education and upbringing had equipped her for working life. In common with most middle-class women, she hadn't received much in the way of a formal education; she was struggling, she knew it, and it made her cross: '(I don't) understand why I was born if I wasn't to be educated. I waste half my time in the Office not doing things properly.'[28]

And on top of all of this and the absence of her boyfriend, there was something else on her mind, something quite terrifying. It was a fear that many Londoners shared: that war was about to come to them in the shape of German Zeppelin airships. Zeppelins were the largest flying machines the world had ever seen, invented in the early twentieth century and used in Germany for passenger transport. With the outbreak of war, the German army and navy quickly harnessed them for more destructive ends. They had initially been used for reconnaissance, but the British public were terrified that they would unleash a dreadful onslaught on them from the skies; that bombs would soon be rained down upon London.

In the evenings, when she'd left the din of chattering workers and busy machines behind her, Kate tried to recover from the stresses of the day. But the nagging threat that hung over London did not allow her the relaxation she craved – however much she tried to help it along:

> Had supper – half a bottle of claret I brought with me from Worthing and really felt quite drunk but, an effort of mind over matter, got up and finished my jobs – then some writing. The light in Big Ben is not lit at night now. I am near there if Bombs are dropped. Oh dear.[29]

Hallie Miles was even closer to the shadow of Big Ben than Kate was in her Pimlico flat – her restaurant was just a few streets away from Parliament Square. And the famous clock's light was not the only one that had been extinguished in the city. In September, the provisions for the dimming of lights in the Defence of the Realm Act – which initially applied only to defended harbours – were extended to allow the Secretary of State to order the dimming or extinction of any lights, anywhere.[30]

By day, in the right part of town, away from recruiting offices, it might be possible to forget the war. But at night, the reality was there for all to see: a cloak of darkness, punctuated by the searchlights sweeping the sky, reminded Londoners that they were in the capital city of a nation at war. Hallie wrote about the strange transformation:

> One hardly knows London at night now. Scarcely any street lights are allowed, and what lights there are have been painted with some dark stuff half way down the glass to shade them, so that if there is a Zeppelin

raid over London the raiders will not be able to distinguish the lights. London looks as if it were lit only by night-lights. It is, in a way, peaceful and dreamy looking, but very weird, and it is difficult for people to find their way about.

There is a huge erection on the top of Hyde Park corner for a great searchlight which sweeps the sky every night, and one of our airships circles over London every day, keeping watchful guard over us.[31]

Less immediately discernible than the physical changes to the cityscape was the rising fear that was seeping into the city's streets and homes. The bombing of civilians from the air was a totally new phenomenon: it had never, ever happened before. It was, on the one hand, difficult to be afraid of something so abstract; on the other, it meant the imagination could run wild. Rumours flew around as to what was in store for London; and Hallie, living and working in the heart of the city, was afraid:

Everyone says the Zeppelins will invade England. One of the German war cartoons is of an army of Zeppelins over Trafalgar Square, throwing bombs down. It couldn't be much closer to us![32]

All that Hallie could do – all that Britons could do – was wait.

Wait – and do what they were told. If German airships flying high above Britain were to be foiled by darkness beneath them, it wasn't enough just to dim the streetlights. The order was issued by police forces across Britain that all outside lights must be dimmed, everywhere: house lights, shop advertising lights, even car headlights.[33]

Even isolated Great Leighs had to comply. In fact, Great Leighs was on the route that Zeppelins were expected to take to get to the capital.

One morning in October, **Andrew Clark** was walking from the rectory along the Boreham Road. The ploughing was finally completed and the fields and hedgerows that he passed were losing the vividness of autumn and settling into their winter colours. When Andrew got into the village, he saw a new notice had been pinned up outside the little police station:

CITY OF NORWICH.

Lighting Regulations & Restrictions.

SPECIAL CAUTION

Between HALF-AN-HOUR AFTER SUNSET & HALF-AN-HOUR BEFORE SUNRISE, NO LIGHT OF ANY DESCRIPTION shall be visible from the outside of any house, shop, premises, hut, tent, or building of any description.

Any person striking matches, using hand or flash lamps, torches, automatic lighters, etc., in any public street or place is liable to be arrested.

Hotel Keepers, Lodging House Proprietors, etc., are requested to place this notice in a prominent position so that it may be seen by Visitors and Non-residents.

E. F. WINCH,

Guildhall, Norwich, *Chief Constable.*
4th January, 1917.

An example of the lighting regulations and restrictions brought into effect in 1914.

Saturday 17 October: 11.30 a.m. Notice up at the Police Station, opposite the Post Office that:
(a) no lamps must show in shops;
(b) as few lights as possible may show in the streets;
(c) no lights must shine from windows of upper storeys;
(d) no lobby-lights to be used, unless shaded, so as not to show outside.[34]

Later that afternoon, the one regular constable in Great Leighs knocked on the door of the rectory. He was doing the rounds, telling residents of their new obligations in the defence of the realm, adding a healthy dose of fear as an incentive to comply: '1p.m. the Policeman served a copy of this notice on the Rectory. He says this house is on the line along which hostile airships are expected to travel.'[35]

This must have caused Andrew some concern; but he had a lot of other things on his mind as well. The special constables of Little Waltham, down the way, had been as busy as ever. They'd raised their

game and started nightly patrols, although these had not proved popular
with the men:

> A state of things verging on sedition and mutiny is reported among
> the Special Constables of Little Waltham: Sir Richard Pennyfeather,
> their chief, has sent the Little Waltham Special Constables (grocer,
> butcher, baker and other comfort-loving citizens) out as patrols, night
> by night. Unhappy Little Waltham Constables, 'Why should they
> only toil, while Great Leighs outer-darkness takes its ease in full
> measure?'[36]

But Great Leighs was not to be outdone. The squire decided that they
too must take on these vital night patrols. In the dark hours of a late
autumn night, in a village without lights, in a rectory with curtains
pulled, beside the embers of a dying fire, Andrew was getting his boots
on. Tonight his name was on the rota, to patrol the muddy paths and
fields of Great Leighs in the hunt for German spies:

> 12.45 a.m. Left the house to go on patrol. Found a sweetly bright moon,
> a singularly mild air and a gentle breeze from the south-west. Just at
> the end of the Terling Road [Fuller Street] I met my fellow watchman
> on the beat, Mr Edwin Luckock; put the official armlet on his left
> forearm, and handed over to him the truncheon.
>
> Except the coughing bullocks and the three dogs, not a sound was
> heard, from first to last, except the sighing of the telegraph wires in the
> soft breeze.[37]

A German airship, if it had been floating in the skies above Essex,
would have seen little below. But there, hundreds of feet down, on a
bench in the graveyard of a little church in a little village, a cigarette
glowed in the darkness. Nothing else gave away the might of Great
Leighs special constabulary.

By November, **Helen Franklin** and her family had left their country
estate and were back in their townhouse near Hyde Park. Helen's brother
Ellis had left home and was in training nearby. Helen, though still
jealous of his adventures, was getting more of a taste of war herself
than she had anticipated. The great searchlights that were scanning the

city's skies every night were not far from where she lived and, in the absence of definite information from the newspapers, the rumour mill had been working overtime. Londoners now believed a bombing raid was imminent. Helen was still writing to **Norman Bentwich**, and she filled him in on the news:

> I went to see Ellis in his camp last week. He is thoroughly happy there – but the ground is in such a frightful condition, they have all been sent away, into billets, much to their annoyance.
>
> There have been heaps of scares of raids here – I almost wish something of the sort would happen though as everything seems so very secret and nervy. I wish the censor would tell us more, and not treat us like uneducated serfs.[38]

But even against the backdrop of war, normal life had to go on, and a lot had been happening for Helen. Norman came to London on holiday and she spent a lot of time with him. He was an earnest, religious, highly intelligent young man, and very respected within the upper-class, Jewish circle they inhabited. Helen was almost ten years his junior, and saw herself as something of a silly young girl in comparison to him; she was flattered that he had taken an interest in her. In fact, he had done more than that: before he left to go back to his job in Cairo, they went for dinner at The Carlton together. There, Norman asked her to marry him. Afterwards, they walked along Whitehall, the sweep of searchlights occasionally puncturing the darkness above them.[39] Helen had not given him an answer, and still wasn't able to:

> Norman, don't think me a beast for not having said anything sooner about what you asked me before you went away, you can't know how tremendously I appreciated it, because I behaved then just like a baby I was so surprised. I hadn't thought about anything like that and I had no idea that you had either. I had just gone on enjoying every moment I was with you and looking forward to your letters, and I'd never thought once of it leading to something else.
>
> I never seem to realise yet that I am properly grown up and I forget that I must seem so to other people. So when you asked me then I couldn't realise it at all. Will you forgive me if I had seemed a beast? And I have been thinking about it ever since, all the time – but I want

you to let me go on thinking about it still longer. Do you mind, will you go on writing to me anyway?

Anyway Norman, I know you will understand.

Yours ever, Helen Franklin.[40]

Norman did understand; he was prepared to wait. Helen was still young, and as she seemed to realise herself, she still had a lot of growing up to do.

One autumn evening, **Kate Parry Frye** had finished yet another gruelling day's work in the office:

Walked all the way home – via Hyde Park Corner. The search lights on the top of the Arch are most fascinating to watch. But the neighbourhood itself is dark as a bag – I was amused to see the news vendor at the corner lighting up his posters stuck on the railings at St George's Hospital with a small pocket electric light.

Bought a hat in the Buckingham Palace Rd for 7s 11d and brought it home in a paper bag – along with a cutlet, tomatoes and fish for breakfast.[41]

She was feeling increasingly lonely, and had been thinking a lot about John. She had been accustomed to have him always on hand for her, unfailingly loyal, but she had hardly seen him since he'd left for training. In the middle of October, he finally got some leave and came down to visit her. They were heading to the south coast to see her family, and Kate was glad of the chance to tell him, in person, what she'd been thinking on recent nights alone in her rooms:

[John] came along at 1 o'clock and helped me to balance accounts and run messages and generally excite the office – and we got off about 1.30. He has got leave till tomorrow. [Got] the 4.30 to Hove. Had a carriage to ourselves as far as Brighton – and I suggested we should get married at Christmas and share a Flat. I have been so miserable all the week – tears trickling into my boiled egg at supper – that I feel something must happen.

Of course it's a very rash suggestion – but John was pleased at the idea. It would be very peculiar – but I don't see I could be much more miserable married – and if we don't make some sort of effort it will never happen.[42]

It had been over a decade since John had first asked her to marry him. The next day they found themselves, serendipitously, in exactly the spot on Hove seafront where he'd first proposed. They had been young then and war had been the last thing on their minds. But things had changed. Now, in the army, John had a regular income after years of insecurity as a jobbing actor, and Kate needed support now in a way that she never had before:

Walked right along the Front as far as the Metropole – the same old crowd – but plenty of khaki. Agnes and Mother were very impressed by the saluting of John that went on – he did look nice – much nicer than any of the other officers.

We stood at the corner where eleven years ago all but a few days he proposed to me. I was fearfully indignant. I thought he oughtn't to have done anything of the kind, but I suppose he couldn't help himself and he doesn't seem to have thought of a single creature other than myself ever since. It's a good long slice out of life – 11 years.[43]

John and Kate said goodbye later that afternoon. He headed back to Shoeburyness, while Kate had a few days off which she was spending in Worthing. Back in her mother and sister's rooms that evening, Kate told them that she and John had finally decided to become man and wife:

We three sat round the fire and I told them the conclusion John and I had come to. Of course Mother was a bit shocked but I have known her take things worse. Agnes was very sympathetic and she thinks we should be doing quite right, if we really want to.[44]

As the nights grew colder and the searchlights silhouetted bare trees in Hyde Park, **Hallie Miles** sat by the window in her study, scribbling in her diary. Beneath the slight melodrama of her words, she captured the fears and feelings of a nation still slowly coming to terms with the brutal reality of the war:

It is so sad how many important people are dying (at home) from the shock and strain of this awful war. I do not wonder at it, for sometimes everything is so ghastly and the dread of what may be coming so horrible, that it seems much easier to die than to live! And yet I pray to live through it all for Eustace's sake.

We were saying last night as we walked through the dim streets (I clinging to Eustace for safety) and every now and then casting our eyes up to the skies to look for Zeppelins, that we could hardly believe or realise it was the same world as we used to live in; and that we are the same people.

And then, on the other hand, it is so strange that we are hardly able to remember or realise the old life of peace and safety, when war seemed a thing only to read of, as one reads history, and not a thing it was possible to actually live in.

There are no little things any longer, for there is too great a purpose in our lives now.[45]

5

THE WESTERN FRONT: THE FIRST BATTLE OF YPRES

October–November 1914

The trouble with the Germans is their enormous numbers.

Andrew Clark's diary, 21 November 1914

October 1914 had been dry and mild, though persistently dull and overcast skies served as a constant reminder to Britons of the oppressive war that hung over them. Then, at the end of the month, the temperature dropped and the sun came out.[1] On a bright, crisp morning, **Andrew Clark** and his wife were enjoying a hot bowl of porridge in the rectory. The reverend might have been a loyal citizen of Great Leighs, but he was resolutely Scottish when it came to the first meal of the day. He might even have been treated to hot scones, fresh off the griddle in the kitchen.[2] That morning, his cook also brought some news that left the Clarks rather bemused:

Tuesday 27 October: This morning our cook, Lizzie Oddey, a village woman, brought a village report she had heard last night: 'The victory of the English is now quite sure. Lord Rayleigh has been looking at "the thing" in the sky. He told one of his workmen that if it turned to an eagle, the Germans would win; and, if it turned to a bear, the English would win. It has turned to a bear.'

So far as I can conjecture, this 'dark speech' bears this interpretation. Lord Rayleigh, at Terling Place, has a powerful telescope and has been studying the comet. He may have made some joke about the astrological inference from its position in relation to the constellations Ursa and Aquila.[3]

Lizzie, like many other Britons, still dared to believe in a quick, conclusive end to the war, so that things could get back to normal for Christmas. On this day, as the Clarks ate porridge by the fire, in Belgium one of the most crucial battles of the war was under way: the first Battle of Ypres. After the early defeats of the war, in September the British and French forces had prevented the taking of Paris and had pushed the Germans back over the river Marne. They'd also recaptured lost ground in Belgium, including Ypres, which was the last obstacle between the German army and the Allied ports at Calais and Boulogne. Now the Germans were trying to take it once more. The battle for Ypres was Germany's last chance to bring about the swift victory in the west that their generals had planned.

As the fighting raged and the glorious medieval town of Ypres burned, little real news of the battle filtered back to people at home. Britons were left with rumours and hearsay to fill in the blanks left by the rigorous censoring of war news – though they were aided, in Great Leighs at least, by prophesies written in the stars. The only definite news that reached many Britons was that which they most dreaded: telegrams and letters from the War Office, reporting a casualty or a death.

In mid-October, news of the first such loss reached Great Leighs. One grey afternoon, Andrew Clark answered his door to a newly bereaved mother:

> 3.45 p.m. Mrs Sophia Fitch, wife of Walter Fitch, agricultural labourer, came to have their application signed for the effects of their son, Dick Fitch, of Second Essex Regiment, killed in action. Dick Fitch was a lad of just 19 and enlisted so recently as a year ago last June.[4]

It was the same in communities all across Britain. The most dreaded but the most carefully read war reports in the local newspapers were the casualty lists.

On the last day of October, in a welcome moment of quiet that Saturday afternoon, **Frances Evans** was reading the *Hertfordshire Gazette*. She would wrap it up to send to Reg just as soon as she'd finished. This week, the paper worried her a bit. It had news of a local woman who'd already lost two sons to the war, and another young lad's death was also reported.[5] The casualty lists seemed to become more prominent each week. One thought eased her anxiety a little: Reg, who was in billets in Bury St Edmunds, had told her he hoped to come home on a couple of days' leave next weekend.

But the escalating events overseas would prevent this. The following day, 1 November, the news that Frances had been dreading reached her in Hemel Hempstead: orders had been issued for the 1st Herts to depart for war. Reg and his fellow soldiers were not going to a far-flung corner of the Empire as they'd initially thought; they were going to Flanders, where, as the Battle of Ypres dragged on, reinforcements were desperately needed.

In the camp at Bury St Edmunds, the next few days were spent in furious preparations for the departure. All the men were issued with rifles.[6] Finally, on his last night on British soil for the foreseeable future, Reg found a moment to sit down and write a letter home:

Dear Mother,

As I daresay you have heard by now the 1st Herts are off to France tomorrow. I am jolly sorry that we have had to go in such a hurry as I was looking forward to coming home this weekend. I should have written to you yesterday but was not sure that the news was correct. You have not got anything to worry about over me at all. I am in excellent health.

I know you are disappointed that I haven't been able to see you again before I go on this little journey, so am I, but then that we cannot help. It is hard for you but remember Mother it is hard for me as well and you can make the parting easier or harder according to how you take this. After all you know I am only doing the same as thousands of other fellows and you would not be proud of me would you if I acted the coward now and tried to evade my Duty would you?

I can't promise of course when I shall be back home, that is not a matter I or any other man can settle, but please God we shall not be long now. Goodnight Mother I shall often think of you and always, as you know, with the best of thoughts, Reg.

Address letters only with name Regt etc. and add: On Active Service.[7]

The next day the battalion set off in two trains from Bury St Edmunds towards the coast, where they boarded the *City of Chester*. At midnight, they set sail, leaving behind the island nation that most had never left before. They landed at Havre at 11 a.m. the following morning and marched three and a half miles to a rest camp outside the town. The weather was good and Reg was enjoying his first trip abroad. He found time to write a brief note home, since he knew his mother would be worrying already:

> We have arrived safe and sound after a delightful voyage. A lovely spring-like day and everything O.K. Don't you worry about me. Remember me to all at Hemel Hempstead. Don't forget to send papers please. Much Love, Reg.[8]

The 1st Herts stayed in the rest camp outside Havre for two days, where they were issued with kit and practised their (generally non-existent) French. Then, on the morning of Sunday 8 November, they were instructed to move on. They boarded a train, travelling through the day and a sleepless night, before arriving at St Omer.[9] They were now very close to the Belgian border, and the rumble of the war could be distinctly heard. They were just thirty miles from Ypres.

Alan Lloyd was also on duty now, but further behind the lines. Much further, in fact – back across the channel in Swanage on the Dorset coast. One block from the promenade, in De Moulham Road, he and Dorothy had set up temporary home. It wasn't the farmhouse either of the newlyweds had envisaged, but Alan was a soldier now, in training with the 78th Brigade, Royal Field Artillery.

The couple had arrived in mid-October, fresh from their honeymoon, and after a week at the Royal Victoria Hotel, Dorothy had found them some rather fine rooms to make their own. As an officer, Alan could live as he pleased, and Dorothy wrote to her new in-laws, gushing about the great time they were having: 'Alan is very pleased with himself and is getting on well . . . We are lucky to be here, it's a most charming little place.' The men were in tents at the camp not far away, hoping that the huts they'd been promised would be built before winter set in.[10]

Within a few weeks, Alan had taken on the job of acting adjutant; it became his responsibility to look after the wellbeing of these 500 men, all new recruits to the army like himself. Alan, by his own admission, struggled a bit with the administrative work such a task generated. But as usual his car was also preying on his mind. He couldn't bear to think of it languishing un-driven at the family home. He wanted it fixed up and brought down to him by the family chauffeur so that he and Dorothy could enjoy some winter excursions in it, and wrote to his father with strict instructions:

> My dearest Papa,
>
> I have had a wire from Lyon and Co (the dynamo people in London) to say they are sending a CAB dynamo to Heath's Garage. It should have arrived there by the time this gets to you. If so, please let Walduck get it fitted to the DFP. Could you spare him to drive the car down here at the earliest opportunity? Please see that both our oilskins and the tarpaulin cover are brought in it together with any little present which you feel you would like to give.
>
> Take care of yourself, I now write reams of letters quoting about a dozen references and send wires all day at Govt expense, which I love![11]

It appears that Mr Lloyd obediently fulfilled his son's wishes because on 11 November, Dorothy wrote to her mother-in-law to thank them. Although Alan was now in khaki, it did not seem to be encroaching on his and Dorothy's happiness at all. Her biggest concern was that she was going to have to move her marital home once again:

> My dearest Mama,
>
> Please thank papa ever so much for letting Walduck bring the car down. Al has got a soldier servant who has been a chauffeur by name of Polly!
>
> We have to move our quarters next week as Al's brigade will then get into their huts and this house is too far from the huts so I've taken rooms up on the other cliff but they aren't half as nice as these. I have been trying to find a tiny house but haven't yet succeeded.[12]

Beyond the cliffs and back over the Channel, the struggle for Ypres continued. On 11 November, the Germans launched another general assault, their heaviest bombardment yet. The British Expeditionary Force, which had been under severe pressure for some time, was on the verge of being wiped out altogether.[13]

That day, **Reg Evans** and the 1st Hertfordshire Regiment, in France for less than a week, received orders to continue to the front lines. The

British army defending Ypres was in dire straits, and the 1st Herts was new blood that was desperately needed.[14] From billets near St Omer, they were directed into forty-five ordinary London buses, complete with London bus drivers who had volunteered for war transport. The journey eastwards over the French-Belgian border took them over five hours, with the drivers taking pains to avoid the channels of deep mud on either side of the road that threatened to trap them. By the end of the journey they were travelling in total darkness, the flashes of guns on the dark horizon growing nearer and nearer. The Germans were pressing in on Ypres on both flanks.[15]

London buses transporting men of the 2nd Royal Warwickshire Regiment through Dickebusch on their way to Ypres, 6 November 1914.

They were offloaded just outside Ypres, the beautiful city illuminated by gunfire. Reg and his comrades marched through ruins, the light from unquenched fires flickering on their faces. Then, for the first time, the battalion came under shrapnel fire. One officer and one ordinary soldier were struck, but fortunately neither was seriously injured. The 1st Herts travelled on, along the Menin Road beyond Ypres, and finally stopped in relative safety about two miles outside the city, just as dawn broke.[16] They snatched some sleep in bivouacs. It was Reg's first night of real war.

The next day, the weather had become decidedly wintry; the rain was almost turning to snow.[17] The British had succeeded in holding off the fierce German attack, but the battle was far from over. The BEF was being obliterated, and the British Army needed all the men it could get. It was only a matter of time before the 1st Herts were deployed into the heart of the fighting. Reg, thinking of home, wrote to his mother, though he didn't want to worry her:

> Hoping you are well. I am fine. You would laugh at the sights here and the way the people go on. It is fine-fun talking to them. We have trav-elled far. I thought of you a lot last night.
>
> Am afraid I shall not be able to get a pass for Xmas so save a little pudding for me. If you see anyone belonging to the Hempstead boys tell them they are all in good condition and there is no cause for any body to worry. Please send papers as we shall get no news here I feel certain.
>
> Give my Love to all and accept the same for yourself, from Reg.[18]

On the 14th, the 1st Herts received their orders to move up to the front line trenches. As territorial soldiers, they were factory workers, farmers, servants; very few had any actual war experience. Besides, this war was turning into something no one had experienced before: a war dug into the ground. After the mobile battles of the first weeks of war, when in September the British and French forces had started pushing the Germans back, the German commanders – keen to hold on to hard-won territory – ordered their men to dig themselves into trenches to halt the advance of their enemies. The Allies, on meeting this line of defence, had little choice but to dig their own line opposite. Trench warfare had begun.

That night, in the pouring rain, the 1st Herts entered the British trenches near the Nonnebossen woods, just east of Ypres. They were relieving the Oxfordshire and Buckinghamshire Light Infantry who had had a terrible time over the previous days. The Germans were a few hundred yards away, in their trenches. The worst of the German assault had passed, but the British trenches were still under fire, and the pouring rain made conditions unbearable. Reg didn't have time to write to his mother again – or perhaps didn't know what to write in the circumstances. But he scribbled a note to his brother Will, who worked on the railways at Coventry, and he passed the message on:

Have just had a card from Reg written last Friday – he says he is quite alright and asks me to let you know as he cannot do much writing. He is in the trenches which he says are pretty comfortable but the mud is nearly up to their knees – raining all the time.[19]

Reg's first experience of trench warfare lasted only two days. On the 16 November the 1st Herts were marched back three miles behind the lines to billets on a farm. But the battle for Ypres was not over yet.[20]

Great Leighs had received news from the front at Ypres in the form of a letter, slightly muddied, to the squire and his wife at Lyons Hall. It was from their son, Alan, who had been with the Coldstream Guards in the thick of the battle, in the same army brigade as the 1st Herts. The squire's wife had written immediately to her friend, the vicar's wife, with the news. **Andrew Clark** swiftly appropriated the letter and stuck it into his war diary – it was vital intelligence, especially valued because he got a personal mention:

Letter from Mrs JH Herbert Tritton to Mrs Andrew Clark, 16 November 1914:

We are deeply thankful again for good news of Alan today although he is still, of course, in great danger at Ypres. He was eleven days in the front row of trenches within 200 or 300 yards of the Germans. Now he has moved to the second row, but I do not think there is much more rest there as they are shelled apparently night and day still.

In his letter this morning he sent his very special remembrances to Dr Clark.[21]

A few days later, Andrew had the good fortune to get another genuine report from the front, first hand. He'd been up to Oxford for the weekend, and on the train home he found himself in a carriage with two soldiers in khaki. He wasted no time in mining them for information about experiences across the Channel, and faithfully recorded what they'd shared in his diary when he reached home. They clearly left quite an impression on him, and gave him a flavour of this new kind of war:

I left Oxford at 10.30 a.m. by a very good train: I was very fortunate in my compartment. On my left hand was a sergeant of the South

Staffordshire, a strongly built man with extremely clear-cut and pleasant features. He told me he was now completing his seventeenth year with the Colours. In several of the actions he had seen more shells discharged in twenty minutes than he had seen in the whole course of the South-African War. He said that this war is 'not fighting, but murder'.

Opposite me was a very tall young fellow, of the mounted ASC [Army Service Corps] men. He was badly wounded in the left leg. He said the destruction in France and Belgium was inconceivable. The trouble with the Germans is their enormous numbers. All the while our men are thoroughly beating the German force in front of them, another German force, equally strong, is entrenching itself further back. If we had as much as three against four Germans or even one against two, our men would sweep the field.

The ASC man showed me specimens of the bullets of the three armies. The British bullet, which is clean and makes a merciful wound; the French bullet, which has a long copper head and may be poisonous; and the German bullet, which has a disc at the back-end. When the point penetrates a body the disc causes the bullet to expand, so causing a terrible wound in the flesh.[22]

As dusk fell beyond his study window, Andrew closed his diary and put down his pen. He thought of Alan Tritton, and all the other young men from Great Leighs who were out in France and Belgium on that cold November night.

Exhausted after his second stint in the trenches, **Reg Evans** was marching along a snow-covered road. At every step the half-frozen mud swallowed his feet, which were now really starting to hurt him. The 1st Herts were going into billets after a traumatic time in the front line. The weather had been desperate: terribly cold and wet, the worst possible combination, turning the trenches into a freezing bath they'd had to sit in for four days straight.[23]

On 17 November, whilst supposedly resting after their first two days in the trenches, the 1st Herts were surprised by German shell fire. They were camped at a farm, but it was almost completely destroyed under a hail of shells when the Germans opened fire. Three men were wounded. After this 'rest', Reg and his comrades were sent straight back into the front line. By this point the rain had turned to heavy snow, and the men were without blankets. They sheltered, shivering, under waterproof sheets. The Germans were only twenty yards away in wet, freezing trenches of their own. The shelling was almost non-stop.[24] German planes overhead marked out the men huddled below as targets. Reg later wrote to his mother about his first brush with death:

As soon as the observer on the aeroplane sees anything which will make a good mark he drops coloured lights and the artillery take the range and before many minutes screeching and roaring come the shells. I can tell you once when one dropped a signal near us I felt as if my death warrant had just been signed, but the firing was right on our flank when it did come.

The shrapnel makes a noise like the howling of a dog but as long as you hear them you are safe because you know they will not burst near you, but the others the 'Jack Johnsons'[25] as they are named, well!!! They come through the air three or four at a time and without a word of exaggeration the noise can be compared to nothing but the rush of an express train. Then high up in the air shoots a huge column of smoke and dust then others, and a terrific roar goes up as they explode. If they hit the ground they leave a hole large enough to bury a motor bus. That sounds tall doesn't it but it's a fact. One burst amongst one of our companies in the trenches and nearly buried some of them.[26]

Finally, at 11 p.m. on 20 November, Reg and the 1st Herts set off for safety. The ground was white in the moonlight. It was freezing and the men's feet were in a terrible state, so progress was achingly slow. They walked all through the night, leaving the screech of shells behind them as they crossed the border into France. In the darkness just before dawn, they stopped for tea. They arrived at their billets at Méteren at 11 a.m. on 21 November. They were exhausted, but they were safe. The battle was petering out behind them, and their work, for now, was done: the Germans had not broken through the line.[27]

The following day, with worsening winter conditions and soaring losses, the Germans halted their attack and the first Battle of Ypres came to an end. The Hertfordshire Regiment had lost many men, but Reg's company had been lucky, relatively speaking. Reg was in comfort now, billeted on an old couple who were treating him and his comrades like heroes. He was as cheerful and optimistic as ever, despite suffering from frostbite.[28] He was also overjoyed to receive packages from home: some cigarettes from his sister and a pipe from his boss at the brush factory, as well as a letter from his mother. The day the battle was ending just across the border, Reg wrote to her in reply. He downplayed his recent experiences somewhat for her sake, but his bravado only partly hid how shaken up he was, and the distance he felt from the life he'd left behind just a few weeks before:

Thank you so very much for your long letter. I have always enjoyed hearing from you but your last letter I have read and re-read till I know it almost by heart. It has been a treat to hear from England.

Well you will want to know how I am, won't you? Let me tell you I am in a fine condition, the only inconvenience being the damp and cold from the trenches and dugouts. However, we are a distance from them for a day or two having all been sent inland for a rest.

It is not nearly so exciting as you might imagine out here as we have not seen any Germans (only dead ones) although so near to them. Their shells and Jack Johnsons we see and hear, plenty of the latter making a noise which I can only describe as equal to that of an express train, as it rushes through the air, and when it bursts it makes a hole large enough to bury a horse and cart. This is not an exaggeration by any means.

I don't know if we shall be back by Christmas or not but anyway save some of your own pudding for me. I am often, I might say always thinking of you and have resolved when I do return to be a 'fire-side lancer' only. We will have some good times together again yet and you will find me a stronger home bird than ever.[29]

The Battle of Ypres ended on a Sunday. That day, as Great Leighs awoke to a still, frosty morning, Lyons Hall was astir with excitement: Alan Tritton, the squire's son, had arrived home on leave. He had sailed for France back in August. Whilst Reg recovered from the trauma of battle and his frostbite in a French farmhouse, Alan would finally be able to relax in the comfort of his own home. That morning, he walked into the church and surprised **Andrew Clark** as he prepared for the Sunday service.

A few days later, the 3 p.m. post brought a letter from Mrs Tritton to the rectory. She had written to Andrew's eighteen-year-old daughter Mildred, studying at St Andrew's, who had knitted some socks for the

The Cloth Hall (Lakenhalle) in Ypres, before and after the German bombardment of November 1914.

men in Alan's regiment. Once again, Andrew took the letter and stuck it in his diary:

25 November 1914

How very kind of you to have sent off the beautiful socks. To our great joy and delight, as you will hear, Alan walked in on Saturday night late, being given a week's rest. He had been in the trenches up to midnight on Friday and he had to march his men 20 miles.

He goes back next Saturday to relieve the other Officers who are then to have a week. Alan is having severe work from the dentist and has so many people to see, relatives of his brother Officers who have been killed and visiting those who are wounded etc.[30]

Alan Tritton was lucky to be alive. The British had suffered 58,000 casualties at Ypres. This was far fewer than the German army's 130,000, but it represented the near decimation of the pre-war British Army.[31] This meant Alan could not be spared for long.

After the failure of the German assault on Ypres, the Allied and German commanders realised that they were engaged in a type of siege warfare. The front line had frozen into a 475-mile-long line of trenches.[32] The French, British and Belgians had held off the German war machine, but it had been destroyed in the process. Winter would provide some respite from the worst fighting, but it would not be long before it would all begin again. The nation's hopes now rested on the shoulders of the territorials like Reg and Kitchener's new recruits, still currently training in Britain.

Dorothy Lloyd was not thinking too hard about the responsibilities that lay ahead for her new husband. She had been far too busy moving house and getting used to being the wife of an officer, with all the social obligations that represented. She'd been too busy even to write to her family. She finally managed a few lines to her mother-in-law at the end of November, to thank her for some packages she'd sent. Along with some final wedding gifts, Mrs Lloyd had sent some extra clothing for Alan's men, now better accommodated in huts but still vulnerable to the cold winter that was setting in:

At last I have time for letters! The linen arrived beautifully packed. It really is lovely and my linen cupboard is a great joy. I have been very busy marking everything and am keeping a very neat catalogue of it all. I don't think there is anything more we want, thank you. The shirts and socks arrived quite safely and I am going to take them down this afternoon. They will be a great boon to some of the men, they are splendid things and we are most grateful to you.

By the way, are the servants to have the small Turkish Bath Towels as they were put down under their linen on the list that came and they seem much too good!!!

I must go and pay calls now, there are heaps of Majors' and Captains' wives to call on now. With tons of love and again many, many thanks.[33]

At the beginning of December, Alan Tritton was back with his regiment and **Reg Evans** was still behind the line in France. It was now apparent to even the most hopeless optimist that they would not be home for Christmas. Along the nearly 500-mile line of mud and sandbags running from the Belgian coast to Switzerland (only twenty-one miles of which were watched over by the British), it was realised that they would be there for the winter, at the very least.[34]

Reg Evans had reluctantly accepted this. Now he was preparing himself for another stint in the trenches. In early December, he wrote home again:

Hope you are keeping well. The weather here is very pleasant again though a trifle cold. We shall soon be shifting back to the trenches I expect as we have had quite a long rest now.

I often think of you, you will believe that, I know, and please God we settle this affair all right as I feel confident we shall, and when I get back home nothing shall come between us for the rest of our lives to make me leave a good home and make me go prowling off on such funny errands as this. You bet I have laughed when I've thought how you used to get on to me about not stopping in of an evening and now, well, here I am and can't get the chance to. Such is life.

Mother, don't you worry about me. I've got no wants in life except a safe return to you and dare I mention it, some chocolate.

Your Loving son, Reg[35]

6

DEEPENING SHADOWS

Christmas 1914

We have got a pack of cards here with which we pass the time away, and
taking it all together we are all as well off as we can reasonably expect to be.
Reg Evans, letter to his mother from the front,
December 1914

It was the first Friday in December, and dusk was robbing London of
the last of the day's pale light. The shoppers on Oxford Street started
to thin out very quickly. The Christmas displays in shop windows –
more understated than usual, with as many Union Jacks as Christmas
trees – were disappearing into darkness. Arrangements of patriotic cards
could still just be made out, with rousing messages for 'our boys at the
front' and 'our Tommies in training'. And beneath them were arranged
all kinds of useful gifts for the serving soldier – from pocket-sized
writing utensils to vacuum flasks, to Christmas hampers designed for
men on army rations.[1]

The headlights of buses and motorcars were very faint, as though
seen through thick fog. There was nothing to keep the shoppers out
any longer, no glittering displays to marvel at, and the weather was wet
and miserable, most un-Christmassy.[2] Eager to get out of the wind and
rain before it was really dark, men and women hurriedly descended to
catch the underground or piled onto the buses that wove slowly down
the dim streets. They carried bags of gifts, many of them for loved ones
who would be far from home, in muddy foreign fields, for Christmas
this year.

Near St Paul's, whose grand dome was also fading into the night, a
couple walked hand in hand, seemingly oblivious to the drizzle and
the gloom. He was in uniform, as were many of the men who bustled

past them. It was **Kate Parry Frye** with her fiancé **John Collins** and, unlike many sweethearts, they would not be parted this Christmas.

That night, once Kate was safely home and her wet things were drying by the fire, she turned to update her diary. Though her day had started with the now customary stress of the office, it had ended on a high note – they were now all set for the wedding:

> To Office and hurtled through my work. First a telephone wail from John. He couldn't get the Licence because he didn't know the name of the church. Then just before 12 he turned up and we went off together. Walked to Hyde Park Corner though the rain had started. It didn't damp our ardour and we were in holiday mood.
>
> First to the A & N Stores – and to buy the wedding ring. I asked in a most careless tone as if I was in the habit of buying them daily. The store was packed with officers – it was most exciting.
>
> Then to Ludgate Circus and to Creed Lane in the shadow of St Pauls to an office that has been in that locality for 300 years and we bought the Licence. It was most thrilling, like a scene out of Dickens – a musty old-world place – no telephone, no typewriters or central heating and 2 old gentlemen who wrote everything in the most perfect handwriting.[3]

She was brought down to earth again soon enough though – back to work as usual on Monday. The workload was as overwhelming as ever, and production showed no sign of winding down for Christmas: 'A busy restless day in the office. An order for a thousand shirts and now we are all over business again and goodness alone knows when we shall any of us get any holidays.'[4]

But later that week, things did finally take a festive turn. To reward the workers for all their toil over the past three and a half months, the workshop was shut up for the afternoon. As the machines sat idle, Kate and the girls walked across Hyde Park and headed to the lavish home of one of the society's organisers near Paddington. She had thrown them a party:

> To 14 Warwick Crescent and a party given by Miss Green for the Work girls. It was a great success – the girls were as happy as possible. The entertainment delighted all. It was really good – Margaret Balfour to sing and lots of other real singers. Of course they sang tosh – including

Tipperary, and we all joined in Chorus – and there was a splendid conjurer who afterwards did ventriloquism with the loveliest doll who moved all over and even wept – squirted a stream of water out of one eye.[5]

The entertainment might not have been quite typical of the Christmas season, but then it wasn't a typical Christmas.

Patriotic songs were what were called for this yuletide. **Hallie Miles** liked to be in vogue and she had set up a choir of her very own. It was called, simply yet elegantly, 'The Loyal Choir' and with the impeccably turned-out Hallie at the helm it performed in hospitals and at patriotic events. 'Tipperary' had been heard endlessly in London over preceding months, and was becoming a favourite, as Hallie noted: '"It's a long, long way to Tipperary" has become one of the most loved patriotic marching songs, although it has nothing whatever to do with patriotism!'[6]

Hallie was also hoping the choir would liven up her restaurant. Unlike in provincial towns, where the huge influx of troops in training gave a boost to local businesses, in central London the movement of men was mainly away. Each meal service at the Eustace Miles Restaurant saw more meticulously set tables remain pristine and untouched. Once such a fashionable destination, through whose doors hundreds of adventurous diners passed daily to sample the latest vegetarian delights, it just wasn't the same any more. But Hallie was determined to bring some life back into the place and, ever-adaptable, she decided that all she could do was embrace the new, wartime reality:

> We are having a series of Patriotic Teas in the E.M. Restaurant for our wounded soldiers once a fortnight, and a concert afterwards, with a collection for one of the War Funds at the close. The 'Loyal Choir' sang at the first patriotic Tea last week. The Collection was for the 'National Food Fund'; we had a number of wounded soldiers as our guests. Some of them were Belgians. It was very funny to hear them singing the chorus of Tipperary in their broken English.[7]

And of course it wasn't just the customers that had left the restaurant behind: members of the staff had also gone to war. One day in early

December, Hallie received a surprise visitor at the restaurant during yet another quiet lunchtime:

> The shadows have deepened lately. We are losing friend after friend. Our front-door porter, who was one of the first men to go to the Front, is back in England with a fractured ankle. He was blown off his horse by a shell, and then was dragged by the stirrup a long way. At last someone shot the horse and released him and took him into a café in Ypres until he could be fetched by an ambulance.
>
> There was great excitement in the restaurant when he came in limping to see us. You never saw such a hero in your life! And now he is home again until his ankle is well; and then he will have to go out and face it all over again.[8]

He was a hero; but this was not the heroic return any of them had expected when they'd waved him off four months earlier. Then, when the days and nights were warm and the war had only just begun, they'd expected to be welcoming all the men home within a few short months.

Throughout mid-December the weather was still terrible; it had been raining for days and gale-force winds were buffeting most of the country. **Frances Evans** was keeping dry at home in Hemel Hempstead and had just received another letter from Reg. She'd read all about the 1st Herts' ordeal in the trenches – the local paper had run an article on it, and the town council had passed a resolution expressing its pride in the regiment.[9] She was proud too, of course, but she was glad to learn from his familiar handwriting that Reg was still resting.

As she sat reading the letter, footsteps overhead reminded her of the men who'd taken her son's place in her home: soldiers themselves, billeted with her. She had plenty to keep her busy, and she wanted to make the men as comfortable as possible, but of course her thoughts were with Reg. She had already sent him some Christmas gifts. They'd been parted for most of his childhood, when Reg was in an orphanage, but that didn't make the separation easier this time. They both tried to reassure the other; and Reg was, as ever, trying to make the best of things:

> Thanks very much for the parcel just received. Your letter was quite in your best style and I quite enjoyed it and have read it through again

and again till I can quite remember it. I am glad that you are keeping in such good spirits for believe me there is not the slightest need for worry where I am concerned. We have got a pack of cards here with which we pass the time away, other duties of course permitting, and taking it all together we are all as well off as we can reasonably expect to be.[10]

You would enjoy being where we are billeted now, with an old French couple. They simply worship everything English. The old lady knows a word or two of our language and I know a little of hers and between us we get on alright. They are of course Catholics and have given me one or two souvenirs, a crucifix and a medallion from Lourdes where it appears the old gentleman went on a pilgrimage and had his sight restored, though as he cannot see now without his glasses I suppose it was not a complete cure. However he seems to be satisfied.[11]

It was only a matter of time before he was due back in the freezing, muddy, sleepless trenches. This time, he knew what was coming, and the thought of it made him miss his life back in Hemel Hempstead. Perhaps he even slightly resented the men who had taken his place at home:

You tell those soldiers with you that I don't think they would be as anxious to get out here after a week or so in the dug-outs or trenches and whilst they are with you they must make the most of things.

I am afraid you will not hear quite so frequently when we move again. Remember me to all at Hemel Hempstead. Well Goodnight mother, I am always thinking of you.[12]

Andrew Clark wasn't able to stay inside out of the terrible weather. Festive season or not, storms or not, his work defending Great Leighs from the enemy went on. On a particularly vile night in mid-December, he was up and about in the darkness, getting his things together for another shift on duty:

1 a.m. A wet night with wind blowing, but light enough to see. Met Major Wm. Brown outside his house (Bishop's Hall) to begin patrol duty. Rain and wind at times severe. Both of us soaking wet. Not a living creature seen or heard of.[13]

They might not have seen anything at all in Great Leighs, but as they walked the deserted paths in the pouring rain, their country was in very real danger. In the North Sea, under the cover of darkness, a number of German vessels were making their way through the waters. A squadron of battle cruisers, light cruisers and destroyers, were headed directly for the east coast, with the entire German High Seas fleet standing by. If the squadron made it, their guns would be turned on Britain. As Andrew Clark and Major Brown got wetter and wetter in Great Leighs, the vessels were steaming northwards, evading the British fleet.

On the morning of 16 December, at 0800 hours, the people of Scarborough were awoken by the thunder of guns. They were under attack. Crowds filled the streets as people rushed for safety, desperately trying to escape the town. Shells rained down: Scarborough Castle, The Grand Hotel, churches and homes were hit. Further south, Hartlepool was also under attack – the steelworks, the gasworks and three hundred houses were ablaze. At 0930 the battle cruisers turned their guns on Whitby, too.

War had come to Britain: cities were burning and British civilians and soldiers had been killed on their own soil. One hundred and thirty-seven people were dead; almost six hundred more were injured.[14] Word quickly spread, and it reached Andrew Clark that afternoon:

> 4 p.m. Miss Madge Gold says that the Tufnells of Langley, Great Waltham, report German bombardment of Scarborough and Hartlepool, but 'our fleet is in attendance.' (It was Mrs Bristowe, a county lady, who made use of the delightful phrase, 'our fleet.')[15]

The Royal Navy did give chase to the attacking German vessels, but the damage had been done: it had failed to stop the attack and the long-held belief in British superiority at sea was shaken.[16] The government, however, determined to turn this serious blow to their advantage. Posters emblazoned with 'Remember Scarborough' appeared in towns up and down the country. One million men had enlisted by the end of 1914, but the War Office made it clear that this was not nearly enough to stop a nation that had shown itself intent on destroying Britain.

The campaign was not universally well received. Andrew Clark recorded that the local men resented the moral pressure they were being

A propaganda poster in response to the attack on Scarborough by German gunships.

put under to volunteer. He was inclined to agree with them that making service compulsory would be better all round:

> <u>Tuesday 22 December:</u> 10.20 a.m. PC Coles, on his round, obligingly left me specimens of recruiting hand-bills. These show the obstinacy with which, to save itself the confession of past error, the Government shirks its plain duty of compulsory service. The country lads say, and to my mind say justly, 'If so many men are needed by the country, let the country say ALL must go.'[17]

Kate Parry Frye was distracted. It was the last week before Christmas, and she was out doing her shopping. This year, the gifts she bought were smaller than normal, but not because of the economies of wartime – her mind and budget were focused on her imminent wedding:

It seems a selfish Christmas – I have only bought such little things for everyone and such lots of things for myself – simply throwing about money. I do feel reckless. New vest, knickers, a nightdress – bodice material to make under clothes – all sorts of things. But though I started out with the idea I wouldn't get anything – like everything it has grown and grown. I should like some nice frocks and things too. I do see it wouldn't really make any difference to John's happiness, but it would make me feel nicer and daintier.

I do hope it will be a success. It rests with him – if he doesn't prove disappointing and take too much for granted. He is a dear but a little careless. I expect we shall have some wild moments of miserable unhappiness when we shall say or feel 'Oh how could you' – but I hope such feelings won't last. I have got such a queer horrid nature – I don't easily shake things off – I can't forget – and for that reason – I pray God he is careful. And I want to be awfully nice to him too – and I want him to be able to see and appreciate what is really nice. Oh I hope we shan't spoil it all. Starting out in a mood of doubt is disastrous – and foolish.[18]

On the last day before the Christmas holidays began, the workshop took on a festive feeling at last: 'The girls were crazy with excitement all day.'[19] Whilst the workers looked forward to a few days off, Kate had been thinking further into the future: after eleven years of resistance, she was giving up her independence to become someone's wife. Someone she didn't seem to be passionately, blindly in love with. Kate wasn't a naïve young bride-to-be. She was well aware of the lifetime commitment she was making – if John survived the war:

I had a thorough clear out and tidy up of everything – then locked up – at 8 o'clock. Had such a queer feeling as I came away – like locking my old self within – because probably my old self never will return – if I am married by then it will be so different.[20]

Kate and John were not alone in seizing the chance to get married whilst they could. In the first two years of the war, more people got married than at any time since records began.[21] The future for everyone was uncertain.

*

In France, **Reg Evans** was on the move. The previous day, the 1st Herts had travelled twenty miles down the line from their comfortable billets. They were now near to Béthune, where the British section of the line was under attack again. Alan Tritton was part of the same brigade, and had also arrived in the area.[22] They were getting ready to enter the frontline trenches.

The weeks since Ypres had been a period of relative calm on the Western Front. The British army had spent the time refitting and regrouping their battered forces, and working on the trench systems and other defences in which they would sit out the winter. But when intelligence suggested that the German army was removing some of its troops from the front lines, it seemed to present an opportunity too good to miss. In the middle of December the French army launched a series of attacks on the German line in conjunction with the British, but terrible mud and heavy German defences ensured these ended in failure.[23]

The Germans retaliated. On 20 December they launched a colossal bombardment of the line near Givenchy, held by the Indian Corps. They followed this up with an infantry attack that made 300-yard inroads into British territory. Things were looking serious, and the colonial troops of the Indian Corps were suffering unsustainable losses. The 2nd Division, including the 1st Herts, therefore received orders to move down the line to relieve them.

On Christmas Eve, Reg and the 1st Herts went into the trenches. By then the Indian Corps had suffered almost ten thousand casualties, and over a thousand more men would be lost during the relief operation. It was a terrible loss of life for the already much-diminished British force, with nothing at all to show for it. Reg spent 25 December 1914 in a battle-scarred trench, with freezing cold water sloshing at his ankles. It wasn't much like Christmas at all.[24] But there was at least post, and there were presents.

The British army postal service was deemed essential to morale; and during any one week, twelve million letters and parcels were delivered to the frontline trenches. On this day, the Christmas Day that few had expected to spend at war, there were a few extras for everyone. Princess Mary had sent a present to every man in the BEF: a box with cigarettes or a pipe; for the Indian soldiers a box containing sugar candy and spices. King George V had also sent each soldier a Christmas card. Its message read: 'May God protect you and bring you home safe'.

In many parts of the line, the soldiers unofficially called a truce. It was a chance for each side to gather up their dead from no-man's-land and finally bury them. There were also reports of more festive occurrences: football games and carol singing, even the exchange of gifts between German and British troops.[25] Reg Evans, unsurprisingly, was thinking of home, and of his mother:

> Don't overwork yourself or try to do too much, for I shall be back soon, you must keep well and strong so that we can have many, many happy days together when this wretched business is over and we can sit and talk of the part we have each of us done to secure that our righteous cause triumphed. We have been back in the fighting again. Won't these days be landmarks for future years eh? I'm not going to talk to you of mud and water in the trenches but I must tell you that in spite of everything I am keeping in excellent condition and I really believe am beginning to get fat. What do you think of that?
>
> We have been so near to the Germans this last time we could hear them singing on Christmas Eve and in one of our advanced trenches in which I was on guard one night we were not 30 yards away from them and I could hear them talking quite distinctly.
>
> We had a Xmas card from the King and Queen and a box of cigarettes and tobacco and also a Xmas card (which I am enclosing) from Princess Mary, so you can see we have been quite amongst the nobs.
>
> I am not troubling much about souvenirs – quite enough to bring myself back as one, but I shall try to keep my box or one or two other little things I have got. I don't expect you will hear very often from me for a little while but you will know I am alright.[26]

The 1st Herts lost one officer and one man on Christmas Day. There was clearly no truce on Reg's part of the line.[27] They were to remain in the trenches until the New Year.

In Britain, Christmas had been subdued and foggy; now gales and heavy rain dampened festive spirits further still.[28] **Andrew Clark** had led a congregation from which many young men were missing, some permanently. The Fitch family would never have another Christmas with their son Richard, who had been killed in action in October. His grieving family were a stark reminder to everyone else huddled in St Mary's Church of the fate hanging over their own boys' heads.

On the morning of 28 December, Andrew was sitting at home, noting the day's events. There was clearly not much going on in Great Leighs in the post-Christmas lull, bar the noise from the artillery training camp nearby:

> 10.25 a.m. a heavy thunderclap of a big gun fired in Shoeburyness direction. Others, at intervals, later.
> 11.30 a.m. Day of singular gloom, but no rain as yet – Vanity of conscientious note making! Rain began just when I had dried the preceding entry, and closed the notebook![29]

But there was a shock on its way to the heart of Great Leighs. The following day, a telegram arrived at Lyons Hall, home to the squire J. H. Tritton and his family. Their son Alan, whose regiment, the 3rd Coldstream Guards, had been involved in holding the line near Givenchy alongside the 1st Herts, was dead. Andrew Clark ended his 1914 diary with a letter in the squire's hand on black-fringed paper. It had arrived at the rectory with the morning's post. Andrew stuck into his diary with great sadness:

> 29 December 1914: The blow has fallen – (Alan) killed in action Dec 26th. Is the brief official – and only – communication. We shall doubtless hear other particulars soon. We give thanks to God for him and ask prayers for ourselves.[30]

Mrs Tritton added:

> Our loss is so great – Alan was such a perfect son and brother, as you know, and the blank can never be filled in this life. But we are very proud of him.[31]

In those first, optimistic weeks of war, Andrew had entitled his diary: *Echoes of the 1914 War*. But he had crossed it out now. In its place he wrote: *Echoes of the Great War*. And he was on his eighth volume. This war was indeed great: bigger than anything that had come before it; longer and more brutal than anyone had ever imagined.[32]

He closed the exercise book, put it on the shelf with the others, and got up. Nineteen fifteen was looming, and he prayed that it might bring brighter times to Great Leighs.

THE LONG WAR

7

NEW TERRORS ABROAD:
GAS AND SHELLS

January–June 1915

I don't know how long this job will last but shouldn't be surprised if it is over by August. Then what a time we will have eh!

Reg Evans, letter to his mother, January 1915

I write with a feeling of profound gratitude to my God I am still alive.

James Butlin, letter May 1915

The New Year in Britain dawned ferociously. The first grey light of day revealed wind-lashed fields and dismal cityscapes; waves tearing at the white cliffs of Dover and the rocky headlands of Cornwall. In Great Leighs such weather seemed appropriate: the little village was still in mourning.[1]

The windows in the rectory rattled. The Rev. **Andrew Clark** was wondering what to do. He felt it his responsibility to mark the loss of the squire's son – a blow felt by the whole community. Later that day, he braved the grim weather to get a message to the bereaved Tritton family, suggesting he lead the village in a memorial service. Their reply, stuck faithfully into his diary, was generous; they wanted to share the service with the other family in the village who had lost a son to the war:

Thank you so very much for your telegram and the kind thought. We are very anxious that it may be for young Fitch also if you would be so kind as to talk it over with his parents. Would Mrs Fitch choose a hymn too?[2]

Richard Fitch, the son of a village farmer, had been serving in the army
before war broke out. He had been amongst the first wave of soldiers
to depart for France, and his had been the first war death for Great
Leighs. He was survived by eleven siblings, including a brother, Arthur,
who was serving in the navy.

Arthur had at least stayed closer to home; he was stationed at
Sheerness guarding against a possible German invasion. However, on
New Year's Eve his vessel, HMS *Formidable*, had moved into the English
Channel near Weymouth for gunnery exercises. The seas were rough,
winds fearfully high. It was some consolation that enemy submarine
attacks were ruled out in such conditions.

But in the first hours of 1915, in total darkness and amid howling winds,
HMS *Formidable* was struck by a torpedo. The captain gave orders to
evacuate. As the crew tried desperately to get to safety, the ship was struck
a second time. She capsized, taking many of her crew down into the
freezing water with her. A total of 512 men and 35 officers were lost.[3] The
news that Arthur Fitch was one of them reached his family a few days
later. Andrew Clark was in bed fighting flu when he heard:

> <u>Monday 4 January:</u> Arthur Fitch, of this parish, is supposed to have
> gone down with the *Formidable*. I was too ill to stay up and consequently
> let my notes slide.[4]

HMS *Formidable*, the ship on which Arthur Fitch of Great Leighs served
and died.

The following Sunday Andrew led the residents of Great Leighs in the memorial service he'd planned. It was now in memory of three of the village's own who would never come home.

Great Leighs had not been singled out for heartbreak, though it might have felt like that to the congregation huddled in St Mary's Church that cold January morning. Pews in churches all across Britain were left with unfilled spaces; thousands of churchgoers would never feel the reassuring presence of their fathers, or husbands, or sons sitting beside them again. As 1915 began, 175,000 British soldiers had already been killed, wounded or were missing.[5]

The nation was faced with a stark and painful truth: so many lives had been sacrificed, everything had been thrown at the colossal struggle – and yet, the war had not been won. As 1915 began, the original BEF in poor condition, all eyes turned to the new army in waiting, the one million ordinary men who were being transformed into soldiers in training camps across Britain. It was their turn now.[6]

James Butlin had grown up in Weymouth in Dorset. A bright young man from a solid middle-class family, he'd left home to study Classics at Oxford University. But his studies had been put on hold by the outbreak of war: 18-year-old James had applied for a commission and, just before Christmas, he'd joined the Dorsetshire Regiment stationed at Wyke Regis. To the provincial teenager it was all very exciting, and seemed tremendously grown up. He wrote to his friend Basil, still studying at Oxford, full of pride in his new role as a soldier:

I have now been in the army over a week and find life pretty different from the Varsity. We have to get up at an unearthly hour, have breakfast and go to a physical drill. The rest of the morning is taken up with various parades and during the afternoon till 4 o'clock. The life is extremely healthy and you are not allowed out under any conditions after 9 o'clock so I go to bed early every night. I must confess I eat more and sleep better (if that is possible) than ever I did before in my life.

I have fallen in love with Madge Green, or very nearly. She is so jolly pretty. When are you going to join the army? It is the duty of every able-bodied citizen to defend his country.[7]

The regiment James had joined, the 3rd Dorsets, was a pre-war, special reserve battalion. In August 1914 it had been tasked with defence: guarding bridges, railway tunnels and waterworks. But as the weeks rolled on and the losses at the front mounted, it took on the role of a training battalion. By the time James arrived at the end of 1914, a routine had been established whereby new recruits flowed in to the camp and trained men left it to join other battalions already at the front. It was all quite chaotic: huts were still being built, and uniforms were in short supply – around the time James joined, a batch of Welsh miners were training in their Sunday best until uniforms could be provided for them.[8]

As an officer, James was in billets, and so was spared the worst of the disorganisation. In fact, he was having a great time. Best of all, he still had plenty of time for extracurricular activities – most importantly, courting girls. Now he was in khaki, he seemed to finally be having some success. He wrote to Basil of a trip to London in February, 'the most enjoyable part of my life for many years.' He'd moved on from Madge Green by now:

> I taxied (to Kensington) and found my beautiful Edythe. I took her out to tea and booked stalls at the Vaudeville as she wanted to see the show there. After tea we strolled up The Strand and went into Horret's. Fortunately there was no one in the drawing room so I spent a very happy hour there talking to her. We taxied to the Vaudeville which was a screaming show, nicely improper in parts. After the theatre we taxied to Allen Street and the chauffeur took us round the longest way, a thing which I didn't mind in the least, I assure you. I need hardly add I kissed her in the taxi. That is enough detail for the present.[9]

By early 1915, many recruits to the Dorsets were being sent out with no more than three months' training. James was right to be making the most of his time in England.

Alan and Dorothy Lloyd welcomed 1915 in together. It was their first New Year as husband and wife. They'd recently moved from rented rooms to a fine furnished house, and were very happy there, enjoying their shared new life and regularly playing host to Alan's fellow officers.[10]

The 78th Brigade Royal Field Artillery was part of Kitchener's New

Army, on which so much now depended. However, Lord Kitchener didn't want to rush the New Armies out to the front. He thought the Germans should exhaust themselves a bit, allowing his brand-new soldiers more training in the meantime.[11] As a result, Alan's soldiering career was not progressing as quickly as he would have liked. His temporary position, as acting adjutant in charge of administration and the men's welfare, was coming to an end, and he was yet to secure a permanent promotion. He wrote to his father in early January, rather impatient with it all:

> I go for a course of 'one man range finding' on 25th. There are four officers going from this division and so I applied and have got it. Now that my days as adjutant are numbered I'm tugging strings, all I know, to get given courses and to fit myself to go to front as soon as poss.
>
> The colonel recommended me three weeks ago for a Captaincy but the General wouldn't sanction it. I must know more gunnery first, he said, and quite right too. However, the Colonel now sent in my name to be made Lieutenant so he's keen on me, which is something at any rate. It's been a grand training for me, this three months of adjutant, and had I been a Captain I'd undoubtedly have kept the job. It seems my fate in life to just miss everything I go for, like my [Cambridge rowing] blue.[12]

The following week Alan set off to London, en route to the artillery training camp at Shoeburyness. This was the first separation of his married life. Alan wrote to Dorothy from his hotel in Mayfair, missing her very much, despite the many attractions London offered to a 26-year-old man like himself:

> This is the first letter I've written you since we were married. We had a great run up here. We actually got to Sunningdale – 20 miles from here – at 1 o'clock, I think it's about 120 miles from Swanage and as we started at 9.30 we averaged something good! Last night we flew round Alhambra and Tavern Nightclub. But it didn't interest me and I was really bored, though I should have loved it a year ago. Such a difference does a little wife make to me. My little bed here was so lovely and I almost cried for my small wife. It's no fun without you, small wife.

*

Reg Evans had seen the New Year in from the bottom of a trench. So far, 1915 had not been kind to him. In France, January was a month of rain, of snow, of floods. The British line was dug into flat, low-lying land with clay subsoil that held water very near the surface, so the trenches were perpetually waterlogged. On top of this the shelling and sniping rarely ceased. The German army had plenty of ammunition; the British were running frightening low and were limited to four rounds per gun per day.[13]

On 10 January, it was Reg's 27th birthday. That very day, he left the safety of billets – where he had been having a reprieve from trench life – to go back into action, southeast of Richebourg. The men of the 1st Herts rotated in and out of trenches and support positions in a small village on the front line. Neither detail was safe.[14] Reg's mother Frances had not forgotten her boy on his birthday, of course, and after two dangerous days, Reg arrived back in Richebourg to find a parcel from her waiting for him, to add to the other birthday presents he'd already received from home:

Just a line to say I received your parcel safely today. How I shall enjoy the many good things you have sent. I shall be able to have a proper birthday spread and no mistake. Your letter too was a pleasure to read (when indeed are they not) and I am eagerly looking forward already to another one. Cissie sent me a nice little parcel the other day and I have also received one from Daisy as well.

We were in a little village just in the firing line for my birthday. Not a single house had a complete roof and all the while we were there bullets were whistling down the narrow street which the Germans commanded from their trenches. This was the place where Mr Snowden got killed. The poor fellow was shot right in the chest and fell without a word. His grave goes to make another melancholy mark along the roadside of this stricken country. We tried to put ourselves in a state of defence by carting sandbags up to the roof of the cottage where we lay in readiness, but unfortunately the Germans noticed our fortifications and late in the afternoon started sniping, so we got down in a hurry.

I don't know how long this job will last but shouldn't be surprised if it is over by August. Then what a time we will have, eh! You will be pleased to hear that I attended a celebration of Holy Communion one morning recently. It was held in a public house near here but the service

I am sure was just as acceptable as if held in a cathedral. All the churches here are in ruins.

Well goodnight Mother. I am often thinking of you.[15]

Reg was a brave man, but he might have said a prayer or two for himself at that service – prayers that he would be home again soon.

The British army had other plans for him in the year ahead. At the end of 1914, Germany had moved many of its forces from the Western to the Eastern front, where fighting with Austria-Hungary had begun in August with the Russian invasion of East Prussia and Galicia. The Allies were planning a large joint offensive in the spring whilst the enemy was distracted by this second front. Until then, the priority was improving the trenches and getting reinforcements ready.

Even in this lull, small outbreaks of fighting did occur – the worst of it on the part of the line that Reg was in.[16] On 25 January, the Germans attacked and made minor inroads into British-controlled territory. A British counter-attack followed. In the darkness before dawn on 6 February, Reg's battalion moved into trenches near Cuinchy in support. A heavy bombardment was unleashed on them for two days, but they held firm, and the ground was won back. It cost a number of officers and men of the 1st Herts their lives.[17] One of Reg's pals from home, who had worked with him in the brush factory, died from his wounds.

Reg's mother, at least, was trying to look after him. Back in rest, he received another parcel from her – though not everything she intended for him survived the 200-mile journey from Hemel Hempstead:

Just a line to let you know I received the parcel safely and to thank you very much for it. The tomato was not, I am sorry to say, a success, but everything else came O.K. and the candles were very useful.

What do you think! Last week I had a real hot bath and a complete change of underwear!!! We were marched down in batches to a large town about six miles from here to a place which I think has been a Catholic College or Monastery but is now in the hands of our R.A.M.C. All our clothes were taken away, our Service dress being ironed and steamed and our underclothing replaced. You'd hardly believe what a treat it felt to be clean and free from our (I regret to say) many tormentors.

I daresay you have heard that one of our chaps from 'Kent's' has died from his wounds. Now don't you worry about me I can assure you I take care of myself.[18]

In February, **Alan Lloyd**'s training was going rather better. Or perhaps his mood had just improved as a result of some very exciting news: he was going to be a father. He wrote to his beloved Dorothy from another artillery course in Shoeburyness, now thoroughly enjoying himself:

> Just a line to tell you I'm flourishing, that the course I'm with is much better than the one I was with before. I've got the car in a garage, safe and sound, and at last she's happy. I do want my small wife so and I do hope she's happy and got no bad pains??
>
> We are working hard and digesting lots of valuable information for which I hope we'll be the better. Tomorrow morning we have a day in the country, map-reading. Tons of love, your hubby

James Butlin had gone through less than four months' training in total. In spite of this, at the end of March, he was rushed out to France to be attached to the 2nd Battalion Yorkshire Regiment, known as the Green Howards. He had just turned 19.

A week earlier, the Green Howards had suffered serious casualties at the Battle of Neuve Chapelle, the first entirely British offensive of the war. Although it had initially been a success, in the end it had done little to change the strategic situation.[19] The Green Howards had lost 93 officers and men, almost 200 more were wounded, and 25 were missing. As the battalion recovered from the ordeal, James Butlin was amongst a batch of reinforcements sent to join them. He wrote to Basil with glee from the other side of the Channel:

> What a tremendous series of adventures I've been through in the last fortnight! Enough and more than enough for a lifetime.
>
> We left Southampton about 7.15 a.m. in the (I can't very well tell you the name of the boat). There were about 1000 on board and the other Dorset officers who had been sent all over the country like myself to fetch drafts all crossed over in the same boat. We consequently had a merry time and after some adventures reached Rouen at 12 noon going right up the river Seine.[20]

However, as James progressed, the reality of war started to sink in. After a few nights under canvas in a camp at Rouen, his journey to the front began:

> One of the 1st things that really woke me up was the ruins of towns and villages which the Germans have shelled. Whole streets lie levelled with the ground – churches, factories etc have remnants of spires, towers or windows to show what they were. If only the people of England could see what I have seen, they would be a sadder and wiser lot.

After a sleepless overnight journey, James arrived just behind the front line a few miles north of Neuve Chapelle, where the Green Howards were now back in trenches.[21] He was taken to join them – suddenly, he was in the thick of things:

> That same day I walked to the firing line. I went into the trenches under the guidance of another officer. By this time, as you may imagine, I was pretty tired and the chance of getting sleep in the firing line is not much. To begin with the cold was intense and a sharp frost every night. Secondly, the Germans keep up a tremendous fire all night, far more than in the day time. Of course all the time bullets keep whizzing over your head and shells bursting all around. But you get used to these things. After a few days we got relieved by another regiment and are now in (rest) for which I am duly thankful.[22]

Once in rest, he recovered some of his usual enthusiasm, and Basil had sent him a treat to cheer him up. But he was struggling with a new shock, seemingly even more serious than that of trench warfare. He was coming to terms with the lack of eligible girls in war-torn France:

> You are a most colossal sportsman. Today about 2 o'clock two most lovely boxes of chocolates arrived and your letter inside. Thank you.
> I have so far had no luck with French or Belgian girls. All decent girls have left this part of France months ago and those girls who are left are village wenches whose style of beauty (which isn't easy to discover) does not appeal to me. I haven't seen a single girl worth looking at. If you see my beloved Edythe give her my love – Take her out to the theatre and treat her handsomely.[23]

*

At the end of March, **Reg Evans** was feeling much perkier than during
the miserable days of January and February. The weather had improved,
and the 1st Herts had been spared the full force of Neuve Chapelle.
They'd been in support on the La Bassée Canal, before going into
trenches five miles down the line as the offensive waned. Since then,
they'd been busy digging new trenches. It might have sounded like
relatively safe work, but it was not: the regiment lost four men – privates
like Reg – as they carried out their nightly labours. But by late March
things were quieter, and by day there was even opportunity for some
recreation:

> The position we are holding here is a bit more exciting than our last
> one where we were practically in reserve all the time. We are doing
> digging 'in' and the same out in the deserted houses behind the lines.
> This particular bit of work is a real joy to me because it is so annoying
> to the allemands. We dig at night and they shell it in the daytime and
> try to smash our work up but we are winning through in spite of that.
>
> The feverish longing I had on me to return to old Hempstead has
> with the better weather nearly evaporated. Of course I really do want
> to see everyone again and especially M.O.T.H.E.R. but I'm beginning
> to enjoy myself thoroughly now.
>
> One day all our fellows sat on the canal bank fishing for tiddlers. It
> was a ridiculous sight, as you can imagine, but anything does for a bit
> of fun here. There are a lot of dogs round about and they are all more
> or less attached to the Regt, one or two of them are even coming in
> the trenches with the men.[24]

At the end of March, French and British planning for a combined
attack on a large section of the Western Front was resumed. The French
Commander-in-Chief Joseph Joffre asked his British counterpart, Sir
John French, if he'd be ready to go in five to six weeks' time. He agreed.
Preparations were under way when, a few weeks later, the German
army made a devastating move.[25]

The twenty-second of April was a glorious spring day in Belgium. The
countryside to the north and east of Ypres had remained remarkably
untouched by the war so far, the tiny villages intact and the fields still
farmed. But the rumble of battle was near: the Germans had been

bombarding Ypres itself for days. Its cafés and shops were abandoned once more, and many more of its fine buildings had been destroyed.

The front line here was now held by French, Algerian, Canadian and British troops. The Allies had more men, but the Germans had more guns and ammunition. They also had a secret weapon. At 5 p.m., a colossal bombardment started up, and two greenish-yellow clouds began to roll inexorably forwards towards the Allied defences. Behind it, the enemy was advancing. Suddenly, news reached the British of French and Algerian troops fleeing. When their guns fell silent, it was apparent that something very serious was wrong.[26] The first mass poison-gas attack in the history of warfare had just been carried out.

As the rules of war were changed forever at Ypres, **James Butlin** was in the trenches 20 miles down the line. Although the Green Howards had been moved up as reserves, should the line at Ypres need reinforcing, in the end they were not called up. James had had a lucky escape:

> We had a big move [on] Wednesday and marched from 12 noon till 5 o'clock in the boiling heat. We had breakfast at 8 and consequently by 6 o'clock when we got another meal, we were pretty done up. We marched, of course, in full kit. It was thought that we were off to Ypres but from latest account things there have gone all right. I expect you've read about the asphyxiating gas the Germans use now. We're all being given bits of stuff to put on our face so that we shan't be suffocated.
>
> The last 3 days have been gloriously hot and if you had weather like this at Oxford, summer ought to be in full swing. It was Snark's annual I mentioned, but look for any shady publication on some bookstall.[27]

James had avoided the second Battle of Ypres, but his turn to see action must come soon. The planned Allied offensive had been delayed by the German attack, but not abandoned. And now there were gas attacks to add to the list of terrors a British soldier might face.

Alan Lloyd had also had a near miss: he'd been in a minor car accident. Whilst down in Devon with his brigade, he'd collided with a car coming round a blind corner. He was angry but there was one mercy: Dorothy had not been involved. Alan wrote to his father immediately after the scrape, desperate to sort out his beloved motor:

Allied troops had to react quickly to the new threat of gas attacks. Here, a
sentry sounds a rudimentary alarm.

> I have had a smash with my own car, a female named Mrs Larden, (the
> vicarage Okehampton) driving a Ford car ran into me at 8 o'clock tonight.
> The damage to my car was not great, smashed off side wings and steering
> rod buckled, and footboard smashed. (Won't Walduck be angry, but I
> know he agrees with me that women ought not to drive cars.) Fortunately
> Dorothy was not on board (here Mama heaves a sigh of relief) but three
> other officers were. No one hurt in either car.
>
> My insurance policy is in one of the pigeonholes in my desk in the
> billiard room. Could you please see the motor union who have a place
> in Birmingham and tell them that I am forwarding the estimate for
> repairs to you for transmission to them. Do you know a chauffeur to
> drive Dorothy for a few months? Possibly you could get one in Brum.[28]

And Dorothy was doing well. Now three months pregnant, she wrote
to her mother-in-law: 'I am keeping awfully fit and am having no
troubles of any sort.'[29]

The Anglo-French offensive was scheduled for the beginning of May.
They had neither enough ammunition nor men to undertake a push
all along the Western Front, so the decision was made to concentrate
on the Artois area, north of Arras. The British target was the Aubers

Ridge on the southern part of their line; the French target, further south, was Vimy Ridge. The date for the French attack was set for 7 May; the British would follow the next day.

From the beginning of May, preparation was intense. Disused trenches were reclaimed in no-man's-land, tunnelling for mines was under way, and the French began their bombardment. The British artillery approach would be different – they had only enough shells for an intense bombardment just before the attack. Troops were moved into position, including Reg Evans and his battalion, who were placed in the La Bassée Canal sector on 3 May. Owing to the importance of that part of the line, the 1st Herts were to remain there to defend it. The actual attack would take place a few miles north. And it was to there that James Butlin and his brigade began their journey on 4 May.[30]

In the event, serious mist prevented the attack going ahead as scheduled on 7 May, but plans were hastily revised: now both British and French troops would attack simultaneously, on the 9th. Everything was ready; it was only the weather that needed to cooperate. And it did. As the first light of a fine day suffused the sky above north-eastern France, the shelling began. Beneath the flare of explosives in the grainy early morning light, thousands of troops were waiting in their trenches, poised to go over the top.

By early afternoon, however, the British attack was in chaos. The leading battalions had suffered horrendous casualties – whole lines of men had been mown down in one go. But still the orders came for further bombardments and further attacks. **James Butlin** remained in the trenches in reserve. His regiment was standing by to be moved into battle, but this attack was held back until dark. Finally, at 6 p.m., as reports of the chaos in the trenches and roads leading to them reached the High Command, that too was called off. It was another lucky escape for James. More than 11,000 British casualties had been sustained that day, many within only a few yards of their own trenches. No ground had been won.[31] James wrote to Basil:

> I write with a feeling of profound gratitude to my God I am still alive, since we have been through a terrible time. By the papers you will see there was a battle on the ninth. Between ourselves it was not an overwhelming success. We were in reserve on that occasion in open trenches

about ½ a mile from the firing line. We saw all the wounded coming
back and had 1st hand news of the battle all the day long.

The fierce fighting was not over. The next morning, James and the
Green Howards were moved further up the line. From there, they were
to take over the front line north of Festubert. The battle of Festubert
would be the second phase of the battle of Aubers. On 12 May, James
entered the frontline trenches. This time he would be in the thick of
the battle, fighting for his life:

> After manning various reserve trenches, went into the firing line on the
> night of Wednesday the 12th. This was the beginning of tribulation. The
> Germans had concentrated their artillery near this point and shelled us
> continuously for five days and nights, Jack Johnsons, shrapnel, quickfirers
> etc. made life a veritable hell.
>
> Worse even than that, our own artillery – a territorial battery, I am
> practically sure – blundered. They dropped shells into our own trenches
> which were meant for the German trench some 300yds away. We were
> caught between two fires and no place was safe. The trench we were in
> was very bad and at the best of time gave little cover from shellfire. We
> sent messages, messengers etc. up to this battery but all to no avail.
>
> Each day was worse than the one before, Our Colonel was killed by
> one of our own shells, my Captain was killed by a German shell and
> Montesole, one of my brother subalterns, was killed by one of our shells.
> Every day I had miraculous escapes from shells.[32]

The next day, the weather broke again and rain turned the trenches
and shell craters into mud-wallows. Communications began to break
down. Some gains were being made, however. Two companies of the
Green Howards advanced to occupy a gap that had been made in the
German line; James's company remained in support in the British
trenches. As ground was won, German troops began to surrender.[33]
James had now been in the trenches under a hail of shells for more
than five days without a rest:

> On Monday the attack was pushed on and on Monday morning some
> 100 or more Germans who had got cut off surrendered to our company.
> As they came running across to us holding up their hands (having
> dropped their rifles), their own men fired at them and I ordered my

men to fire on them as we were still being sniped at by the Huns but a British Tommy <u>won't</u> shoot a man in cold blood and unarmed. The Germans came scrambling over our parapet many of them blubbing and in an awful funk, obviously expecting to be shot. I wish I could have shot them down then and there. This was Monday morning, one of the most awful days of my life. About a dozen prisoners were standing in our trench when our own artillery dropped a shell (one of many I regret to say) right into our own trench. This was the shell that killed Montesole, 4 of our own men, 3 Germans, besides wounding 18 men. It was impossible to bury the dead and I can never forget the sight of that trench.

That night, we left the trench to follow in the wake of the great advance and hold captured German trenches. Here again we were open to awful shelling as the Germans knew the range of the trench we were holding to a foot or less. For a week I, and no one else for that matter, had no sleep, for 3 days we had grovelled in mud and clay till we were wet through and unrecognisable. The mud was awful and one stumbled blindly over dead and dying.[34]

On the evening of the 17th, **Reg Evans** and the 1st Herts – part of the 4th (Guards) Brigade – were getting closer to James's sector of the line. As James was given orders to move into the captured German trenches, the 4th (Guards) had been called out of reserve to support the advance. The ground was by now a muddy quagmire of shell holes and bodies, so progress was terribly slow; Reg and his battalion failed to reach their destination before darkness.

The following morning the advance was set to resume, but mist prevented an early bombardment, pushing the attack back to the afternoon. Again the conditions meant both communications and the movement of troops were all but impossible. Added to this, ammunition was now running dangerously low. But at 4.30 p.m., the 4th (Guards) were ready to make their advance. Reg Evans was in to the rear, in support. What no one knew was that the German lines had been moved back, meaning the British artillery had failed to even touch them. As a result, when the 4th (Guards) attacked, they were met with a hurricane of bullets.[35]

By 9 p.m., after heavy losses, the attack was called off. Reg and the 1st Herts moved up to occupy the new frontline trenches. Twenty-four hours of hell began. Reg later wrote to his mother, trying not to worry her by implying he hadn't been part of it, though of course he had:

> I'm not telling you this for swank, but one night recently some of our Regt went up in the trenches. They were under terrific shellfire and all through that night and the next day it rained unceasingly. They supported another Regt in an attack which resulted in the capture of a German Trench and then had to go out and dig all the night a new trench, right out in front. By next morning they occupied it and had to sit tight in the pouring rain and a practically endless hail of high explosive shells and didn't get back til nearly mid-night again.[36]

That day, 19 May, the 1st Herts suffered over 100 casualties before they were relieved, including 17 men killed.[37]

The Battle of Festubert came to an end a week later, and Reg again wrote home. In spite of the horror of his recent experiences, he had some genuinely good news to report:

> I am writing to you whilst I have the opportunity as we are now enjoying a rest in the rear. I know you will be pleased to know that my promotion to Corporal was published in orders last night.[38]

Reg had entered the army at the bottom of the hierarchy, as a private. Now, as a 'non-commissioned officer', he had won himself the charge of a section of men. He had obviously handled the horrors of Festubert well, and this courage and composure had not gone unnoticed:

> You will be pleased to hear that the other morning I was sent for by our Commanding Officer who thanked me for my behaviour during our last affair in the trenches and said I well deserved my promotion. This sort of thing doesn't happen every day you know, so I take it as a bit of an honour.
>
> I received the parcel on Sunday but the specimens of salad were not, I am sorry to say, a successful consignment, so I don't think I should repeat the experiment.[39]

In spite of Reg's unfailing optimism, **Frances Evans**, like most Britons, now knew that the war could be going better. The news in the papers had not been good. On 14 May, as the battle of Festubert raged, an article had appeared in *The Times* under the headline: 'Need for Shells:

British Attacks Checked: Limited Supply the Cause'. Based on information from the commander-in-chief, Sir John French, it claimed that the British did not have enough shells to fight and win the war.

It made alarming reading: 'We are suffering from certain disadvantages which make striking successes difficult to achieve. The infantry did splendidly, but the conditions were too hard. The want of an unlimited supply of high explosive was a fatal bar to our success. We have had many casualties this week.' It concluded, under a heading, 'OUR URGENT NEEDS: Until we are thoroughly equipped for this trench warfare, we attack under grave disadvantages.'[40] Picked up by the popular press, especially that under the control of the press baron Lord Northcliffe, the story swept the country: British men were dying unnecessarily, for want of ammunition.

The result was an outcry and Asquith's Liberal government did not survive the ensuing political storm. After a cabinet split, a new coalition government was formed on 25 May. Crucially, the political organisation of the war quickly became more serious: a Ministry of Munitions was established on 9 June.

But the ever-patriotic Reg did not approve of the furore:

> You know, I hope you don't have the *Daily Mail* or any of the Northcliffe Papers in the house. I think it is a scandal that they have the power to make so much mischief. The Germans must laugh at us. [41]

Alan Lloyd must surely have taken an interest in it all – he was, after all, in the artillery – but he didn't mention it in his letters. He was in the final stages of his training, and, coincidentally, firing his own guns for the first time. His father had been helping out with car-related matters again, having just sent the family chauffeur down to them in Devon. Alan wrote to thank him:

> Just a line to thank you awfully for sending me Walduck who was awfully useful to Dorothy and me. He tuned up the car and sweated at it for two days with very beneficial results.
>
> We fired our guns today – great excitement – for the first time. All the men were very excited and frightened of them! They certainly do make a row. I had to 'conduct a series' i.e. work out the angles and give all directions to open on a target – great sport.

Hope you're all well. I bought a topping fine horse or rather Mrs
Hewetson bought him for me in Yorks, and I sold him to the Govt. for
same price, so I did well. The arrangement is that I'm allowed to have
sole use of him and he's fed and kept at Govt expense of course. So
now I've got a gee to carry me.

Meanwhile, the weary troops in France and Flanders pressed on. In
early June, things had quietened down after the carnage of Festubert,
giving a chance for some welcome rest. Letters flowed home. Young
James Butlin was recovering, helped by a few local residents:

I am still safe and sound, which is after all the main thing. My new
captain (Hanbury) thought I looked 25 when he saw me after I had just
come out of the last show.

Just opposite our billet is a bridge. On the other side there lives a
farmer and his wife with two daughters. One, about 18, is the prettiest
girl I've struck since I came out and it has bucked me up immensely.
To be accurate she is the only pretty girl I've seen since I left England
nearly 3 months ago.[42]

But James did not have long to relax. In the middle of June he was
back in action in the Givenchy sector as part of an attempt to capture
some key points on this section of the line. The Green Howards led
the charge. It was another terrible, costly failure. Limited ammunition
supplies and poor observation meant the British bombardment barely
touched the German defences. As the men went over and into no-man's-
land, they were mown down.[43] James was lucky again:

Once again I have been made to realise how narrow is the line that
divides life from death. I was sitting down to lunch last Monday at 10
o'clock in billets when Hanbury told me that I would not come with
the battalion into action. I have seldom been so surprised and glad (as
I had cause to learn later) in all my life. Owing to the loss of life among
officers, our battalion was forbidden to take more than 20 officers into
the battle.

I remained in a village about 2 miles from the fighting. The Germans
knew the time and every detail of the attack as well as if they themselves
had planned it. The heroism of A's and B's officers will never be forgotten

in the regiment. As they fell dying and wounded they shouted to their men to advance.[44]

Five officers and 170 men from A Company went over; only 40 were not hit. Five officers and 180 men from B Company went over; only 1 officer and 31 men escaped unhurt.[45]

James was sick of the danger and pressure of the front. Even his new love interest, a local girl, couldn't help – he was longing for home and was slightly resentful of Basil for being there:

> Our division has been in practically every fight since the war began and there are rumours of being relieved by Kitchener's army. Whether there is the slightest truth in it I cannot say. I went to see Aurelia on Sunday and told her of our heavy losses in the last attack. She was awfully cut up about it and shed a few tears. Aurelia is really quite pretty but I long for the sight of a real English girl.
>
> Later 6 p.m. Have just received a most interesting letter from you. You have been giving yourself up to unlimited enjoyment while your brothers in Flanders have been engaged in one of the most sanguinary battles of history. How wrong of you! I am glad you were at 'the top of your form' in tennis. From my experience of the bottom of your form I could appreciate the change.[46]

But James was right: Kitchener's recruits would finally be joining them in France.

Reg Evans had been making the most of the relative calm on the Western front, and he too had been fraternising with the locals. He was staying in billets at Cambrin, a few miles south of Festubert. The weather was fine and Reg was sitting on a tree stump, the pleasant gurgle of a stream at his feet, enjoying another letter from his mother:

> The first thing I did with the parcel was to find your letter and then I took myself off with it (the letter, I mean) down by a pretty little stream which runs near us here to read it in quiet. Quiet I say – well, comparatively. Nearly all the trees round here have been cut down or knocked down by the heavy guns and so I had a good range of rustic seats to choose from.

How I did laugh over your enclosure. It is to be hoped that all the girls whose acquaintance I have made won't take to writing to you for information because just between ourselves you'll get your hands full, for I know one or two, but never met one yet to come up to M.O.T.H.E.R., though I have told several out here that '*apres la guerre*' I'm going to come back and marry them'. Don't get alarmed though – they're always being told that.[47]

Alan Lloyd's last day on English soil had finally arrived. He was at Southampton Docks, and a boat was waiting to take him into the war he'd dreamt of for so long. He was alone: Dorothy could not come with him this time. He scribbled her a final farewell:

Belovedest little small wife,

Just a line written in a stiff breeze on the quay with a bit of note paper bought for a penny off a small boy here! We arrived 7am this morning and embark at 6. So we have had a nice long wait doing nothing here.

We shall cross by the very fast boat *Zulu*, which can do 24 knots, whilst Humphreys has to go by a slow transport with all the guns and horses. I have 59 men and no horses or guns so am lucky. I haven't even a rifle!

I will write as soon as I possibly can from the other side and tell you all the news, you little angel. You were an amazingly plucky little small wife when I went away and hubby was awful proud of his small wife, hubbins was. Hubbins didn't want to leave her a bit and feels very sorry now he has done so. But he'll soon come back.[48]

Dorothy was now six months pregnant. She had walked some of the way from their home to the camp, from where he was setting off, with him. As they finally parted on the road, Dorothy had pressed a present on him. It was a small good luck charm, to keep him safe and bring him home to her and their unborn child. Alan wore it around his neck as the letter in his hand fluttered in the breeze coming off the sea.[49]

8

THE RIGHT TO SERVE: WOMEN AT WORK

Spring–Summer 1915

We're all striving now for the same thing, and the artificial barriers, which used to matter so much, are now forgotten.

Helen Franklin, January 1914

Dorothy Lloyd was now facing life without her husband by her side – but in that she was hardly alone. By the start of 1915, one million men had hung up their morning dress, factory overalls, butchers' and bakers' aprons, saying farewell to family and friends as they donned khaki instead. And as the months rolled by, more and more of them were sent over the Channel to war.

Hallie Miles decided that she should see for herself these last goodbyes. As a journalist, she felt it was her duty to record such scenes for posterity in her war diary. So it was that one afternoon she made her way down to Victoria Station:

When I got to Victoria Station, the train was waiting in the siding which is always kept entirely for these goings and comings. At first the platform was empty – only the train with steam up, waiting. And then there began to arrive, the Tommies, and the Officers, and the Mothers, Wives, and Sisters and Sweet-hearts. The men looked very brave, but their faces were very set. Some of them hardly dared to look at the brave women walking by their side. Soon the platform was crowded with this wonderful army of men and women who were fighting back the tears so bravely, and each helping the other by their own courage.

Then came the moment when the first dreaded whistle sounded; it seemed more like a trumpet call than the whistle of an ordinary engine. The very air became suddenly charged with intensest feeling. We all held our breaths; perfect silence reigned, for we knew the good-byes were being said; we knew that for some the last kiss was being given. Then there was the banging of doors, and the last whistle sounded. The train slowly moved off, as if it could not bear to go. I never saw such a sight as it was when the khaki arms were waving out the windows to those dear ones who were left standing on the platform as long as the train was in sight.[1]

Such a trauma still lay ahead for **Kate Parry Frye**. But not yet. She was first braced for something quite different. On 9 January 1915, her thirty-seventh birthday, she was standing at the altar of All Saint's Church in Hove. She was wearing her best black dress, her silk hat and squirrel coat and muff. In the pews at the front sat her mother and sister; the church was otherwise empty.

Kate turned as the doors at the back of the church were pushed open. In stepped John in his uniform:

> I saw John coming from the Vestry. I was only conscious that he looked alright and not nervous. I spoke very, very slowly, I noticed, as if I were weighing every word – and I said 'obey' most deliberately and carefully. I would have rather had it left out altogether – but had come to the conclusion that if I had the Church of England marriage service at all, there wasn't much more objection to that one word than to much of the other. It probably sounds lazy – one ought to battle for one's conviction.
>
> Brighton was all *en fete* as the King and Queen had come to visit the wounded – and as chance would have it when we were turning off the front, we saw a little group of people, and finding the King was expected we waited for about 10 minutes. Then past they came – the King quite deliberately turning to John and returning his salute – it was exciting – and on my Wedding day too. I wanted to stop them and tell them all about it.[2]

The newlywed Mr and Mrs Collins walked back to Portland Road in Hove, where Kate's mother and sister were staying. They had a celebratory tea, including a small cake covered with white icing, which Kate cut with John's sword. They had a few presents, and then Kate and John said their goodbyes – they were going to spend their first night together as man and wife. At 37, Kate was as nervous and excited as a teenager:

Caught the 4.40 train. It proved slow – but it didn't seem to matter – we just sat and hugged each other – government compels us now-a-days to travel with the blinds down so it was alright. [At Victoria] taxi to the Great Central Hotel. I suggested we had better not pay too much, but it was really rather nice on our arrival not to be consulted and just taken to the first floor – No 123.

I suggested to John – my husband – that he could go on down while I changed but he flatly refused, so he sat and watched me do my hair and then did my dress up for me. We went straight into dinner about 8.15 and had 9 rather bad courses. I was hungry and ate quite a lot. Then we both said we were tired so I said I thought I had better go to bed. John said he would come – but I told him not for 20 minutes and I went and got the key and went up alone.

I was so excited – who isn't at such a moment – I undressed all backwards and was only just done when John arrived. Ours was a gorgeous room, the bed in an alcove. We had meant to have a fire – it would have been nice but really the room was so warm we didn't need it. I laughed at first. Later I shed a tear or two and John would turn up the light to look at me – then he saw my tears and wept himself. We did try to go to sleep – but I don't think John had more than 2 hours and I had considerably less. But we were very, very happy.[3]

Kate Parry Collins awoke early the next day, exhausted but happy. She watched her husband put his uniform on. They had been married less than twenty-four hours, but their wartime work would not wait. Before long they'd left the hotel and kissed each other goodbye. John went back to his barracks at Shoeburyness, while Kate returned to her office: 'a mental and physical wreck is all I can describe myself – a face like chalk and eyes like stars – strangely and utterly happy. It all seemed just too wonderful. I could think of nothing else . . .'

Kate had been fighting for women's rights for many years. The war had changed everything – for her, and for women everywhere. Ironically, in some ways it had made Kate more conventional. Though she had taken on war work she'd also finally decided to marry, and even promised to 'obey'. But in truth, for thousands of women up and down the country, along with its painful goodbyes, the war had also brought them new challenges and opportunities.

Millions of men were away from their normal jobs, and it was becoming apparent that this would not be a temporary state of affairs. At the same time, there was more work than ever to do: this was a war that demanded equipment and weapons on a scale never before imagined, and women's work was no longer governed by social etiquette – it was a matter of urgent necessity. In 1915, the strictures that had long kept women confined to the home or to certain spheres of work were suddenly loosening. And the doors to gilded cages were among the first to be flung open.

Twenty-two-year-old **Helen Franklin** began 1915 working in a factory – though it wasn't functioning as a factory any more. Normally used for the production of rivets, the building on the outskirts of Aylesbury had been commandeered by the Royal Army Medical Corps and turned into a hospital. Helen no longer needed to envy her brother who had joined the army, for here she was getting a taste of wartime adventure herself. She'd joined the Voluntary Aid Detachment, an organisation providing medical assistance in time of war. By the end of 1914, thousands of other women, mainly from the middle and upper classes, had done the same.

In the middle of December 1914, Helen had packed up a few things – with the help of the servants – and travelled in her chauffeur-driven car to Aylesbury, where she'd been billeted on 'an old maid with a very nice house'. It was quite unlike anything she'd ever done before. On her first day, Helen was given a uniform and shown into the kitchens. That evening, she wrote to Norman, still her suitor, rather shaken up. She'd never cooked, cleaned, or washed up before, not even for herself. And now here she was, elbow deep in food waste and dishwater, working in an industrial hospital kitchen:

> My dear Norman, I am now in Aylesbury, billeted out, with no friends except new ones in the make, and I've got to let out on someone.
>
> I work every morning from 8–2 in the military hospital a mile away from here. I've only been here 2 days so far, and for the first week we are in the kitchens, to get used to discipline etc. I've never really worked

A Voluntary Aid Detachment nurse dresses the hand wound of a
German prisoner.

before in my life, til now. Talk about menial duties – why it's the hardest
thing in the world to wash up properly, and clear away, and peel potatoes and carry things without smashing them.

I am such a hopeless duffer at it all – it's so humiliating, because
really, being educated ought to help in things, but the stupidest skivvy
girl can do these things instinctively and I have to be taught how, and
then do them badly. There's such a lot to remember, which plates go
into which cupboard, and to wash the silver before the plates, and where
things are kept, and which vegetables are peeled and which scraped, and
which only washed.

It's very tiring.[4]

The hospital was set up to tend to Kitchener's New Army, still in
training. Some 500 soldiers a day were being inoculated against
typhoid at the hospital before being sent to the front, and staff had
to be inoculated too. A few weeks into her work, Helen was in bed
suffering after her first typhoid jab. But she was not suffering any
more with self-doubt – she had found a genuine satisfaction in her

new, simple work. She couldn't hide how happy she was, and how proud of herself:

> I still do washing up and peeling potatoes at the hospital and it's perfectly extraordinary how keen I've got on it. I'm going into the wards when I'm typhoid-proof. All the nurses and people at the hospital are simply ripping. I'm getting quite a good 'kitchen's help' now and never spill things and set about things in the right way.
>
> Did you read an article in *The Times* one day last week on 'The Temptation of Simplicity'. It said how many people found it such a tremendous relief to have a really simple routine – work to perform such as soldiering or nursing, instead of the ordinary varied responsibilities of daily life. That's exactly what I feel, and that I want to stay here as kitchen-maid.[5]

Helen had taken a pretty big leap, away from her cosseted, upper-class life. And now the door to this new world had been opened, she would struggle to close it again.

Lady **Diana Manners** had done the same, though perhaps with rather less naïve enthusiasm and a rather greater sense of rebellion against her mother. She was the same age as Helen, 22, and from a background even more privileged: Diana was an aristocrat, daughter of the Duke and Duchess of Rutland. A famed society beauty, her life was a whirlwind of parties and dinners with the in-crowd of her generation, known as 'the coterie' – of which she was the glittering star. But the war reached deep and it reached high; and it was changing all their lives too.[6]

Lady Diana had a seemingly infinite number of suitors, from counts to princes to dukes. Most of the Eton- and Oxford-educated young men in 'the coterie' were more or less in love with her too, including **Alfred 'Duff' Cooper**. Duff had been at Eton and Oxford with the rest of them, but was the son of a society doctor, with only a modest income from a career at the Foreign Office to look forward to. With no title, he was not on a social par with Diana.[7] That had not dampened his enthusiasm for her – Duff had first proposed to her in a letter in 1913, in the wonderfully wry style that would characterise their long and voluminous (he sometimes wrote to her three times a day) correspondence:

I always meant to ask you whether you would marry me or not. Probably not. I am mouse poor and should be a vile husband. But there is only about one person as far as I can remember whom I love better than you but she won't marry me, so I could promise at the altar to love you quite, to cherish you a good deal and to endow you with nearly all my worldly goods which wouldn't amount to much. I should in return require implicit obedience and scrupulous punctuality. Think it over at the end of the season.

Yours almost, Duff.[8]

That summer of 1913, Diana had been floating from party to party, champagne flute in hand, wrapped by her servants in the latest and most expensive gowns, garlanded with jewels, living in rooms overflowing with flowers from rich suitors. She was all the clichés of Edwardian decadence personified.[9] Now, in early 1915, she was wearing a rather severe nurse's uniform, tending to the needs of ordinary people on a hospital ward, living in an austere little room.

Diana had joined the Voluntary Aid Detachment like Helen, much to her mother's horror. In October she had started work at Guy's Hospital. A few of the hospital's nurses had gone abroad with the forces, and VADs were needed to fill the gaps they'd left. Diana had initially wanted to go to the front herself with the Red Cross, but this was something her mother, the duchess, would not countenance. Guy's Hospital was the compromise: a world away from their castle at Belvoir or their London mansion next to The Ritz, but at least still just down the road from the latter.

It captured the public imagination that Lady Diana Manners was toiling in a menial job. A music hall ditty even did the rounds: 'I'll eat a banana, with Lady Diana, aristocracy working at Guy's.' With no experience at all (she'd never even been inside a hospital before), Diana found herself, for the first time in her life, at the bottom of the hierarchy.[10] She was just another tired, hard-working nurse, on her feet all day. Duff remained as keen on her as ever:

When does the nurse's cap, so terribly like a nun's, come on and the tango curls fall off? And may I please be given one of the fallen curls – a wanton scented tress, which I will treasure in a golden box.

This morning I am acutely, achingly conscious of the privilege that I have in knowing you. I realize that you are the most remarkable woman of my generation. I have been fortunate in finding the mate God meant for me. But God's schemes never quite come off and it seems highly improbable that I shall ever marry you, though two people so perfectly made to fit have never been turned out. But if you ever should happen to want a husband in a hurry (and who hasn't occasionally?) be sure to ring me up. The devotion of a lifetime will always be waiting for you at 3446 Mayfair.[11]

He wasn't being completely serious, as Diana well knew. She was not Duff's only love interest – not by a long way. But she was fast becoming one of his favourites.

At the end of January, **Helen Franklin** had a few days off her own VAD work and was spending the weekend at her family's townhouse in West London. She'd spent half her life there – whenever she wasn't at their country house – but it felt a bit strange to be there now and to be so well looked after. Now she knew what hard work went on below stairs to get her dinner on the table or to keep her in clean clothes and linen. She knew, because she'd done it herself.

After her baptism of fire amongst the potato peelings and pots in the hospital kitchens, Helen had now been made a VAD nurse, like Diana. On the wards she'd come into contact with people she would never have encountered in the rigidly hierarchical society of pre-war times. She was inquisitive and open-minded, and it had made her think. Lying on her bed at Porchester Terrace, she wrote to Norman. She might have been propped up on the finest pillows, but her mind was on the patients in the makeshift hospital beds at Aylesbury:

We get a most interesting set of men at the hospital – they are all newly enlisted and have had such varied careers before. They are the sorts of people one never comes across in ordinary life. We've had a sailor on a tramp steamer, a stevedore, a half-cast clerk from a Shanghai tea-merchant, a Mexican oil borer, heaps of coal miners and iron smelters, a professional footballer, navvies, waiters and all sorts of other things.

The extraordinary part is that they take no interest in the war. They'll dash at a paper as soon as one appears; and if we ask them if there is any news in it, we get the invariable answer 'News! We're sick of the War. We only read the football.' Football is the common bond among them, from whatever part of Great Britain, and we now have men from all parts of Great Britain. There was intense indignation the other day because one man had enlisted who, one of my ward told me, was one of the best forwards in the North. 'What does he want to spoil the team for?' was the universal comment![12]

Helen's family were part of the elite. Her parents were less conservative than many of their contemporaries; they were Liberals who did a lot of charitable work amongst the poor Jewish community. But they respected the established order, in which everyone had their place and in which they, the Franklins, were comfortable near the top. But Helen had started to notice that things were changing – and she was excited by what that meant for Britain:

> The great beneficial change here, which is becoming more and more marked, is the great sense of equality in the whole nation – the idea that we're all striving now for the same thing, and the artificial barriers, which used to matter so much, are now forgotten. The 'people that count' are those who are doing something to help – and the 'nobodies' are those who are slacking. The badge of distinction is a wound. I only wish we could keep from going back to our former snobbery after the war's over. I wonder when it will be over.[13]

Diana Manners was 'a person that counted' – both in the pre-war terms and in the new way that Helen Franklin described. And she was having a great time. It wasn't that she particularly enjoyed the hard work, though she did it willingly; it was her freedom that she was relishing. At home she was under constant surveillance by her very protective mother, and never allowed out without a suitable chaperone. Now, in the few hours she had off in the evenings, she could do what she liked – as long as she was back through the hospital gates before they closed to be in bed by lights-out at 10.15 p.m.

In early 1915, most of Diana's male friends had enlisted in the army. The coterie had been scattered by the war. But for now, Diana's social life whirled on; whenever any of the men were in town, on leave from training or back from the front, they passed through London. Nurse Manners would change her clothes and run out of the hospital gates to a dinner party, as beautiful Lady Diana once again.[14]

Duff Cooper was one of the few men of the coterie still hanging around London. By the time the war broke out, Duff's career at the Foreign Office was underway, having started at the bottom as a resident clerk he'd moved up to the Commercial Department, which he hated. His work was in London and due to its importance he was required to stick at it. Duff didn't mind too much; he was a notorious party animal, heavy drinker and womaniser, and London was his stomping ground. Needless to say Diana's mother, the Duchess of Rutland, did not approve of him.[15]

Still, it was Duff who was there to keep Diana's spirits up when her war work was interrupted by a bout of measles. She wrote to him from her sick-bed:

> It is pleasant to think of two million germs lost in me – all treating this undefiled temple as an hotel, brothel, battleground, see-saws on my heart. Envy them Duffy. I envy them myself. Dine tomorrow at Carlton with George and secure Pinafore room at the Savoy. D[16]

And his reply came promptly, as it always did:

> Oh my measly love-bird, how you must weep to be the victim of so unaugust a malady. Don't think that I should be afraid to visit you, or that disease could ever turn me from you, however loathsome it might be. Oh the presumption of those half-witted germs – it fairly staggers one. How dare they pasture in those luxuriant fields of firm white flesh that should have been all mine. Father, don't forgive them, for they know not what they do and that's what I hate about them. Duff.[17]

The war would bring Duff and Diana closer together than the duchess could have feared or Duff could have dreamt of.

However, while Duff must remain in London, Diana's hopes for getting closer still to the conflict were suddenly reignited. Her mother, the duchess, had decided it was appropriate for someone of her station to open her own hospital. And it was to be in France. Diana, naturally, would go too. There was a lot of setting up to do – and Diana's career at Guy's came to an end.[18]

Helen Franklin found her work cut suddenly short too. The measles outbreak had reached her hospital in Aylesbury, the patients were quarantined, and the wards closed off to newcomers. As the workload fell, the staff was reduced accordingly. Helen was back at her London townhouse. And measles had made her think of her suitors too – with some time on her hands, she'd been seriously thinking about Norman's marriage proposal, which had taken her by surprise back in November. She wrote to him now, three months later, with her answer:

> I've been thinking an awful lot lately, and I've come to the conclusion that it's not very good for either of us to be so uncertain as to our future, and that it's not exactly fair on my part to leave you in doubt when I have already made up my mind. I imagine you can guess what it is – anyway, I'd be a pretty big rotter if it were anything else, after having had such a splendidly intimate correspondence with you during the last few months. I can't tell you how badly I'm longing for when I'll be able to see you. I think about you all the time, and wonder what you'd think of all the things I do. I'm sure you'll think I'm an awful kid when you know me very well – but perhaps I'll grow out of it soon.[19]

Helen had made a tough decision. She had hoped to continue her nursing in a new post, but she had been asked to sign on as a VAD for the duration of the war, and to be prepared to be posted anywhere. Now that she was to be married, she felt that wasn't possible, and with regret she ended her short-lived career.[20]

Kate Parry Collins's marriage had not changed much for her. Work, and the war, rumbled on. But despite being separated from John from the very first day of their marriage, and despite the usual din of sewing machines and her habitual rushing around, she felt rather special. She had surprised herself – she was thoroughly enjoying her new status as a married woman, in spite of mixed reactions from her former suffrage campaigning comrades:

> To Office. I was glad I was in my best and looking nice as a bride should. I still look rather pale and large-eyed but it's an exciting time – 'all soul' as Alexandra puts it.
> We had a meeting in the Office at 3. Mrs Chapman had greeted me kindly – also Mrs Hartley who kissed me twice and said she had seen the announcement in the Times and it looked 'very nice'. (I had bought

a Times and been reading it at intervals all day on the quiet – it does look very nice.) I had the usual up and down afternoon and a lot of congratulations when the meeting broke up. Some were quite nice. Mrs Innes very indignant – had not thought it of me.[21]

And things were changing for the workroom:

> Monday 1 February 1915: To Office. Then at 11.15 I had to come along to the Army Clothing Factory at Pimlico. Saw a nice official but don't know whether he will help us to get any shirts to make. Work is getting rather slack in the Workroom just now. [22]

Six months in, British industry seemed to be adjusting itself to wartime conditions, and regular trade was recovering. Charitable organisations like the National Constitutional Suffrage Society's workshop weren't needed to plug the gap any more.

Things got worse and worse, until finally, in March, the decision was made to shut the workroom down. Kate was put in charge of administering this. And closing the place down was going to take almost as much organisation as starting it up.

Women's war work was expanding rapidly – in more traditionally female jobs like nursing, clothing manufacture and food provision, but also beyond. **Helen Franklin**'s own war career had come to an end and she was now busy planning for her married life, but she was still aware how much the world around her was changing:

> It's so funny, but we are getting quite used to seeing girls and women do jobs men used to do. There are girls at the bookstalls on the Underground, women milkmen for the dairies; women porters and ticket collectors on some lines; women drivers of lorries and cars; women lift-boys in all the big shops – but still, for all that, there are hundreds and thousands of men who ought to go fight.[23]

Not everyone approved of women stepping into men's shoes. Helen's father certainly did not want these changes to reach his own household. Helen's brief sojourn into the world of work in a caring profession was permissible, but it had not won her any right to do things

A female tram driver and conductor at work.

differently at home. She wrote to her fiancé Norman at the end of April, the day that the family chauffeur swapped one uniform for another:

> I had another harrowing farewell this morning. Our chauffeur has joined the transport corps and came to say good-bye. He's over age, with a wife and family, but he's awfully fit, and a very good driver, so he's quite right to go. What upset him much more than the separation from his wife and children was the thought that perhaps he would not be here to drive us when we had a wedding. He almost wept to think that I could get married without his driving me and I said he'd have to get special leave if the war wasn't over.
>
> The car's been put away, because father won't have a female chauffeur – not even one of us if we learnt to drive it – and he couldn't patrioti-cally get a man now. [24]

Helen was expected to concentrate on becoming a wife, not learning to drive a car. Her mother was worried that she was a bit distracted by her recent adventures, and decided Helen needed something to focus her efforts. At the end of April, she was enrolled on a 'domesticating' course to learn to be a good, proper, old-fashioned housewife, despite – or perhaps because of – the increasingly permissive attitude to women's lives.

Of course it was not just in the big cities that women were taking on work they would never have done before the war. Men were leaving rural towns and villages too, and women were stepping into the gaps they had left behind in these places as well.

In Great Leighs, the Tritton family's support for the war had not died with their son Alan. The family continued to encourage recruitment in the village, through a poster campaign. Their own household set an example: their butler and two of their footmen left Lyons Hall in May 1915 to enlist. But while the squire's household might have been able to cope with such absences, they were causing problems for the farmers.

On a walk through Great Leighs early one May morning, **Andrew Clark** stopped for a chat with the squire's farm foreman, who was worried about how he was going to manage the year's harvest:

> Saturday 1 May: 7.40 a.m. at the gate into the meadow by the spring I had a conversation with Wm. Milton, foreman of Lyons Hall Farm. He does not approve of the profusion of recruiting posters, which on their present visit the squire's daughters have put up on all tree-trunks, gate posts, barn walls next to the road on Lyons Hall estate. 'Enticing more men away from the land, when too many have gone already. Unless the war is over before August, and some of the men come back, there will not be enough men to get in the harvest.'[25]

And some of the locals were shocked by a highly unconventional means of getting the work done at Lyons Hall Farm in the men's absence – allowing women to do it:

> Mrs Phillips (wife of the cowman) and Constance Stoddart the dairy-maid had been at the end of last week, hoeing turnips. Phillips, I heard, was very indignant and vowed that if his wife was to work in the fields,

he would stay at home. Other workmen have asserted the same of themselves.[26]

But the unavoidable reality was that new ways had to be found of doing things in wartime. The crops would not wait for the men to return from war. By May 1915, thirty-six men of military age had volunteered for service in the village; another thirty-six had not yet done so.[27] In the absence of half the men of prime labouring age, farming had to be kept going – even if it meant upsetting social mores.[28]

In May, **Diana Manners** had just returned from a trip to Boulogne. She was having lunch with her parents at their London mansion, along with Duff who'd hurried round to see her.[29]

The duchess's hospital was now well under way. The great and good of London society had rallied behind it – thanks in no small part to Diana's charms. Mr Selfridge had donated £2,000; and George Moore, a famously rich American businessman (and one of Diana's many suitors), had found a chateau at Hardelot for them to use, as well as donating a few thousand pounds himself.[30]

But despite the excitement of their new venture, Diana was finding it tough being back under the watchful eye of her mother. Her temper was frayed. The trip to the chateau had been exciting – its transformation into a hospital was very much on track – but her mother had irritated her more than ever. Diana had written from Boulogne to a friend about the developing tension between them:

> She said tonight sadly, does everything I do make you uncomfortable? By Jove it does, every bloody thing: squabbling with the base commander over the rent of the chateau; forcing useless and unwelcome objects – calendars, napkin rings etc. – on the officers.
>
> Worst of all staring at and questioning of the wounded. That eternal asking them where they are wounded, and the answer is always 'Buttocks, lady' or 'just here' with an ominous pointing index, or else a crimson face and a trembling lip from a sensitive man who wants no-one to know he has lost both hands and a leg.[31]

If Diana was to realise her dream of getting out to France, she'd have to bite her lip. And their plans for the hospital still needed final approval from the Red Cross.[32] Without it, neither Diana nor the duchess would be going anywhere.

Helen Franklin, meanwhile, had now started the domestic course designed to turn her into a traditional wife. She couldn't stand it. Whilst she should have been learning how to run a household, manage the laundry and choose the daily menu, she was sitting in the garden soaking up the May sunshine and writing to her fiancé:

> I've written to you in many funny places, but I think this is about the queerest. I'm in a little back garden of a little house in a little back road up in West Hampstead. The house belongs to the domesticating place. There is a theory lesson in housewifery this afternoon – but I struck.
>
> I told Mother this morning that I was not coming to this rotten old hole any more, as you said that you'd help me out. She said we'd soon get sick of that, and wish we knew how to do things properly.
>
> You said you wanted me to be myself, and if I became the thrifty housewife all these respectable females would like to see me, I wouldn't be. You take me for better or worse – and my housekeeping will probably be the worse part.[33]

The wedding was fast approaching; whether a good housekeeper or not, she was soon to be a wife.

The Duchess of Rutland's plans for a French war hospital had been thwarted. The Red Cross had refused to sanction it. But, still desiring a hospital in her name, the duchess decided to use the money to set one up closer to home. At home, in fact: in their Arlington Street mansion.

Diana Manners' life went through another change as her home was transformed into a hospital – unsurprisingly, one exclusively for officers. The changes were dramatic: the golden drawing room was turned into a ward for ten patients; the ballroom into a ward for an additional twelve. The beautiful floors were disguised under practical linoleum; glazed linens hid the walls. The duchess's bedroom became an operating theatre and Lady Diana was moved to a tiny room at the top of the house – formerly the servants' quarters.[34]

*

In May 1915, as the British army in France picked up the pieces after the battles of Aubers Ridge and Festubert, at home the furore over the shell crisis led to not only a new coalition government, but a new way of thinking about how the war must be fought. **Kate Parry Collins** followed the unfolding crisis:

> The papers are uncheering reading just now. We are not getting on – awful things keep happening – squabbles on all sides – unpatriotic attitude of many – now a coalition government called up. Well this one does seem to have been inefficient – all these months and only now beginning to organize. It's all too sad.[35]

The coalition government, with Lloyd George at the newly established Ministry of Munitions, realised that with the continued demand for men at the front, and the continued demand for industrial production at home, there was only one thing to do: get more women out of their homes and into war production factories.

On a grey, damp day, Kate braved the rain to do something she'd done many times in the days before the war: join with other women and march through Westminster. Back then she had been marching against the government, demanding the vote for women. Today was a march in support of women's war work, organised by former suffragette leader Mrs Pankhurst, in partnership with the government. The banners fluttering above the crowd read not 'Votes for Women' but 'We Demand the Right to Serve'. Kate was there as an organiser:

> A very dull morning and it just started to rain as I went out. I was prepared – a short grey linen dress – a woollen coat to keep me warm – Aquascutum – boots and rubbers – a small cap tied on – and an umbrella. I went by bus to Westminster and walked along the Embankment.
>
> Just before 3.30 we discovered if we were to march we must arrange ourselves – so a few people did one thing – a few another. I ran down the line telling people to come along and so we caught up with the front. Banners and bannerettes were hastily pulled out of carts and we were off. I went up and down giving directions and making us as trim as possible. We were a motley crew but we had some fine banner bearers and the greater number of us looked very neat in rainproof coats. And so off again on the great Women's Patriotic Procession organised by Mrs

Pankhurst and led by her. Mr Lloyd George received a deputation of women concerning Munitions.

The route was long – Embankment, Whitehall, Cockspur St, Pall Mall, St James, Piccadilly, Park Lane, Oxford St, Regent's St, Haymarket, Northumberland Avenue on to the Embankment again. At intervals were tables with ladies taking signatures of women ready to do munitions work. It was very inspiring and invigorating, though I felt very tired and seedy before.[36]

At the end of the march, as was the norm, rallying speeches were given. Mrs Pankhurst was there to oblige as she always had been. At her side was Lloyd George, previously a hated target of the suffragettes. But on this day, he took to the podium and made a speech that even Kate, miserable and damp, was roused by. He told the crowd that women's work was not only now possible, it was vital. The government was assuming control of munitions factories; 50,000 women were already working in munitions production; more were needed. And they would get the same pay as men. He concluded, to a thunderous round of applause: 'Without women, victory would tarry. And a victory which tarries, means a victory whose footprints are footprints of blood.'[37]

Alan Lloyd, whilst at Cambridge University.

Dorothy Lloyd (née Hewetson).   Kate Parry Collins (née Frye).

Queues outside the Whitehall Recruiting Office in London, shortly
after England's declaration of war on Germany in August 1914.

Reg Evans in uniform as a territorial soldier in the
Hertfordshire Regiment, c. 1914.

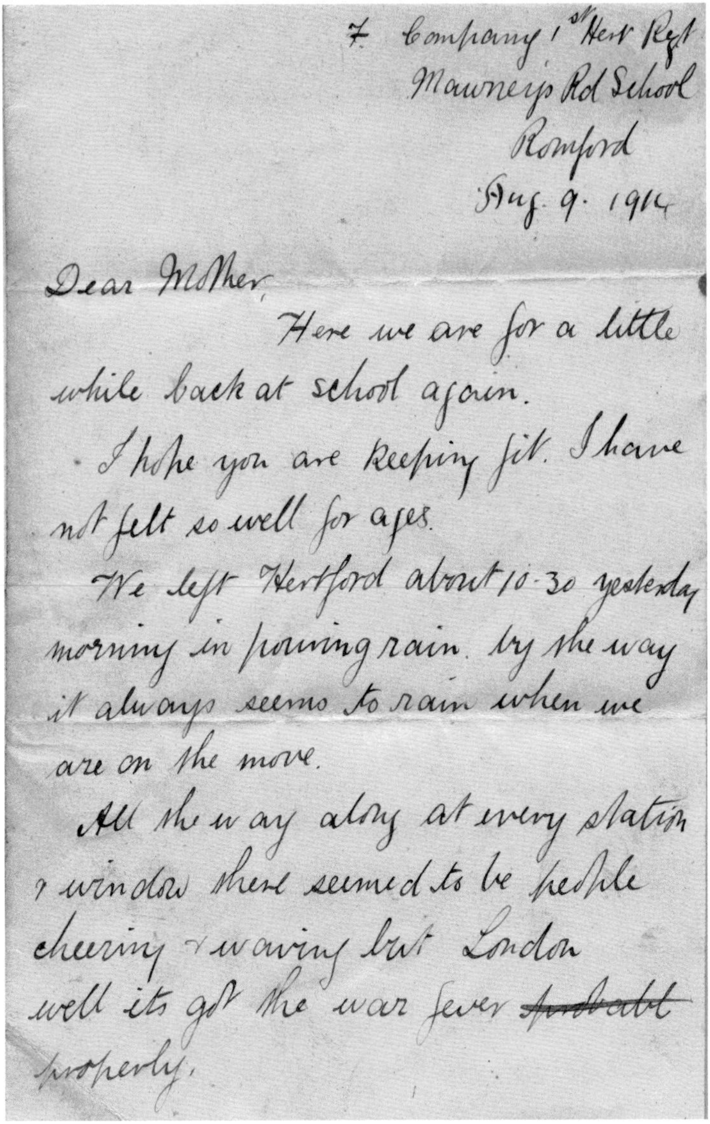

7 Company 1st Herts Regt
Mawneys Rd School
Romford
Aug. 9. 1914

Dear Mother,

Here we are for a little while back at school again.

I hope you are keeping fit. I have not felt so well for ages.

We left Hertford about 10.30 yesterday morning in pouring rain. by the way it always seems to rain when we are on the move.

All the way along at every station & window there seemed to be people cheering & waving but London well its got the war fever ~~no doubt~~ properly.

A letter from Reg to his mother, Frances Evans, written from his training camp in Romford, 9 August 1914.

Alan and Dorothy Lloyd on their wedding day in Boston Spa,
West Yorkshire, 1 September 1914.

James Butlin in uniform, c. 1915.

Lady Diana Manners in her uniform as a nurse in
the Voluntary Aid Detachment, collecting funds for
a soldiers' charity, 19 October 1916.

An Australian officer struggles
through the knee-deep mud of
the trenches in Gueudecourt,
during the Battle of the
Somme, 1916.

A recruitment poster for women munition workers, 1916.

The telegram informing Alan Lloyd's mother of his death. It reads:

'OHMS War Office, London
To Mrs Lloyd, Edgbaston Grove, Birmingham
Deeply regret to inform you that Lieut. A S Lloyd, RFA, was killed in action August 3rd. The army council express their sympathy. Secretary War Office have not informed Mrs Alan.'

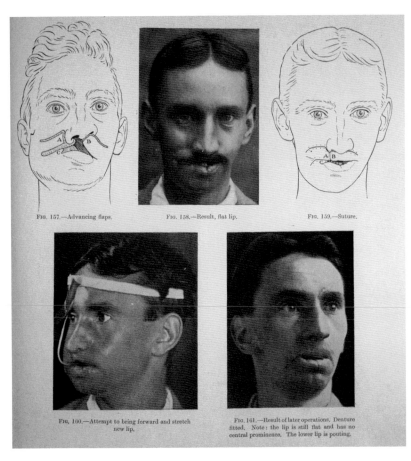

FIG. 157.—Advancing flaps.

FIG. 158.—Result, flat lip.

FIG. 159.—Suture.

FIG. 160.—Attempt to bring forward and stretch new lip.

FIG. 161.—Result of later operations. Denture fitted. Note: the lip is still flat and has no central prominence. The lower lip is pouting.

Illustrations and photographs showing the surgical procedures used by Harold Gillies to reconstruct Reg Evans's lip following the injuries he sustained in February 1916.

9

NEW TERRORS AT HOME: AERIAL CHARIOTS OF A FOE DESCENDING

January–September 1915

Such awful things are being prophesied: it makes one's heart stand still to hear of all that may be going to happen to our beloved England.

Hallie Miles's diary, early 1915

Although London had never suffered a Zeppelin raid, the people going about their lives in the darkened city feared it was only a matter of time. The first-ever air raids on civilians had already been unleashed on the East Coast, supposedly on military targets but in reality causing much damage at random. On the night of 19 January 1915, two Zeppelins aiming for the Humber had dropped high-explosive bombs on the Norfolk Coast. It had shocked the nation. Once again, the rules of war had been changed.

Hallie Miles learnt of these raids some days later – censorship meant that such news was tightly controlled:

It is a specially anxious time just now. Last night there was a German raid on the East Coast by Zeppelins and Aeroplanes. They attacked Yarmouth and King's Lynn, and even Sandringham. There have been several killed by the cruel bombs. So we are on the tip-toe of expectancy that they will continue these visits, and try hard to get to London. Such awful things are being prophesied: it makes one's heart stand still to hear of all that may be going to happen to our beloved England.

It is strange to read of trenches being made in England, and full of soldiers too, all ready and on the watch. And yet with all the watchfulness from air, land, and sea, the Germans seem able to slip in and take us unawares. God grant they may never reach London. We have to be prepared to fly to our basements, and have candles ready, and 'lamps trimmed'; for at the first sign of a raid over London all the gas and electric light will be turned off at the main, and everything will be in pitch darkness.[1]

The destruction caused by the early raids was not inconsequential: in the attack on Norfolk, four people were killed and thousands of pounds' worth of damage done.[2] But the real impact was on civilian morale. Flight was a relatively new idea to the world: the aeroplane had been invented just a decade before the outbreak of war, and aviators were seen as a new breed of heroic pioneers. But along with tremendous excitement over the power of flight, there had also been a sense of its threat from the very beginning. When Alberto Santos-Dumont flew a fixed-wing aircraft in France in 1906, Lord Northcliffe famously claimed that Britain 'was no longer an island' and feared that, if war were to come now, 'there would be no sleeping behind the wooden walls of Old England with the Channel our safety moat. It means the aerial chariots of a foe descending on British soil.' H. G. Wells had prophesied an air war that would bring the end of civilisation. And now, in early 1915, it was as though all these fears were being realised.[3]

Britain was on the alert. Londoners dared to hope that the Kaiser would not authorise an attack on the capital, with no legitimate military targets to justify it. But they were warned to be prepared. Hallie Miles was determined not to be caught unawares:

By way of preparation, all the basements and cellars are being got ready to flee to. I have piled up the parcels and books and literature all round the sides, and have left boxes for 'seats'. I have a table in the middle, and also a lamp, candles, matches and an oil stove, and lint and bandages, and even brandy! I have brought down a lot of furs and rugs and blankets in case we have to fly down at night. This is, of course, supposing the Zeppelins ever reach London.

We are in a most dangerous zone in Chandos Street.[4]

IT IS FAR BETTER
TO FACE THE BULLETS
THAN TO BE KILLED
AT HOME BY A BOMB

JOIN THE ARMY AT ONCE
& HELP TO STOP AN AIR RAID

GOD SAVE THE KING

A recruitment poster depicting a Zeppelin against the London skyline.

Hallie was not just worrying about herself, though, she also wanted to set an example to the people of London (or at least to her own fans): her preparations were so exemplary that a photograph of her basement was featured in the *Daily Graphic*.

As winter turned to spring, the bombing raids on Britain continued, though the capital remained untouched. Raids on Ipswich at the end of April and on Southend in early May proved the Germans were not giving up on aerial bombing of Britain, despite the limited strategic damage they were causing. **Helen Franklin** found she couldn't take the panic seriously, however, especially given the news in May of truly devastating losses in the spring campaigns in France:

> Some people take [the Zeppelins] awfully seriously, and go about with respirators in their pockets for the poisoned gases. I do wish I could see

one, it would be so thrilling, and so awfully nice to swank about after. I can't get up any panic about it, and nor can any of the family, but various relatives take it all very seriously.

Statisticians say that there have been more deaths due to poor lighting in the streets on account of the scare, than could ever be caused by a Zeppelin raid. There's a fate looking after us somewhere with a jolly huge sense of humour, isn't there? How it must be enjoying all this holocaust now. The casualty lists in the papers are too ghastly for anything, and we can't see any ending to it at all. It's so horribly depressing.[5]

But Helen's mind was really on other things. She wanted to thank Norman, who was in Cairo, for the wedding ring he'd just sent her:

My boy, the ring is so absolutely what I longed to have, that if all our tasks coincide in the same way, we'll do. It's the prettiest thing I have ever seen, and so rippingly uncommon. I can't thank you properly for it – you're giving me such a lot in life, that if I once started thanking you I shouldn't stop . . . woa back. I'm exceeding the speed limit, and waxing damned sentimental. Guilty my Lord, and I won't do it again.[6]

Norman was due to arrive in England in July; the wedding was scheduled for September.

It wasn't just from above that Britain was being threatened by German military might. The threat was also coming from the seas that encircled her. After the sinking of the HMS *Formidable* on New Year's Day, German submarines had continued to bring tragedy to British seas – and now merchant ships were the target. On 30 January, a British merchant ship was torpedoed without warning. The following day, the German navy was given permission to launch submarine warfare against all ships bringing food or supplies to Britain, even neutral ships. The reason given was that the British mining of the North Sea was a 'hunger blockade' of Germany – and this was their retaliation.[7]

Food shortages resulting from this submarine blockade could, of course, spell disaster for the Eustace Miles Restaurant, but **Hallie Miles** was nothing if not inventive, and was optimistic she could turn things to her advantage. After all, it was a vegetarian restaurant, and it was the supply of meat that was worst affected. Prices were already beginning to rise and Britons were being asked to get used to eating less of it:

> I am very busy over many things. My cookery book 'Economy in War-time' is to be published by Methuen as soon as ever I have finished it. It is exactly the right time for it to come out, for the price of meat is becoming so awful that many of the butcher shops are closing. Eustace and I are tremendously in requisition about meatless foods. I am trying to start a campaign in people's own kitchens for demonstrations in meatless cookery, especially as Thursday is now the 'Meatless Day' in England.[8]

But Hallie had not dreamt that submarine warfare would reach the level it did.

On 1 May, the British liner, *Lusitania*, left New York for Liverpool. Six days later a single torpedo was fired at her, without warning. The ship sank in just eighteen minutes, and 1,198 passengers were drowned. Hallie was preparing the Loyal Choir for a concert at an exhibition on Women's War Work when news of the disaster reached London:

> I shall never forget that evening. The Choir all met beforehand in the EM Restaurant, and I gave them dinner. In the middle of dinner, we heard the dread news of the *Lusitania* having been sunk by the Germans. The customers came in looking stricken with horror; the most awful silence and solemnity seemed to fill the place. I asked the orchestra to play very softly 'Eternal Father, Strong to Save'. It seemed the only thing to do.[9]

With the sinking of the *Lusitania*, which was a passenger liner rather than a merchant ship, Germany had made it very clear that in this war no one was safe. The German argument was that the *Lusitania* was carrying arms, but the message was clear: civilians – even foreign civilians (128 Americans were drowned) – had become legitimate targets of war. Britain was shocked; the USA was outraged; the German press celebrated.[10]

Helen Franklin was appalled by the sinking of the *Lusitania*. It registered with her in a way that the first air raids had failed to do. Perhaps it was because it felt closer to her; she had been a passenger on an ocean liner herself, and Norman travelled by ship regularly between Britain and

Egypt. Helen was not alone in her horror. A wave of anti-German riots swept London. Helen was volunteering with the Girl Guides in the East End at the time, as well as doing her domestic course.[11] And from her girl guides she had first-hand accounts of the spate of 'anti-German' lootings. She wrote to Norman a few days after the disaster:

> Everything seems so very black & terrible, & one hears nothing but death & misery from all around, that it almost seems wicked to have so much happiness of our own. But I know it isn't – it is right. And it is one of the wonders of this good universe that joy & sorrow are always strangely intermingled.
>
> The feeling of hatred towards Germany is very marked since the *Lusitania* disaster & the poisonous gases; & people who are, naturally, good Christians & love their enemies, are very bitter in all they say of the Germans. That, I think, is very sad – but it is inevitable.
>
> These 'riots' are put-up jobs by gangs of hooligans & rough women, & are done for loot under the name of patriotism. They are mostly cried up by the papers to encourage recruiting – and people destroy the property of Germans & British indiscriminately. Sarah Laginsky says she now knows what it feels like to be a German! The shop where she works in Islington was sacked by the mob and every blessed thing taken out of it, nearly all by women and children. She said the shop people stood and looked on, and could do nothing.[12]

Duff Cooper had seen a different response to the sinking of the *Lusitania*: the political reaction. From inside the Foreign Office, he couldn't understand the popular outcry – if anything, he thought, it must be a good thing for the British war effort: 'The *Lusitania* sunk. People seem very worried about it, as though it were a defeat for us, whereas of course it makes not the faintest difference to the war and only stirs up America against Germany.'[13]

The USA had so far remained fiercely neutral. President Woodrow Wilson was determined to keep America out of war. But popular opinion in America, like that in Britain, was demanding a reaction to the atrocity. Duff didn't discount the moral weight it would give the Allies:

> The feeling in America is so strong that they may be forced to go to war, if they do not they will simply be playing into Germany's hands.

Here is another example of the truth that it is not statesmen and diplomats who are responsible for wars but the people themselves, a truth that socialists and diplomats fail to recognize.

I cannot help feeling that in the long run neutral nations and even the more thoughtful of the Germans could not fail to be impressed by the spectacle of all the most civilized nations in the world joined in alliance against one enemy.[14]

On 13 May, President Wilson issued a note to Germany, urging them to abandon their policy of unrestricted submarine warfare. Duff felt that America was on the brink of joining the war: 'America's note to Germany today looks as though war is inevitable. America can hardly with dignity avoid war.'[15] Wilson sent two further warnings, each increasingly aggressive. But the will to fight was not there, yet, and Wilson managed to keep America out.

Duff turned his attention back to his social life:

In the evening I had a men's dinner party which made all the women furious but we adored it. It was the greatest fun and was followed by a glorious party at The Cavendish which was really the best of its kind. I climbed up the wall to the roof at juncture, putting my foot through the window and cutting my ankle. Those who were left wanted to have breakfast at a cab shelter at about 5.[16]

The Cavendish was a favourite hangout of the coterie. In the first half of 1915, **Diana Manners** was frequently to be found there, and neither she nor Duff seemed to mind that they were often with their other love interests:

At 12 o'clock we both went to a small supper party at The Cavendish. It was great fun and everyone was very drunk at the end especially me. As Diana was going off with Hallam and I with Marjorie, Diana said to me in the hall that although we both had our stage favourites we really loved each other best, and kissed me divinely, which nobody noticed, though they were all standing by.[17]

The set-up at her mother's new hospital suited Diana very nicely: she could do the war work she'd craved, but in a far more agreeable setting. At Arlington Street there was none of the austerity of Guy's – morning tea now consisted of cream cakes and sherry, as befitted the officer-patients. And, best of all, her mother had rather tired of the venture already. She spent an increasing amount of time at the family's estate, leaving Diana with plenty of time to do as she wished.[18]

It was a time of hedonism for Diana and for her set. Not because the war seemed distant, quite the opposite: with most of the men in the army, life seemed short and needed to be grabbed with both hands. Diana's rich American suitor, George Moore, threw wild parties in her honour for the men on leave, called 'Dances of Death' because no one knew who would be there for the next one. For Diana, it was a time of abandon. One of her favoured suitors at this time was music-hall star Basil Hallam, and after the parties they would sit in a taxi for hours, circling Regent's Park, so they could spend time alone together.[19]

But at the end of May, the war was no longer something that could be escaped in London. On the last day of the month, the long-dreaded zeppelins arrived in the skies above the city.

It was a Monday, and a clear night had taken the place of a sunny day over London. The Houses of Parliament were disappearing into darkness, and from Westminster Bridge a dark mass could be made out where Big Ben stood. Drawn curtains hid the lights of late workers in a scattering of windows in Westminster Palace. The new coalition government was only a few days old; the public anger over the losses at the front due to lack of shells had been sated for now, but there was much work to do.

Duff Cooper had spent a long day at the Foreign Office. Perhaps he was still there at this late hour, hunched over a desk in the grand building on King Charles Street. Or perhaps he was out enjoying a drink somewhere.

A mile along the Thames was Pimlico, and Claverton Street, and **Kate Parry Collins**. She was probably already asleep, exhausted after the stresses of the workroom, a letter from her husband and a burnt-down candle on the little table.

Three miles north, through the gloom of Green Park and Hyde Park, **Helen Franklin** was back at number 35 Porchester Terrace, after a weekend at the family estate in Buckinghamshire. Outside, the darkness of the park was occasionally broken by the sweeping beams of search-lights.[20]

And back east, off the Strand on Chandos Street, **Hallie Miles** was saying goodnight to the staff of the Eustace Miles Restaurant.

All this, the human detail of the sprawling capital city, could not be seen from 10,000 feet above. For Erich Linnarz, the commander of the LZ38 Zeppelin now entering the skies above Margate, such detail was of no concern anyway. The LZ38, loaded with incendiaries, was moving west through a moonless night to London, which had now been declared a target of war.[21]

The Zeppelin reached the British coastline just before 10 p.m. on 31 May. This was the same airship that had perpetrated raids on Ipswich and Southend in the previous weeks and had so far proved immune to the efforts of the Royal Naval Air Service to stop it. Zeppelins could simply fly higher than aeroplanes. It was now to carry out its most significant mission yet: the first-ever air raid on the capital. By 11 p.m., the airship had reached its destination. British planes, searchlights and anti-aircraft guns failed to prevent the LZ38 as it dropped ninety small incendiary bombs and thirty grenades on East London.[22]

Kate Parry Collins slept through it all. Down in Pimlico, she didn't hear the bombs hit the ground; or the crackle of burning buildings; or the cries of the seven Londoners killed and the thirty-five injured that night. She only learned of the raid the next day:

> To Office and a very busy day. News of a raid on London last night – Zepps – and bombs have been dropped – some deaths. No places mentioned but I know they went to the East End. So it's come at last. It is a horrible feeling.

As Kate walked home she had a lingering sense of foreboding: another dark night approached. The details of the raid – a terrible blow to British morale and a worrying demonstration of the inadequacy of the capital's defences – had been heavily censored. But rumours flew around the city, and Kate was nervous:

> I continued my ramble to Marble Arch. Stopped on my way to send post cards to Mother and J. to let them know I was safe. Of course all the talk was of Zepps – everyone feverish with the subject and none of us too comfortable about the matter.[23]

*

As Kate posted her postcards near Marble Arch, on the other side of Hyde Park, **Helen Franklin** was getting the gossip about the raids from her father, who had returned from his work in the city. Unlike Kate, Helen refused to be rattled by this latest development in the war and seemed to feel most people were equally stoical:

> Father has brought in more news of the Zeppelins, tho' it's not allowed in the papers. One bomb was dropped in Osborn Street and many all round Whitechapel & Shoreditch. London's taking it all as a matter of course, & all the notice taken of the raid is that a few more German shops are being sacked. We are a funny people – but I'm jolly glad I'm English, all the same. We'll muddle through the war somehow, & come out grinning on top.[24]

The following day, she got to hear from sources that had been even closer to the action, thanks to her East End Girl Guide troop:

> Last night I was down with the kiddies and heard all the latest versions of the Zeppelin raid. The Yiddisher Zeit published the names and addresses of the wounded and killed (rumour has it that there are more than are allowed by the press bureau) and the streets and localities bombarded and so the editor has been arrested and the paper suppressed.
>
> I wish the Germans could see how their terrorism acts on the minds of the small girls of Whitechapel: 'Isn't it a shame, Mother never woke me up to look at the bombs.' – or 'Let's stay here til 11, and then we can see the Zeppelins if they come again.' – or 'Oh they never threw any down YOUR street, they did down OURS.' – these are the stock remarks of the youths and maidens of Whitechapel. All rushed out to see the bombs fall.
>
> The man who teaches my guides First Aid is a member of the St John's Brigade and he lives in Mildmay Park, near Dalston. Two people were killed in the next street to him and he was out all night attending to wounded, and picking up bombs. They picked up 20 there, and took them to the police. Father has heard that both Zeppelins were destroyed by our men, but it's only a vague rumour. It seems too good to be true.[25]

It was too good to be true: nine aircraft had tried to catch the Zeppelin, but had been totally powerless to stop it. One British pilot and plane were lost in the attempt. The LZ38 dropped its deadly load and then left, untouched.[26]

The press were forbidden to report the location of raids, and only the official Admiralty communiqué could be published. In the absence of detailed reporting, Londoners relied on snippets of information, and the rumour mill.

Kept in a fog of uncertainty by the censorship of the press, the rumours **Hallie Miles** heard did nothing to quell her deep fears that a bomb would find her home:

There has been a horrible Zeppelin Raid in the East-End of London. All details are kept out of the papers but of course one hears a good deal privately. It was a much bigger raid than was announced. Some of our employees were actually in it. Our two charwomen were close to it and saw houses being burnt down. They gathered up a few belongings, and with their little bundles walked about the streets all night, afraid to go to their room at the top of some high flats.

A very touching story did get into the papers at one of the Inquests. When the Fireman entered one of the houses that had nearly been destroyed by an awful bomb, they found a husband and wife, with all their clothes burnt off them, kneeling in prayer at their bedside. The husband's arm was still round his wife's waist. One can hardly tell, or think of it, without tears. I sometimes wonder if Eustace and I shall be found like that. It all seems coming so near us. Every night it seems to me like preparing for the Judgement Day.[27]

There were further attempts to bomb London in the following weeks, but none of them succeeded. The Zeppelins dropped their bombs elsewhere in error. On 4 June Gravesend was hit; two days later, Hull, causing considerable damage. And in mid-June, a raid planned for Tyneside met its target: a shipyard was hit and seventeen workers were killed.

But then Britons had some respite. The long summer days made it harder for Zeppelins to make the run to and from Britain and remain under cover of darkness. But summer couldn't last forever.

*

At the end of June, **Helen Franklin** was in a wonderful mood. Norman was arriving in just a few weeks' time; they were to be married in early September. She was beside herself with excitement. She was in Cambridge, staying with her future sisters-in-law, and lapping up the English summer:

> A heavenly June morning, when all the world is sunshine and roses, & just as it should be, & I'm waiting for your sisters to come & take me on the river. A whole day on the water in June! It sounds ripping, doesn't it? I am having such a fine time here, & getting very, very fond of your sisters.
>
> It's rather heavenly to think you'll be down here in a fortnight, & will come in time for the roses after all – and the strawberries, do you like strawberries? There are masses now, but I can't promise there'll be any left in a fortnight. Let Ellis or I loose in a strawberry bed, & we do our duty manfully & like true-born Britons.[28]

Kate Parry Collins was also on a break from life in London. The workshop had now been closed down, and Kate had some time off. At the end of July she went back down to Hove and spent a few weeks with her mother and sister. Then, in mid-August, she finally had the chance to spend some time with her husband and caught the train to see him in Shoeburyness. The sun had come out and all seemed well with the world:

> It was a lovely day, the weather seems to have got summer like at last. John was at the station to meet me and we drove to our diggings – very nice – light and clean rooms. Tea was soon ready and I had brought some new laid eggs with me.
>
> John is to stay here with me as he doesn't seem to have anything to do and his new Major is very easy going. I didn't expect he would be able to be with me – it is very nice. He looks well. It will be a lovely three weeks.[29]

Kate also glimpsed a little of the latest defences being put in place. Shoeburyness had long been home to Royal Artillery and Gunnery schools, and the newest addition was an anti-aircraft gunnery school:

We caught the garrison train at 2.20 to the new ranges and saw the lovely anti-air craft gun there. It is a beauty and one would [wish] for Zepps to come along. Then we walked back to the Adjutant's house and had tea in the garden with Major Notley. Mrs Worthington – a doctor's wife who I remember something of – told me they have just had the top of their house blown off by a Zepp bomb – fortunately they and their children escaped.[30]

Another sunny morning a few days later, Kate and John saw the anti-aircraft guns in action, as troops trained for combat against Zeppelins:

Walked to Garrison where John came back for me – and watched the Anti-Air Craft Gunners firing at a balloon went up on the sea. It was very exciting but they didn't hit it. Such a noise and all sorts of different shells.[31]

After lunch we walked to Thorpe Bay and train to Southend. Tea at Garons. The place was packed and it was most amusing – the lovely ladies with or hoping for officers. Then we strolled about and out on the front. It was a very heavy close evening. We kept expecting Zeppelins as it was so dark. We sat and listened to the band from 7.45 to 9.30 and came back by the 9.45 train.[32]

Kate and John made the most of their few precious weeks together.

In August, as the nights drew in again, the Zeppelin raids resumed: Kent, Suffolk and Essex were bombed.

Duff Cooper and **Diana Manners** had been enjoying the summer in a suitably luxurious fashion. But an especially drunken weekend in Brighton had ended in disaster: after a boozy lunch, the pair had suffered a nasty fall while walking down the steps to the beach together. Duff got off pretty lightly with some terrible bruises. Diana broke both her legs. A five-week spell in a London nursing home followed.

Against all odds, this was the start of a wonderful summer for her. She held court in her flower-filled private room in the nursing home near Regent's Park. Even the prime minster, Herbert Asquith, came to see her, much to the surprise of the nurses. And she was still out of the controlling gaze of her mother, who had by now added to the hospital in their London mansion by turning their country estate into a convalescent home.

Duff, working nearby, was making the most of the duchess's absence:[33]

> Dined at Manchester Street alone with Diana. One of the most delicious evenings of my life. I was beautifully dressed – silk shirt and big black tie. A very hot night. Diana in a night gown only. I brought a bottle of champagne, we broke the cork but with the help of the nurse eventually opened it. We sat side by side on the sofa and ate a cold grouse off one plate with a knife and one fork and I also ate some Camembert cheese.
>
> After dinner Diana was divine. We went further than ever we have gone – but with such art and distinction. She is the only person who is worth making love to, who understands the game and how to play it. There is a great deal to be said for love-making that sends one away hungry, exasperating though it is. She assures me she has never abandoned herself to anyone in this fashion. I am inclined to believe it. How I adored her.[34]

All his other love interests were forgotten, for the time being at least. He wrote to Diana shortly afterwards, truly smitten:

> My darling heart, this is the third time I have fallen into love with you, Oh see to it, my lily, that I do not fall out. I wish I was more beautiful so as to be worthier of you. I should like to marry you and then go round the world to look for lovers lovely enough to deserve you. I should like to find a nearly perfect one, and bring him back and prepare him and coach him in every engaging artifice of love, and then I would serve him up to you – a morsel for a goddess – and you would kill him in a fortnight and love me better than you did before. Duff.
>
> I shall wait longingly for you to telephone tomorrow.[35]

Diana left the nursing home shortly afterwards, and enjoyed another few weeks off nursing, hobbling between social engagements on crutches. On 7 September, she was at a dinner party with a friend. Suddenly their meal was interrupted – by a loud noise from above. The Zeppelins had reached the capital for a second time. This time, they were directly above central London. Diana and her friend clambered onto the roof to watch the show.[36]

There had been a number of unsuccessful attempts to reach London in late August. This time, two military Zeppelins made it. For the second time in history, bombs rained down on the capital. They hit the Isle of Dogs just after midnight, and were scattered over a swathe of southeast London as the Zeppelins continued their progress. Eighteen high explosive bombs and twenty-six incendiaries fell; six men, six women and six children were killed.[37]

Following on from this success, German naval Zeppelins had a go the next night. Four set out: one barely made it off the ground; one headed for industrial targets in the north but its bombs failed to detonate; one reached the Norfolk coast. The final airship steamed straight to London, arriving at 11 p.m. **Hallie Miles**'s worst fears had come true.

Hallie and Eustace were hosting a dinner party at their flat. Eustace's close friend, the novelist E. F. Benson, was amongst the guests. There had been much discussion at dinner about the previous night's raids, and Hallie had proudly told the writer about her model preparations, much to his delight:

> E. F. Benson had been dining with us, and of course we had all been talking about the raids. I described to him all my preparations for a Zeppelin raid; bags; dressing-case; long coat; Eustace's 'Zeppelin trousers'; and my 'Zeppelin hat'. He was very amused by it all, and begged to be allowed to see these grand preparations, including the 'alarm trousers'. So I showed him the little pile at our bedroom door. He thought it all very funny, and said, 'I'm afraid you will be disappointed, and that you won't have any use for all these things' to which I replied, 'Perhaps you will have a surprise when you get home!' This was prophetic!
>
> We were very anxious about E. F. Benson that night, for the first bomb fell just after he had left us. He had to walk home with the bombs and shrapnel falling all around him. But he was as brave as possible, and said it was the grandest sight he has ever seen; he would not have missed the experience for anything. He saw some of the fires too. It was such retribution on him when he had been mocking me for my wise preparations, every one of which was the greatest use, and prevented our having any panic or bad forgets![38]

Hallie's preparations may have stood her in good stead, but those of the nation had been exposed as woefully inadequate. Twenty-six anti-aircraft guns in and around London had opened fire on the Zeppelin, seven aeroplanes went after it, searchlights scanned for it; yet on it went on its deadly course. The results were shocking: fifty-five high explosive and fifty-five incendiary bombs struck the heart of London. The City and Bloomsbury and Holborn burned. Two buses were hit directly. Twenty-two people were killed and seventy-eight injured.

The aftermath of the 8 September 1915 Zeppelin raid, showing damage caused to buildings on Bartholomew Close in the City of London.

The next day, Londoners were outraged that they had been so poorly defended. In response, Admiral Sir Percy Scott was tasked with the creation of a London Air Defence Area. Sir Percy went to France immediately to get hold of 75mm auto-cannons mounted on armoured vehicles, which arrived in London within days. He urged that a fleet of planes armed with guns be made available to him. And the calls for control of lighting were renewed: apparently the Zeppelin pilot had seen the glow of London from Cambridge.[39] Hallie Miles, patriotic and dutiful as ever, was quick to do her bit:

> I have had curtains made to draw right across our windows. I hope others will do the same. We feel much safer now that Sir Percy Scott is in charge of the safety of London from Air Raids. We have a moon on just now, so it is a respite.[40]

But whatever efforts were made now, the vulnerability of civilians in this war had been underlined. For Britons at home, including Hallie, it was a turning point:

> We have now entered upon such a solemn and awful phase of the War. The music of life seems so deep and vibrating; it is as if all the stops of an organ were out; the very ground and, alas!, our hearts, seem to tremble and shake with the deep thunder of this terrible music.[41]

Helen Bentwich was sorry she'd missed it: 7 September was her wedding day, and straight after the ceremony – a traditional white wedding, save for the guard of honour provided by her Girl Guides – she and Norman had headed off to a hotel in Kent on their honeymoon.[42] She wrote to her mother the next day:

> So far, it doesn't seem very different to not being married. We were very dead beat last night, & retired to bed about 9.45, & had breakfast this morning about 10.30. They've arranged everything rippingly for us here – even to treacle for breakfast and we haven't to do anything except enjoy ourselves. The house is packed full of flowers for us.
>
> You are lucky people to be having Zeppelins – it's we really that should be having them here, not you there. Do you all put on respirators when they come, & go into the cellars? Or do you all dash to look at the instructions posted up at the street corners, to try & remember what to do?[43]

The newlyweds' big trip was yet to come. At the end of September, 23-year-old Helen, armed with her new housewifery skills, was off to set up home in Cairo, where Norman worked in the law school. They travelled via Paris and, accompanied by their maid Esther, Helen and Norman explored the French capital. Helen was not impressed:

> Paris isn't a patch on London. It's not nearly so sanitary or so interesting. Also, all the traffic goes on the wrong sides of the road which annoys me. The tea is foul, another reason I'm glad I'm English.[44]

But while Helen was finding fault with the quality of French tea, just 100 miles away, the biggest battle of the war was under way.

10

FAILURE ON
ALL FRONTS

Summer–Autumn 1915

There are no signs of the end whatever. It is questionable if flesh & blood can stand another winter.
Letter from James Butlin to his friend Basil Burnett Hall, July 1915

June 1915 was a relatively quiet time on the Western Front. The armies were recovering after the traumatic months of April and May, which had seen the arrival of gas at Ypres and huge losses in the offensives at Aubers and Festubert. Now there was a respite, a chance for each side to consolidate their positions. The British took over further sections of the line from the French, north of Ypres, south of Cuinchy and later in the Somme valley.[1]

Meanwhile, the war had widened and spread. The Eastern front, running from Lithuania, through Poland, to Galicia, was the focus of German efforts in 1915, and their advance into Russia continued. New powers had entered the fray: most recently Italy had joined the Allies in May 1915; most significantly, Turkey had declared holy war against them in October 1914. By summer 1915, the fighting had spread to Italy, the Middle East, Africa and Gallipoli. It had become the First *World* War, though it would not be so named until much later.[2]

Turkey had proved a more formidable opponent than expected. Russia was being stretched to the limit by the Turkish army in the Caucasus, on top of fighting the advancing Germans on the Eastern Front, and pleaded for help. In response, a plan was formulated for a diversionary attack on Turkey in the Dardanelles. It was hoped that the breakthrough that was proving so elusive on the Western Front could be made there. The French were reluctant but complied. At the end of April, just days after the gas attack at Ypres, British, Indian, French, Australian and New Zealand troops landed in Gallipoli. But here, too, fighting quickly descended into a hopeless, bloody stalemate. Valuable troops and resources had been diverted from the Western Front and nothing was gained.[3]

In mid-June, the British and French Allies met at Boulogne. They'd been fighting together for almost a year. The French proposed another offensive on the Western Front before the winter; this time, they suggested attacking on a broader front, with more divisions than ever before. The British, still the junior partner in the alliance, doubted they would be ready in time. The woeful inferiority of the Allies' heavy artillery was discussed. The new British Ministry of Munitions knew that much work lay ahead before they could even come close to matching German firepower.[4] Yet plans for a Big Push in summer 1915 were set in motion. The belief that one massive effort could break the stalemate and end the war was one that many wanted to cling to.[5]

The indomitable **Reg Evans** was missing home. He had now been on the Western Front for seven months, and it was almost a year since he had left Hemel Hempstead in a blaze of patriotism. It all felt a lifetime ago. Now a corporal leading a squad of men, he had just gone into the trenches again, in a part of the line the British had taken over from the French near Cuinchy.[6] Reg wrote to his mother from the trenches, shells exploding periodically nearby. It was her birthday soon:

> I am writing in plenty of time as I do not know when it will be possible as we are now back in the trenches. Before I get any further, let me wish you 'very many happy returns of the day', your birthday I mean, not the wicked Huns' Der Tag. I wish I could have been with you but never mind Mother dear, we'll have all the more to celebrate when I do return. Be sure and let me know who you hear from and if you have anything special to mark the day, won't you, for I shall like to hear all about it.
>
> The trenches we are in are a fresh section we have lately taken over. Paraphrasing the psalmist, the allemands appear to say 'at morning noon and eventide will I hate thee' and at these times send over some shells

as tangible proof of their feelings and have busted in one section of the trenches no less than five times in less than two days.[7]

Reg and the 1st Herts spent much of July enduring the constant sniping of the Germans. On 10 July, Reg was commended for his conspicuous bravery in the field, though the records do not note for what.[8] When they weren't in the trenches, they were resting in Bethune. Reg had already spent time there earlier in the year.[9] Being back again, with no progress having been made, despite all the death he'd seen and his own acts of bravery, brought home how differently the war was proceeding to his initial, enthusiastic predictions:

> Oh dear me, it doesn't seem as if this war will be over for years. Here we are again back in the same place we were in in February. The same old billets and the trenches not advanced a bit. The only changes are that the place is smashed up a bit more and there are fewer inhabitants. I reckon old Kitchener knew what he was doing when he enlisted men for three years or duration of the war.
>
> You ask me whether I am likely to get leave and I can only reply by saying, ask me another. I may strike lucky. We have been back for a rest but the huns won't let us rest, dropping a few shells into the town to strafe us, though fortunately without doing us much damage.[10]

While passing through the ruined town of Cuinchy, Reg picked up a piece of stained glass that he found amongst the rubble of a churchyard. Reg was religious, and he kept it with him, perhaps as some kind of a lucky charm. He was longing for home. It was in the lap of the gods whether he would get there before the next big push began.

In July 1915, **James Butlin** and the Green Howards were still near Festubert, not far from Reg and the 1st Herts. James too came across a destroyed church:

> The village here which is blown to pieces has not been inhabited for a long time. The church & grave yard are sights never to be forgotten. Tremendous shells have ploughed up the graveyard so that tomb-stones & vaults have been scattered, broadcast as though they were pieces of match-board. The bones of those buried there are all laid bare & thrown

yards from the graves. A certain amount of the church still stands. It is very strongly built, otherwise it must have collapsed ages ago. There still stands in the church a huge crucifix, untouched by shell or shrapnel.[11]

James was still struggling to adjust to the privations and danger that were the lot of the soldier. Summer brought a whole new set of enemies:

We are still in reserve trenches & I don't know when we shall be relieved. I hear that the 17th Division is going to relieve us. The plague of flies here is unspeakable: they settle on everything. By means of flypapers we catch millions daily but it doesn't seem to make much difference. There is a battery of 9.25 somewhere behind us. They fire intermittently all day & night. The din and shock are perfectly appalling & get rather on one's nerves. However one has to put up with it.[12]

James was right: in late July, the 17th Division – Kitchener's army – was on its way to the war zone. The 78th Brigade of the Royal Field Artillery, including **Alan Lloyd**, was amongst them. The massive Anglo-French offensive planned for the summer would require all available forces. The date for the joint offensive was set: the end of August.

Alan Lloyd arrived in France on 13 July, travelling by train to Wizernes, near the Belgian border. Accompanied by the good friends he'd made in training – including fellow officer Arthur Impey, known as Mark II to Alan's Mark I – and still a way from the fighting zone, it felt to Alan more like a summer holiday than a deployment to war. Two days into their travels, Alan wrote to Dorothy to fill her in on their adventures so far:

Here we are comfortably installed in an old chateau, nowhere near the firing line for a while. Mk II and I are sharing the hayloft which makes a good bed place except for the fleas which are already beginning to tickle! When we move up to the line I don't know, but I think very shortly. Everybody is fit and well after the long journey here. Mk II is a good caterer and we live quite well.

Lovely country about here of crops, awfully peaceful, one would never dream of war at all. Small wife would love it. When the war's over, she and Hubbins will have a little honeymoon and see some of these places which we pass through now. Well little wife, Hubbins is tired, So good night, beloved.[13]

On 19 July, the brigade moved closer to the fighting. That day at Hooge, just twenty miles away from their new position, the British army launched one of the only attacks of the summer, an attempt to strengthen a weak part of the line. The Royal Engineers exploded a huge mine beneath the German defences, creating a crater 120 feet wide. Alan went up to visit the line the following day, with his battery commander, Captain Humphries.[14] Afterwards, he wrote to Dorothy, excited by his first taste of war, but eager to reassure her that he was fine:

Humphries and I came up to the line yesterday morning – joined the Battery which we are going to relieve. I went up this morning to the Observing Station with one of the subalterns to see how things worked. The station is within 800 yds of the German front line. Of course as soon I got there, they must needs start shelling and I didn't mind a bit. They dropped 8 shells all round and one fell within 15 yards of me. So I'm the first of the Bty. to come under fire!

My little Arab charm I'm sure is devilish lucky and I've now great faith in it, for already it's saved me 2 or 3 nasty accidents. Apart from the shells, as we came up in a motor, a wire across the road, stretched taut, caught my cap and of course took it right off. Had it been 2 inches lower it would have taken my head off as we were going fast! Hubbins blessed his small wife's luck! MkII calls it 'Alan luck'. We are quite comfy here and very safe so don't be anxious and take care of your beloved self always.[15]

As an officer in the artillery Alan's experiences of war would be different to those of infantry soldiers like Reg Evans and James Butlin. The 78th RFA, a mobile artillery brigade, was equipped with 18-pounder guns which were moved into position by a team of horses. Their job was to break down German defences and cover infantry attacks. For now, Alan felt confident he'd have plenty of free time on his hands, adding to his wife: 'You might send out my Kipling poems which are in little leather case in my old bedroom. We have any amount of time to read and I should love some Kipling.'[16]

On 25 July, Alan's battery went into action. A few days later, they had their baptism of fire: spotted by a German aeroplane, the battery's

Gun crew of a Royal Field Artillery 18-pounder battery.

guns were shelled mercilessly. Alan was in the observation post at the time – riding his luck once more – but still had his own introduction to the incessant shelling on the front line:

> Just one scrap to say I'm right as rain, tho' the Battery had 62 shells pumped into it yesterday while I was in the O.P. and all 'crumps' i.e big 6-inch or 8-inch shells which made a terrific noise! Just like Hubbins's luck to be in the O.P at the time. I had 5 shells on top of me the same morning but the dug-out is very snug. Humphries says his nerves 'have gone completely'. They have, too.

He was already thinking of when he might get home:

> A lot of people think the war will be over in the autumn. I want to see small wife very bad! I hope you are alright. I expect the baby will be a wopper.[17]

The following night, 30 July, it was eerily quiet at Hooge. Suddenly, at 3.15 a.m., a hissing sound came through the noise of shells and bullets. Jets of flame lit up the night sky. The German army had come to regain their lost land with the help of a devastating new weapon: the flame-thrower.[18] Alan's battery had been moved to a new position, just 10 kilometres away from Hooge. Two weeks into active service, any visions he'd had about the glamour of war were long gone:

> Such a big show this morning further up the line, terrific commotion for 1½ hours, result a slight loss of ground to us I hear.
>
> We are now in a new position and it's better than the old one. Not so many rats or mosquitoes but swarms of wasps. You are always saying you would like to be here but this is no place for a housewife. There's never a minute of the day now that guns aren't firing. I write from my dug out in the O.P. Aeroplanes overhead, guns booming, rifles cracking, bullets swinging away, it's the same thing day after day.[19]

At Hooge, the German army had shown itself to be a step ahead in terms of innovations and equipment once again. The British had only just started to come to terms with their previous surprise weapon, chlorine gas – and now came the flame-thrower. Both sides were seeking the weapon that would prove decisive. The Lewis gun – a light automatic weapon – had been issued to British infantry battalions in mid-July, and turned out to be extremely effective. And an experimental section of the Royal Engineers was constantly trying out new weapons, from kites that dropped explosives to giant hoses to flood out trenches.

But the real, pressing problem remained the lack of ammunition and heavy artillery.[20] The Germans had plenty, and could terrorise British troops day in, day out. The British artillery, on the other hand, was rationed. The urgent need was building sufficient stocks for the Big Push, scheduled to take place in just a month's time.

James Butlin was not apparently aware that a war-winning offensive was planned. He was already worrying about the coming winter in the trenches:

> I would have written to you yesterday but I was feeling too ill. I have been a bit bilious during the last few days & yesterday was the culminating point. I lay down and tried to sleep but without success. To add to my troubles the Huns started shelling a point about ½ a mile off. Fortunately they kept on the spot & didn't switch on us.
>
> Both sides are making strenuous preparations for a winter campaign

. . . There are as a matter of fact no signs of the end whatever, nothing
to lead one to suppose that there will not be another winter in the
trenches, yet somehow, I believe there will be no winter campaign. It is
questionable if flesh & blood can stand another winter.[21]

In August, James returned to his original regiment, the 1st Battalion
Dorsetshire Regiment. They were sent to the Somme area, as part of
the Third Army's takeover of that section of the line to free up the
French in advance of the big offensive. Over the following month, they
were in and out of the trenches. It was relatively quiet but James was
becoming less and less able to cope with the constant stress[22]:

My nerves are not what they were & I can tell you I could do 3 months
in England with advantage. John Bull is as optimistic as ever but then
he writes in England & in peace. Let him sit here in the trenches with
a few trench mortars & rifle grenades falling round his way & write the
same tonight. I am feeling a bit vicious tonight. Also I have not been
up to form these last ten days, not feeling ill enough to be really bad
but just bad enough to make me look on the gloomy side of things.[23]

In August 1915 it was beginning to look as if the war might soon be
over; but not in the Allies' favour. They were facing failure on every
front. The Gallipoli campaign had gone from bad to worse, with a
second assault in August ending in carnage and huge losses for the
British and Allied troops. Italy had failed to hold off Austrian forces.
Bulgaria had joined the Central Powers. The Russians had suffered
defeat after defeat and it was questionable how much longer they could
hold out. The Allies were realising the terrible price of disconnected
campaigns on separate fronts. The appeal of a huge, unified offensive
on one front grew.

After months of wrangling over whether the British army would be
ready for an attack in late summer, Kitchener himself visited the French
army headquarters in mid-August. In spite of limited resources, he
finally committed the British army. He had reservations, as did his
General Staff: the ground for the attack was deemed unfavourable, no
more than a quarter of the troops they felt necessary for such an attack
would be ready, and munitions were still in short supply. Yet Kitchener
saw no alternative. It was agreed that the First Army would attack

south of the La Bassée Canal, with all available resources, in a few weeks' time.[24]

Meanwhile, the fighting continued and **Alan Lloyd** endured day after day of heavy shelling. Men and officers were injured, guns were destroyed. Alan found escape in daydreams about home:

> Beloved little small wife, How's David? How's yourself? I'm writing from the O.P about the Bicho [Alan's car]. There's the cushions of the front seats which must be well stuffed. They are getting too thin. They should do this and the buttons for nothing, also another coat of varnish all over. You little beloved, she'll look as smart as when we set out from B'ham together in her.
>
> I want another little honeymoon with small wife, I want it so awfully badly . . . We will have such a long honeymoon when we get it, Devon and Cornwall and Scotland and all over the place, staying and browsing away at all the nice comfortable old-fashioned pubs we know, and everywhere we've enjoyed our little selves so much. We'll motor all over Perthshire and Argyllshire and away up to the wilds of Caithness and the Bicho will hum with that lovely dreamy humming sort of hum which it has when it's going away with small wife and Hubbins on a long, long joy ride, and won't it sing when it knows that war is over and small wife and Hubbins together for always. So take the greatest care of your precious little beloved self.[25]

Dorothy was now seven months pregnant. The Anglo-French attack was scheduled for 8 September, just a few weeks away.

On 31 August, the attack was pushed back until 15 September, because the French were having transport issues.[26] And **Reg Evans**, it seemed, might finally get home for a bit:

> Dear Mother,
>
> Just a line to tell you that I don't think it will be very long now before I get leave but from what I can make out there isn't much opportunity for sending a wire or anything of that sort, so don't be surprised if I happen to walk in unannounced one morning.
>
> On Saturday evening I was told that I was one of 5 going home next day. In the morning we set off to the town about three or four miles off,

and though it was jolly hot marching, we stuck it well. Arrived there we found that the headquarters of the regiment were in a little village a mile or two further on and that our passes would have to be fetched from there. Luckily we had plenty of time so I suggested we ordered a jolly good dinner (I'm a rare lad for grub) and then I set off for hdqs. They told me they hadn't got the passes yet but would send them by a motor-cyclist orderly to the station. Well, to cut a long story short we arrived at the station but the passes didn't, and so as leave has been dropped for the present I shall be one of the first to benefit when it starts again which may be any day. I don't fancy it will be long now before I see you and till then I must sign myself your affectionate and wandering son, Reg[27]

Sure enough, one day in early September, a train arrived at Victoria Station. Its doors flew open, disgorging a mass of khaki-clad soldiers who hurried to mingle with the expectant crowd gathered on the platform. One young man, short and slight and nimble, made his way quickly through the throng – he needed to catch the next train to Hemel Hempstead.

Reg had made it back to Blighty, after ten months of some of the bloodiest fighting the world had ever known. In his pocket, he had his small piece of stained glass from the churchyard at Cuinchy. He planned to give it to his own church, a token of his gratitude that he'd made it this far.

He made the most of his leave, of course, spending precious time with his mother and sisters at home, and paying a visit to the brush factory as a returning hero. But the war could not be forgotten. The newspapers were full of news of the imminent Big Push. Reg was in no doubt as to what awaited him when he got back. The days passed all too quickly.

Dorothy Lloyd was living with her parents-in-law in Birmingham. She was nearing full-term and was awaiting her confinement. On 1 September, it had been her and Alan's first wedding anniversary. Alan celebrated by surviving another day of constant bombardment, so his letter home told his wife:

Our wedding day to-day! It doesn't seem like it but we've just had a good 'crumpeting' to make me think of it. About 700 or so of the little pets came round us but their hymn of hate did no harm and we're just the same as before. This is no rest camp! Neither is there tennis or polo.[28]

In early September, Alan swapped places with an officer from another brigade for training purposes. The 23rd Brigade, which he joined, was at Hooge, which had been blasted only a few weeks earlier with liquid flame-throwers. The country wore the scars to prove it, and still the shelling went on. Alan was spared none of it. On his third day, he experienced his first death of the war: his bombardier was hit whilst he was in the O.P. Alan was cut up, but told by his major to get used to such things. And so it went on, Alan trying to remain cheerful against all the odds:

> I'm still going strong though this is a most objectionable spot! In addition to all our troubles, there is a stream running through the position, a terrific big shell yesterday dropped right into it and you should have seen the fountain. I should think it was quite 100 feet high. The result is it has now flooded the dugouts. The trenches of course are perfectly fearful, a foot of water already and where I sleep 6 inches. So I slept on a frame exactly 6 inches wide, with my air pillow and slept like a top, though why I didn't fall off I can't think. Wonderful what one gets used to. My feet and legs were of course soaking wet, I had only my oilskin coat to cover me and the rain dripped through the roof.
>
> When I tell you that this is the worst spot in the whole British line and that our battery position is supposed to be the worst of any round here (so the General says, and he should know) and when you know that we have only 2 Subalterns instead of 3, the Captain away on leave, you will realize that there is plenty of invigorating exercise or work for me.
>
> I'm as happy and fit as a fly-catcher and when the General remarked yesterday that he supposed I'd be jolly thankful when Wednesday came and I got back to peace and comfort, I told him that I should be quite sorry as the excitement of here was so invigorating and meant I could not possibly suffer from constipation! He seemed very amused.[29]

Despite his bravado Alan was, of course, thinking of Dorothy. He knew she would be worrying about him. And now he was worrying about her too, soon to go into labour:

Well, little beloved small wife (or rather well beloved) I must shut up. Don't be nervous as Hubbins is awful well and very happy but he does so want to see his small wife. Let me know the exact date when you think the Babe will come. Hubbins will be dreadful nervous. Don't worry if it's a girl, belovedest, I shan't care a hang which it is. It might be another little small wife for someone.

Don't worry your round head about Hubbins, all will be well and you'll be quite alright I know. The old Arab charm hangs round my neck and I have named it 'Heart of the Luck of Small Wife' which is good and rather poetic! Hubbins wants his small wife, his strong dog, and his car, but he wants the first of these so much that he wouldn't mind if he never saw the others or anything else ever again so long as he had small wife. So there![30]

Leave was over all too soon for **Reg Evans**. On 15 September he was back in France, travelling to rejoin his regiment. All along the way he passed troops on the move; the atmosphere was one of feverish activity.[31] He went into the trenches the very morning he got back, but found time to drop his mother a note:

Just a line for you to see that I have got out here alright. I arrived at the railway station here about 6 o'clock this morning and by about 11 was up in the trenches so you can see I didn't waste much time.

We had it very pleasant all the way. In the train the fellows were all showing photos of their wives, girls or kiddies and relating the different welcomes they received. I slept both in the boat and after leaving Boulogne on the train but I'll give you my word I have slept better in a bed. Well I'm awfully hungry again all ready so order me 1 stuffed lambs heart with vegetables and some plum tart.[32]

On 21 September, the Allies began their preliminary bombardment. The attack was planned to take place over a 25-mile stretch – a much broader front than previous battles, which German artillery had been able to cover from the flanks. Bombarding such a stretch was a huge effort for the British artillery, working with limited resources, but it was hoped that another weapon would make up for any inadequacies: the British were preparing for a first gas attack of their own.

The weather was fine, but the clouds of chalky dust raised by the bombardment made it difficult to observe how successfully it was breaking down the German defences.[33] There was only one way to find out if it was working: send out soldiers to have a closer look. On 22 September, Reg's company officer asked to see him:

> He said that headquarters wanted a volunteer to go out that night and report what damage had been done to the enemy's wire and front trenches by the intensive bombardment. The artillery would receive orders to cease fire for an hour whilst the reconnaissance was carried out but so as not to raise suspicions at the lull, machine guns would carry on covering fire over the German lines. Whoever took the job on would have to go alone. It would probably mean death but would certainly mean glory. Then after a pause, he came to the point. 'Will you go?' he asked. For a few seconds I hesitated. What could I say?[34]

That evening, Reg undertook the most dangerous mission of his life: he slipped out from his trench into no-man's-land, alone. Although the Allied bombardment had paused as planned, enemy shells continued to fall, and bullets from his own side flew across the open ground in the dark. Crawling on his belly in the mud, he managed to cross to the German trenches and inspect the damage to their barbed wire without being spotted. His work done, he turned to head back to safety. That was when the danger really began:

> Suddenly as if Inferno was let loose, the artillery bombardment burst out anew. All around me fell the shells, with tremendous explosions. The earth seemed to rock as I lay stiff and scared on its surface, and the sound of the broken metal was like the rattle of a hailstorm as it pattered to the ground with a noise incessant and penetrating even amid the louder roar. I really thought that my end had come.
>
> The state I was in when finally I did reach our trenches can be imagined. Challenged by a sentry, I was almost too exhausted to reply. Plastered with mud and clothing literally in shreds I was almost unrecognisable even by men of my own company.[35]

It was a miracle that Reg had survived. He passed out in the nearest dugout. He awoke the next morning to a letter from the brigadier general, commending him on his staggering feat:

I congratulate you on the excellent reconnaissance you made last night. The information you sent in was most valuable and the pluck displayed in going out alone, on a moonlight night, (exposed not only to the enemy's fire but to risk from our own machine guns) is worthy of the highest traditions of the British soldier. I shall take an early opportunity of bringing this act to the notice of the Divisional General.[36]

It was 23 September. The Allied attack was now only forty-eight hours away.

On the evening of the following day, the wind was scrutinized by the British High Command. Forty gas officers reported every hour from along the 6 1/2-mile stretch of front that had been selected for the British gas attack. The conditions were not good, but seemed to be improving. At 9.45 p.m., orders were given to attacking troops to get into the trenches and prepare. By 2.30 a.m. on the 25th, all the attacking brigades were in position. But the wind, essential for a successful gas attack, was dropping off. As deliberations went on, men tried to snatch a few final minutes of sleep.

Finally, at 5.30 a.m., an intense bombardment was followed by the release of 150 tons of chlorine gas. It formed a dense, yellowish cloud 40 feet high along the entire battlefront. Unfortunately, the wind was not distributing it as intended. Nonetheless, at 6.30 a.m. the infantry emerged from the trenches. The bombardment ceased; the advance was begun.[37]

The previous night, **Reg Evans** and the 1st Herts had been moved out of the front line trenches and into reserve. The 1st Kings relieved them, and were to participate in the attack on the section of line astride the La Bassée Canal. The 1st Herts were waiting in support. At 5.35 a.m., the gas officer covering that part of the line sent word that he refused to carry out the attack as instructed, since the conditions were so unfavourable. He was overruled.

The gas released blew back into the faces of the 1st Kings. Those who weren't severely affected then went over the top as instructed. There was no cover at all in no-man's-land, and the Allied bombardment had left this part of the German line relatively unscathed. The advance was met with unbroken machine-gun fire. The few who made it across were confronted by completely intact barbed wire. The general, on learning of the failure of the advance, ordered another bombardment. The 1st Herts were then due to follow up the attack. However, at 9.45 a.m., recognising the futility of further action given the lack of damage to the German defences, orders were issued that no follow-up attack should be made here. Reg had had a lucky escape.[38]

A view from the front line, as British troops advance through a cloud of poison gas on the opening day of the Battle of Loos, 25 September 1915.

Elsewhere, the Battle of Loos went a little better. Despite heavy casualties, by midday many sections of the German line had been broken. At one point British troops had advanced by 4,000 yards. However, by nightfall things were not going so well – there were insufficient men to exploit the advantages gained and it had begun to rain heavily. The attack was paused for the time being. On the 26th, the 1st Herts were moved onto the front line.

Another push was planned for the evening of the 27th, and at 5 p.m. another gas attack was carried out. To ascertain whether it had been effective, a patrol was sent out from the trenches – and immediately fired upon.[39] Reg Evans might have been one of the patrolling party. Whether it was out there or back in the trenches is not recorded, but Reg had a very near miss. A bomb exploded very close to him. He was sent back to the dressing station and put in an ambulance to be taken to hospital. But before the motor started, Reg decided he wasn't injured badly enough to merit it. He got out and walked back to join his regiment in the trenches. He later reassured his mother that it had been nothing:

> You have no doubt seen by the papers how things are going and of course you want to know how I am getting on and that is only natural so I'll relieve your mind and tell you the truth at the same time. I am really in the best of health and spirits, all ill effects of my little shock having quite passed away bar my torn trousers which are a constant nuisance to me. I didn't tell you, I think, that Captain S was hit at the same time as myself and also young Shibbington from along Marlowes. Fortunately I believe neither are seriously hurt.

In fact Shibbington would later die from his wounds. Trying to be positive as ever, Reg concluded: 'Have you hung your flag out for our victories yet eh?'[40] His optimism was unfounded. While the French were enjoying some success on their part of the 25-mile battlefront, the British section was littered with thousands of corpses. The fighting continued nevertheless, though the 1st Herts were still not ordered to attack.

Alan Lloyd and the 78th Brigade RFA were further up the line but still had their role to play. To distract the enemy from the main battle-front, three subsidiary attacks had taken place. Alan had been involved in one of them, at Bellewaerde. It too had ended in failure, with the troops retreating to their own trenches.[41] But despite the dangers he was facing, Alan was much more concerned with how Dorothy was faring:

> Just a scrawl at the OP to say your hub is very well. Don't be anxious about me if you don't hear regularly for a bit as post will probably be very erratic indeed. Will send you news when I have it but you'll probably hear more in the papers than I shall know.
>
> Hubbins is beginning to get quite excited. I feel sure that my little wife will be alright about her babe and I know that Mama will take great care of her and have everything cosy and comfy. But I know how much you'd like Hub near you.
>
> It's a funny thing but sometimes I feel awfully close to small wife and can sort of see her sitting and thinking of Hubbins. Then I get very

bucked and jump about and yell. I did this on the way down from the O.P at a quarter to seven in the evening about 2 days ago. I could see small wife sitting in the library with a book on her lap which she wasn't reading but she was staring away at nothing and thinking of Hubbins. I was by myself in a field on a lovely evening and I shouted out 'small wife' and I capered about like a small boy.

Hubbins wants to see his small wife very bad. Are you still quite alright? You must tell me all the time how you are. Take care of your beloved little self because Hubbins is just mad about you.[42]

By the beginning of October, things had quietened down. Alan and his battery were relieved.[43] Alan knew that his child was due any day now – and scribbled Dorothy another note:

Beloved little wife, I am wondering whether the babe has arrived and how you are and whether you're alright and everything else. We are moving tonight, don't know where but perhaps to rest. Am hourly expecting news of you.[44]

Reg Evans went into rest in Bethune on 3 October. There, he wrote home to share some rather remarkable news:

I expect by the time you receive this letter you will have heard the news that our Commander in Chief has conferred upon me the D.C.M. [Distinguished Conduct Medal] The news was conveyed to our Colonel in a special telegram and when I tell you that I must have been the recipient of genuine congratulations from our Colonel downwards you will understand how really pleased I am and share more fully in my pleasure.

The Colonel made a splendid speech to our Company this morning and I can assure you it has been the most wonderful experience of my life to know that I have got the confidence and honour of such splendid fellows. I do hope that I shall never in the slightest degree forfeit their esteem and I only wish that you could have been with me to share my happiness. As you know I have always tried to do my duty and serve my country and with the help of Providence I shall always be able to look back after this terrible war is over and have the knowledge that I have been able to do so.[45]

Still the Battle of Loos rumbled on, not officially coming to a close until the middle of October, though the bulk of the fighting was over in the first few days. It was clear this was not the decisive victory everyone had hoped for. Eight thousand yards of German line had been taken, and in some places Allied troops had advanced over two miles. But the losses were heavy indeed – of the 10,000 British soldiers who attacked at Loos, over 8,000 were either killed or wounded.[46]

James Butlin was stationed in the Somme valley, some forty miles south. It had been quiet there. Although James had escaped the terrors of the battle, he knew what its failure meant: that he was now facing, as he had feared, another winter in the trenches. And his health was starting to suffer:

> I went up to the trenches last night with the battalion but as I had been feeling ill all day I went to see the doctor as soon as I arrived there. The result was that he sent me back to billets to stay with the Quarter-Master until I feel on form again. I am much better today but I don't expect I shall go back to the trenches this time as the battalion is only up for 3 or 4 days. Did I tell you that Rogers, my captain, was wounded about a week ago? He was shot right through the lung.

James was too traumatised even to take much interest in the local women. He wrote to Basil about a so-called 'camp follower' he had come across:

> The next information I give you is for your own edification, pure and simple. I do not want to go any further. In my last billet, where Gomez and I stopped there lived a woman (aged about 30) who was of low (or rather no) morals. So to put it plainly she was a harlot, pure and simple. She would come into your room at all hours of the day and night & dress or undress in your room. I didn't have much to do with her person-ally as she wasn't at all my fancy.[47]

Alan Lloyd had gone into rest on 6 October. The following day, he learnt there was a telegram waiting for him at his old position. He was desperate to know its contents. He had to wait, however, until the next day, when he got another telegram, this one from his brother:[48]

My ownest belovedest little wife,

The first news I got was Eric's wire saying he was an uncle! So I knew you were alright but I didn't know if it was a boy or a girl! Then I got all the letters together and your Hubbins was off his head with glee. I did love it when I saw there was actually a letter from you. I never dreamt you'd be able to write and I don't suppose you ought to have done so, you little ownest. It was a lovely little letter and Hubbins nearly blubbed when he read it, for he knew that all was well with his little wife and that she had got her heart's desire – a little Allieboy. I bet he's a topping little kid, beloved, and I know I shall love him awful much, more because he's his mother's son than for any other reason.

Take great care of your beloved self, ownest, and soon get well again and then your Hub will try and come and see you and your little baby. At present I couldn't get leave. Bye-Bye my little beloved. If anything had gone wrong with you I don't know what I would have done . . .

P.S. All the brigade have been round congratulating me and we had two bottles of bubbly last night.[49]

The brigade had little else to celebrate. Another winter in the trenches awaited them. The Allies had tried everything to break the stalemate, and everything had failed.

II

ANOTHER YEAR OVER
October–December 1915

I suppose there are other people who have lost as many friends as I have but it seems hardly possible.

Duff Cooper's diary, November 1915

It was raining heavily. The fields were sodden; the pathways dotted with muddy pools; livestock cowered beneath dripping trees. Nevertheless, in Great Leighs, the doors of cottages were opening and people were emerging. Feet were disturbing the puddles on School Lane, on the Boreham Road, on Main Road as they picked their way to the corrugated iron barn that functioned as the community hall. Inside it, the Reverend **Andrew Clark** was looking through his notes. The noise of the rain hammering on the roof was mildly distracting but not unpleasant. And Andrew was pleased to see the villagers flowing in, in spite of the terrible weather. The audience grew, one wet family at a time.

In summer 1914, the people of Great Leighs had assembled in the same hall to hear rousing recruitment speeches and to make plans to help win the glorious war. Now, as the Battle of Loos limped on in France, the community had gathered to hear a lecture on the progress of a war they had expected to be long over. Once everyone was settled, Andrew surveyed the sea of expectant faces, cleared his throat, and began:

I suppose the first feeling in thinking over the war is a feeling of disappointment, of sorrowful disappointment. It seems such a long time to look back upon; we are aware of enormous efforts which have been made in the country; we know about the terrible losses which have been sustained abroad and yet so little seems to have been accomplished. On the one frontier, things are no further on than they were a year ago. On the Eastern battle-line, they seem much worse. So there is a feeling of disappointment and discouragement.

That feeling is, I think we must admit, quite natural; but it is not well-founded. The war has lasted for one year, one month, and twenty-four days. Now that is not a long time as wars go. We have to remember that this war is, in the full sense of the word, world-wide. It has not been confined to one continent only but has spread over every continent and every ocean.[1]

Outside the rain continued to fall, and Andrew spoke on. He talked about the new dangers this war had presented: the floating mines and submarines that were terrorising the navy, and the Zeppelin airships that they all had cause to fear.

He spoke also of the men in the trenches in France and Belgium. He tried to be positive: had these soldiers not endured, were they not still holding firm? The war had not been won; but neither had it been lost:

> The fiercest attempts of Germany against our lines with over-powering superiority in guns, with terrible, unexpected, forbidden weapons of poison gas and liquid fire, have been shattered. And our men, and with them Belgians and French, have held fast. We are not only to think of the battle-front, but of what has been going on behind it. Could anyone have said that a great new army could be sent into the field in less than a year? Yet that has been done.[2]

But the villagers knew the price that had been paid for struggling on. The newspapers had been full of the human cost for days: casualty lists stretching over pages for each day that the Battle of Loos went on. The mood was sombre in the tin tabernacle as Andrew came to an end. The following day news reached the village of the death in action of Willie Hughes-Hughes, who'd grown up just down the road at Little Leighs.[3]

As the villagers filed out of the hall and into the dark, wet night, **Duff Cooper** was out for dinner in London. He looked sharp, as always, in immaculate evening dress: tails, waistcoat and bow tie. He'd been to Diana's house for lunch; now he was with another of his love interests, the divorced daughter of the Clerk of Parliaments. The news of the severe losses at Loos had reached him too, of course – though his mind was on other things as he worked through the courses:

> Lunched at Arlington Street. Gerald Thorpe was there and spoke of our enormous casualties – 30,000 men, 1,400 officers he said. Dined with Nancy, Marjorie and Hugo. After dinner we went back to the House of Lords, from which Marjorie's parents were away. My only breach of chastity in September.[4]

A few days later, the news of the enormous losses was made more personal, more palpable, when word reached him of the death of one of his friends. Tommy Agar-Robartes, a Liberal politician, had died at Loos rescuing a wounded comrade. Duff's sister, Steffie, had been in love with him. Duff experienced something of the wave of grief that was sweeping over the nation in these terrible weeks, though Steffie's reaction to the blow was far from typical:

> Heard this morning at the Foreign Office that Tommie Robartes was killed. His brother come in on that account and rang up and told us. Came home and found poor little Steffie half mad with misery. She was really in love with him. I am so sorry for her.
>
> We had a terrible night with Steffie. She and Sibbie are both staying here. Steffie had sent Sibbie to buy her a lot of morphia and Sibbie had told the chemist to give her something that looked and tasted like it but was innocuous. Steffie discovered this the moment she tasted it. Terrible row ensued. I was woken up. It was 1.30. Sibbie insisted on going out to try and get some real morphia from a doctor.
>
> After she had gone I heard Steffie moving about and went to her room. I found her with a fur coat on over her nightgown and a pair of shoes, on the point of going out. Tried to dissuade her without success. So thought it best to follow her, which I did having put an overcoat and a pair of trousers on. She insisted on going to Berkeley House to look for some chloroform she had left there. This we eventually found and came home to bed.[5]

Steffie dealt with her grief in a manner appropriate to the hedonism of their set. Morphine was an increasingly fashionable drug. Even Lady Diana was growing rather fond of it, though Duff preferred good old-fashioned drink. Over October, Duff and Diana shared some memorable, drunken nights together – and more kisses. But then the war forced its ugly face into their world again. In the last gasp of the Battle of Loos in mid-October, another of their close friends, Yvo Charteris, son of the Earl of Wemyss, was lost:

> Dined at Queen Anne's Gate. Cheerful dinner. Afterwards we played bridge. I saw a letter lying open on a table and, starting to read it, learnt suddenly that Yvo had been killed. The news apparently arrived on the 19th and nobody had told me because everyone thought I knew. It was a terrible shock. He was so young and so delightful. How I pity them all, especially Lord Wemyss, whose favourite child he was. I slept badly and woke early and felt miserable.[6]

By the end of the battle, the British army had suffered 50,000 casualties; a staggering 800 officers and 15,000 men were reported killed or never heard of again. That was three times higher than the German casualty rate – though that was the usual price for going on the offensive.[7]

Reg Evans was now a hero. Over October, letters poured in from his friends and family back home, congratulating him on his Distinguished Conduct Medal. Enjoying a few weeks' rest, he wrote to his boss at the brush factory, with whom he'd kept up a frequent correspondence and who had been worried by news of the injury he'd sustained in the battle:

> Just a word or two to let you know we are all still getting on 'tres bonne'. I paid the Doctor my last visit yesterday and got the M.D. [Medicine and Duty] so I've got nothing to complain about. We are back resting and having a jolly nice time too.
>
> Our Colonel has had the Company out on the square here and publicly thanked and praised them for their share in the recent doings. I have got my D.C.M. ribbon and we are all anxiously waiting for the Honours List as we hope and believe there are several others here have been recommended for distinction. I can say without swank with such stuff as this in our Territorial Regiments what ruddy hopes for Germany!
>
> We have been issued with some jolly fine underclothes and woollen cardigans so are alright for the colder nights which are unfortunately so near us. I had hoped that there would not have been another winter

campaign but am afraid it is unavoidable. Still never mind, it's as bad for them as it is for us, that's something to be thankful for.[8]

As the weather started its painful deterioration into winter, Reg also wrote to his mother, putting on a cheerful front as ever:

We have been swarming the ditches again and oh, the weather. Still never mind we do get dry again sometime if I remember rightly. Now that the long nights are with us once more I should be glad if when you send you would put in some candles.

We have been out here a year this next week. You wouldn't have thought the Germans could have held out so long after my arrival here would you?[9]

Although **Alan Lloyd** was still in the midst of the fighting, he could think of little but his wife and his newborn son, David. Alan believed he would get leave in just a few weeks' time and he couldn't contain his excitement. His optimism was also spilling over into his view of the state of the war:

Be of good cheer beloved. By the time I come you will be as fit as a fiddle and we shall have to be careful! Hubbins is rather pash and I don't care if the censor knows it. I have quite forgotten what it feels like to sleep between sheets and we shall have a honeymoon again . . .

The war is like that great race I saw at Henley between Leander and the German Four, the Huns led from the start and were a length up at Fawley (1/2 way) but then the Leander crew shook together (having got munition!) and forged up till they were level at Phyllis Court, close to the finish, then with a sudden crash the German 4 collapsed and stopped rowing and Leander paddled in easy winners after the best race I've ever seen. This was Henley just before the war broke out and I've always called it a rare good omen.

How's Davison and is he behaving and what's his chest measurement and has he got spine curvature and flat feet and ear trouble like Joan or is he healthy like his darling Mummy? I bet he's alright. Hubbins wants to see his son very badly.[10]

*

The casualties at Loos had been high. But it wasn't only physical injuries that were becoming a problem. Medical staff on the ground reported a surge in cases of 'definite hysterical manifestations (mutism and tremors)' especially amongst the young recruits.[11] The constant danger and terrible discomfort of daily life in the trenches was taking its toll on the mental state of the men.

James Butlin and the 1st Dorsets were still in the Somme region. The fighting there was currently mild, but the weather started to close in, and alternate snaps of frost and rain played havoc with the trenches, which were already in very poor condition. There was also a particularly large and aggressive breed of rat, known as the Somme rat, which was a far from welcome guest in the trenches.[12] In the relative quiet, James Butlin's health had improved, but his mood was much the same. He was sick of war. His tone in writing to Basil betrayed his growing frustration and his resentment towards those who remained at home:

> My dear old Burnett,
>
> We still continue our ceaseless vigil in the trenches, which was brightened last night by your interesting epistle. Your efforts to secure work are as indefatigable as they are futile. I think after all you will have to join something as a private and do your bit properly. I just got to this point when a whizz-bang landed nearer to me than I cared about, so I've shifted into a dug-out about 100 yards away.
>
> I wish they'd get on with conscription at home as they will need every man they can get. I can't make out how they expect to carry on without it.[13]

Over the course of the year, the issue of conscription had been a dark cloud over Parliament – now, after the failings at Loos, it had worked itself into a storm. The overwhelming rush of British men to enlist had initially enabled the government to evade the highly contentious issue, which was so at odds with the English liberal tradition. But recruitment was falling off, and the casualties suffered over the course of 1915, especially at Loos, meant calls for conscription were building. In July, the first tentative steps had been taken by the coalition government, with the establishment of a national registration scheme to gather information on the occupation of men of military age. Now, there was a furore over the next step: calling up those who weren't working in vital industries.[14] Parliament and the British public were divided.

James certainly hoped it would come. Not least, perhaps, because the thought of Basil – free to chase girls, out of danger, doing nothing for the war effort – was too much to bear from the bottom of a cold, muddy trench:

> I am sorry you persistently shirk work in a munitions factory. Of course you'll have to work hard, and why not? At present you are doing nothing except eat, sleep and run after Oxford flappers.
>
> I have hopes of leave in the near future and you must be ready to meet me at any time and at any place if humanly possible. This seems rather a tall order but I can assure you it's nothing compared with what we are doing for you out here.[15]

He might have been hundreds of miles away from the front, but **Andrew Clark** was still doing his best to contribute to Britain's war effort. It was a rather gloomy October night, and he'd just left the rectory for his shift on patrol. The particular priority of the special constables of Great Leighs was currently looking out for Zeppelins, which had darkened the skies over the village a number of times since the summer. At their latest meeting the previous week, the special constable had discussed but rejected a proposal to follow the example of the neighbouring force at Chelmsford, where 'extra-special constables' had started a Zeppelin warning system:

> These 'extra-specials' are to have long poles, with pads on the end, to reach up to rap upon upper-storey windows. Major Brown says that this is utter folly, because the first action of every sleeper so aroused will be to light gas or candle, and every street will be alight in a moment.[16]

So Andrew and his partner on duty that night continued as always, walking the paths and roads of the village, looking up at the night sky, listening out for a telltale rumble overhead. But another commonly felt concern was also on Andrew's mind: conscription.

As in many rural areas, it was felt that the working men could simply not be spared. The squire, disregarding the needs of the farms, had been aggressive in his efforts to increase recruitment in the village, and his daughters regularly badgered the men even as they worked in the fields. Recently, the squire had laid off his own estate carpenter, who he deemed fit for military service or munitions work. Andrew was furious, writing with atypical emotion in his diary: 'It will be an unhappy parish when all the good men are driven out of it!'[17]

In October, a last-ditch attempt by the government to avoid conscription but boost recruitment came in the form of the 'Derby Scheme'. Lord Derby's idea allowed men to 'attest' their willingness to serve, and these recruits would only be called up when they were needed. Andrew was asked to help publicise the scheme locally:

> <u>Monday 25 October:</u> Major Brown called. He had been asked to find someone who would canvass for recruiting under Lord Derby's scheme. I said frankly that I would not. It is quite contrary to my opinions which are (i) that enough men have been taken off field work, leaving idle youths loafing about town; and that (ii) at the beginning of the war, government ought to have adopted some equable form of compulsory service.[18]

Most Britons realised that conscription was now probably only a matter of time. Andrew hoped it would come soon and stop all the fuss, and take away the moral vagaries of any voluntary scheme: 'Conscription, being just, would be welcome.' He believed he spoke for the village on this matter.[19]

Loos had not been the only failure for the Allies that autumn. The Gallipoli campaign in the Dardanelles had been disastrous. The Ottoman forces had put up a formidable defence, and terrible conditions had further worn down the Allied soldiers: after a nightmarish summer of intolerable heat, insects and dysentery, the men now battled rain and cold. Their evacuation would begin in December. In mid-November, **Duff Cooper** received news of the death of another of his close friends: George Vernon had died after catching dysentery at Gallipoli:

> This morning came the terrible news of George Vernon's death. We had heard some days ago he was seriously ill with dysentery but lately the news had been better. I suppose there are other people who have lost as many friends as I have but it seems hardly possible. Diana telephoned the news to me in the morning. We went to the Hannover restaurant

and drank mulled claret which helped us to call up our last reserves of
courage and gaiety to face the new blow.[20]

Like most of the men of their set, George Vernon had carried a torch
for Diana. She was terribly upset about his death. A few days after the
news reached her, George's last communication to her arrived, written
from his deathbed. Duff found her heartbroken:

> Went round to see Diana. Poor child, she had been crying all night. She
> had received a letter from the doctor who was with George when he
> died – such a kind, well-written letter and at the bottom of it George
> had written in his own hand with, the doctor said, 'almost superhuman
> effort'. He had made the capital G and then wanting, I fancy, to write
> something more meaningful than his mere name in the last moment of
> life he had written quite distinctly the one word 'love'. It was too sad.
> I sobbed and she cried again.[21]

A few nights later, high on morphine, Diana scribbled a note to Duff.
Now, more than ever, he seemed to be the only man amongst those
she knew who was safe from the hand of death that was plucking their
friends one by one:

> My darling – it's eleven and for two hours I can't stop crying – if only
> you were by me I would. O Christ the misery and the morphia not
> working. O Duff, save yourself – if you die, where shall I be? – my poor
> George, if only I could stop.[22]

In December, representatives of the Allied High Command met at the
French HQ at Chantilly. The mood was sombre.

The year had been a failure. Nothing had changed on the Western
front and on the Eastern front the Russians and Serbs had been routed.
With the end of the Gallipoli campaign, there came a final, reluctant
acceptance that this war would be won or lost on the Western Front.
The decision was taken to begin planning for another combined assault
in the spring, even more ambitious than the offensive at Loos. More
casualties and more suffering were inevitable.[23]

The burden would fall on men like **Reg Evans.** Reg had had a
remarkable year, and his fortunes had just taken another turn for the

better. In November, he had been promoted yet again, from a corporal to a sergeant. He was enjoying the privileges that came with his status, such as better conditions when in rest: 'I have got a nice comfortable cellar in an old broken up house which I share with the other N.C.O's of the platoon and got a ripping fire.'[24] But in the trenches, the cold and the danger was the same. He had suffered badly from frostbite the previous winter and now his feet were troubling him again. And over little more than a week in late November and early December, four men in his regiment died[25]:

> We are having by no means as easy a time as we had a week in straight off and have only been out three days and go back tomorrow. I think we accounted for some of the Germans last time we were in but unfortunately had several casualties ourselves. Still as the French people say 'c'est la Guerre' – it's the war.
>
> Well I don't know how long the war is going to last and at times I quote to myself the lines of that hymn 'We bear the burden of the day and often toil seems dreary' for indeed we have been bearing the burden and oh what a heavy one no-one knows who hasn't been out here. But then, what is the next line? 'But labour ends with sunset ray and rest comes to the weary', that's just it. Isn't it a glorious thought and won't it always be a real joy to know after it is all over that not only have I sung about my country but that I have laboured for it and I hope, with God's help, not unworthily.
>
> Well au revoir and mind you have a jolly Xmas, I shall be thinking of you all. We must look forward to next Xmas for a re-union.[26]

People at home were thinking of Reg too; hoping that there would indeed be a reunion next Christmas. They were starting to worry that this young man's luck must run out. Shortly before Christmas, Reg got a letter from his old boss at the brush factory, asking him in no uncertain terms to take better care of himself and stop playing the hero:

> There is no question about you being absolutely without fear, all your comrades know that, but they are likely to lose a very valuable NCO if you are so foolhardy. So don't take any risks when they are unnecessary as you will be missed.[27]

*

In spite of his initial high hopes, **Alan Lloyd**'s chances of getting home to meet his son before the year was out were not looking good. Firstly, the allocation of leave had gone wrong. Then a number of his fellow soldiers fell ill with dysentery, including his good friend Mark II. Alan, by then back in Belgium, could not leave until another fellow officer was back from his sick leave:

> I'm fed up to the neck with that chap. But of course he's pretty bad with dysentery poor chap. Still, poor old Hubbins is stuck here and can't get to see his small wife.
>
> How are you and small David? All accounts of you both seem very good which pleases Hubbins awfully. I want you so awfully badly, little beloved, and this is a most desolate and boring spot, nothing but ruined houses and brick heaps and old iron. It just makes my head swim to think of hugging you, you little belovedest of all.[28]

For now, Alan had to content himself with the photographs Dorothy sent out to him. David was now six weeks old, and Alan longed to meet him. But whilst his family gathered for David's christening in Birmingham, Alan and the 78th Brigade RFA were being kept very busy near Ypres. Alan's battery commander Captain Humphreys, who had struggled with the pressure ever since he'd arrived, had now gone off sick. Alan was put in command of the battery. He enjoyed the responsibility, but it made his chances of leave even more remote:

> Col. Willis came round this morning to see how I was getting on and seemed quite pleased with everything. He tells me there's practically no chance of Humphreys coming back again – nerves quite gone! I should call it another name myself.
>
> The General of Division issued an order the other day, saying that our division had the honour of holding the worst piece of the whole British line, and that we were doing awfully well so far. The other divisions on each side of us and other troops call us the 'strafing' division because we are never quiet but always going for the Hun full out! We are a lucky battery, the last position we were in and which was taken over from us by another battery has been crumped out, lots of fellows wounded and killed, but we live happily in another spot. That's the luck of small wife working well!

Poor little angel wife, I must get to you somehow and we'll manage to get a couple of days or more in bed![29]

About a hundred miles further south, **James Butlin** was still loathing life in the trenches, which the weather was making steadily worse:

We got back to billets just before midnight last night after six days, the most muddy six days I have ever spent in my life. When we went in it was freezing hard. This frost lasted about 24 hours & we had 10 or 12 degrees of black frost. Cold in trenches is bad enough and I felt like (& was) an icicle during that time.

Suddenly the thaw came and it rained solidly for 24 hours & on & for the remainder of the time. The trenches fell in, the dugouts collapsed & the mud & slosh was anything from knee- to waist-deep. From the weather point of view they were the worst days I have ever spent. When I came out my clothes were solid with liquid mud & weighed about a ton. One sergeant was buried alive and crushed to pieces by a dug-out falling in on him. A fellow in my platoon was buried alive, with the exception of the head. We got him out and have hopes that he will live.[30]

There was one bit of news from home that might have cheered him: conscription was now looking inevitable. It seemed likely that Basil's fun was about to come to an end, and James would no longer have to be reminded in such enthusiastic terms of the life he'd left behind:

Doubtless by this time you will be a conscript in his majesty's army, drawing the princely wage of 1/1 per diem. If however (which I hope is the case) you still succeed in hoodwinking the doctors that you are weak & puny, I take it you will be in 42 Grosvenor Gardens by the side of a roaring fire. I, on the other hand, will be standing, in a few hours, shivering in a trench full of mud and water and cursing the Kaiser and his abominable hordes. Hurry with those cigarettes.[31]

The weather was pretty awful back home too. In Great Leighs, **Andrew Clark** had sloshed his way to the church school for the monthly meeting of the special constables, ankle-deep in muddy water every step. His trousers were now wet through, as he sat listening to Major Brown explaining his progress with the Derby Scheme. Not a single married man had expressed a willingness to serve, though the major had managed to get the assent of five unmarried villagers. But nobody seemed to feel very positive about the scheme:

> The general impression of the meeting seemed to be that Lord Derby's scheme would prove a failure, and that the government would be compelled to resort to a militia ballot, or other form of compulsory service.[32]

The following weekend the issue came to a head in Great Leighs. The doctor was in town and although conscription had not yet been introduced, the pressure on the villagers to enlist was ratcheting up:

> There has been a great turn-up in the village yesterday and today. Some of the farmers had notice to send all their men to be medically inspected for service. They came in a body to Mr Caldwell. He advised them to go. If they were called out, their master would be able to say whether they could be spared or not. If they did not put down their names now, it was doubtful whether, if they were called upon, there would be any possibility of appeal. This is not voluntary recruiting, but compulsion in dishonest form. The officer who attended at the council school this week said that, if men hung back, they would be hauled out with a rope round their neck. This is voluntary enlistment![33]

In the early hours of 19 December, the German army at Ypres began another new kind of bombardment: phosgene gas shells fell from the pre-dawn sky to land amid the British lines. It had been a year that had seen the deployment of many terrible new weapons, and this was the final one. British gas masks were not designed to cope with high concentrations of phosgene. Thousands of men quickly developed symptoms: coughing, nausea, vomiting and headaches. The worst afflicted drowned as their lungs filled with fluid. Over 1,000 men were incapacitated, 120 of whom died.

Alan Lloyd's battery were sleeping unawares when the phosgene attack occurred. Their dugout was shelled – one man was killed instantly and all telephone lines were severed. The men struggled against the

effects of the gas and, in the absence of any communication, shelled
the enemy as best as they could, hindered by gas masks, sickness and
fatigue. It was a traumatic day in the battery's history.[34]

But while his men battled poisoned air and the thunder of falling
shells, Alan Lloyd was waking up in bed next to his beloved Dorothy.
His leave had finally come through and he had arrived home in
Birmingham just before dawn. He'd met his son David for the first
time. At last Alan could realise the dreams he'd enjoyed on the battlefield; Alan, Dods and David would spend their first Christmas together
as a family.

British children making the most of Christmas in spite of the privations of war,
December 1915.

Though it was cut short: on Christmas Day itself, after just a week
at home, Alan's leave was up. He arrived at Victoria Station, which
was awash with the other officers and men who had been lucky
enough to get Christmas leave, all now returning to war after an
agonisingly brief reacquaintance with the warmth and normality of
home. This was not the excited departure of troops leaving for the
front for the first time. These men knew what awaited them at their
journey's end. Above the noise of footsteps and cases thrown down
and doors slammed, a song could be heard, sung by the soldiers
milling on the platform:

I don't want to die,
I want to go home.
I don't want to go to the trenches no more,
Where the whizz-bangs and shells do whistle and roar

I don't want to go over the sea,
To where the Alleyman will shoot at me,
I want to go home
I don't want to die.[35]

Alan got on the train.

TOTAL WAR

12

COMPULSION COMES
Winter–Spring 1916

When I cannot sleep I try to picture the distant time when the Days of Peace will be with us again. I try to recall what it will be to see happy faces once again.

Hallie Miles's diary, 1 January 1916

The year 1915 was very nearly over. Britain had been at war for over 500 days and nights. Almost two and a half million men had left their homes and volunteered to fight. And still it went on.

In Bray in Northern France, 19-year-old **James Butlin** was in rest, and had interrupted a game of cards to sing 'Auld Lang Syne' outside the general's house. He'd been at war for ten months. Twenty miles away, **Reg Evans**, also in rest from the trenches, had been at war for over a year. Thirty miles away in Belgium, new father **Alan Lloyd** was in action at Ypres, the town now little more than a pile of rubble behind him. He had been at war for six months.

Back in Britain, as the last seconds of 1915 disappeared, Big Ben was in darkness; its bells did not chime. But the celebrations shuffled on away from the gloomy streets, behind the blackout curtains. **Hallie Miles**'s choir was singing 'Auld Lang Syne' in her restaurant near Trafalgar Square; **Duff Cooper** was drunk on punch at a New Year's party with the prime minister; in Great Leighs, the Rev. **Andrew Clark** was tucked up in his bed, but not asleep. And then, 1915 was gone.[1]

As 1916 began, the peace of the past had faded into memory. This nascent year would see liberal traditions abandoned; control of the population tightened; battles fought on a scale never before thought possible. The war of attrition was beginning.

Still, **Hallie Miles** looked to the year ahead with cautious hope and optimism:

> When I cannot sleep I try to picture to myself the distant time when the Days of Peace will be with us again. In my imagination I see all the windows once more brightly lit, the streets a blaze of light, and I hear the bells daring to peal and clash in the old sonorous way, and Big Ben striking the hours again. And I seem to see all the windows open in the evening, as of yore, with the glimpses of happy home life that one used to see through the open windows instead of the windows with curtains tightly drawn across as they are now.
>
> And I try to recall what it will be to see the happy faces once again: the faces one sees nowadays are so drawn and sad; if by chance one hears a hearty laugh one wonders what it means: it sounds so new and strange, like something one used to hear long, long ago. God grant that this year my dreams and visions may come true.

On New Year's Day in Northern France, **James Butlin** was feeling a little the worse for wear after a night of drinking. But he was relatively content, away from the front line and buoyed by the news that conscription would almost certainly be introduced at home. Basil claimed he was unfit for service because of a weak heart. After months in the hell of the trenches, James had little patience with any excuse he might offer:

> Dear Old Basil,
>
> We have moved a bit and are now further away from the line in fairly comfortable billets. I have recovered from Christmas & am now flourishing!
>
> Is the compulsion for single men terrifying you? Have you presented yourself for an armlet? I expect you've got wind up now the Daily Mail is so hot on your track. You, remember are one of the 400,000, branded in the eyes of the world as a slacker. Never mind, Basil, take heart and breathe through your heart muscle (if your heart is weak) when you go before the local tribunal.
>
> I hope you didn't drink as much as I did at Christmas. Your

chocolates were most acceptable. I can thoroughly recommend a second issue of the same.[2]

On 3 January, Butlin and the 1st Dorsets marched from their comfortable billets back into the front line near Albert, on the Somme. This was one of the areas that the French commander-in-chief was considering for the location of the big offensive this summer. Now it was quiet, and the weather was relatively mild. But it was winter, and in the trenches the nights were cold; the water always sloshing, seeping, soaking; the lice always scratching, the rats scuttling; and trench foot came for many and stray shells for a few. James would at least have been cheered by the news that arrived amongst these torments: the conscription bill was passed in Parliament on 5 January.[3]

It was not the first New Year that **Reg Evans** had seen in away from home. But a lot had happened to him since the outbreak of war: he'd been decorated for bravery and twice promoted, first from a humble private to corporal, and more recently to a sergeant. He was a respected and well-liked leader of men.[4] And he was pleased to be able to tell his mother that he had been asked to take on yet another responsibility:

> I don't know whether you have heard but I have now got a position of somewhat more importance i.e. on our Divisional Intelligence Staff. This is also quite between ourselves though I daresay the news will get around in some other way as of course all our fellows know. This is rather fortunate for me getting an appointment of this kind for it is not usual for any but an officer I believe.[5]

Reg's star was rising. He had been selected from amongst his peers to work under the Divisional Scouting Officer, gathering intelligence on the enemy's line. From now on, Reg would be responsible for observing the positions of enemy machine guns and trench mortars, noting any changes to the enemy line or the habits of enemy soldiers, and the results of the British artillery fire. As well as his own observations, he was to gather information from conversations with the other NCOs and men in the trenches, and to report his findings daily (or immediately if he felt anything was significant) to the Divisional Scouting Officer. It was a big responsibility. Observing the enemy line from the trenches would inevitably mean exposing himself to greater danger, but that was not something that generally bothered Reg Evans.

For now, Reg could relax. He was in rest in a little village near Bethune, some twenty miles behind the line.[6] On the eve of his twenty-eighth birthday, he sat down to write to his mother, who hadn't forgotten the occasion, of course:

> You really are too good and kind to your wandering son and I shall never be able to repay you for your kind thought and loving care. Everything is splendid & the cake just arrived looks glorious. And what a lovely day it is too. Here I am sitting in a little cottage in a faraway village in France & the sun shining in bright & warm through the open door.

News of Reg's successes was travelling fast. To his friends at home, he was a war hero – the rest was mere detail:

> Percy wrote me a nice letter and said something about me being on the Divisional Staff. Please correct him as he is not correct at all in his ideas. I only hope nothing I have said has led him to think that I am shortly to be a general, only of course don't hurt his feelings.[7]

Reg had another week in rest before he went on duty again. This time, when he entered the trenches, he would carry with him greater responsibilities than ever.

Alan Lloyd had arrived back at Ypres from his leave to find his battery recovering from the terrible ordeal just before Christmas. His sergeant was dead; a fellow officer had had an arm amputated; men were recovering from the horrible effects of gas. But in early January they left the rubble of Ypres behind them for an extended rest, and a chance to regroup.

The quiet was also an opportunity for training: the preparations for the great, extended offensive were already beginning. Effective artillery was understood to be of paramount importance – proven by the tragedies at Loos when men ran into untouched enemy defences – and new techniques were being sought. Much to his excitement, Alan Lloyd and C Battery of the 78th Brigade had been chosen to trial new methods of cutting enemy barbed wire.[8] It helped him swallow the bitter pill of renewed separation from his family:

> Lovely day to day so Hubbins is happy and not miz!
>
> We have to go to Calais in a week for a shoot on the sands. One battery had to be selected from the division for an exhibition shoot at barbed wire entanglements and we've been chosen. This is a great compliment and I only hope we live up to it. Really, old C battery seems at last coming in to its own.
>
> Hurry up and learn to drive Bicho car and tell Hubbins when you can do 60 and Hubbins will give you a little kiss and perhaps something else if you're very, very good!
>
> Bye-bye ownest, Tons of love,
>
> Your own Hub[9]

Dorothy wrote to him daily over January. Alan was in good spirits, and – with a new officer in command, Captain Marshall – he was finally getting the recognition he'd sought for such a long time:

> Marshall wrote to the Adjutant the other day and asked why I hadn't been promoted long ago and said he wanted me promoted at once. The adjutant replied that my name had been sent forward 3 weeks ago for 'special promotion'. So I think the old Colonel thought I did alright in the last position when I was carrying on the battery.[10]

Alan would soon have the chance to prove himself further.

In January, the evacuation of Gallipoli was completed. With that mammoth, resource-draining campaign over, the Allies could focus the bulk of their energies and resources on the Western Front. In February, the British and French were thrashing out the details of the campaign for this summer. The spot was chosen: The Somme. The date was agreed: around the beginning of July. So confident were they of their success, the British and French governments issued a joint declaration that there could be no peace with Germany until Belgian neutrality was restored and reparations paid.[11]

The British knew that they had work to do to get in shape in time. There was a need for better strategy, for more training, for new tactics, for better intelligence, but at the most basic level, the requirements were simple: more men and more weapons. On 27 January, the Military Service Act was passed. Every unmarried man aged 18 to 40 was deemed to have enlisted, and their calling up was under way.[12]

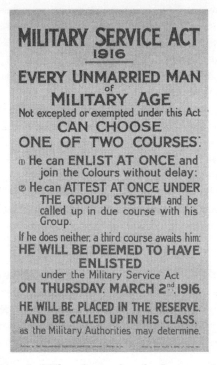

A poster publicising the Military Service Act of 27 January 1916.

In February heavy snowfall turned Great Leighs into a winter scene worthy of any chocolate box. One morning, the postman arrived, late and red-cheeked, his breath steaming the air as he crunched up the path to the snow-clad rectory. He had a letter for **Andrew Clark**'s groom-gardener, Charles. It was a notice to present himself for service. Many other young men of the village received the same letter.[13]

Conscription had come to Great Leighs.[14] Worse, it had come to the rectory. Andrew was outraged; he sat down at his desk and wrote to the recruiting office to tell them Charles could not be spared. A few days later, he got their reply:

I had written to the Recruiting Office, Chelmsford, asking notice of holding of tribunal to ask exemption or postponement of service of my lad, Charles Henry Ward. I had by this post very courteous letters in answer. C. H. W. is a very useful lad, in this house – where everything has to be done by hand – water pumped from a deep well, drains flushed weekly, as well as the garden tilled and the pony attended to. The place cannot do without a man. On the other hand he has not stamina for service. To take him out in wet would be to send him to hospital with chest trouble, and I do not imagine that recruiting is intended to provide inmates of hospital.[15]

Andrew received notice to present his case at a tribunal a few weeks hence.

James Butlin was, like Alan, in training in the first weeks of the New Year, learning how better to use the new machine gun, the Lewis gun. He was temporarily safe, but that didn't seem to cheer him; he was angry to see how the instructors at the training school lived. He wrote to Basil:

You may perhaps be wondering what has become of me so I hasten to reassure you. I am in a small village about 6 kilometres outside St Omer. I am here for 5 days only learning the Lewis automatic rifle and all the wonders connected therewith. I cannot help being struck by the enormous numbers of officers and men who live miles behind the line, apparently doing dawn all. Yet after the war these fellows will presumably wear the same medals as myself and you can't even hear the sound of the guns from this place. [16]

Meanwhile the German army was preparing for a massive assault of its own. They too hoped to grind their enemy down through the biggest, most sustained assault of the war so far: theirs focused on the French-held fortress at Verdun. And unlike the French and British, the Germans were almost ready to go.[17]

Writing to his mother while back in rest, **Reg Evans** was allowing himself a bit of well-earned pride in his achievements and the recognition he was still receiving for them:

Of course you know we have a V.C. in the regiment don't you? Well the other day when we were relieved from the trenches the whole battalion was formed up and our Brigadier General made a speech and then this V.C. chap who is in our company and about three more of us who have got the D.C.M's had to go out and he shook hands with us and the Regiment had to march past and salute. (Swank eh!)

The General said 'We don't need any introduction to Sergeant Evans, for I think he is about the best known man in the brigade and we are always hearing of some good deed or other of his doing.' So the Colonel added 'If we'd only got two or three hundred more like him I think the Germans would have a more uncomfortable time.' (Swank!)[18]

After just a few days' rest, the 1st Herts were preparing to go back into the trenches, this time at Festubert, the site of the terrible battle the previous spring. From the trenches, Sergeant Evans left behind his company to undertake divisional intelligence duties. We do not know his movements in mid-February, but whatever they may have been, we do know that Reg Evans was not to be found with 'F' Company, the 1st Herts Regiment at that time.[19]

The German army meanwhile wanted to distract Allied attention from their preparations at Verdun. Therefore, on 14 February, an intense bombardment was unleashed on the front astride the Ypres Canal. The 78th Brigade RFA had been covering the line for some days already. **Alan Lloyd** had just been promoted – finally – from second lieutenant to lieutenant. As the day went on, the artillery was asked to retaliate whilst the infantry was warned to prepare for an assault. Alan's battery was eventually shelled out of its position. The remaining artillery supported attempted counter-attacks as best they could over the course of the night. But the frontline trenches were lost, and bloody attempts to reclaim them over the coming days were unsuccessful.[20]

By the afternoon of 17 February, casualties had reached 67 officers and 1,227 other ranks. A friend of Alan's was killed:

It was poor old Slavey who was killed by a shell. We all had a rough time about then and since then. You see those blessed trenches were lost and we covered them.[21]

The British were determined to win back the lost trenches, and started preparations for a counter-attack. Meanwhile, the shelling went on and on. On 27 February, it began to snow, but the British plans were not given up on. An attack was set for 2 March. At 5.15 p.m. on the 1st, Alan's battery began the preliminary bombardment of the enemy's support trenches. Much damage was done. At 4.15 a.m., under the cover of night, the assaulting infantry troops moved forward into position. There, they waited: at 4.30 a.m., they were to attack their old lines. Alan was amongst them. He had been chosen as forward observation officer, tasked with liaising with the battalion commander from the midst of the assault.[22]

At 4.30 a.m., the order was given. Alan and the infantry climbed out of the trench. As they scrambled in the dark across the frozen no-man's-land, the artillery barrage was unleashed on the lines they were running towards:

> I was F.O.O. in the trenches for the attack and saw a bit of life! We bombed them right out and they bolted like rabbits and we potted them with rifles, I claim to have got one myself, about 25 yards range. It was exciting work and the Hun had had enough by Jove, he came over holding up his hands in hundreds, we got over 500 prisoners and about 7 officers. We were all at the end of it on top of the trenches and having a tremendous time shoving the prisoners into the trenches and sending them down to H.Q. One Hun officer came up to me and told I was to take charge of him as he was an officer. He said in French I was to take him to his place of captivity! I told him I wished I could as it would be England! All the Tommies roared and bellowed with laughter at this.[23]

The attack was a total success. The lost trenches were won back, and some extra ground gained. But the transient nature of these minor successes was made clear: in one trench, shelling had revealed the bodies of soldiers of three different nationalities, who'd all occupied this part of the line at different times. The snow was getting heavier.[24]

The main event was now underway at Verdun. However long it took, however many of their men were lost, the Germans intended to exhaust the French army, still the main player on the Western Front. The Kaiser proclaimed proudly: 'This war will end at Verdun.'[25]

On 21 February, 850 heavy guns began a nine-hour bombardment along an eight-mile front, unprecedented in warfare. Phosgene gas shells and 140,000 German infantrymen advanced in its wake. One corporal remarked that for every five French soldiers in defence, two were buried alive under collapsing fortifications, two were wounded and one was waiting to be hit. On the second day, flame-throwers were brought out; by the third day the Germans had advanced two miles.[26]

James Butlin was crosser than ever. His leave had been stopped. The day after the key fortress of Douaumont fell into German hands, James wrote to Basil, from his position one hundred and fifty miles up the line from the battle that might end the war:[27]

> I am almost too angry to write letters. All leave is stopped, just before I was to go. The irony of fate is that the C.O. (commanding officer) could have sent me off as soon as I came back from my course but said I could wait a few days. Then the inevitable happens and leave is cancelled. I am terribly disappointed.
>
> Today is very wintry, snow falling fast. It freezes all night and most of the day. The snow is setting quite deep. I rather welcome this weather as a change. It must be awful for the poor devils in the trenches. I forgive you for forgetting my birthday. To tell you the truth I nearly forgot it myself.[28]

James had just turned twenty.

Now that conscription had come into force, the British army was growing in size again: over the first half of 1916 it would grow by 1.5 million men.[29] **Andrew Clark** was determined that his groom-gardener Charles would not add to the numbers, and in March he went to make his case. It did not go well:[30]

> Went to the Recruiting Tribunal Office; waited three-quarters of an hour beyond time; and was refused leave to keep my man, Chas. Henry Ward, til a later date. The tribunal consisted of a dozen or more country people – with military assessors – told off to compel them to refuse exemptions.[31]

In the middle of March, Andrew had to watch the first batch of conscripts leave the village and the surrounding district. The squire, who had been such a champion of recruitment, lost nine of the thirty-six men who worked on his farms. He told Andrew he was going to have to take on women workers.[32] Getting ready to go out the following night on patrol, Andrew was feeling ill and decidedly grumpy about it all:

> This is my night of Special Constable patrol: I am not in love with the prospect. I am worn out with a bronchitic cough, and consequent fever-ishness; and am singularly nervous and inclined to be quarrelsome. 1130pm: dark, cloudy, still, damp night: not a creature about, nor a sound to be heard.[33]

Alan Lloyd was still in action at Ypres. A week after the successful assault in which he'd taken part, the adrenalin had long since faded and battle-weariness had set in. He wrote to Dorothy with unancharac-teristic bitterness, cross that his brigade's efforts – risking of all their lives – had gone unrecognised:

> By the way, don't think I'll get anything out of our show because I know I shan't. There have been no awards for the old 78th and won't be. I did nothing at all, tho' as a matter of fact they sent my name forward for both shows. The Hun attack and ours a fortnight later, but I don't know why and shan't get anything and don't deserve anything so don't expect it. Are you expecting to get a V.C or note to come?! Cause if so you'll be disappointed.

Alan then regretted his tone, and tried to rectify it with a postcard. But he was clearly exhausted, and couldn't keep his frustration at bay:

> P.S I just adore you, you darling, and so I put this P.C because thought perhaps small wife would be hurt at what I said about getting a V.C But I do hate the people who expect their men to do the Death or Glory stunt! It's not easy in this war, and for a gunner his duty is gener-ally inconspicuous, an F.O.O must tend his wires and communication, and this isn't a spectacular show. I should say it's far easier to do a balaclava charge – all your pals round you just like a rugger scrum – than

to go out on your wires on a dark night with 5.9's falling round you and a thousand other shells and no trenches to protect you, all by yourself with one signaller. I can tell you, my darling, it's not too easy.

But don't worry, I'll not be again in such a show for a long time probably. Bye bye ownest.[34]

In early March, **James Butlin** had gone back into the trenches in the snow and sleet. He was in a section of the line very close to the Germans, where mining activity – and the threat of being blown up from underneath – was constant..[35] Two days into this stint, James had fallen ill. He now wrote to Basil from the comfort, and normality, of a hospital well away from the line, in Rouen:

> Last Monday I had to go sick with acute otitis – for your benefit that means inflammation of & discharge from the ear. I went off Monday morning to the 92nd field ambulance & stayed the night there. Tuesday morning I left for Amiens and after lunch at the hospital there was sent down by the hospital train to this place.
>
> I have been here ever since and am much better We are most awfully well treated & looked after, best of food etc and as you may imagine it makes a glorious change after a year of trenches. I am allowed out and go down into the town every afternoon with a man in the Manchesters, Robertson by name. I have my head all bandaged up so pass for a wounded hero! There is an excellent tea-shop which we patronise, it is full of British officers and all the tarts in Rouen.[36]

Following a few days of rest and treatment, James was something like his old self again.

Reg Evans would never be the same again. In mid-February, whilst on special duties away from his company, he was hit by a bullet. This time there would be no jumping out of the ambulance to go back to the fray: half of his jaw had been shot off.

By the time he arrived at no. 7 general hospital in Rouen, he was also seriously ill. His mother Frances got a letter with the devastating news, and little information:

Dear Mrs Evans,

Your son, Sgt. Evans was admitted to this hospital last night; suffering from a gunshot wound of face and scarlet fever. He feels very seedy at present; he sends his love and says you are not to worry, he will write when he is able to and I shall write again very soon and let you know how he is progressing.

Yrs sincerely, I.P. Stratton (Sister)[37]

The 1st Herts Regiment was distraught that they had lost a much-loved, well-respected soldier, and the commander wrote personally to Frances to express the deepest sympathy of the regiment:

I expect you will have heard by now that your son has been wounded rather badly. I am very sorry I was not able to see him before he left us, but he was doing duty with another Company at the time and there was no means of communication.

I thought I would write and tell you what a tremendous loss he is to the Battalion and his Company in particular. I have never met anybody so amazingly cheerful under every possible condition – the worse the weather and the more awful things were the more cheerful he would become. His effect on the men was marvellous. Then again he was very hardworking indeed and was never happy unless he was doing something useful. Lastly but not leastly he was as fearless a man as I have seen – his courage was absolute and whenever there was any trouble of any kind he was always one of the first to come along and see to things. I am a bad letter writer, but I would like you to know that he has a great reputation in the battalion and was respected, admired and loved by every man in the company whom he came into contact with.

I do not generally write to the relations of any men who are wounded, but your son was such a personality and such a fine soldier that I had to write and try and tell you what a lot we all thought of him.[38]

13

ENDURANCE AND
EXERTION

April–June 1916

It is going to be a long job, but I am resigned to that.
Reg Evans, letter to his mother, April 1916

It was a mild spring morning in Hemel Hempstead. The postman made his way through town, a large bag slung over one shoulder. On Broad Street, in her guesthouse at number 12, **Frances Evans** was clearing up after breakfast. She was anxious. She'd been waiting for further news of her wounded son every morning for days. Today, the postman knocked at the door: in his hand was a letter from France.

The handwriting on the front was not her son's. But as she ripped open the envelope, its contents were revealed to be a long-awaited letter from him. The tone was unmistakably his, though less perky than normal:

Very many thanks for your letter. I can tell you I was jolly glad to get it. I am afraid that you won't get a letter from me in my own handwriting whilst I am in this hospital, because all our letters have to be copied for fear of infection . . .

I am thinking of you all and am looking forward to my leave and a pretty long time at home. I expect I shall get moved to a hospital in England in three weeks' time, then that will seem nearer to you all. Please thank everybody for their kind enquiries and you can tell them all that I am getting on splendidly. I shall be glad of a letter from anybody just to let me know how things are getting on.

You needn't have the slightest worry about me, as I am getting on fine and don't have any pain. There is nothing you could send at all bar reading matter as I cannot eat or smoke. I am afraid you will have to prepare yourself to receive rather an uglier duckling than before.[1]

No matter what Reg might say, the last bit did worry Frances.

The ear infection that had got **James Butlin** out of the trenches had been bad enough to get him sent to Blighty, to no. 5 General Hospital in Southsea. Now it had developed into an unspecified illness, which was not then deemed to need hospital treatment. James had suffered some kind of breakdown and was being sent to his family home in Weymouth to recover. He wrote to Basil, now in his final year at Oxford University, to tell him how pleased he was to be on English soil once again:

> I can tell you I am thankful to get to Blighty. I don't know of course how long I shall continue to remain in England but you can take it from me that it will be as long as human ingenuity and cunning can continue. I've done 12 months of it and that's enough in the infantry. We are on the eve of great things – perhaps – in France, great things mean great slaughter, at least so it appears to me, as I for once am thankful to be out of it for a bit.[2]

As James gazed out of the window of his ward, a classroom in a girls' secondary school not so long ago, over the sea the preparations for the great battle continued. By the end of March over 170,000 men had been wounded or killed at Verdun, but the French support for the joint offensive was not dimmed. It would be the Allies' turn soon.[3]

Dorothy Lloyd was also about to go home. Since Alan had left for the front she'd lived with her parents-in-law, John and Gertrude Lloyd, in Birmingham. Alan's family were Quakers, and the Quaker community, as pacifists, had been struggling to come to terms with the war and particularly with compulsory military service. John and Gertrude had never really understood their son Alan's desperation to become a soldier, which was so contrary to the principles of the religion he'd been bought up in. Dorothy, though she loved Alan's family deeply, was a little tired of being around people who were opposed to the war he was fighting.[4]

Dorothy was going to live with her parents in Yorkshire – a week later, she was back in Boston Spa. Her father was a retired army surgeon and her brother Richard, once a locomotive engineer, was now serving in France. War was a part of this family's life; and Dorothy liked the change. But best of all, a letter that arrived early in April made her think that she might see Alan again very soon indeed. He had left Ypres, was now in France and hoped to be in London any day now:

> This place is very quiet and it's great fun to be snugly in bed and hear the guns booming away to the North and think we're out of that dreary region of mud and blood!
>
> When I'm coming on leave I'll wire you just 'Come, Alan'. Then you will come down to Grosvenor Hotel, Victoria, which is quite comfy and close to the station. I'll not send the wire till I'm quite sure I'm off and when you get the wire send a reply to this hotel saying what time your train arrives and what station so that if I reach London first I will know where to meet you, tho' probably you'll get there first as we may be delayed as I was before when I came on leave. But the meeting place will be Grosvenor Hotel, Victoria and we'll both make straight for that. The one who gets there first to book a room with a big bed! (small wife!)
>
> I just long to have small wife again and see her lovely little face and press it close to mine and squeeze her little body.[5]

Britons everywhere were enduring separation from loved ones; loss of loved ones; injury of loved ones. And meanwhile the attack on their own lives and their own homes continued. In spring 1916, Germany launched a series of air raids on Britain, designed to break morale at home whilst they broke armies on the battlefields of Verdun. London's defences had been much improved since the first bombs had fallen on the capital almost a year earlier, and though attempts were made to reach the city in early spring, they failed. The rest of the country, however, was as vulnerable as ever. In early March three airships arrived in the night sky above northern England, and discharged a volley of bombs on Hull. The casualties were severe.[6]

The nation was once again on the alert. One cold night in March,

Hallie Miles found herself fleeing to the shelter she'd carefully fashioned in her basement:

> Oh! The grim horror of it all, and the chilly feeling on entering the basement, not knowing what was in store for us. I lit the little lamp and got out all our warm rugs and blankets, and we sat with them spread on our laps as if we were in a railway carriage. It was very funny how strangers came wandering along the passages that led to our basement. A young man in evening dress and wearing an eye-glass walked in. He was trying to find the basement of some friends who had invited him to dinner and were hiding in their own basement instead of receiving them in their flat! We invited him to remain with us, but he continued his search, and we never saw him again.
>
> We sat shivering and expectant; every door that shut with a bang we thought was a bomb. We were down there an hour and then news was brought us that the Zeppelins had been turned back, and we might go upstairs again. How gladly we all left our 'Dug-Outs', and how beautiful our flat looked as we entered it again! The wicked Zeppelins wended their way to the Midlands instead, and did frightful havoc there.[7]

On 31 March, the Germans launched a hugely ambitious attack, designed to wipe out the munitions factories in the east of England. The Zeppelins were also determined to get to London once more. As **Andrew Clark** lay in bed in Great Leighs, five airships were entering the skies above England. One of them was on course for Essex:

> At 11 p.m., just as my wife had come up, there were two tremendous explosions, just to the north which shook the house, and caused her to call out, involuntarily, 'Oh! Oh!' The second call woke me, and I got up to find my daughters disturbed by the great bangs, and the dog roused and barking.
>
> At 11.10 p.m. I was dressing-gowned and out. It was a starlit night, slightly foggy. By this time the Zeppelin was roaring like a railway somewhere nearby, apparently somewhere over the rectory stables. For an appreciable time it continued to roar but make no progress, like a big engine letting off steam on a railway siding. I tried every way to locate it against the stars, but did not succeed. Then the noise began to be louder and louder as the machine began to move from the

over-the-stable-yard way. The movements were ridiculously, so far as could be judged by their sound, like those of a crow, flying over a pasture field.

11.50 p.m. Several explosions in the south, followed by lights (probably searchlights). Just as the clock struck 12 midnight, sound was heard of one Zeppelin coming back. When it got this length, it hesitated; hovered about (as if uncertain how to proceed) over N.W. corner of this house, and over the Stokes's cottage opposite the Rectory Gate. It was now distinctly seen – a long, black thing against the stars. [8]

That night, eastern England – from Woolwich in South London to Cromer in Norfolk – was subjected to widespread bombing. Bury St Edmunds was hit at midnight. Another airship reached the outskirts of London, but was stopped by searchlights and anti-aircraft guns and a plane, which drove it out to sea. Another airship got as far north as Cleethorpes, bombing a chapel that was being used as a billet, killing many soldiers from the 3rd Manchester Regiment. The airship that Andrew saw above Great Leighs dropped its bombs on Sudbury, Braintree, Blackmore, Springfield, Stanford-le-Hope and Thames Haven. Braintree was just a few miles away, and Andrew discovered just how lucky he'd been the next day:[9]

Village reports as to last night's raid: at Braintree bombs were dropped in High Street, in Martin's Yard, and in 'Rifle Hill'. Much glass was broken, the chief damage being to shop of C. Joscelyne, my pet stationer, in High Street. In St Martin's Yard five people are reported killed; ninety bombs were dropped in all.[10]

The Zeppelins came back the following night, bombing Sunderland and Middlesbrough. On 2 April, Edinburgh was the target. Two nights later they reached Norfolk; the night after, Durham, Hull and Skinningrove.[11] Britons were subjected to a week of terrified, sleepless nights.

Helen Bentwich had missed the Zeppelins again, this time because she was on the other side of the world, in Cairo. She'd moved there with Norman just after their wedding. But she found herself suddenly alone in the strange city: Norman had left his job at the law school to become an officer in the Camel Transport Corps. The Allies might have pulled out of Gallipoli, but the war against Turkey was not over, and fighting continued in the Sinai Peninsula and in Mesopotamia. The Camel Transport Corps offered vital support to the Egyptian Expeditionary Force fighting in Sinai. Helen wrote to her mother with the news, excited but frustrated as usual not to be in the thick of things herself:

> Don't get a horrid shock – but Norman left me this morning in khaki (which suits him uncommonly well), is now at this moment in camp 10 miles away and has just rung up to say that 'it's all ripping'. There – has that taken your breath away? If you have recovered read on and you will find out the details. Ever since we came out here we both realized that the law school job was a most unworthy one at the present time and Norman has had the most violent fits of depression, especially after reading the recruiting articles in The Times.
>
> There's only one objection. The colonel won't let me join too (I don't believe Norman really asked him) but it does seem such fun – plenty of riding and trekking about and I'm sure I'd be good at it. It makes me feel so wild that I'm just a female – and I feel as jealous as I did at the beginning of the war, when Ellis and all the other boys went off and I couldn't. I won't say damn being a female, but I'll think it.[12]

A soldier in the Camel Transport Corps, near Shellal.

*

Frances Evans's children were all far from home. Her son Will was fighting in Egypt, her son Edgar was fighting in France, and her son **Reg Evans** was fighting for his life in a French hospital. She had received a few letters from him now, and he seemed to be doing much better. He was winning his battle against scarlet fever, and his words were written in his own hand. In spite of everything, he was still being cheerful, and was more concerned with his sister's pains than his own:

> You will be glad to know I have nearly finished with the fever and hope soon to be moved to another hospital, in England I trust, where I can undergo an operation to my face and then we shan't be long.
>
> How are you all getting on? Has Daisy's neuralgia finished troubling her? I do feel so sorry for her, for I know only too well how queer it makes you. There is one thing I shall be jolly surprised if I ever get it again in my teeth at any rate. You wait till I come swanking home with my false teeth and artificial jaw, I'll show some of you up.
>
> Don't imagine me as pale faced and anaemic looking, for I'm not and there's absolutely nothing in my condition for you to worry over at all. The doctors I have seen so far have said how well my wound is getting on.

If all went well and Reg was transferred to England, Francis would soon be able to see for herself how his recovery was going.

Dorothy Lloyd already had her weekend bag packed, waiting for when she got word from Alan that he was en route to London. But in the middle of April she received some very disappointing news: leave had been suspended. It was bad enough to have her hopes of being together as a family for the Easter weekend dashed, but she was also worried about Alan. He was bad-tempered, which wasn't like him, and obviously run down. She read his increasingly frustrated letters over April, frustrated herself that there was nothing she could do to help:

> By gad I do love the staff, they take damned good care of their own leaves, they and the cavalry every 8 days or less to the day, and do damn all. The more you do in this war, absolutely the less you get.
>
> I have got a boil on my neck which the professor has been tormenting. He is not much good and has filthy hands for the job! Beloved little

angel Are you sorry for your hubbins with a nasty boil? . . . It will all be gone when I come home on leave and otherwise I am very fit as you'll find out. I just long to hug you all to bits. Soon with luck I'll be with small wife and then she'll be as happy as she can be and we'll first laze away all the time in bed!

Bye-bye ownest. Small kiss to small son on his funny little nose and two for small wife on her darling little mouth, Your Hub.[13]

At the beginning of April, Asquith and his War Committee had convened to discuss the plans for the upcoming offensive on the Western Front. Ministers were told that more prolonged fighting and heavy casualties were inevitable, but not wanting to jeopardise their alliance with the French, the committee finally endorsed the plans for a joint offensive on the Somme. They accepted that it would be an enormous sacrifice of British life. The government started discussing the extension of conscription to include married men, to keep the numbers up. It was clear that Britons would be asked to give more than ever before.[14]

Easter 1916 was sunny and dry in Great Leighs. It had only been a few weeks since so many of the village men had been conscripted. **Andrew Clark**'s groom-gardener Charles Ward had left him at the beginning of the month, and Andrew was struggling to keep up with the outdoor work himself. As he walked to church on Good Friday morning, his hands were only just healing after he'd torn them open trying to clear away thorns from his garden.[15]

Andrew was surprised by the large congregation that turned out for his Good Friday service. But then the villagers were anxious. In the wake of the Zeppelin raids at the end of March and beginning of April, all sorts of rumours had been flying around about a possible German invasion. After the service, Andrew learnt how seriously the community was taking them. They believed an invasion of Britain to be imminent:

Yesterday I had a report that certain excitable people had been greatly distressed by a report that a meeting was to be held in the school in view of invasion. All I had to say was that I had not heard the faintest whisper of it. Today Mr G.S. With, the parish church-warden and Headmaster of the Council School told me: Major Wm. Brown had asked use of Council School on Thursday for such a meeting.

4 p.m. Dr Smallwood called: A Zeppelin raid is expected tonight, tomorrow night and Sunday night; with this raid, an attempt at invasion is expected, and the moment the approach of the Zeppelins is notified, the military are to be on the qui-vive, and everyone who is on leave is to be recalled. One recent attempt at invasion is said to have been turned back by our fleet, but, of course, there is no certainty as to that.[16]

Elsewhere, events more significant than gossip and hearsay were unfolding: an anti-British uprising took place in Dublin. Home Rule for Ireland had been passed in May 1914, but its implementation had been interrupted by the outbreak of war. Amid fears that conscription to the British army would be introduced there, Irish Republicans seized the moment: on Monday 24 April, over a thousand armed fighters stormed the Post Office, the Law Courts, St Stephen's Green and several other locations in the city. An Irish Republic independent of Britain was declared.

Irish Rebellion, May, 1916.
Holding a Dublin street against the Rebels.

British soldiers hold a street in Dublin during the uprising.

In a proclamation made from the steps of the Post Office, the rebels described the Germans as their allies. They had attempted to support the uprising with a shipment of weapons, but it had been intercepted.[17] The fear was that Germany might indeed do more and launch an invasion of Britain. On the morning of Easter Monday, as the republicans stormed the centre of Dublin, eight Zeppelins left the north coast of

Germany. They did little damage, but another raid followed the next night. Tensions at home were running high.[18]

In Essex, Andrew noted real fear among the populace:

> I hear that on Tuesday night many people in Bocking and Braintree did not go to bed but sat up prepared to flee inland. A report had got about that the Germans had actually landed.[19]

After six days the Dublin rising was brutally put down by British troops and its leaders executed. The supposed German invasion never materialised. But the people of Britain had been rattled. The unified nation that rallied behind King and Country in August 1914 was suddenly not looking quite so solid.

The act that extended conscription to include married men was passed at the end of May. Parliament and the population was divided on the issue, but the government knew that if the huge offensive of the summer was to go ahead, they would need as many men as they could get. The French had now suffered more than 115,000 casualties at Verdun, and would be unable to provide as many troops for the offensive as they'd originally promised.[20] The pressure on Britons was mounting.

Alan Lloyd was fed up with reading about the debates over conscription in the papers that reached him in France. He wrote to Dorothy, angry at what he felt was the dwindling of support for men like him at the front:

> It makes one annoyed out here to think of all this bleating of married men and shrinking of single men and general unwillingness at home to really take their coats off and get on with it. On top of this they keep the best aeroplanes and anti-aircraft guns at home to stop a few bombs being dropped and leave us here to sacrifice pilot after pilot in fighting superior machines. Really, one day there'll be some hanging in the streets if this sort of tomfoolery goes on.
>
> It's very uncertain about leave, the Colonel has been altering things and generally interfering and I don't exactly know when I'll get away. So don't expect me til you get a wire. It might be a long time. Please stop all hams and pork pies. They won't keep. I asked you a month ago to stop pork pies and they still come. Have you sent out 2 pairs of

stocking puttees yet and also all thin underclothes. Please get them off
as quick as possible, it's awful hot in long pants.

Hubbins is rotten 'snarly owl' today.[21]

The night after this latest letter was delivered to Dorothy, the Zeppelins
returned in force. This time Scotland, the East Midlands and Yorkshire
were the targets. York was bombed; nine people were killed and thirty
injured.[22] Dorothy and David were just fifteen miles away in Boston
Spa – perhaps Alan felt differently about the 'tomfoolery' of Zeppelin
defences when he read about this latest raid.

Frances Evans had been eagerly waiting for word that Reg had arrived
in hospital in England. But, instead, she received another letter from
France: Reg wasn't coming home as expected. He didn't say why, but
the extent of the treatment ahead of him was obviously dawning on
him.

Frances was in her sixties, running her guesthouse on her own, and
suffering constant anxiety about the wellbeing of all three of her sons,
not just Reg. It is perhaps unsurprising that in April, Frances fell ill.
Reg was terribly worried when he heard:

I was so sorry to hear you are not well and do hope by now you are
better. Now is the time when you must be extra careful for the weather
is so changeable and treacherous so guard against it all you possibly can.
Certainly see a doctor and get some thing for that cough of yours and
don't try to do too much. Then above all don't worry . . .

It is going to be a long job but I am resigned to that, all I want is
to get to England so that I can have a chance of seeing you. I am getting
on as well as can be expected and have practically no pain so you see
dear Mother if I've no troubles then you need have none for me. I am
well looked after here and fed every two hours with a variety of drinks.
Fancy I have been nearly 8 weeks in hospital. Still, what's that in a
lifetime, eh?

Please write toute suite and say how you are and ease the mind of
your loving son Reg

pour Mother XXXXXXXXXXXXXXXX[23]

*

As the months went by, **Helen Bentwich**'s enthusiasm for Norman's military adventure dwindled. Left behind with their servant Esther in a rented flat overlooking the Nile, she was lonely, and thoroughly bored:

> It's a bad confession, but although I've only been married 7 months I'm sick to death of having to think such a lot about meals and talking of food and I can't get up any enthusiasm for housekeeping of any sort and have a very profound pity for all my friends who have to do their own. And they envy me – which just shows that it's only pretence that all women like it and they only do it as they've got to.[24]

She had had enough. She decided to leave Egypt, and wrote to her mother at the end of May, excited about her imminent departure:

> I suppose I'd better tell you the boat I'm coming home on is the *Caledonia* – the same I came out on. Don't worry about submarines. I'll bet my bottom dollar that we'll be safe. By the way, I warn you, I smoke a good deal. It's very much done out here, so I'll smoke just like a boy when I come home and not just privately in my bedroom.
>
> Well good-bye and hurrah for being back in Blighty soon. Keep me heaps of strawberries![25]

Her family *was* worried about submarines, and rightly so; the war at sea was intensifying. On 31 May, the British and German navies met near Jutland, Denmark. It was a terrible battle in which neither side could really claim victory. More than 6,000 British sailors were killed. The Germans decided not to risk open naval battle again, but ramped up their policy of submarine warfare.

On 5 June, HMS *Hampshire* was en route to Russia when it struck a mine laid by German submarines. On board was the people's hero: Lord Kitchener.[26] Helen was among those left in shock:

> The news of Kitchener's death was so sudden and appalling that people laughed at it as a rumour and at first said 'how absurd'. Of course everyone knew him here and the natives are very upset. Norman says it's bad for our prestige for them to think we couldn't even look after such a marvellous man as Kitchener. It does seem great carelessness somewhere doesn't it? And what a beastly crow for the Germans.[27]

Kitchener's death was a terrible blow to British morale, which was already faltering. He had been a key advocate of the summer offensive on the Western Front. On the day of his death, the last division of his New Army crossed the Channel ready to take part.[28]

Helen's plans to come home were unchanged. She was to leave on the 21st.

James Butlin was thoroughly enjoying himself at home. He had been given light duty on grounds of his poor health, and was based at Wyke Regis in Weymouth. Chasing girls had returned to the top of his agenda and he had just enjoyed a stay with Basil:

> I arrived home safely and without any adventures. There were absolutely no girls about at all. I went up to the club and had quite respectable tennis. I met the Blue Flapper (Lulu) just now on my way down. She was looking prettier than ever and my determination to stay in England at any cost has grown stronger and stronger.
>
> I enjoyed myself exceedingly at your place, dear Basil; I can never thank you enough. I still rather regret the fact that I didn't get off with that girl on the river on Sunday. However, the future is full of promise.
>
> Do all in your power to get me this recruiting job, as I feel quite unable to face the trenches again. What a war this is! I am afraid there are many aching hearts over this last naval affair. Damn all Germans![29]

Life in Britain might have been getting harder, but James knew the horror of the front line of war. Even a Britain of Zeppelins and harder work was paradise compared to the trenches and battlefields of France.

Andrew Clark was tired. In May yet more young men from the parish were called up – the biggest call-up yet. Amongst them were the two farm lads Andrew had been paying to work in his garden since Charles had left. Andrew now had to do all the work by himself:

> Am very tired – heaving wood – cutting grass – sawing wood – mending fence – piling up rubbish on bonfire-heaps.[30]

Andrew turned sixty in early June. On his birthday, he saw the baker's wife pushing the baker's cart around the village. Everything was changing in Great Leighs. Andrew was doing his own manual labour; the squire's daughters now worked in munitions factories; other women were also working in men's jobs. It was all quite a lot to take in at his age. His new circumstances were also affecting him physically, as he discovered in late June:

> 9.25 a.m. started to go to Chelmsford. At my hairdresser's I had myself weighed. If the record is correct (15 stone, 7lbs) I have, in the last few months, lost three stone at least in weight. I never used to be less than eighteen and a half stone.
>
> In the High Street I met two young women, who represented the more swaggering lot of women workers on the land. They had riding breeches, like troopers, of a khaki cloth, with brown boots and leggings, and an overall of holland, white, coming down to a little below the knees. Ordinary women's hats. Carrying shortish rattans, such as grooms might have. They looked as if they had gone astray, out of a comic opera.[31]

Helen Bentwich was now safely back in England, despite a submarine scare on her journey. She wrote from her family's town house in West London to Norman, now 3,000 miles away in Egypt:

> I'm back home again feeling as if I'd never been away at all. It is comic isn't it? And it's awfully cold – the coldest June on record in England, while it was the hottest on record in Cairo.
>
> There were all sorts of yarn when we came off the boat about submarines. Most were untrue but I do believe there were some there. I believe that's why we stopped one night and also that we turned right round one morning. We passed a boat that was subbed just after and got many signals. It all seems a bit incredible after – but I do believe that it's true.[32]

In late May, **Dorothy Lloyd** received the news she'd been praying for: Alan was coming home on leave – and he was already in Southampton. She rushed down to London, and by the time she pulled into King's Cross, Alan was there to meet her. They headed straight for the Grosvenor Hotel, as they'd arranged. They were overjoyed to be reunited, and determined to make the most of this precious gift: a week together, in the English summertime.

In the last week of May, the commander-in-chief of the British army, Sir Douglas Haig, met his French counterpart, Joseph Joffre. Haig wanted to delay the offensive until August. Joffre refused. The last date they would countenance was 1 July. It was agreed.

The battle would commence in just over a month's time[33]

The Minister of Munitions, David Lloyd George – who took over as Secretary of State for War after the death of Lord Kitchener – had transformed the munitions industry in the year he had been at its helm. Two hundred thousand women were now working in war industries.[34] **Helen Bentwich** – who had been taught that housewifery was her calling – was about to join them. She wrote to her husband, hardly able to believe it herself:

> Well now for my news. I've been taken on as principal over-looker at Woolwich Arsenal, with the princely wages of £4-10 a <u>week</u> working from 7 a.m. to 7 p.m. for 6 days and then from 7 p.m. to 7 a.m. for 7 days and starting next Monday! There, doesn't that take your breath away? It does mine! It's the highest up job a woman can get in the factory, bar inspectorships and staff jobs, which I hope to be raised to if I stay a couple of months.
>
> I had to go and see the manager of the factory and he looked me up and down and asked a lot of questions about myself and then suddenly said, 'Are you frightened of figures?' I said no and that I was fairly at home in ordinary sums. Then he said, 'Can you do decimals? I said yes. Then he asked if I thought I could supervise 20 people (men and women) who were doing analysis of textiles and see their calculations and their deductions were correct. I said at any rate I could try it and so he engaged me on the spot.
>
> Then I had to be examined by the Doctor, which was a beastly process. There were a lot of chairwomen being done at the same time. I'd never been examined *en masse* before like they do men for the army and I hated it. You don't mind my getting a job like this, do you? It's hard work, I know, but then my health is one of my assets, isn't it and I do mean to do some real war-work.[35]

The Woolwich Arsenal was a giant industrial complex, which had already expanded massively to accommodate war production and would become the largest and most concentrated armament-manufacturing centre in Britain.

On 2 June, the Whitsun holiday was postponed until July to keep the factories open and turning out the weapons with which the great offensive would be fought.[36] The weapons needed men to use them, of course. On that day, too, **Alan Lloyd** returned to France.

14

DEATH ON THE SOMME

June–August 1916

*We're an old veteran crew, and we got a bad start and Leander got a bad
start, but in the end they won and we'll win and that's all there is to it.*
Letter from Alan Lloyd at the Somme to his wife, July 1916

On 3 June 1916, a train packed with British soldiers steamed through
the flat, spare landscape of Northern France, heading south from the
coast towards St-Omer. Inside sat **Alan Lloyd**, fresh off the boat from
England, in a clean, pressed uniform. With every inch of track, every
puff of steam and every pull of the pistons, Dorothy and eight-month-
old David receded further behind him.

Alan must also have been thinking of what lay ahead of him. The
signs of activity – the movement of men and horses and supplies – had
been obvious at the port and station. To the south, 11 Casualty Clearing
Stations had already been set up; 55 miles of new railway track had
been laid and 17 railheads had been built; roads had been put down
with chalk shipped over from Britain; underground tunnellers had been
at work preparing for the laying of mines; water pumps had been
shipped over and miles of pipes laid. Around 400,000 men and 100,000
horses would soon be assembled there.[1]

Later that day, Alan rejoined his battery in training at Bayenghem-
lès-Seninghem. The troops were not privy to the details of the plans
that were being made, but every man out in France knew that something
massive lay ahead.[2] For now, Alan was 70 miles away from the chosen
battle site. On his first day back, he was upbeat – or being positive for
Dorothy's sake:

Lovely day today tho' we've had showers. Much warmer than England and very sheltered in this little valley. The strenuous training was nicely over when your husband got back, so now he has a lovely slack time and does "damn all"! Does small wife know this expression? I hope not. Hubbins misses you awful. Never mind, get a nice little house and in 3 months back comes Hubbins.

Bye-bye ownest one, Love to David.[3]

A few days later, Alan and the 78th Brigade RFA received news of an imminent move – further south:

Wet day today. We're still in rest and I believe we may go into action soon. I hear it will be a very nice part of the line and I think we shall have a very good time. I hear we are for a cushy spot. So be cheery and your Hub will look after himself! You little angel wife bye-bye, Your own Hub.[4]

The same day that Alan wrote this letter, 8 June, the first trains loaded with ammunition arrived at the railheads in the assembly areas on the Somme. These wagonloads of shells were then taken, generally by teams of horses, to the artillery batteries that would be firing them. Almost all of these batteries were already in place.[5] Alan's would be on the move very soon, to join them.

Helen Bentwich was sitting in a train carriage, scribbling away. It was the crack of dawn, just before 6 a.m., and the first day's light was filtering through the window beside her. Like most Britons, she was still getting used to daylight-saving time, introduced in May. It was a wartime economy measure, and had caused much confusion and grumbling. It was Helen's first day of work at the Arsenal, and she was writing to her husband:

Train to Woolwich 5.45 a.m. fancy time. 4.45 a.m. real time.

My dearest Boy,

What's your definition of patriotism? Mine is turning out of a comfy bed at 5 a.m. and wandering off through pitch dark anti-Zeppelin streets to one's work. That's what I do now, with only one definite advantage in the shape of a ridiculously cheap workman's ticket which takes me from Notting Hill Gate to the Arsenal and back for 7d.

I'm absurdly excited to see what it's all going to be like – I couldn't sleep last night for excitement and for fear I'd not be able to do it. I've got all sorts of maths tables and things with me, to look impressive anyway. I change here – more later, when I know more where I am, and have more to say.

Mother told me not to forget I had a husband in the excitement of new work. Do you think I was likely to? Now I'm in the other train from Charing Cross. They took me in first, to keep the roughs out, they say. Only everybody seems a little drunk this time of the morning – I think it's the end of night work. It was nice coming up from the Embankment just as it was getting light. I'm enjoying this awfully.[6]

The train pulled into Woolwich Arsenal station, and Helen was one of hundreds of workers who poured onto the platform at the massive industrial complex. The site stretched for miles along the Thames, and was expanding all the time. Buildings housed gun factories, shell factories, chemical factories, textile factories, canteens, shops, stalls and hostels. It was only a year since women had been allowed through the gates; now a female superintendent had been appointed, and the numbers of women workers were growing every day. Helen, amongst the chaos of the morning crowds, made her way to the textile department where she would be working – from where she resumed her letter:

Later. Oh I've been waiting for such ages for somebody to come and talk to me and they won't come, so I'm going to talk to someone else instead, to while away the time. I'm sitting in the ante-room of the tailor's shop, along with 16 other females of various ages, degrees and sizes and nobody seems to want us. I wonder whether we will still be sitting here when you come home at the end of the war? Will you come to see my skeleton if we are?

Coming into here at 7 is like going into a huge fair. Crowds and crowds of men and women – chiefly women – pouring in to day and out from night work; strings of motor lorries, with soldiers on them; trains careering madly and imprudently wherever they choose all over the place and outside the gates, ice cream and milk and cheap sweet vendors galore. Plenty of love making of a serious kind goes on between the men and girls, as well as much chaff and cheap banter – but I suppose it's all inevitable. After all, I suppose it's not necessarily the highest type of human nature that comes as a factory hand or a cleaner to this old Arsenal.[7]

Helen's life was now tied up with the lives of such factory hands and cleaners. Everyone working the long hours in the hot, dangerous conditions at the Arsenal were united in a mammoth task: keeping the guns firing at the front.

Women munition workers finish small arms cartridges, Woolwich Arsenal, London.

Alan Lloyd and the 78th Brigade RFA had been on the move, marching south every day. On 18 June, they arrived at their destination: Ville sur Ancre, a few miles north of the Somme river.[8] Alan was set up in a tent on the wagon lines, where the horses were kept and along which supplies were moved. From there he wrote home for the first time in days:

Have had no time absolutely and no post for last few days. We are now in a very nice peaceful country, rolling hills and valleys and the Professor actually caught a fish in a stream here in the wagon lines yesterday. So cheer up, we're very fit and well. I am doing Captain work and am very comfy with a tent all to myself and no trenches to do so be cheery.

Bye-bye ownest, Hub.[9]

That same day, the 78th Brigade received the detailed orders for the bombardment to precede the assault. It was to be bigger than anything ever attempted before, with three times the number of guns that were engaged in the Battle of Loos. Following heavy losses at Verdun, Joffre had asked Haig to bring forward the Somme offensive in order to divert the enemy's attention and ease pressure on the French troops. A new date of 29 June was agreed for the infantry assault, with a five-day bombardment starting on 24 June – less than a week from the date that orders were given. Alan's battery was to be heavily involved in targeting the barbed wire of the German defences.[10]

Like Alan, Dorothy had been on the move: she'd travelled to Devon to look at houses for the family. She'd found one she liked in Shropshire – but Alan didn't seem too keen:

> Yes I think Church Stretton would be alright if Devon wasn't any good, but I much prefer Devon and Little Stretton is much better than Church Stretton which is a habitat for business men of Shrewsbury and Wolverhampton, and Birmingham tourists. Devon is far better and warmer in winter for David. By now you will be in Devon and I do hope you find something nice. There must be a little garden if possible where we can sit and gossip!
>
> Well beloved, things are quite quiet here and it is a nice peaceful spot miles and miles from anywhere we've been to before. How is your beloved self and David? I am very fit and well.[11]

Two summers before, Alan had been searching for a home for him and his young bride. Now his young bride was the mother of his child, bringing up their son without him, whilst Alan was 300 miles away, in a tent in a field in France, on the eve of the largest battle in human history.

A few days later, the War Committee met in London. The final go-ahead for the battle was yet to be given. The greatest fear for Asquith and his Cabinet was that they would face a repeat of the debacle at Loos and its political aftermath – all down to a shortage of shells.

At the meeting on 21 June, Lloyd George, Minister of Munitions (and later Secretary of State for War), was there to report to the committee. What he told them was music to their ears: in the year since he'd taken control, munitions production had soared. While France was making 20–30 heavy guns each month, British factories were now turning out 140–150. He reported that there would be enough shells for the artillery to fire almost 300,000 each week of the battle.[12] The only problem was, he admitted, a slight issue with fuses. But that was overlooked amongst the very 'great progress' he had to report, noted by the committee in its minutes.[13]

Helen Bentwich was at the coalface of Lloyd George's war production, and kept Norman informed about her new role as a supervisor in the textiles department:

Whew I'm hungry. It's now 12.30 and I've only had a cup of tea since 5. I've had a jolly morning. I'm in a department called the tailors shop where all that has to do with textiles takes place. My particular department is the testing room where every sample has to be tested. I'm to be in charge and there are about 9 or 10 men and the same number of girls (everything female in in the arsenal, even proud mothers, are girls) under me and two boys. They all call each other by their first names, not I, of course, as I'm the boss. I have to go through it all thoroughly. Today I was pulling sacking stuff to bits & testing its pulling strength.

It had been made clear to Helen the huge importance of the work that she and her team were doing:

The manager interviewed me yesterday evening and impressed on me the necessity for being accurate and checking everything. Apparently, we are known as the Royal Laboratories and everything used in any of the munitions factories in England in the way of textiles, paper, or leather, has to be examined here. And I'm between Scylla and Charybdis because if I let bad things pass I am too lenient, there'll be dud shells and internal explosions inside guns and all sorts of things. And if I refuse things without very good cause, then the contractors take it up before the chamber of commerce and if we are wrong – well, the manager explained we never had been wrong, so that was a reputation to live up to.[14]

There was more than Helen's department's reputation at stake, of course. Tough lessons had been learnt from the failures at Loos – failures that had cost thousands of lives and which it was hoped would never be repeated.

On 23 June, in the rolling countryside of the Somme Valley, thousands of men were on the move. Violent thunderstorms tore open the summer sky and rain poured down onto them as the ground became churned to mud. The communications trenches which had been dug to allow the troops to move into the front lines became flooded.[15]

Alan Lloyd and the 78th Brigade RFA were to go into action that day.[16] As they waited for the order to be given, Alan scribbled a note to Dorothy:

> Perhaps by now you're back at Clifford but I don't know so I'll send the letter there. Mails are a bit erratic at present so don't be alarmed if you don't get a letter for a bit.
>
> Interval while Hubbins gets his tea, 19 cherries, strawberries, 2 peaches and some cake! The doctor comes 'round and unfortunately being hungry eats two of Hub's peaches and some of his cake! The vet has also called in on his rounds and had two glasses of Hub's whiskey! Haven't I got a lot of callers Beloved, in my little tent in the wagon lines.
>
> Does you love Hubbins much or only a little bit? And do you think he's rather mad at present? Hurry up and get your house at Endleigh. I should like to feel you're settled in comfy with David.[17]

The next day, 24 June, the preliminary bombardment was to commence along the 15-mile front chosen for the attack. One thousand field guns had been amassed for the bombardment. The aim was to smash not just the frontline defences, but also the German second and third lines, to prepare for a possible breakthrough of the infantry followed by the cavalry. It was a massive job, and a strenuous time for men like Alan who would be manning the guns and observation posts.[18]

The 24th was a dull day, wet after the storm. Aircraft were not able to make the observations on enemy batteries as planned, but the bombardment commenced all the same. It continued the following day, and even intensified the next. The noise was incessant and so loud at times that no one and nothing else could be heard; the sky was lit up like a firework display.[19] Alan scribbled a note to his Dorothy amongst the maelstrom. She had taken a house and he was relieved:

> All well and flourishing here. Got no proper paper so have to use this. Am awfully glad you've got a house – a good little one. I want to come and live in it very badly please small wife. How's David?
>
> All well here tho lot of wet weather. It's really topping country here and we can get a gallop on the downs. It's spiffing after that beastly other country. All rolling undulating country and nice little villages.
>
> Tons of love, Your Hub.[20]

Patrols were sent to examine the damage being done to the enemy front lines: conflicting reports came in. The weather took a turn for the worse and misty mornings were followed by heavy rain. On the 28th, the day before the assault was due to commence, 'zero day' was put back because of the poor weather and due to questions over the effectiveness of the bombardment. That night, raiding parties found German trenches more strongly held than ever. Many of the shells being fired were duds; two-thirds were shrapnel, rather than high explosive.[21]

On 30 June the War Committee met again in London. A report was given of the situation on the Somme: 26 British divisions and 14 French divisions were ready to attack, facing only 6 German divisions. The final decision was given: the attack would go ahead the following day.[22] The reports of the state of the German wire varied. It was decided that there were gaps large enough to pass through in most places, though some reports were ominous.[23]

Dawn on 1 July 1916 revealed a beautiful summer's day. In his battery position, **Alan Lloyd** waited. His lucky charm from Dorothy hung around his neck. At 6.25 a.m. Alan and the 78th Brigade RFA commenced a bombardment of the German line in front of Fricourt, at precisely the same moment that their fellow artillery brigades opened fire on other areas. Nearly a quarter of a million shells were fired in the next hour, an average of 3,500 a minute. Beneath that din and hell, the infantry troops assembled in the trenches.[24]

At 7.28 a.m., less than two miles north of the 78th Brigade RFA battery position, a huge mine that had been placed beneath the German front lines was detonated. Earth was thrown 4,000 feet into the air. Alan would have felt the ground rock beneath him. Sixteen other mines went off elsewhere. At 7.30 a.m. his guns suddenly stopped firing, and all along the front there was silence. Then whistles signalled zero hour had come. Fifty-five thousand British and French soldiers climbed out of the trenches, from Gommecourt in the north to Maricourt in the south.[25]

A frame from the 'Battle of the Somme film', depicting troops going over the top, 1 July 1916.

The guns that fired that morning were so loud they could be heard on the other side of the Channel. In Great Leighs, **Andrew Clark** listened to the booming as it echoed over the summer fields, wondering exactly what the source was:

> All this morning the Flanders (as it is supposed) guns have been booming forth, making the house quiver at times and shaking window sashes. At 10 a.m. they made almost an uninterrupted roll of sound, like a long roll of distant thunder. The Post Office people say that 'it is unofficially reported that a big naval battle is raging in the North Sea.' Heavy concussions of big guns at a distance continue to shake the house.[26]

When the infantry soldiers of 11 British divisions climbed out over the top of the trenches and into no-man's-land, every man was carrying 66 pounds of equipment. Many of them had been instructed to walk at a steady pace over the battered ground to the German lines. Then, in the eerie silence after an unbroken seven-day bombardment, the German machine guns opened fire. Their defences were still intact.[27]

Arthur Burke of the 20th Battalion Manchester Regiment was in a section of the line near Fricourt. He was one of 100,000 British and French soldiers who waited, ready to advance in support of the first attack.[28] He went over the top much later in the day:

> We covered ourselves with glory, but we paid a terrible price. It was our colonel's idea that we should take it cool and easy, and go over at the slope, and this we carried out even so far as having cigarettes in our mouths.
>
> Not until 2.30 p.m. did they get the order to advance. All those weary hours the lads remained calm, but very eager to get it over. They did not go over after a strong ration of rum as some people imagine these affairs are carried out, no, they went over feeling themselves. The colonel watched them mount the steps, and his last remarks were 'Isn't it wonderful'. The way they walked over at the slope one would have thought they were at Belton Park or our other training quarters. Our reserves were calling out 'Bravo Manchesters' 'Good Luck' 'Cheer-oh' and every word of praise that such calmness could bring to their minds. Down they fell one by one.
>
> It was Hell, being so late in the day many of the devils were taken unawares, and were asleep in their dug-outs. We thro' bombs of every description down, smoke bombs especially, and as the hounds came up, crawling half dead, we stuck the blighters and put them out of time. In one dug out there were about 25 in, and we set the place on fire, we spared them no mercy, they don't deserve it. They continued sniping as we were advancing until we reached them, and then they thro' up their hands 'Merci Camerade', we gave them mercy – I don't think. We captured many guns, all sorts of souvenirs, but the souvenir I treasure most is my life, pray to God and thank him for sparing me, such mercy.[29]

There were more than 57,000 British casualties that day, of whom a third were killed. On two-thirds of the front, the advancing troops were met with machine-gun fire and fell in droves, not making their objectives. The British assault on the line near Fricourt and Mametz was successful, and the French had successes to the south. But the great breakthrough had not materialised.

More soldiers had been killed in that single day than in the first four months of war.[30]

That was not the news that reached Britain. The following morning, **Andrew Clark** took his usual Sunday service at St Mary's Church in Great Leighs. The congregation was animated:

> Sunday 2 July: All the village was talking about 'the good news' of last night, the 'push' of the British troops in Flanders (apparently successful) begun.[31]

In the window of the village post office, Saturday's official news bulletin confirmed the rumours of good news from France:

> British Official: Attack launched 7.30 a.m. north of Somme combined with French. British broken into German forward system on 16 mile front. French attack equally satisfactory. Remainder front successful British raiding parties.[32]

The villagers of Great Leighs could not know the catastrophic cost of human life that lurked behind those simple sentences.

As the battle raged across the channel, positive reports of Allied gains continued to be circulated in Britain. Then the telegrams began to arrive. **Diana Manners'** sister, Letty, received news on 3 July that her husband Hugo Charteris, who had been missing, was dead.[33] It was yet another loss for **Duff Cooper'**s circle of friends:

> I met Diana here at a quarter to one. She had had such a sad time with Letty. She lay in my arms and sobbed . . . I nearly cried too.[34]

He wrote to Diana that evening:

My own darling – I am so sorry. Oh the cruelty of life. I am almost
crying at the thought of you and poor darling Letty. I wrote to her this
afternoon and told her to hope; now I have nothing to tell her except
to give her my love and sympathy which are so useless. Oh dear, miserable we shall all be. Duff.[35]

The next day, the first wounded from the Somme arrived back in
Britain.[36]

Alan Lloyd had had a busy few days. After the failures in other parts
of the line, British efforts were focused on the southern sector he had
moved to, near Mametz. Just after midnight on 5 July, they began a
concentrated bombardment of the next German line, then lifted it to
allow for a surprise infantry assault. In the rain and darkness, many
units charged into the enemy lines, but the key objectives – including
Mametz Wood – were not gained.

After another day's fighting, Alan's battery moved forward again.
The bombardment continued.[37] Alan found a moment to write to
Dorothy for the first time since the battle had commenced six days
earlier. He can't have had much sleep and must have been running on
adrenalin:

> We are very flourishing and are not having a bad time at all. It's great
> sport advancing over the Hun trenches and I hope it will continue. It's
> also much more comfortable because the Hun has to take back his heavy
> gun and has only small stuff against us. And we go for him with heavier!
> Lots of loot in the Hun's country and the Professor pokes about in the
> Hun Dug-Outs for all sorts of nick-nacks! So don't be uneasy about
> your hub.
>
> The photographs of David were topping. The whole mess roared with
> laughter when they saw his pugnacious expression![38]

The Battle of the Somme had become a daily struggle for woods and
villages, and Mametz Wood was the largest on the Somme. The intelligence reports suggested that there were only 15 German battalions on
that part of the line, and that they'd suffered heavily. The reality was that
there were 33, and 40 more close at hand. But at 2 a.m. on 7 July, an
infantry attack was commenced. The artillery barrage continued over the

following three days, and the infantry captured some of the wood.[39] Whereas many infantry soldiers were pulled out of the battle after a week, Alan had now been in the midst of the fighting for ten days straight:[40]

> We are quite alright tho' of course have had a hard time. Still, it hasn't been nearly so rough as it might have been and we have done pretty well so far and hope to do better still. Probably they'll relieve us shortly. We are all very cheery and bright so don't fret your little self beloved. The Hun is having a rocky time with the French and us and the Russians all together. He shoved in the Prussian Guard when we'd burst through his first line the other day to try and stop us going further. But we got on to them with machine guns and nearly annihilated them. They had to go out and reform and did no good at all.[41]

By 12 July the whole of Mametz Wood was in British hands. Hundreds of British soldiers had died for it, thousands more had been wounded.[42] The commander-in-chief, Sir Douglas Haig, was pleased with how the battle was progressing. He started to plan the next phase: sending in the cavalry.[43] The focus was now on the enemy's second line, with an assault scheduled to begin on 14 July. Alan Lloyd and the 78th RFA kept up a continual barrage over the days leading up to it.

Then, in the darkness before dawn on the 14th, an intense five-minute bombardment of the German second line preceded an infantry assault by 48,000 men.[44] This time, Alan was not manning the guns behind – he was with the advancing soldiers, rushing forwards in the night, signalling back to his battery. He didn't tell Dorothy, but he did write about it to his brother Eric:

> I have been over several times, once in the big attack on his 2nd line which was very successful. On this occasion I was right up with the infantry and got a machine gun bullet thro' my tunic on the right elbow, it tore the shirt and vest and never scratched the skin! This was a very exciting day and I enjoyed myself. I was signalling back by flag. Topping weather now and I'm on great form.[45]

The wood and village of Bazentin was taken. It was a longed-for success, seeming to suggest lessons had been learnt from the massacre of 1 July.[46] But, from there, the British push forward was met with stiff resistance. In four days there were 10,000 casualties.

Nearby High Wood was on a slight hill; it therefore had huge tactical significance, and became the new target. The infantry briefly took it, but a German counter-attack won it back. The fighting there ground on for days. On 20 July, the British infantry retook it. Alan had now been in the midst of battle for twenty continuous days, on top of the seven-day bombardment he'd carried out prior to that:

> I keep on looking at the photos of little David and I think he looks an awful little sportsman and you can see he loves the dogs and doesn't care a button what they do. His face when Spot surfaces to play with him is topping and he's wise to like old Rodger the best for he's far and away the best of them and a great old aristocrat in his way. I can see he's awful fond of little David. His great big fists and puckered forehead are ripping and I know how you'll love watching him grow up – and so will Hub.
>
> Here we are going strong and peppering the Hun night and day, very hard work it is, continuous shooting, but I think he's giving way alright. We are gradually beginning to slowly heave him back and after a while he may very likely go with a run. We got a very important wood last night, without much resistance, and his counter attacks are not what they were. Hub will bring you and David a little souvenir if he can, and in fact has got a nice little one already.
>
> Bye-bye ownest. Don't worry at all for Hub thrives on this hard life.[47]

But High Wood was lost again. The attacks and counter-attacks continued. The bombardment continued. Finally, on 23 July, after 30 days in action, Alan and the 78th Brigade RFA were relieved. At 11 p.m. that night, they marched five miles in the darkness to Dernancourt, and sleep, though the noise of battle still reached them.[48]

As July came to a close, the reality of the cost of the Somme offensive started to dawn on people. The wounded had come back in their thousands; there were also the dreaded telegrams. Due to the local patterns of recruitment (and especially the 'pals battalions', when men served alongside their friends and colleagues), many communities were devastated by a single day of fighting.[49]

On a weekend at her family's country estate in Chesham, Buckinghamshire, **Helen Bentwich** reflected on the bleak mood. Her own brother Ellis, at war, was safe for now, but human life seemed increasingly disposable:

> Today has been rather a black one in the village, as the loved battalion of territorials has just been badly cut up. Sir Arthur's adopted son has been badly wounded & the vicar's son is killed & Mary Hancock's young man is badly wounded too & his brother is killed. And many other local people also. It seems so ghastly coming together like this, doesn't it?
>
> I saw an officer from Ellis' regiment; 25 officers went in – they were the first over the trenches in our attack at Fricourt – & only 100 men & 1 NCO came out. Fortunately, many were only wounded. But a great many have been killed. Now Ellis writes they are behind the line & out of things for a while. I suppose they are too cut up to go on. And it seems to be going to end in a second Verdun doesn't it! People seem to be losing their first optimism – wondering how long we will be able to throw away troops at this rate.[50]

Great Leighs was also dealing with the first of the losses from the Somme. At the end of July, **Andrew Clark** was in Oxford, but his daughter Mildred maintained his notes for him:

> <u>Wednesday 26 July:</u> Two boys connected with these parts have lost their lives in the 'big push.' (a) Victor Carpenter, in the Somersets, son of the housekeeper at Little Leighs rectory. (b) – Fitch. The family is a large one consisting of 12 children. They have lost heavily in the war – one son was killed at the front in 1914, a second son went down with his ship the Formidable. Yet a fourth son when home on leave was out with a gun, which exploded and badly damaged his right hand.[51]

Many Great Leighs boys were also due to go out for the first time to take the places of the men already lost:

> Charlie Collins is coming home on leave. He is under orders for France, but doesn't want his mother to know til he has started. Major Bibben Allen, of Black Notley, says that there are a million men, almost fully trained, who will be sent out almost at once.[52]

*

Alan Lloyd was finally in rest. Three days into this stint of relative peace and safety, Alan received notification that he had been awarded the Military Cross, recognising acts of gallantry in the field:

> *NOTICE OF MILITARY CROSS: TEMP LIEUT A S LLOYD*
> *Always ready to volunteer for dangerous work. Absolutely fearless and can*
> *always be depended on to carry out orders under most difficult circumstances*
> *and has also made bold reconnaissance and shown pure initiative.*[53]

Sitting in the sunshine, the boom of guns at a safe distance a few miles away, Alan's mind wandered. Back to an old life; a life before world war and 18-pounder guns and 60,000 casualties on a single day. He thought of the Thames, and well-dressed ladies and gentlemen on its banks at Henley, and the glint of summer sunshine on the water, and the rhythmic plunge of oars into its sparkling surface. The dull barrage of shells in the distance became the cheers of the crowd:

> There are a lot of indications that the war will not last a vast time longer. I think the Hun is getting enough of it now. We've got the race well in hand, but as we quicken the stroke a really good crew has its work cut out to keep well together – and that's what we've got to do. Remember, the Hun boat cracked opposite the Grand Stand when to all appearances it was as fresh as Leander and then it went with a punt.
>
> So cheer up! We're a big heavy boat, and clumsy, but we're going well together now and the coaches on the bank seem to know what they're driving at and when to give her ten slick 'uns. The people in the Grand Stand are beginning to stand up, ready to yell, and we're going up, my dear, up, up, up! I can almost see the crowd again – Leander, Le-an-der, well rowed Leander, you have them, shove 'em in! Got 'em by Gad! And the terrific crash of God Save the King as Leander rows in ahead. We're an old veteran crew, and we got a bad start, and Leander got a bad start, but in the end they won, and we'll win and that's all there is to it.
>
> Bye-bye my ownest, I just adore you.
>
> Hub.[54]

On 1 August, Alan and the 78th Brigade RFA went back into action. Just before they set off, the heat of the day fading, the light flattening out on the countryside around them, Alan scribbled Dorothy another note:

Just a scrawl to say all well and flourishing and still comfortably in rest. Awful hot and dusty but much better than rain. You'll be in Devon now I expect, I wish your Hub was there too. What a time we'd have and we'd bathe together and do all sorts of funny things there! Bye-bye, beloved.[55]

At 6 p.m. they set off, marched for ten miles and took up position behind the line at Longueval. Alan's lucky charm from Dorothy was, as ever, around his neck.[56]

In early August, Dorothy was in Devon. She'd finally found a house, at Budleigh Salterton, a pretty little seaside town on the south coast with a stretch of pebbly beach. David was now almost a year old. The only thing missing, of course, was her husband. One morning in early August, she got a letter from him: a muddy, scribbled note. It was a small piece of war in her hand, out of place in the tranquillity of an English seaside resort at summertime:

Excuse this dirty paper but war is war and dust is dust and here we've plenty of both and very warm too, little wife, hot as heaven! You thought I was going to say something else but I wasn't. Please would you like Hubbins with you at Salterton? Cause he'd like to be there. Here, we go steadily on bit by bit, smashing the Hun with guns of all sorts and the heavier accounted for 31 batteries yesterday which is awful good.

Please, is small wife very well and David too?[57]

In August, **Duff Cooper** and **Diana Manners** got the news that Basil Hallam, the music-hall star and Diana's suitor of the previous summer, was dead. He had fallen from a balloon whilst conducting observations over the Somme battlefield. Diana was very upset at this, the latest in her litany of loss.[58] And just a few weeks later, while Duff was attempting a holiday in Scotland, the war dealt them the greatest blow yet:

I felt depressed and was still more so on arriving at Glasgow after nine to find that it was too late to get anything to drink. I had an indifferent dinner at the Great Central Hotel and afterwards, looking at the news telegrams in the hall, saw 'Prime Minister's Eldest Son Killed in Action'.

It was the worst shock I have ever had. I shall never forget that awful moment or that horrible place. What an end to what a day! I wished I were with Diana to comfort her. She will be very miserable and all alone.[59]

Raymond Asquith had been yet another of their close friends. He was married, but Diana had always been a little in love with him – Duff only realised how much so when she wrote to him that night, desolate, inconsolable:

Oh my sweet Duff. I would really as soon be dead – Raymond killed – my divine Raymond – killed – has hung in my head for twenty-four hours – and tonight it's all coloured and true. I don't think you know how I adored Raymond – certainly he didn't – more perhaps than you – so had you not known him his loss might have been your gain but, knowing him, there is no gain in possessing the world if he is not in it.

As to you my Duff you know that whatever you feel I feel it for you – and love you always. Diana.[60]

At 9.21 a.m. on 8 August, a black-rimmed telegraph was received at the post office in Edgbaston Grove, Birmingham.

Its contents were brutal in their simplicity:

TELEGRAM from London War Office – 8th August 1916
To Mrs Lloyd, Edgbaston Grove, Birmingham
Deeply regret to inform you that Lieut. A S Lloyd was killed in action August 4th
The army council express their sympathy. Secretary War Office have not informed Mrs Alan.[61]

The news that shattered **Dorothy Lloyd**'s world reached Budleigh Salterton post office at 6.57 p.m. that evening, passed on by Alan's parents. Shortly afterwards, in the dying light of a summer's day, it was delivered to Dorothy's new home by the sea.[62]

A few days later, with Alan's parents now at her side, Dorothy received a letter from France. It was from Alan's closest friend in the battery,

Mark II. She opened the envelope and unfolded the letter. Inside it was hidden Alan's lucky charm:

Dear Mrs. Mark I,

Before you get this, I hope you will have been told that poor dear old Mark I was killed very early yesterday morning. I know only too well that nothing I can say at all can make any difference to what you will feel. The loss to me personally makes me feel done right in – I couldn't tell you how much it means to me. Feeling as I do, I am able to realize, I think, how terrible it will be for you. He often used to talk to me about you, and I think that I, probably more than anyone else but you yourself, know how much you meant to him, and how true he was to you.

I have read letters written at times like this that didn't sound quite true, and I don't want to convey the impression that I am writing in that spirit – it would be an insult to his memory and to you. But it is the simple truth that he was the bravest man I ever knew. During the time he's been out in France he has done far more than his share of the nasty jobs, and has done far more than many men who have got DSOs. It is easy to say these things, isn't it, but in this case my feeling is that it would be wrong not to, because you will be proud of the knowledge confirmed of what I expect you already guessed, and you and he have a son who will want to become as fine a man as his father was, and will be proud to know what his father's pals thought of him, and in saying this I am saying what I know is thought by every one in the brigade.

He was up at the observation post with Marshall, at night, relieving me there. It had been fairly quiet all day, and I never expected they would have a bad time, but they did – one gun kept on dropping near them, and the wire was cut, so he went out with another officer to mend it. They hadn't gone 50 yards when a whizz bang dropped right in amongst them. Poor old Alan was very badly hit. He never had a dog's chance, and died in about 20 minutes. He was quite conscious, and asked if he was badly hit – they told him no, and he seemed quite happy and in no pain, and said he would be all right soon. He never knew what was really the matter, and died without knowing what was happening. Yateman was badly wounded and two of the signallers, and the rest went away for help. Eventually whilst they were away (all this happened in the dark) someone came along and took all the things in his pockets, and his watch, I think they must have taken them to hand in to someone and I am trying to trace them. The enclosed I found as I knew he had it and looked first for it.

We got him back to the battery, and eventually right back to a military cemetery behind shell fire. I am just back from his funeral. About 40 from the battery were there and I have arranged for a plain oak cross to be made by the wheeler – I didn't like the crosses provided by the cemetery people – and I am having this inscription put on it:

IN
LOVING MEMORY
OF
LIEUT. ALAN S LLOYD
C battery 78 Bge RFA
KILLED IN ACTION, AUGUST 4 1916

I don't think I can say anything else now, no loss that I have had to stand has ever affected me as much as this because I was so very fond of old Mark I. He was a brave man and died a brave man's death. I know that you are brave too, and will be proud of him, but I know too that nothing can soften the blow of losing a fellow as good as he was. And I am very, very sorry, I won't say the conventional things, I'm sure you know what I do feel and I want to say, only words won't convey it, so I won't try.

Yours ever, Arthur E. Impey[63]

Aged 30, Dorothy was now a single mother and a widow. Alan had died aged 27, killed two years to the day into the war.

His lucky charm was cold in Dorothy's hand.

15
BROKEN BODIES
October–November 1916

It's all so terrible and unnecessary . . . it's just a vast, crushing war-machine.
Helen Bentwich, letter to her husband, October 1916

More than a million soldiers, from all sides, were dead or wounded when the battle of the Somme limped to a close on 18 November. Over the course of the four-and-a-half-month-long campaign, the War Office sent 420,000 telegrams (for officers) and letters (for other ranks) to homes across Britain, notifying families that their loved ones had been killed, wounded or were missing.[1] Almost 100,000 men were dead.[2]

Of those soldiers who did survive, some would never be the same again. The wounded arrived back in Britain from early July: men without limbs; men blinded; men maimed for life. Men bearing the scars of war became a feature of daily life at home. **Hallie Miles** was deeply moved whenever she encountered them:

It is impossible to tell all the touching and heroic stories of courage and patience that we come across in our work. At one of our last Patriotic Teas a young soldier beckoned me with his head and eyes to come to him; I went to speak to him, and he whispered to me 'would one of your young ladies feed me, please? I have no arms!' I went up to one of our waitresses and asked her if she would, but we both cried so that we had to hide ourselves for a few minutes. Then one of the waitresses came to me and asked if she might feed him. The soldier who sat next to this armless hero was so tender too and held the cup of tea for him to drink from, and put bits of cake into his mouth.[3]

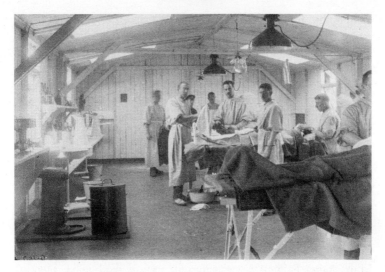

An operating theatre suite at No 3 Casualty Clearing Station on the Somme.

Injuries on this unprecedented scale triggered medical innovation. Roehampton Hospital opened in summer 1915 as a specialist treatment centre to cater for some of the quarter of a million men who underwent an amputation after injury over the course of the war. At Roehampton thousands of amputees were fitted with prosthetic limbs and taught how to use them. It marked a watershed in the rehabilitation of disabled Britons.[4] It was not the only pioneering medical institution set up. In early 1916, a young army surgeon from New Zealand, **Harold Gillies,** was given a ward at Cambridge Military Hospital in Aldershot to experiment with new methods of treating the facial wounds that were so common in trench warfare. It was the first plastic surgery ward in the British Empire. Gillies was just 33 years old when his radical work began:

> My days and nights were filled with a steady flow of injuries. I just had to go ahead with the ingenuity of my own mind and the principles of surgery behind it. Little by little those principles evolved.
>
> All the time, we were fumbling towards new methods and new results. My small staff and I felt that we were on trial.[5]

The steady flow of injuries turned into a torrent after 1 July 1916. Gillies had been allocated an additional 200 beds in anticipation of the increased patient numbers in the wake of the Battle of the Somme. But 2,000 new patients arrived – and the challenges they presented him with were unprecedented:[6]

> There were wounds far worse than anything we had met before. Men without half their faces: men burned and maimed to the condition of animals. Day after day, the tragic, grotesque procession made its way towards us.[7]

So disfigured were these men that mothers in Aldershot would call their children inside when the patients were out in the town, to prevent them seeing their wounds and scars.[8]

Amongst Gillies's very first patients was **Reg Evans**. Reg had arrived in the spring, before the onslaught of men from the Somme. His new home in Aldershot was just 50 miles from his home town, Hemel Hempstead. Ernest Kent, his boss at the brush factory where he had worked in his distant civilian life, was one of his first visitors. After Mr Kent had left his bedside, Reg wrote to his mother in excellent spirits:

> Dear Mother,
>
> I was jolly pleased to get a letter from you today and do hope you are really getting better. The idea of you referring to me as being 'bedded down' allows me to inform you that I am up all day now. But before I get any further I must tell you about Mr Kent's visit today. He was very kind indeed and so surprised to find me as well as I was. Mrs Kent had sent a lovely huge bunch of daffodils and he had bought me several books and in case I was short of money he also gave me a pound. I really don't know what I have done to deserve such kindness.[9]

In spite of his good cheer, Reg was in a bad state. His upper lip had been blown away. Not treated in France, it had partially healed; now there was a distorted, dysfunctional mass where his mouth had once been.[10] Gillies would do what he could, but he was working in a brand-new field, by guesswork and intuition as much as knowledge.

*

Dorothy Lloyd was still reeling from the news of Alan's death and trying to find solace in his heroism. On 1 September, less than a month after Alan's death, it was the second anniversary of their wedding. She spent it with her mother-in-law at Torquay, and wrote to her on her return home:

> My dearest little mother,
>
> I did so love being at Torquay and I'm sure it did me good and it helped me over the 1st too, though it was agony living through it without him but I still feel his wonderful love for me just as I did when he was alive and I know that will never leave me – and every hour that goes past shortens the time of waiting.
>
> I've had another letter from Capt. Marshall sending me the original wire announcing the award of the military cross. The colonel had asked him to send it to me and on it the colonel has written 'thank God he has left a son, let him always know what we all thought of his father.' Captain Marshall says that Gunner Manning has gone sick with shell shock but that before he left he wrote in pencil on the cross they put up: 'He died as he lived, a splendid English gentleman, brave and fearless to the end.'
>
> How Allie would love to know, and he did know, how his men idolized him. Oh, how proud I am – I never dreamed how it could make me feel so sort of uplifted and able to face the world with my head up. And oh, how he is helping me and I have got to live so that when I go to him he will praise me as he always did – he seems even closer than he has ever been now, and when I am quite alone I almost feel he answers my thoughts.[11]

Helen Bentwich was lying in bed in her townhouse near Hyde Park in London. It was late on a Sunday morning, and she was making the most of a day off, writing a long letter to her husband Norman in Egypt. Helen had herself come into contact with the horrors of total war of late, far from the battlefields of France. She'd been at the other end of the war machine, and needed to share her traumatic experiences with someone. She began:

> 'Pack up your troubles', that's one the boys sing on the night shifts and very useful it is at times. I like my job mostly as I'm always telling

you. And that's no swank but honest injun truth. So don't think I'm not happy there because of some of the things I'm going to tell you. You see, they don't affect me in the least, but it's all so very, very ghastly and ugly and tragic for the poor devils in the shops and at the machines who can't leave there and go any place where they work them less hard if they want because of the Defence of the Realm act and who are worked and worked until they drop by their machines, really and literally.

I think something that happened on Wednesday brought it home to me more than anything, what a hell life was for some of them. It was an awfully hot, muggy night and the factory was simply fugged up with bad air. One old cobbler collapsed by his machine and they carried him out. It was the third time he'd done it and he was always allowed back to the same job, without anyone caring. Three or four girls fainted and then at five in the morning, we heard that some poor devil just couldn't stand it any longer. He ran outside with one of his tools in the dinner hour and trying it first on his hand and arm to see it was sharp enough, he then cut his throat for 5 inches and when he was found he was still alive. One of the lads found him.

The horrid callousness of it all – nobody properly in charge, no proper first aid outfit, the difficulty of getting the train, nobody to quiet down the girls, who were all in groups discussing it with white faces. I felt as bad as any of them, I couldn't get it out of my mind and got that sort of feeling inside that makes you feel like a squashed bicycle-tire. And – worst of all – to be told that was nothing very new and that there are many cases of suicide each week in the arsenal. It's all so terrible and unnecessary and comes from the fact that the whole thing is impersonal and callous and nobody cares about the individual, it's just a vast, crushing war-machine.[12]

Another summer had passed in Great Leighs; another harvest had been brought in, with difficulty in the absence of so many of the farm workers. It was over two years since the first Great Leighs boy, Arthur Fitch, had been killed. Now his two brothers were also dead; and a further six young men from the village had been sacrificed to the war.[13]

At the end of October, **Andrew Clark** himself had cause to be at the local undertaker's parlour, in Chelmsford. His wife Mary had died at home, after a long and painful illness. She was 65.[14] Andrew did not allow himself to indulge in personal sadness in his war diary. But he did note down what was of interest in terms of war news: so many local people had lost their sons and husbands that the undertakers were overwhelmed:

> Recent casualties have been heavily felt in Chelmsford and district. The undertaker Mr Bond said this forenoon that the mourning orders during the last three months had been overwhelming. They cannot get in materials fast enough to meet the demand.[15]

Andrew Clark returned home to the rectory, standing dark and silent in the Autumn afternoon. His wife was not there to greet him. His male staff was long gone; the pony and trap were up for sale; his grounds were overgrown and wild. He saw only ghosts there now.

Just a few miles east of Great Leighs was Witham. In a muddy field at the back of the town, a crowd of army tents withstood the unsettled autumn weather.[16] This was the new home of the Royal Devon Yeomanry, in training for the front. On this blustery October evening, the notes of an enthusiastically bashed piano were ringing out from the YMCA hut on site, where most of the men were gathered, including **Will Martin**, who was writing a letter.

Will was a 19-year-old lad from Cornwall, a farm worker who had lived with his aunt near the quiet town of Helston before the war. He'd volunteered for service in 1915, and had spent this past summer stationed at Thorndon Park, just outside Brentwood. There he had met a young servant, called Emily, and it was to her that he was writing that evening:

> My Dearest Emily
>
> We have arrived at Witham. We have got tents and also a plenty of mud. It is very inconvenient here, there is no place to have a wash even, so I had to come into Witham, and have a wash at a public house, with several others, and to be honest I had a port and lemon.
>
> It is sickening, to be out here, and to be thinking of you, and not able to see you. You must forgive me if I was reserved on Tuesday night. I wanted to say a lot, but I knew that you couldn't stand it, I didn't want to make it worse for you. I know, dear Emily, that you do not doubt me, but I want to reassure you that you are the only girl I love. I may

make a muddle of things but I am sure dear that you will understand me.

You must excuse mistakes, as there isn't half a din going on here, what with the piano playing, chaps playing games and clapping – you can just fancy what it is like. It will be an awful suspense until I get a letter from you, but I don't know of anything more to write, so I will conclude with fondest love and kisses.[17]

The letter arrived the following day at the large farmhouse in Herongate where **Emily Chitticks** worked. Emily was also 19, and lived just up the road with her family. Her father was a farm labourer.[18] Will's presence nearby had brightened up her otherwise rather routine life over the past few months, and she was ecstatic to receive a letter from him:

My Dearest Will,

I was so delighted to receive your letter this morning to hear that you are arrived at Witham quite safely. I do miss you terribly Will, but it won't be for long will it, dear? So I must try and cheer up until you come back. I am so sorry to hear that you are having such a hard time of it. I don't blame you for having that port and lemon as I am sure you were in need of it, and I know very well you would not take more than was good for you.

You are everything to me, and I don't know what I should do without you, I only wish that this wretched war was over. We shall not have to part from each other so much then, shall we? It was terrible parting from you on Tuesday, Will, I am glad you didn't say much to me, as I could not have borne it. I tried to be cheerful, Will, for your sake, because I could see that you felt the parting as keenly as I did.

You know dear, although I have talked to one or two different boys, you are the only one that I have ever loved with my whole heart and soul, and if anything came to part me from you now, Will, I believe it would kill me. I feel more convinced than ever that we are made for each other, don't you dear?[19]

Harold Gillies was under tremendous pressure to fix the patients on his ward. Not least so they could be sent back out to fight as quickly as possible, and to make room for the new patients that were streaming in all the time. Of course, he was also painfully aware that the future of each of his patients depended entirely on the pioneering work he was doing – not just to make them healthy again, but also to make them socially acceptable.

Reg Evans's injury was not one of the most extreme Gillies would confront – some men had most of their faces blown away – but it was very complicated, because of the functionality of the upper jaw as well as its aesthetic importance:

> In comparing it with lower lip repair, it would seem to me that the shortening of the upper lip is a much greater defect than a similar shortening of the lower. In a few words it is quite possible to sew up a lower lip which has lost nearly a third of its bulk without causing a serious functional or aesthetic deformity, whereas a similar loss of the upper lip cannot be produced without very serious impairment of function, accompanied by a most unpleasant effect.[20]

However, Reg was in reasonably good spirits, as always. His mother had now been down to see him from Hemel Hempstead, though she was still unwell herself. Typically, he was more worried about her health than his own judging from his letters to her:

> We have spent hours on those puzzles between us and had a lot of sport over them. I was sorry you were not up to the mark on Wednesday and you must not think of coming down again yet as I am afraid it is too much for you. I will make haste and get better so that I can come home, don't you worry about me for I am alright.
>
> I am enclosing a little snapshot one of the nurses took the other day, which reminds me you must have taken that photo of me away with you on Wednesday.
>
> Well goodnight and I do hope you are better, but don't attempt to come down again yet as I am sure it is too much of a strain on you. Perhaps I shan't be so very long before I get home for a bit.[21]

However, good spirits could not alter the medical reality. In a few days' time, Reg would be undergoing his first major operation at Gillies's hands. Neither of them knew how it would turn out.

*

Helen Bentwich was on her lunch break at the Arsenal. The din of the machines could be heard, even in the canteen – though the piano-player and singers were doing their best to drown it out. Helen was sitting separately from the mass of men and women, writing to her husband Norman:

> Being here I seem to see a good deal of the back-wash and underside of war. I think I'd sooner be a soldier than a munitions worker, if I had leanings towards being a conscientious objector. It seems more personal and less conscientious and calculating. I am confident that democracy and brotherhood will be the outcome of this war. We must just do our little bit, this has to come to an end – and then we'll be rebels for all we are worth.
>
> But I don't seem to be able to put my thoughts down clearly here – a piano playing rag-time and talk and joking going on all around. You say I must waste my rest-time writing to you – but it's the only pleasure in life now.[22]

Helen had previously done more than most people of her social background to help the poor but she had never before experienced the privations of their daily lives at such close quarters. Helen might have had a mansion house on Hyde Park to retreat to, but she shared their working hours. She was increasingly shocked by the lack of concern for the individual – and starting to wonder what she could do to help. She wrote to Norman a few weeks later, at the end of October:

> I'm again in bed after finishing off my week's night work – and again bubbling over with righteous indignation at the arsenal scandals. One feels impotent – nobody seems to bother or take any notice. You see the work in the shops is well supervised, but outside it's a little hell. Last night, for instance, when we went in, there was mud and water inches deep which couldn't be helped. There were deep trenches by the side of our road which weren't lit up. There were surging crowds of girls coming and girls coming out and a rowdy, ganging crowd of men wanting for their pay. Then, four or five huge trucks were driven right through the crowd – the result, one girl ran over and badly injured and one fell into the trench and broke her leg. A girl elsewhere in the arsenal fell into a vat of boiling water coming from the canteen in the dark and died. The arsenal was censored for gross negligence at the inquest. But it does no good.

You don't mind if I get mixed up in rows and things about the munitions workers, do you? It's all in a good cause and I've got better opportunities than anybody else! They can't shoot me up and if I do go to prison – well it's all experience. Still I don't expect I'll get as far as that and it's all swank really, because I've done nothing but talk yet.[23]

Reg Evans had left his bed on the ward for the first time in ten days. He was recovering from a major operation on his injured jaw and mouth. He seemed to think it had gone well – or at least that is the news he reported to his mother:

I am up today as I have had all the stitches out of my face, which feels a lot better in consequence, and it is only a question of a few days before I have my final operation. You will see that under the circumstances it will not be worthwhile coming down again, but if you are sending I should be glad of some cigarettes.[24]

His operation was not the only excitement he'd experienced in recent days. Gillies's pioneering work was attracting attention – and Reg, as one of his current patients, was getting his share of it too:

On Thursday The King and Queen came without a minutes notice. They only came into No 1 and 2 wards to see the face cases and they came separately to each patient and spoke to them. They were as nice as could be and it was all so informal. They just drove up and said they wanted to see the 'plastics' wards (that's us) and were shown along. Somebody ran for the Colonel, somebody else for the matron but they (the King and Queen) were in our ward before they arrived. Capt. Gillies was doing an operation at the time but came up later and the King said how interested he was in his work and how splendid it was to think that men who might have been hideously disfigured for life could now look forward with hope to the future. Of course yours truly came in for a little attention, just a little informal presentation, my dear, that's all – still it's stimulating isn't it?[25]

However the operation might have gone, his recovery did not go well: just days later, Reg contracted bronchitis. His body rejected the dental shield Gillies had made for his new lip, and the coughing undid a lot of the careful work Gillies had attempted. Reg was seriously ill.[26]

Emily Chitticks had also had some excitement – **Will Martin** had sneaked out of camp to come and see her:

> Oh you reckless boy coming out of camp when you ought not to, I am afraid I shall have to severely reprimand you when you come home again!
>
> Sometimes it seems too good to be true that one day I shall have a home of my own and a dear good man like you to love and be loved by. I often wonder what the future really holds for us, I wonder where we shall live, and all sorts of different things, don't you? I think it is wonderful how we came together. The more I think of it the more wonderful it seems. Well you know, dear, I hadn't been talking to you long the first evening we met before the thought came to me that you were the boy that I could really love, and it has been proved right.[27]

Will was now back at Witham. He was finding army life boring, and missed his new love:

> I'll see whether you will reprimand me when I come back or not, I'll be on my guard, and I guess you won't catch me napping very many times, or if you do it will be something unusual!
>
> Well little girl it is a very great pleasure to be writing a letter to you, it occupies my thoughts, and it makes me wish that I was back in Herongate. Never mind, dear Emily, it won't be for ever, that is one consolation, but it was hard to part. I don't see any reason why we should not be happy together, dear, for as long as we have known each other, we have always agreed together. You are already mapping out the future in your imagination and I must own that my thoughts have corresponded with yours, on more than one occasion. It will be a happy day when the war is over, and we shall meet again darling, to part no more as we have to be parted from each other now. I can manage well enough during the day when I have work to do to occupy my thoughts, but the evenings are monotonous.[28]

*

Reg Evans's plastic surgery was put on hold whilst he battled his illness, and he was moved out of the specialist ward to an auxiliary hospital at Waverley Abbey. There, his health took a turn for the worse: his bronchitis developed into septic pneumonia.[29] The chaplain at the hospital kept his mother informed of his progress, and in mid-August he was pleased to be able to give her better news:

> Dear Mrs Evans,
>
>   You will be glad to hear that your son at Waverley is getting on splendidly – I saw him yesterday walking about on the cricket field and in very good spirits. I go off on Wednesday for 12 days' leave, but hope that you will be able to come over on my return, if not before then.
>
>   Yours sincerely, B K Cunningham[30]

A few weeks later, Frances got a letter from Reg himself. He was keen to get back to the plastics ward, and finish the surgery that Gillies had started:

> I am sorry that I must ask you to give up the idea of coming down here as I do not know from one day to another whether I shall be here or not. I may go back to the Cambridge or may come home for a while first but cannot say what will be decided – in any case it is not worth your while coming down as the time cannot be long now before I am finished with hospital for good. So I hope you will instead of counting on coming to see me build on me coming to see you and save your strength so that we can get about a bit while I am home.
>
>   I am enclosing one or two photos; you will see by them how well I am getting on. They brought a famous French Surgeon round the other day, he was very interested in me and thinks my career (from a doctor's point of view, I mean) wonderful and my recoveries from the various ills I have had to combat, splendid and my looks a great improvement on the various photographs he was shown. I am sure you will agree with me that even you with your many and various ailments have never had the amount of tip-top advice that I am getting for my one.
>
>   Yesterday when Canon Cunningham was preaching he was saying that it was everybody's duty at a time like this to dress as nicely as they could and also to cultivate these good looks and make themselves as beautiful as they could. It rather tickled me and I started smiling and to my horror saw that he had seen me. He continued 'In God's sight

those with scars honourably won were more beautiful than anybody and with them there were no aids to beauty needed' and so on and so on. How I managed to sit still I don't know but I don't want you to be alarmed when I come home to find I've got quite conceited.[31]

Kate Parry Collins was by now living just a few miles away from Waverley Abbey Hospital. Her husband John had been in training since 1914, and had been promoted to Acting Major in the Royal Garrison Artillery, with whom he was stationed in Farnborough. Kate and John had been living apart for the past year; she had been ill, and living with her mother and sister. But in October, feeling better, she had moved to be with him.

At the end of October, as the Battle of the Somme was in its final stages, John received news that his deployment was imminent, though his destination was not yet confirmed:

> [John] met the Colonel who told him his Battery is due to leave here on the 19th for Larkhill and then on to Codford, Wilts, to mobilize. It's just like a stab every time a bit of news like that comes. I suppose it will be France but it may be Salonica or Egypt. Well I am glad, as his time has come, that he has got his battery and is in such a good position. No sign of a Major coming to take command and, though it is a responsibility, I am sure that he is pleased. As for our parting, let me think of it as little as I can and let me retain as much hope for his return as is possible.[32]

Reg Evans was feeling better. Well enough, in fact, that Mr Kent from the brush factory could finally arrange the hero's reception he'd long planned for him. Reg went home to Hemel Hempstead for a few weeks' leave. He had made many friends at the hospital and was sorry to leave them behind – in particular, one of the nurses, Nurse Oakes, an upper-class woman who had taken a shine to the high-spirited Reg.

On Friday 22 September, Reg Evans walked through the doors of Kent's brush factory. Things had changed dramatically since he had worked there, over two years earlier. Many of his fellow workers had hung up their overalls and were now soldiers, like him; some had not survived this far. And of course, Reg was not the same man. He wore a medal on his sergeant's uniform; and his face was not the one he had left with.

He was with his mother Frances, and Nurse Oakes had travelled up to be there too. Mr Kent made a speech and presented Reg with a ring. Nurse Oakes was impressed, but her first thoughts were for his health. She wrote to him a few days afterwards:

> I thought you were looking rather thin; so you must be sure to eat well and get up your strength as Ashwood tells me you were quite ill after the last operation – I thought you got through the presentation very well indeed and I feel very much for you because it was a tiring thing to stand and listen to Mr Kent's speech; but when you began to speak yourself you were alright and spoke jolly well too. The memory of this day will always remain in my mind as a very pleasant and happy one. Please give my love to your Mother and I am sure she was a proud woman on Friday.
>
> Yr sincere friend
> Nurse C Oakes.[33]

Reg spent the next few weeks at home. He needed to recover his strength before the next phase of his gruelling surgery could take place.

At the end of October, **Will Martin** was moving again, this time even further from **Emily Chitticks**. He was destined for a camp in Norfolk. He'd managed to see Emily before he left and they had made a life-changing decision. They were to be married:

> Just a few lines to let you know that we have arrived quite safely. It is very much better than Thornden Park, only there is one thing missing, and that is your dear face, but we shall have to face that matter as well as we can. But oh it was hard to part from you last night. We had a nice ride, much better than I expected, I rode in the rear guard, and you can just imagine what we were up to – we were all on our own. I galloped one of my horse's shoes off.
>
> It is hard lines, to be parted from each other so soon, and just as we have realized that we cannot do without one another. But I do feel happy to think that we belong to each other. It doesn't seem nearly so hard, as it would have done had it been otherwise.[34]

Emily replied at once:

> It nearly broke my heart to let you go on Saturday, and yet, dear Will,
> I am very, very happy now I really belong to you. You cannot imagine
> what happiness you gave to me on Friday, I did not expect it then, but
> that was what I had been hoping for, darling. Of course I knew that
> you loved me, but yet I did not feel so near to you then as I do now.
> Really I don't think I could live without you now. What a happy day
> for both of us when we shall be joined together never to part any more.[35]

And once Will arrived at camp in Holt, Norfolk, he was keen to press
on with the engagement:

> You will think I have been busy, sweetheart, when I tell you that I have
> been to a jewellers and chosen your ring, and have been to the post
> office to arrange to get some cash through dear, so I daresay you may
> hope to get it by the end of the week. It is plain dear but I thought
> that it would be better quality.[36]

A portrait of Emily Chitticks, c. 1916–17.

And Emily was keen for Will to go through all the proper formalities:

> I say dear when you get a chance you might write to Dad will you, I
> am sure he would love to hear from you. And you might mention our
> engagement.[37]

At the end of October, **Reg Evans** was back in a bed on the ward at
Cambridge Military Hospital. He had undergone another operation
under Gillies's knife. He was suffering severe discomfort and then had
to endure the bad news that the operation had not gone well.[38] As
irrepressible as he was, even Reg found it hard to be cheerful as he
wrote home:

> I have been feeling so rotten though I am glad to say I am a lot better
> now, though I'm afraid the last operation was not a success and I shall
> have to undergo another. The look of my mouth is completely altered
> again now and not I am sorry to say for the better but I suppose it'll
> all come alright in the end.[39]

It was the anniversary of the day that Norman had proposed to **Helen
Bentwich**, while searchlights scanned the sky above them from the top
of Marble Arch. In the few minutes she had to relax in bed before
leaving to catch her train to the arsenal for work, Helen scribbled a
note to him in Egypt:

> Two years ago this afternoon a very scared girl and I believe a very
> scared man, were wandering up and down the Mall settling their future.
> Today one of them is riding camels in the desert and the other is resting
> in bed (at the moment) preparatory to turning out on the filthiest night
> imaginable, to start her ninth week at the arsenal. It's a comical world,
> I wonder where we'll be next Guy Fawkes day? . . . I've got to get up
> now and get ready to go out, despite the vileness of the weather. Oh
> damn kings and countries and patriotism but bless searchlights and
> horseguards and camels and husbands and I do love you very very
> much.[40]

*

Dorothy Lloyd had just watched little David turn one. She was trying to be cheerful, and wrote to her mother-in-law to thank her for the presents she'd sent:

> Thank you ever so much for the lovely present. You know you couldn't have given me anything to touch the photos of Allie, it is such a joy to have them, oh I do hope David will grow like him.
>
> Thank you so much for David's first football. He loves it and bangs along the floor after it as hard as he can go. He has had 18 presents spoilt boy. He was simply full of life and enjoyed the party more than anyone. He played with the others in the drawing room after tea and did all his stunts and screamed with joy. He loved his birthday cake with its one candle and tried to blow it out.
>
> Yesterday I found a letter written to you thanking you for asking us to come to you for Christmas. I should simply love to come, it will remind me of last year when he was there too and I know he will be very near to me and it will be lovely if we are all together won't it?[41]

The fallout of the Battle of the Somme would last for a generation, and more. David Lloyd's father had not been there when he was born; he was not there on his first birthday; he would never be there again.

In early November, **Kate Parry Collins** got the news she had been dreading: John was to go to France. For months the papers had been filled with news of the fighting on the Somme, so Kate could imagine all too vividly what was in store for her husband. John too, was under no illusions as to what it would be like. On a dark November evening, he came back to their rented rooms, bringing two of his junior officers for tea. These were the men who John would fight alongside, and Kate's worries were not eased by her impressions of them:

> [John] came in with the news that their destination is to be France. It seems to be getting near now. He is quite cheerful about it – that is one good thing. John brought Mr Smith and Mr Turnbull – two of the (Subalterns) – in to tea. I was not struck with either of them. Mr Smith was a schoolmaster at Cardiff and Mr Turnbull, with his father, an estate agent at Manchester. Poor fat podgy soul, I feel sorry for him – he looks frightened out of his wits and hates the whole thing. Mr Smith, one

feels, will see it through somehow. But I don't envy John [his] companions.[42]

A few days later, John left her for further training at another camp. It
was an unhappy foretaste of what lay ahead for them in the very near
future:

> John got up at 6.45 a.m. and had breakfast at 7.30 – brought mine up
> and then at 8 o'clock he went off on his bicycle in the new Aquascutum
> for Larkhill Camp, Salisbury Plain. I watched him off from the window
> and then got back into bed and wept. I felt so miserable – so different
> from last Sunday morning. And what will it be in a few weeks' time
> when he has gone altogether?[43]

For 19-year-old **Will Martin**, on the other hand, the war still seemed
a long way off. He was occupied with the business of securing his
fiancée. He wrote to Emily once more from his camp in Norfolk:

> I am so glad that I met you, I couldn't possibly do without you now. I
> hope that I shall be able to let you have your ring by the weekend, but
> it might be Monday.
>
> I will write to your father, dear, perhaps tonight. But at any rate as
> soon as I can. I thought about it last week, but I hope you forgive me
> when I say that I couldn't summon up the courage, but writing a letter
> won't be quite such a hard ordeal, and it will be the proper thing.[44]

He did write to her father, on 11 November. That same day, a special
delivery arrived for Emily: the engagement ring. Everything was falling
into place. She wrote to Will immediately:

> How can I thank you enough for my dear little ring. I am so delighted
> with it. I only wish that you were here to put it on for me. It fits nicely,
> and looks ever so neat and nice on my finger. I don't care who knows
> that I love you, dear, and I feel a very happy and proud girl because you
> love me.
>
> Oh Will, I do wish that I was with you. I do so long for my dear
> boy to come back but never mind darling, it is not so very long now to

wait until Xmas, what joy dear to meet each other then. I shall jump
out of my boots nearly with delight.[45]

It was indeed only six weeks until Christmas; six weeks until the two
would be reunited.

Reg Evans was still in hospital. He was less optimistic about Christmas,
and his progress remained frustratingly slow:

> Just a line to let you know I am going on alright. I am having Xray
> treatment and massage for my face which is getting on now, though I
> am to have another operation when Capt. Gillies comes back. He has
> gone to a conference at Paris, I think. It's beginning to look as if I shant
> be home for Christmas after all. Still, never mind – Christmas is only
> a name, after all, and we can have our little celebrations just as well if
> they do happen to come a few weeks later.
>
> Goodnight Mother, take care of yourself and heaps of love from your
> redoubtable (that's swank) son Reg.[46]

In France, the Battle of the Somme was finally coming to an end,
though its effects were still being felt in Great Leighs – on 13 November,
Andrew Clark noted down news of another loss in a war diary that
was becoming increasingly sombre:

> Charlie Cook, who worked for Major William Brown at Bishop's Hall,
> has been killed. He was slightly wounded and sent back in to the trenches
> with his hand bound up. This time he was wounded 'from top to toe',
> and died either as he was being taken to hospital or just after he was
> admitted.[47]

A few days later, Andrew received more bad news. His former groom,
Charles Ward, had been admitted to hospital in France:

> Thursday 16 November: Mrs Harry Ward has today had a letter from
> her son, Charles H Ward. He is in hospital, but she does not understand
> whether he is there because he is sick or wounded.[48]

Two days later, on 18 November, the battle of the Somme was called off. In four and a half months of fighting, over 400,000 British men had been killed or wounded. At its deepest point, the Allied advance into German territory was less than six miles.[49]

The commander-in-chief, Haig, claimed it had been a victory. The people of Britain were starting to question whether this war would ever be won. And how much more could be asked of them. The winter ahead looked bleak.

16

A COLD CHRISTMAS

December 1916

So many of our lads have been killed, and often the parents die of broken hearts.

Letter received by Andrew Clark, 25 December 1916

As the battle of the Somme ground to a halt in the French mud, winter began to set in at home, too. In the third week of November the temperatures plummeted.[1] On a bitter Sunday night, **Kate Parry Collins** was writing her diary, the icy rain battering at the window-panes. Tucked up against the cold under blankets, she was thinking of John, whose side of the bed next to her was cold and empty. He had left her that day for training at Larkhill, then on to a holding camp at Codford. From there, he was to be transferred to France. Kate was to join him for his final days in England, but she was feeling lonely already:

> It's been a fearful day raining and sleeting and bitter cold, and now I am just going to bed feeling very unhappy and dreading everything – first – foremost John going and next because it means getting off tomorrow and settling somewhere. But where? Shall I find a room in Salisbury alright and eventually move on to Codford – or will it be disastrous? I am frightened.[2]

Kate closed her diary, put it down next to the bed, and tried to sleep. She awoke the next morning to another miserable November day. She packed a basket with food for her day's travels, and set off for the station. Once again, she was off to set up home somewhere new, in the wake of her soldier husband.

As an officer, John could live where he liked, and when she arrived at Codford Kate was determined to find some nice rooms in which to pass their last days together. But she was taken aback by what met her there; the place was completely given over to the accommodation of the thousands of soldiers who were there at any time, waiting to be sent to the front:

> One can only imagine what Codford was – a pretty little one-street village on the high road Salisbury to Bath – but what it is like now is a mining village. Rows of grey huts built right up to the downs which are the beginning of the plain – right along the entire length of the village and beyond – camp after camp. The gaps in the cottages and shops in the street filled with shantys – wooden or galvanized iron, temporary shops as ugly as can be. The hedges gone – and the fields built over. What used to be glorious cornfields now covered with the engineers. Everywhere soldiers and mostly Australian ones with their picturesque hats and bizarre accents giving a quite foreign appearance to the place. And mud ankle deep in the gutters where one had to go to get out of the way of the great motor lorries and the traffic of all description tearing by.[3]

Kate trudged endlessly round Codford St Mary looking for rooms, to no avail. She was then directed to outlying villages and finally, at Upton Lovell, found somewhere. She waited for John to join her there. The days before his departure were fast disappearing, and Kate spent too many of them on her own before he at last arrived:

> Sat down to my writing of diary. Had just got up-to-date when, about 11, a khaki figure passed the window and I ran to the door. He looks a bit peaky after his week but says he feels better today. Left Larkhill at 7.30 and came on a lorry dragging one of the guns as he did not feel fit to bicycle or march. He was driven by an old Vanguard London bus driver. John had quite a lot of compliments for his battery from the commandant – and for his own shoot. The only battery in the 2 weeks shoots so complimented. I am ever so glad as it was a great anxiety.[4]

In Great Leighs, some good news had finally reached **Andrew Clark**. Charlie Ward, his former groom, was out of hospital in France. He had not, in fact, been wounded; he was only suffering from eczema:

Charlie Ward is, his mother thinks, suffering to eczema to which he has always been subject. He writes home that it is worth being ill to have the comfort of sleeping in a bed again. He was always a great hand for bed and was often late for his work here by delay in getting up.[5]

But news was filtering back to Britons of the true horror of the battle-fields, even to those in isolated Great Leighs. Andrew's friend Major Caldwell stopped by one evening a few days later with news from France:

> 7 p.m. Major James Caldwell called. He was very depressed about both the war and commerce – rather an unusual thing for him. He hears from the officers on leave that the official bulletins suppress vital facts if they are unfavourable. Thus they announce 600 German prisoners at a particular position but say nothing of 20,000 British casualties in taking it. Nearly all the newspapers concur in this policy of hushing up losses.
>
> His nephew, Sidney Caldwell, in the Artillery, writes from France, that the mud at the front is so bad that wheels cannot be used and ammunition for the guns and other supplies, has to be drawn forward in sledges.[6]

At the end of November, the Allied military commanders met at the French headquarters in Chantilly. The Somme offensive had not gone to plan, but they felt that it had achieved its objectives of holding off the Germans at Verdun and stretching the enemy's resources to the utmost. The difference in losses between the two opposing sides was, in fact, negligible: it was then estimated at 660,000 German casualties against 630,000 Allied. But that extra 30,000 was deemed victory enough. The plan for 1917 was set: more of the same.[7]

The politicians did not entirely agree with the military assessment. The same day the commanders met in Chantilly, the statesmen met in Paris. Lloyd George, Secretary of State for War, viewed the Somme as a bitter disappointment and condemned the plan for continued offensives. When he returned to London he started a campaign for closer management of the war effort. But the plan in France remained set. For now, it was a matter of getting through another winter. [8]

*

Will Martin had now moved to Devonport, and was training with the 3rd Devonshire infantry regiment. He was given six days' leave before he transferred, and had been to see his Emily. They had gone up to Southend together. Despite the winter weather, they had wandered along the blustery seafront, hand in hand – just young lovers on a day out.[9] When Will left to rejoin his regiment, Emily had waved him off at the station. He wrote to her as soon as he'd arrived at his new camp:

> Just a line to let you know that I have arrived quite safely. We had a rather tiresome journey but still, we got over that all right. We had a very nice reception. The band was at the station and played us to the barracks, and when we arrived supper was quite ready.
>
> I am sure, sweetheart, that you are worrying yourself, but there is no need for it. I am disappointed about having to come so far away from my little girl, but I didn't have the heart to stay behind when all my chums volunteered – all my schoolmates are here. But wherever I go I shall always be the same.
>
> Well, my dear, I haven't got much to write about. I know that you will forgive as you can understand how I am feeling after leaving you, poor little girl. How are you getting through with it? Left the station and cried all the way home, I expect. Never mind darling, I love you, and nothing shall step in between us.[10]

A few days later, however, the reality was setting in: he was destined for France. And his departure came sooner than either of them might have wished.

Emily received a telegram and immediately sent a brave reply:

> 2 December 1916
> TELEGRAM: Chitticks Heronport Brentwood.
> Leaving Devonport tomorrow on draft. Will

> 2 December 1916
> TELEGRAM: 45631 Pte William Martin
> Received wire don't worry. Emily.[11]

The next day, she got a scribbled note, Will's last chance to say goodbye before he crossed the Channel:

I will give you an address as soon as possible. I shall be longing for your letter. We left Devonport at 9.30 this morning, and we don't know where we are going. You must excuse scribbles as the train is rocking badly. It was a bit hurried. I am disappointed, too, for I so hoped to have taken you to Cornwall at Xmas.[12]

John Collins was luckier: he had managed to get some leave before he had to head to France, so he and Kate decided to go on a trip to London – a final few days of fun together before they had to part. Kate wanted nothing more than for John to enjoy these last preparations:

Out at 11. First to the A & N Stores then walked across the Park to Pall Mall where we went to order John a Bullet Proof coat at Wilkinsons. We have seen all the kinds that are made but this seems the only one any good, but if he will be able to support the weight I don't know. Then we walked to Maule Fox in Piccadilly and arranged for him to be photographed tomorrow and then to lunch in Slaters near by. I never saw John happier. It is a time he will always remember.[13]

Tensions were running high in Westminster, just a stone's throw from the rooms Kate and John had taken in Pimlico. Lloyd George had called for a new, small war council to be formed, that he personally would chair. The prime minister, Asquith, was put in a tricky position. He had sacrificed his own son to the war, yet he was coming under increasing criticism for his management of it. He initially consented to the war council, but then, a few days later, realised that he was being sidelined and changed his mind, insisting that he should chair it. Lloyd George was not happy.

Kate couldn't help but follow the unfolding crisis, even as she tried to savour her time with John:

We walked up to Victoria – the paper posters saying 'Resignation of Lloyd George'. If he goes we are lost indeed – this terrible political crisis.

Ate our sandwiches and made cocoa and John went to bed while I sat and read the paper until 10 and then into bed, when John promptly woke up. Well it was our last night in dear old London. John has kept on saying 'I have never enjoyed myself so much in my life'. It is a great deal to be able to give him so much happiness – he never seems to enjoy himself away from me – or very seldom.[14]

As Kate and John made the most of their last night in London together, **Duff Cooper** was at the very house where Asquith was holding a late-night meeting in an attempt to save his political skin. Lloyd George had not yet resigned, but the coalition government was on the brink of collapse:

> I managed to dine alone with Diana at her bedside. Afterwards I read to her – poetry – and loved her. I went on to Queen Anne's Gate. On arriving I was almost shown into the dining room where Edwin, the Prime Minister and Lord Reading were waiting for Crewe. I stopped the servant in time and went up to the drawing room where I found sitting on cushions round the fire Venetia, Barbara, Lady Wimborne and Lady Goonie. They were all looking very pretty and were beautifully dressed. I liked the scene – lovely women warming themselves at the fire this bitter night while under their feet the fate of the Empire was being decided.
>
> At last Edwin, Reading and the Prime Minister came up – the two first rather white and careworn but the PM happier, less concerned, and I must say more drunk than I have ever seen him.[15]

Asquith thought that he'd saved himself. They all played bridge.

Kate Parry Collins left London the following morning with John. She read the headlines: Asquith was not coming out of it as well as he'd hoped. *The Times* wrote scathingly of the 'dilatory and irresolute manner in which the Cabinet and the War Committee have directed the war.'[16] The next day, 5 December, Lloyd George resigned, hoping to bring the government down with him: 'I am fully conscious of the importance of national unity. But unity without action is nothing but futile carnage. And I cannot be responsible for that. Vigour and vision are the supreme need at this hour.'[17] Asquith followed suit, and resigned too – probably based on the assumption that no one else would be able to form a government.

*

Kate and John were back at Upton Lovell, John back in the camp at Codford, Kate was bored in the house by herself. Their future, like that of the rest of Britain, was in the hands of the new government, which was announced the following day. Kate, feeling in need of some air and time to think, went for a walk alone on Salisbury Plain:

> I was a bit nervous of the matter at first. It was so bitterly cold – so vast and so lonely. I was right up on the plain and there for miles and miles it stretched, the roar of the guns was almost too acute for some time. Some of the Batteries, I suppose, on Larkhill. The news in the papers is that Lloyd George is to be Prime Minister. Perhaps we shall get on now.[18]

With a new leader at the helm, Kate dared to hope that the worst of the carnage was over.

As Kate walked the deserted expanse of Salisbury Plain, **Will Martin** had landed in France. He had never been abroad before. He wrote to Emily:

> Just a few lines to let you know that I am still in the land of the living and keeping fit. I have arrived at the base. We sailed Tues night and arrived in France somewhere at 4 o'clock in the morning. I was a little seasick, but not nearly as bad as some. It is a bit awkward using French money at first. I got done in when I was coming up country by train – we stopped and got some coffee, so I gave him a 2/- note and didn't get more than 9½ back, but I'll watch being done again.
>
> We are still sticking together so it isn't so bad, I hope that you are not worrying, I am quite well and happy, and we are comfortably situated. I am sure, sweetheart, that you must be very disappointed by the way events have taken but I hope that our hopes may be realised at some future date, and the sooner it turns up the better dear, but it's not much use grumbling. I suppose we shall have to make the best of it.[19]

The infantry base at Rouen where Will found himself was one of the holding camps for men being sent from Britain to the front. Following the losses at the Somme, in order to build up sufficient numbers for the next planned offensives of early 1917, Haig had asked for 300,000 new infantry soldiers.[20] Will and the draft he'd come over with were just a few of those who would make up that number, ready for the campaign of the New Year.

Rouen base camp, 1917.

It wasn't just infantry that would be required. **John Collins** and the 222 Siege Battery Royal Garrison Artillery were now ready to go across too. John told Kate on a cold Sunday afternoon two weeks before Christmas:

> John came in at 12 o'clock with the news – the guns go tomorrow – an advance party on Tuesday and the battery on Thursday. It is hard to bear it and I shan't be able to unless I put a tremendous curb on myself.[21]

They had just three more days together. On Thursday morning, they woke up together for the last time in what could be many months. Or worse – but of course neither of them wanted to think about that. Kate accompanied him to the station:

> We woke up fairly early but when we were called at 7.30 it seemed like the death knell. We had to get up soon after. I was the first to get out of bed, as soon as John would let me go, and we both dressed and had breakfast together. I cut sandwiches & stowed them in his knapsack. Packed up also a lump of bread, butter, potted meat etc. Then he has

meat tabloids – malted milk tablets and some cocoa rations and other
food of the kind in case he should not get rations for a day or two.
John's man had come early to help.

John went off at 9.15 with his knapsack, water bottle, glasses etc. slung
on him – on his bicycle. I drove up to the station just as the battery
marched up. John's servant stepped forward to help me and got a porter,
giving my trunk, John's bicycle, the little valise and my basket of food
to him, to be taken to the up platform. I stood talking to John. I stood
quietly apart when the train came in – a special at 10 minutes to 1 – full
of soldiers – another battery. The commandant was there to see them
off.

I walked right up the train when John had found his whereabouts
and carriage and stood talking. I had put in John's hand an envelope
containing a silver identification bracelet with his name etc and on the
back 'Christmas 1916 from K.P.C.' and told him to open it when he
liked. Also a little letter not to be opened until Christmas Day. He got
in and kissed me, and the train moved off. He looked at me – then
turned his head – I suppose he could not bear any more – but I smiled
at him – then the train went faster. I just moved down the platform to
avoid the official group and then turned and looked and waved until he
was out of sight. I think I had a great feeling of thankfulness that it
was over and that I had come through such a terrible ordeal.[22]

Still, more men were required; and for **Andrew Clark** in Great Leighs,
every day seemed to bring some fresh news of a family separated by
conscription: 'The Rayner twins have received papers calling them up.
They will be eighteen before Xmas. It is very hard on their father
because they work the farm with him.'[23]

As the third Christmas of the war approached, the community could
not help but think of those who would not be with them this year, nor
ever again. Nine young men from Great Leighs had already fallen in
the war. In the adjoining village, Little Leighs, the daughter of the
reverend had the idea for a war memorial to commemorate the dead:

Mrs Drummond (daughter of the Revd John Green, sometime rector
of Little Leighs) is going to present Little Leighs with a 'war-shrine',
to be set up in the churchyard there and to have on it the names of all
Little Leighs' men who have fallen in the war.[24]

At a time when he should have been looking forward to the festive season, Andrew was miserable. The year had been a terrible one for him personally, but he was also increasingly disillusioned with the war effort, despite the new man in Number 10. That weekend's official war news made him crosser than ever:

> Sunday 10 December: I preserve the official bulletin for today. It is insolent in its brevity: 'Summary of Saturday's Official War News. There is nothing of importance to report on any front.'[25]

In December, Andrew's daughter Mildred returned home from medical school in Scotland for the holidays, so he had some more company at least. There had been snow – perhaps the most Christmassy thing about an otherwise dismal festive season – but on Christmas Day itself it began to melt into slush. The scene in St Mary's Church as Andrew preached was stark:

> 10 a.m. Cold dreary day, snow is rushing into water. Naturally there was the smallest Christmas morning congregation I have ever had here. Twelve communicants – seven men, five women.[26]

On arriving back at the rectory for Christmas lunch, Mildred had a letter from a friend in another village. The picture there was no more cheerful. Andrew stuck the letter into a war diary that was becoming decidedly bleak:

> So many of our lads have been killed, and very often the parents die of broken hearts. In one family of farmers we liked very much, the sons have been killed, The mother died a week after, and the father twelve hours after her, leaving some daughters all alone.[27]

Kate Parry Collins was back with her mother and sister, who were now living in a cottage near Wooburn in Buckinghamshire. There too, Christmas Day had begun with perfect crisp snow, which melted away over the morning. Kate was, of course, thinking of John:

> Up 7 off 7.45 to Church. A wonderful morning – a real black and white etching. The ground had a good covering of snow and in the light as it

was when I walked down the hill everything showed up jet black against it – except for one patch of egg-shell blue over the hill there was no colour anywhere.

[After church] Coming back up the hill it had begun to thaw and the gorgeously pretty morning – though rather sad and desolate withal – had departed. Kathleen had lit a fire and I had my breakfast in the sitting room. Wrote to John afterwards and got Kathleen to post it when she went off at 12. No letter from him.[28]

John was thinking of her too – he had written to her, a letter that would arrive some days later. He had been in France little more than a week, but already felt a world away from home:

Dearest, this Xmas I hope you are having a peaceful time, don't ask me how I am spending mine, that there exists such places as London, Codford, Wooburn I cannot imagine, even the men who have been out three times have never seen anything like this. Xmas will have more memories for me than I can say.

The great joy of Xmas has however turned up this evening in the shape of 2 letters from you. I am off to bed which is the only comfortable place to be in. Fondest love and many kisses, John. I did love your letters.[29]

Will Martin also wrote a letter home to Emily:

It has been a rather strange Xmas for us, but still I think all the boys are happy. There was a small bit of pudding for dinner, and also some beer and rum, but I didn't have any of the latter two. I could just fancy you today, sweetheart, wondering what I am up to and what sort of time I am having. Things are getting regulated a bit more – we have been split up into companies and platoons. Things are very quiet but the roads are very rough and there is plenty of mud and water about. What looks very familiar out here is the London motorbuses conveying troops from place to place.

Well sweetheart I hope you have had a good Xmas, but I daresay you had a busy time. We are having a concert here tonight in the Church Army hut, we have got no piano but we are making the best we can out of it.[30]

Emily Chitticks had a rare day off on Christmas Day, which she spent at home with her own family. The following day, she was back in her servant's uniform, and wrote to Will from the farmhouse, having not yet received his letter. She was feeling anxious:

> Well dear what sort of Xmas, I wonder, did you have? Mine was very dull. I have had some more unpleasant dreams about you. One in particular, I dreamt that you were home with me, but you had ceased to love me and treated me as cold as ice. I don't know why I dream such silly things, I wish I didn't, because I know you do love me. I hope that you do not think me a funny girl for telling you all my thoughts and dreams as I do, but I must tell you, I can't help it. I feel more happy when I tell you everything.[31]

If Emily was anxious, the next few letters she received from France did nothing to calm her nerves – Will was getting closer and closer to the front line:

> Just a few lines to let you know that we have again arrived at our desti-nation after another 24 hours travelling. We are within sight of the flashes of the big guns. Of course we marched there in full marching order, and you may guess we found it a trifle hard, seeing that we are so green, but still I am feeling all right now, I have had some tea, and I am feeling fit.
> Saturday afternoon we went for a route march, not the way in which we have been in the habit of spending our Sat afternoon, but we are in France now, and we are not out for a picnic, sweetheart. Are you getting used to being alone now sweetheart? I find myself that it takes some getting used to, and I guess you find it the same.[32]

A few days later, it was New Year's Eve. Another year of war had come to an end. It had been the most brutal year of them all. Britain had been transformed. Long-standing and dearly held liberal traditions had been cast aside. Military service had become compulsory. A prime minister had lost his son; he himself had lost power. Women now worked at what had been men's jobs. Britain – her people, her resources, her industry – had been realigned towards a single purpose: victory at any cost.

As the final seconds of 1916 ticked away, **Kate Parry Collins** stood at an open window in her cottage bedroom, her breath visible in the dim light:

> I felt I must wait to see the New Year in. It had been a lovely day and when the time drew near we opened the window to let in the day. Upstairs I opened it wide too, and sent out a message to John. I wondered where he was – asleep in his dug out or watching and listening for the speaking guns. I could not tell.
>
> I read a little, but I was busy with my thoughts. The dying year gives one pause to think but this year one does not so much think of what is past – terrible, tragic and awful as it has been – but wonder what is to come. And what is to come for the nation and for oneself. One is anxious, very anxious – sometimes it seems more than one can bear just to wait patiently. They say the back is suitable to its burden but I feel, I suppose selfishly, that my back and heart or brain won't stand much more. It's weak, I know, and I try to count my mercies – I do realize them – they are very many, very abundant. But I want my own man – I want my own man – it is difficult to say and mean 'God's in his heaven, all's right with the World'.

DARKEST DAYS

17

HARDSHIPS AT HOME

Winter–Spring 1917

We have come to a very intense and terrible epoch in the War. I suppose that the worst part of all is yet to come.

Hallie Miles's diary, March 1917

As the fourth year of war began, eleven European nations – almost every major world power – were battling each other across the globe. The strain was being felt as never before. The war was now costing Britain an estimated £5 million each day, and her people were being squeezed.[1]

The US had so far remained out of the conflict, but the shock waves from it were now starting to cross the Atlantic. The newly re-elected president, Woodrow Wilson, had attempted to broker a peace at the end of 1916. He had failed. On 10 January, the Allies responded to him, restating their war aims. The following day their enemies answered that they were determined to prosecute the war to a successful end. There was no possibility of peace.[2]

Reg Evans awoke on the first day of the New Year in a hospital bed – as he had done most days for the past ten months. On the table next to his bed was his new set of false teeth, specially fitted to his reconstructed jaw. He still wasn't quite used to them, and had to take them out to eat. Having undergone the bulk of his surgery, Reg had left the specialist ward in Aldershot and was back at the auxiliary hospital nearby at Waverley Abbey. He was in the last stages of his marathon recovery, and still not his usual self. He wrote to his mother in low spirits – they had been apart at Christmas, yet again:

Thanks so very much for yours, received this morning, but you know really you shouldn't spend money on me at a time like this when I'm sure you must be feeling the cost of living in so many ways. I'm so sorry that you had such a lonely Christmas – if I had imagined that you were going to be by yourself so utterly I would have insisted upon them letting me out whatever they said.

Well I haven't written any letters this Christmas for I didn't feel like it. I was pretty busy, for one thing, helping in odd ways about the hospital, and then I wasn't feeling particularly fit for another.

Well goodnight Mother, even if I don't write je suis toujours pensee a vous – I am always thinking of you.[3]

Reg was right – like most Britons, Frances was finding it increasingly difficult to get by. Her workload at the guesthouse she ran had not decreased, yet with her sons away she had no one to help her. Food and fuel were in increasingly short supply. In 1917, it was only going to get worse.

The government recognised that something needed to be done to ensure the equitable distribution of food to Britons at home. Farming had suffered as a result of the loss of men and horses to the war; and shipping available to import food was diminishing all the time, thanks to military requisitioning and Germany's increasingly aggressive policy of submarine warfare. Food prices had been rising since 1915, and as the war dragged on the situation was getting more serious – and public discontent was rising.[4]

The Defence of the Realm Act had been extended to give the Board of Trade powers to control the food supply, and in December 1916, a Food Controller was appointed to take the problem in hand. The decreasing supply of cereals was particularly worrying: at the end of November, London had only two days' wheat in store, and imports during the first two weeks of January were half those of the same period a year earlier.[5] Attempts to get more out of what Britain did have ranged from increasing the amount of flour taken from each kernel, to promoting wholemeal bread.[6]

Such measures were not always popular. As **Andrew Clark** noted, the people of Great Leighs, for example, were outraged by the thought of giving up their white bread: 'A village woman's opinion of whole-meal bread – "That will be the black stuff the Germans eat. Fancy bringing English people to eat that stuff. It ain't fit for pigs.'"[7]

Another deeply unpopular measure was an enforced reduction of the output of beer – to a maximum of 50 per cent of 1915 production – to preserve barley supplies.[8] Andrew does not record how the drinkers in the St Anne's Castle or the Dog and Partridge reacted to this, but one can presume it was not with pleasure. Coal was also in especially short supply and had already been rationed, allocated to households based on their number of rooms. Andrew's parishioners were starting to feel the pinch and some turned to him for help:

Saturday 20 January: This is a time when a country parson would need to be made of silver pieces. I preserve the latest arrival of these appeals. This is a large family of young children, nice little things. The mother has the reputation of being 'an awful liar':

Dr Sir,

Could you Please help me to a little coals as the weather is so very cold and baby is not well and I have only my husband's wages to do upon for 6 children and our 2 selves to live out of one man's wages and so expensive are things I can scarcely get enough to eat and can't get anything for boots or clothes and nearly all are without boots if you can spare me just a trifle I shall be extremely thankful I would not ask you sir if I did not need it badly.[9]

That particular woman might not have been entirely trustworthy, but the fact was that by January 1917 the retail cost of food had risen by 87 per cent since before the war.[10]

Hallie Miles was, of course, keen to help out in these difficult times. In the autumn of 1916, desperately trying to avoid a system of compulsory rationing, the government encouraged people to cut down on their food consumption in more inventive ways. Enforced 'Meatless Days' in restaurants was one of the campaigns trialled.[11] Hallie and Eustace had long preached economy and vegetarianism, previously a rather 'niche' message. But suddenly business was booming:

This wave of 'meatlessness' is making us both so busy. My little Cookery Book is selling well. It is just going to have a third edition. People say it is quite the best book there is of the sort. It has got into some very important households. I have been very busy revising it for its third edition.

Now that the Food Controller has limited people in their meals, especially in meat, the EM Restaurant is absolutely packed for lunches. We often have a thousand people for lunch only. We cannot seat them all, and sometimes a hundred or so have to go away because they cannot get served or seated. It is heart-breaking to see them going out![12]

It was not just the healthy wartime profits that were welcome to Hallie. This was a chance to change public perceptions for good, and it seemed that at least some of the public were receptive:

To show how keen people are on the meatless food question, I wrote a letter to the papers offering to send a small leaflet with meatless recipes to anyone who sent me a stamped addressed envelope. In response to this I received over three thousand letters in reply! For several days the letters were brought up to our flat in a black sack! I hear that my recipes have been most useful.[13]

However, many of the measures and campaigns the government pushed out were also met with anger, particularly from working-class people, who were feeling the increased prices the most. For many of the poorest Britons, meatlessness and other economies were not a choice but a fact of life.[14]

Helen Bentwich did not have to worry about the rising costs of living herself, but the people working with her at the arsenal did. And she resented how much they were being asked to give up, when extravagance elsewhere persisted:

The food laws tackle the wrong end. It's the restaurants, extravagant venues and theatres that ought to be banned and then there would not be so much need for these restrictions. If you were here and took a walk down Regent St or Oxford St and looked in the shop windows, you'd say all you read in the papers about shortage of food was lies. But is isn't – for the poor people. The others still have too much.[15]

A poster published by the League of National Safety, encouraging food economy as a means for British civilians to contribute to the war effort.

Duff Cooper certainly did not seem to be going without, and was probably exactly the sort of person Helen was thinking of. At the beginning of January, he was back from a New Year's break in a friend's country house – the only deprivation he had suffered was that they hadn't had any champagne for the few days they were there. But he was not in a good mood and his feelings for Diana were not what they had been:

> Dined at Mulberry Walk with Diana, Viola and Alan. I am not in love with Diana and I am tired of Viola and Alan. This is a terrible thing and is probably only a phase but there it is. We had a beastly dinner except for the champagne which I provided and enjoyed, not having tasted it for a week.[16]

In early 1917, the primary economising measure Duff was trying to impose on himself was the curtailment of a spiralling gambling habit. He wasn't having much success:

> [Ruby] persuaded Diana and me to go to the Carlton where we went up to the sitting room of two Americans and played that silly card game with three cards. I think Marmora is the right name. I, like a fool and being rather drunk, lost £180. I went on from there to the Curzon Hotel and played Chemin de Fer and lost another £200. It is perfectly hellish. I shall have to sell out some more capital. Damn.[17]

Duff's problems were added to when he suddenly found himself without his personal servant, though he did not have to do without for long: 'Holbrook, my servant, left me today – to join the army – a mortal blow at my comfort. However Mother managed to procure me another.'[18]

In mid-January, **Reg Evans** was finally within sight of getting out of hospital. His letter to his mother containing the good news was much chirpier than of late, though astonishingly he was frustrated to be out of action when there was still a war on:

> You will be pleased to hear that I am getting on fine and now being fitted for my final set of teeth. If I do not have a further little operation which the colonel this morning suggested, I ought to be back with you by next month, but of course if I have this other operation it may make it a little longer. Then I will have 10 days' leave before I go back to the regiment and we must have a jolly time to ourselves. No running about to see people, they must come and see us, no going out to tea and leaving you at home, everything together so that all your memories of my leave will be of the very pleasantest.
>
> Oh how I long for my liberty again when I think of getting out it seems so grand. Of course I mustn't grumble because everybody has been so good to me bit still I am weary of doing nothing. Just think I've had just on a twelvemonth of laziness and really this next summer should see the end of the war and I should always regret it if I wasn't in the finishing touch.
>
> We've had a grand concert this afternoon. Do you know the song

'When the war is over Mother dear' a girl sang that splendidly. Oh when it is all over . . .'[19]

January 1917 continued bitterly cold. The weather made life even harder for Britons who were struggling to make ends meet. Through her contact with workers at the arsenal, **Helen Bentwich** was realising more and more just how much ordinary people were suffering – and how removed their lives *always* were from the world of comfort she'd been brought up in:

> It's cold, cruel cold, in the mornings and evening, still I'm one of the lucky ones who can have all the clothes I want and a fire in my room and someone to get up and give me breakfast and I've no right to grouse. Sometimes, when I see some of these poor devils here and listen to their talk and realize all they have to put up with I wonder if I'll ever have the face to grumble at anything again. I've been thinking lately – I don't know how I'll get on when the war's over and I've got to stop working hard. In spite of being away from you and all the sadness of life, because I work like this I'm truly contented and I feel that it will always haunt me all through my life – the misery of those who slave day and night so that others may be wealthy.[20]

Helen had taken the first step towards doing something about this injustice she saw around her – she had joined a trade union:

> I've become more of a socialist lately than I've ever been before and more than any others of the family have ever been. If there's a militant socialism after the war – well, you'll have to spend your time bailing your wife out of police courts.
>
> What a tirade – but it is best really to prepare you for the part I mean to take in the Trade unions campaign after the war. That's why I've joined one now and paid a year's sub in advance so that even if I chuck being a worker in a factory I'll still belong to the union, see? Are you angry, or do you think I'm right?[21]

It was a bold step for an upper-class woman. Trade union activity was seen by most of her own class as deeply unpatriotic, and Lloyd George had moved to control union activity in wartime. But Helen felt her eyes had been opened, and she could not simply turn away from what she now saw.

Aside from the daily privations that they were suffering, the dangerous nature of the factory labour the working classes were undertaking was dramatically highlighted one January evening. **Hallie Miles** was rehearsing with her Loyal Choir at the time:

> There has been a ghastly explosion at the Silvertown Munition Factory. A 'Loyal Choir' practising was going on, when suddenly there was a rending cracking sound, like a bomb or a gun; naturally we thought it was Zeppelins, and how we all flew downstairs, kitchen staff and all! But nothing more happened; only the whole place was filled with the most awful smell of gunpowder and gases. We soon heard what it really was; and terrible news it was too.[22]

Silvertown Munition Factory was just the other side of the Thames from the Woolwich Arsenal. An accidental fire there had ignited fifty tonnes of TNT. The resulting explosion caused a mile of devastation – more than all of the Zeppelin raids on London combined. Sixty-nine female workers were killed and hundreds more were injured.[23] The news shocked the public. But the guns must be kept firing. Workers in Britain would have to keep on making munitions, whatever the dangers.

On 31 January, Germany announced that it was adopting a policy of unrestricted submarine warfare, meaning that from now on neutral merchant ships would be sunk without warning. Germany was also suffering from food shortages – more serious than in Britain – and was looking for a quick way to end the war now victory on the Western Front had failed to materialise. They hoped to starve Britain into surrender, by cutting off even more of the imports that had already been affected by the war.[24] There was a risk that neutral America would be angered into joining the war as a result; but this was a risk Germany decided to take.

On 3 February, the US severed diplomatic relations with Germany.

The ruins of the Venesta factory, which produced wooden packing cases for the tea trade, following the Silvertown explosion.

Over the course of that month, 105 British merchant ships were lost by enemy action – a total of 313,000 tonnes of shipping.[25] The German naval staff had calculated that it would only take the destruction of 600,000 tons of British, Allied and neutral shipping to starve Britain out of the war within five months.[26] The British public was worried. Most of them, anyway. **Andrew Clark** was sceptical of the scare stories that began to dominate the press:

> The Times and the Daily Mail are trying to raise a scare about U-Boats. In their list of ships sunk they include ships sunk as far back as November 1916, leaving people to conclude that all ships in their list have been sunk since the present German declaration about submarine war.[27]

Yet he continued to dutifully – and accurately – report the shortages that were being experienced by Britons at this time:

> <u>Wednesday 7 February:</u> 7.30 p.m.: Major Caldwell called, very cheerful and chatty. I have remembered only a few patches of his most interesting but discursive talk: The 'coal famine' in London is no fiction but a real

fact. Mr Caldwell's firm in London today had to abandon fires in all
but one room. The explanation is that people who have been managing
the railways for the government have sent so much rolling stock over
to France that there is not enough to supply the ordinary needs at home.
Liverpool is just as badly off.[28]

Lack of coal was a hardship, but it was food shortages that remained
the greatest concern. The impact of the German submarine campaign
was quickly felt: in the first quarter of the year, 15 per cent less food
was shipped in than in the corresponding period the previous year, and
that had been down on pre-war levels. The Food Controller, Lord
Devonport, was reluctant to introduce compulsory rationing, which was
seen as very 'un-English.' But something had to be done.[29]

Hallie Miles, of course, followed the discussions closely, and Eustace
was now being officially called upon for advice:

> The food question is becoming a very acute and solemn one. Lord
> Devonport and his Staff have an anxious work before them. Eustace is
> being a good deal consulted on food-values and meat substitutes, and
> spends much of his time at the Offices of the Food Control and Ministry
> of Food.

Whether or not Eustace Miles played any part in the decision is hard
to say, but in February, the Food Controller asked Britons to voluntarily
reduce their food consumption in the name of the war effort. Bread,
meat and sugar were the primary concerns and it was suggested –
though not made compulsory – that weekly consumption should not
exceed 4 lb of bread, 2½ lb of meat and 12 oz of sugar.[30]

Britons were subjected to ceaseless campaigns about economising:
cinemas screened films, speakers toured lecture halls and Food Economy
handbooks were published. Cutting down waste was endlessly promoted.
'Growing your own' was another proposed solution and use of allot-
ments soared.[31]

Hallie was convinced that the only way to beat the submarines was
economy. So far, however, she had been disappointed by how reluctant
Britons had been to rise to the occasion – despite her own example:

If only everyone would really ration, the awful 'U' Boats could not bring the famine that they are striving to bring to England. We ourselves are far below the [suggested] rationing allowance, but it is gladly we go below it. I eat nothing at afternoon tea now: I just have tea. I nearly always feel hungry nowadays; but I love to feel hungry; for I know that it means that I am eating less to help my country.[32]

Helen Bentwich agreed: the system wasn't working. Food was starting to become a problem even in the elite world her family inhabited:

I wish they'd ration us. This voluntary arrangement is stupid. Some people talk as if it were quite beneath them to ration and revel in the amount they can eat. You hear people say 'I can't possibly do without meat at least three times a day. I've had it all my life and I shouldn't dream of surrendering it'.[33]

Helen had other pressing matters on her mind, however. She had not wasted any time in implementing her campaign to improve working conditions at the arsenal:

I've got my union badge – a shield and so fight to struggle, to right the wrong. I think it's a perfectly topping motto to have and makes me simply wild to fight and right things bang off. I composed a long letter to my union secretary this morning, but I've not sent it yet, tho' I think I shall. I've suggested having a branch secretary in each show to deal with all grievances, and every girl being asked to sign on as a member when she signs on at the Arsenal. Also that there be dinner-time speeches and propaganda work.[34]

In Great Leighs the winter continued to bite. In mid-February **Andrew Clark** noted that the ground around the rectory was frozen solid with eight inches of frost. Things were tough for the villagers; as their minister, he was expected to encourage them to economise further still:

Afternoon's post brought me: a circular from the Food Controller urging all ministers of religion to encourage a voluntary cut-back in food consumption to avoid rationing.

5.15 p.m.: Dr Smallwood called: in some of the cottages very little
food is taken except bread. Cottagers are terribly alarmed as to what
will happen if they are put on a fixed rate of bread.[35]

Not all villagers felt they had to put up with the exhortations to
economise. A local domestic servant made the most of her newfound
power in this period of greater employment opportunities:

> A great house in the district, where 'economy' has always been practised
> in respect of servants' food – to the verge of meanness – has now made
> the happy discovery that true patriotism requires still further reductions.
> The cook at once gave notice to leave; she was not going to be put on
> 'one oat a day.'[36]

Helen Bentwich, writing to her husband from her bed, was deliber-
ating on how best to pass on the shock news she'd been given the
day before:

My darlingest boy,

I've disgraced you hopelessly and enormously and you'll have to be
jolly well ashamed of me. I've got the sack! Sad, but true – me, what
used to give select dinners to judges and titled ladies and pay gracious
calls on advisers – me, what am the wife of a captain and brilliant lawyer,
has been kicked out of the factory for disobeying OF rule no 79, which
states that a full day's work shall be done for a full day's pay. I have
been guilty of talking to the girls about trade unions and receiving
payments from them of course. You see, they found they couldn't get
one on the questions of joining or encouraging to join a T.U. because
there's nothing in their blessed rules book about it.

Aren't I a ghastly failure? 7 months' work and instead of promotion
– this! I was pretty blue last night and hadn't hardly the courage to go
home and confess. But I hadn't anywhere else to go, so I went, after
purposely missing many trains. Well, there's an end of the arsenal.

It makes me a bit sad because I don't seem to be doing anything but
am just a hopeless trier after things I can't do. I do so long to be and
do something and yet I don't somehow think I ever shall.[37]

*

Reg Evans's treatment was finally over. Harold Gillies had done the best he could. On 3 March Reg was 'discharged to duty', the final note on his patient records stating simply: 'Functionally the result was good. Cosmetically there is still an ugly arrangement of the lower lip.'[38]

Not yet fit for service, Reg had been sent to a 'command depot' at Shoreham on the south coast, where 5,000 injured soldiers like himself were undergoing rehabilitative training. Reg was having a great time – even though the food restrictions applied to them at the camp too. And yet his improved circumstances did not stop him worrying about his mother:

Dear Mother,

I have been rather disappointed at not hearing from you but only hope that it isn't owing to a renewal of ill-health. Do take care of your-self this treacherous weather. On Thursday it blew a biting freezing gale and on Friday it snowed. Ever since it has rained intermittently until the camp and all round it is practically ankle deep in mud. Still I am having a jolly good time and already have made lots of good pals, both in the mess and out. We have jolly good grub at the Sergeant's Mess and who ever gets the tatties, I can assure you that we don't as I haven't tasted any since Wednesday as we have swedes in their place. Still, we don't mind as long as it helps to win the war.

There is nothing much to do here, we don't have breakfast till 8. Roll call at 8.30. Parades 10.30 and 4.15. So you can tell it is an easy life and I'm going to be as fat as butter here. I went down to Brighton yesterday afternoon. As it came on to rain I put in the afternoon at the pictures and then after tea went to a concert in the aquarium. I can tell you 15/- a week won't go very far down here, for I mean to make the most of this holiday, for that's all it is. [39]

The worst horrors of the trenches had been unable to break Reg's spirit or embitter his cheerful nature. He would always wear the scars of war, but against the odds it looked as though he would one day be able to live a relatively normal life. He would, however, play no further part in the struggle on the Western Front.

Andrew Clark was not getting fat. The stress of the previous year, the extra work he had to do, and likely also the diminishing availability of many foods, had caused a drastic weight loss. And things weren't getting any better:

> I was weighed in Chelmsford yesterday — 11 stone 10 lb. My loss of weight from 18 St. 9 lb., in a year, is not assuring.
>
> 7.30 p.m. Major James Caldwell called. He said nothing is being imported now except food-stuffs and materials for making munitions (especially explosives). Every ton of shipping therefore, which is reported in the week's official return, as sunk, represents so much food gone to the bottom; altho' the ships lost are only a fraction of the arrivals, the food-stuffs lost in them represent a very grave diminution of the food supply.[40]

In March, 127 British merchant ships – a total tonnage of 353,478 – were lost through enemy action.[41] American ships were also being targeted as a result of the German policy of unrestricted submarine warfare. President Wilson had already requested permission from Congress to arm US merchant ships. And in March, a German attempt to entice Mexico into war against the USA was exposed. American neutrality was, surely, becoming impossible.

18

AFTER THE SOMME: TO ARRAS

January–May 1917

Oh my dear boy, I do pray that you will be spared, if I lost you, well dear, I don't know what I should do.

> Emily Chitticks, letter to her fiancé, March 1917

If the start of 1917 was bleak for British civilians, it was bleaker still for the British soldiers in France and Belgium. They huddled in cold, muddy trenches or snatched rest in billets or crowded base camps along the Western Front, which slashed the Continent in two from Switzerland to the sea.[1]

Nineteen-year-old Private **Will Martin** was one of them. Now, four weeks since leaving Blighty, he was really starting to feel the distance between himself and his fiancée Emily. He wrote to her on New Year's Day:

I am quite well and happy, but should be very much more happy if I could only get your letters. It does seem hard lines that we have to be so far apart, and the postal arrangements here are so rotten up to the present, but we are all in the same box. We are getting used to things now. Our sleeping accommodation is fairly good, it is better than being in tents in Rouen, but we have plenty of company by night which get running over our beds, and scuttling over our pillows, and they don't ask permission to eat our bread.

Dear little girl don't worry, for I am all right, but I couldn't help feeling sad on Xmas day darling, when I could see you in my mind, wondering where I was, how I was faring, and what I was doing, and I guess that I am reading you fairly well sweetheart. Well, I must now conclude hoping that I will get a letter soon. Fondest love and kisses from Your Loving Sweetheart,

    Xx Will Xx[2]

Will had arrived in France at a relatively quiet moment. In January 1917, the primary task for the British soldiers on the Western Front was to rebuild and regroup after the shattering five months of the Battle of the Somme. The state of the ground where the fighting had taken place was the worst it had ever been: lacerated by shellfire and the weather.[3] But the respite from the fighting – if it can indeed be labelled respite given the grim conditions – was only to be brief.

James Butlin was desperately hoping he would not be back in France any time soon. Since falling ill the previous spring, he had been on light duty at Wyke Regis, on the outskirts of his home town of Weymouth. He had been rather enjoying himself, not least because he had plenty of leisure time to spend chasing 'flappers'. But in early 1917, the fun came to an end. His battalion was reorganised, and he was found fit for a new job, and moved away to Salisbury Plain. He wrote to his old university friend Basil, who had now graduated from Oxford:

> My luck this year has been absolutely out. To start with they reorganised the battalion at Wyke and under the new arrangement I found myself no longer even second in command of a company. Suddenly, without a moment's warning, I was pitch forked into this accursed job. I am now OC to 3 Southern company non-Combatants Corps in the middle of the Salisbury plain. When I heard my fate at Weymouth I swore terribly and cursed every thing within reach. I was wild with anger and am not yet really myself again.
>
> At present I am sinking into a state of nervous depression. What little work I do here is utterly uncongenial to me. If I stay here a month I shall go stark staring mad. If I stay here indefinitely suicide is not unthinkable. There are of course one or two ways of getting out of this place if only I could get a medical board. I can either volunteer for active service or be too ill to carry on here. There is yet another alternative to

which I do not wish to resort. Push off, stay in town until arrested for
leave without absence.

Yours in great tribulation, James.

p.s. All information in this letter is strictly confidential. Tear it up
when you have read it.[4]

In mid-January, **Will Martin** finally received a parcel from Emily. He
was still behind the lines, but he knew his training must be coming to
an end:

> I have received your parcel quite safely. I must thank you very much for
> your kind wishes. I have been doing some trench digging lately, quite a
> change from drill. A pick and a shovel are not strangers to me, but it
> is the first time in the two years that I have been in the army that I
> have done my part towards digging a trench, and we are still training
> and not trained yet, but I expect we shall be someday.[5]

Will was one of a draft of men who were yet to join the main body of
the regiment they'd been assigned to. In mid-January, whilst Will and his
fellow new recruits practised soldiering and dug reserve trenches, the 8th
Devonshire Regiment was in the frontline trenches near Beaumont-Hamel.
There a series of minor operations had made some gains for the Allies, to
strengthen their position in advance of the next big offensive, now being
planned.[6] On 16 January, the French and British war leaders met in London.
The plans for the spring were finalised: the French would attack on the
Aisne in mid-April, the British would attack a week earlier, near Arras.[7]

Meanwhile, temperatures in France plummeted. The mud froze and
the men were tormented by the cold.[8] Will was casting his mind back
wistfully to former times:

> We are having dry weather, and the sun is shining nicely, but it is cold
> enough to freeze your nose, in fact the cold has got hold of the tips of
> my fingers, and it had made them quite sore. By the way dear, could
> you manage to get me a pair of woollen gloves, I am sorry to trouble
> you, but the ones I had issued are gone done, and I can't see any likes
> of getting any here.
>
> I was just thinking what a contrast the times are now, to what they
> used to be. Wouldn't I just like to be in Herongate today! I forgot to

mention before that one of those books you sent me was the one I commenced and went to sleep holding on the cricket common, the day you caught me napping, so it brings back fond memories.[9]

Soldiers survey the landscape from a snowy trench outside Arras, France, February 1917.

In the last week of January, the 8th Devonshire Regiment, at rest at Beauval, received 124 new soldiers into its ranks. Will Martin was one of them. They started training immediately for the next stint in the front lines. Beauval was just 25 miles from Arras.[10]

In early February, **James Butlin** turned 21 whilst on leave. Now back in camp on Salisbury Plain, he was terribly anxious. His future was about to be decided by a medical board. If he was deemed fit, he would have to return to active service. His wrote to Basil in a dark mood:

> I don't know what to do in the near future. The whole affair is compli-
> cated by several factors. I have a medical board in a few days' time, on
> which of course much depends. The people with whom I live and mess
> here are going out to France in a week's time and I should have to find
> a new mess, if I were to remain here. On the other hand, if I get passed
> I am certain to be sent out for the great push which I understand is
> going to exceed anything that ever was.[11]

After seeing action in the terrible battles of 1915, James did not want to go through such trauma again.

But at the end of February he was passed fit for active service.

Kate Parry Collins always loved hearing from John; she worried desperately when she didn't. In February, she got a letter that pleased her even more than usual:

> A letter from John in the morning to say he has at last got his official 'Majority' – while he is in command of the Battery. I had written to him last night and addressed and stamped the envelope 'Captain' – so added PS of congratulation.[12]

Kate relished John's new status, and soon got used to addressing him properly – she wrote to him again the following day:

> I posted my usual bi-weekly papers to John addressed to 'Major Collins' – it does look grand. To think we have so often talked of him as a Major and it has been so real and then never come – and now it really has come.

With the increased status came, of course, increased responsibility. John's battery, 222 Siege Battery of the Royal Garrison Artillery, was one of those intended to participate in the upcoming offensive. In less than two months, its heavy howitzers would be needed.

Will Martin and the 8th Devonshire Regiment he was now a part of were still in rest behind the lines. Will was now living alongside men who had experience of the front lines of war, and he was realising the gravity of what he faced:

> Well I am still alive and kicking and in the best of spirits, although I wish sometimes that it was at an end, but I suppose we must do as the Chaplain told us on Sunday, dear: that we must get to the end, that the end was fixed, and that it would not come half way to meet us.
>
> We are a happy and fairly comfortable party sitting round the fire this afternoon in our little wooden hut, some talking of the good old

days and others writing like myself. It is certainly very upsetting when
you go to Church, and they start speaking of the war and so on. It
doesn't give anyone a very good heart to go again, but it seems that they
like speaking on the subject.[13]

In the middle of the month, the 8th Devonshire Regiment marched
to Puchevillers, where the entire 7th Division was inspected. The
commander-in-chief of the British Expeditionary Force was present.[14]
He had big plans for them, as Will had guessed:

> I think that we will soon start soldiering now. I am getting somewhat
> used to the pack now, and can carry it with the rest of them.[15]

On 21 February, Will and the 8th Devons marched to Bertrancourt.
Two days later, on the 23rd, strange reports began to reach their
commanders. Three patrols from the 21st Manchester Regiment, also
in the 7th Division, had gone out near Serre, a few miles away. They
had been amazed to meet no resistance. It appeared that the Germans
had vanished.[16]

That afternoon, instructions were issued to all divisions in the line to
send out strong patrols during the night. Four hundred men from the
8th Devons went out. On the entire section of the front between Le
Transloy and Serre, British troops met no resistance. They advanced ten
miles. The Germans had put into practice a plan they had long been
preparing: they had begun the retreat to a new defensive line, known to
the British as the Hindenburg Line, to the Germans as the Siegfriedstellung.
It was a well-defended position, without kinks and salients, and some
twenty-five miles shorter than the previous line they'd held. As a result,
the Allies' plans for an attack were thrown into chaos.[17]

Once the initial bewilderment had passed, the question for the British
commanders was whether to pursue the retreating Germans. The
commanders were cautious: the planned offensive remained the main
objective, but nevertheless, on 25 February, a pursuit was begun.[18] Over
the next few days the 7th Division made significant gains though, on
some parts of the line, resistance was met from parties left behind by
the Germans to ensure that the Allied advance did not proceed too
quickly.

Will Martin and the 8th Devons had remained on standby at first.
Then, on 2 March, they were assembled and moved to the new front

line at Puisieux, where they took over a section running round the northern edge of the village. The village was in ruins and there was heavy shelling all night. The following day, patrols pushed forward, but all ultimately returned. The village and road were shelled all day. The next day was the same – and then it started to snow.[19]

The ruined village of Puisieux, March 1917.

This was Will's first, bitter, and bitterly cold, taste of war. He was relieved after dark on 5 March, and went back into billets at Mailly-Maillet. He received a concerned letter from Emily, and wrote back to her, trying to put her mind at rest:

> I daresay, sweetheart, you have been wondering why I have not written, but I daresay you will understand why I have not written, and I daresay there will be more occasions when I shall not be able to write for a few days . . .
>
> You need not worry the slightest bit on my account, for up to the present time I have got on all right and I am still quite well. You were quite right in your guess, and I have seen a bit of life since that letter reached you.[20]

On receipt of this, Emily's worries became much more immediate and she hastily scribbled her reply:

I have just received another letter from you. I can't quite understand
your meaning in one sentence. It's where you said I had guessed quite
right and you had seen some life since I had that letter.

Do you mean, Will, you have been fighting? Don't keep it from me
– if you have been in the trenches, tell me. I would rather know. I can't
think what else you mean darling.[21]

March 1917 was a crisis moment for the Allies. The Germans had surprised
their opponents, and were now fully committed to a defensive strategy
on the Western Front.[22] It would be harder than ever for the great
breakthrough to be made. And the Allies had other concerns, too.
Discontent over the war had been building in Russia, and on 10 March,
the Soviet of Workers', Soldiers' and Peasants' Deputies challenged the
power of the Russian Parliament in Petrograd. Soldiers joined the crowds
in the street demonstrating against the Tsar, and on 13 March the law
courts and police stations in the city were set alight. Two days later, the
Tsar abdicated and a provisional government took over.[23]

Despite the political turmoil, the new government did not withdraw
Russia from the war effort. But the plans for the spring offensive were
thrown into doubt by the Russian army's increasing weakness – the
Allies could no longer rely on a war on two fronts in the coming spring.
The pressure was mounting on the planned offensive against the
strengthened German line on the Western Front.

By now, **James Butlin** was in France, en route to join his unit. But
first, he had some time to readjust – and have an unexpected adventure:

On Sunday I went into Rouen where I had a good look round. The place
was absolutely chock full of girls, some pretty, some pretty awful. I saw
one in particular about 6.30 p.m. who was most awfully pretty and looked
different from the painted type with which we are all familiar. I hazarded
some of my French (which is steadily improving) and she came and had
a drink with me at a hotel. Her sister also came, who arrived while I was
speaking to her. Introduced her to two other Dorsets who came out with
me and they, (i.e. the two girls) went off at about 7.15 p.m. and asked us
to come to tea at an address they gave us on the following day.

Fortunately for me I was the only man who spoke French and so at
tea the next day I had a pretty good time and took her into Rouen to
dinner. After dinner we were both pretty merry and drove a few

unnecessary miles in a taxi which I enjoyed most immensely. Her name is Juliette and she is only eighteen but most frightfully pretty and very vivacious. By this time I got to know her pretty well and was very much in love with her. I went by invitation to her house last night at 8 o'clock and stayed the night with her till 7 o'clock this morning. However the fact that this letter has to pass through a number of hands prevents me from saying any more except that I am supremely happy.[24]

So far, James's second trip to France had not been as bad as he'd anticipated.

Will Martin spent much of March in training for the coming offensive, and improving the roads in the area in preparation for the movement of troops. But on 26 March, Will and the 8th Devons went back into the front line at Mory, just south-west of Ecoust, an outpost village still in enemy hands that the Allies wanted back.[25] As he marched back into action, **Emily Chitticks** was thinking of him. She interrupted her work in the farmhouse to write to him, and for some reason did so in bold red ink:

I wonder what you are doing now. Oh my dear boy I do pray that you will be spared. If I lost you I don't know what I should do. I do hope I shall hear from you soon. I can't help worrying about you. If only it was all over and you were home again. What a dreadful time you must be going through.

On several occasions I have dreamed that you were back home with me, and the most strange thing about them, you are always in civilian clothes when I dream of you, and I have never seen you in those . . . I only wish you were in civilians now. I do want to see you again so badly, but I must try and be patient. Oh Will it is very hard to be cheerful when I am always thinking of you, wondering if you are all right!

I must close now dear as its time to see about dinner. Heaps of love and kisses from your Loving Sweetheart,

Emily Xxxx[26]

There was a problem of manpower on the Western Front. As the British Army grew and took over more of the front from the French, additional support was required. In 1917, a number of solutions were found to this problem. Firstly, women were allowed in uniform in France and Belgium for the first time; the Women's Army Auxiliary Corps were employed at ports, on the lines of communication and at GHQ.[27]

Secondly, there was to be an expansion in the use of 'coloured' labour. The commander-in-chief requested that 'coloured' workers – from India, South Africa, China and Egypt – take over work on the lines of communication. These civilian labourers would be in addition to the Cape Coloured Labour battalion already working behind the lines.[28] The British army's racist policy allowed Indian troops to serve as fighting soldiers; black troops from the Caribbean or South Africa were only allowed to work as service battalions in Europe, though the British West Indies Regiment did fight in Egypt and Palestine.[29]

In Britain, the recruitment of black Britons to the army was not officially permitted and they were not liable to conscription. In reality, it was a matter left up to the discretion of individual recruitment centres.[30] In any case, in February 1917, **Arthur Roberts**, a black man of Caribbean descent, living in Glasgow, enlisted in the King's Own Scottish Border Regiment in Edinburgh.

Arthur was the son of a ship's steward from Trinidad and Tobago, and a white mother from Bristol, the daughter of a chimney sweep. He had been born in Bristol, but had moved to Glasgow as a child, without his mother. His father was absent a lot of the time, working on transatlantic ships, and Arthur lived alone in a hostel near to his aunt and cousin in the tenements of Anderston. Against the odds he did well at school and had afterwards started an apprenticeship at the famous shipbuilding firm Harland and Wolff. They had constructed the *Titanic*, which had sunk just a few years earlier.

But by late March 1917, he was a world away from the shipyard. He had joined up, against the wishes of his father, who had wanted him to continue in his apprenticeship. From his training camp in Portobello, Edinburgh, Arthur wrote to his aunt:

Dear Aunt,

I have thoroughly recovered my health and am progressing finely. I hope you are drawing the half pay alright. I suppose the old boy would be kicking up a dust about me but just let him talk till he is tired then he'll dry up.

I've seen two or three drafts going away since I've been here and it feels so funny while the men are passing. The bands are playing good O and you feel as if you were going too, but when one sees the mothers and sisters and sweethearts crying as they keep step with their loved ones and the fathers walking silent with eyes red and shining with unshed tears it makes one feel creepy, especially when the big drum booms and the kettle drums roll, but somebody must go.

In the draft that went away today there were three men taken out from the guardroom, that's our prison, handcuffed and marched off to France without being able to shake hands with some of their friends who were waiting on them at the gate. I hope when I go that I'll be able to walk as straight as any man in the draft.

Wishing you and Lily the best of health and that you practise economy. I remain your loving nephew,

Arthur Roberts[31]

Arthur would not be long in training. With the spring offensive on the horizon and the Germans in stronger defensive positions, the need for fresh blood at the front was greater than ever.

Emily Chitticks had not heard from Will for several days, and she began to fret. She knew the post was erratic, but it was hard not to think the worst. She continued to write to him, in the same bright red ink she had used last time:

I feel I must write to you again although there is not much news to tell you. I wonder how you are getting on. I shall be relieved to get a letter from you – I can't help feeling a bit anxious. I know how you must have felt, darling, when you did not get my letters for so long. Of course I know you will write as soon as ever you can, but the time seems so dull and weary without any news of you. If only this war was over and we were together again. It will be one day I suppose.

Don't think I am worrying unnecessarily about you, because I know God can take care of you wherever you are, and if it's his will darling he will spare you to come back to me.

I can understand darling your not being able to write so frequently. I shall get used to waiting for your letters soon I guess, but at first it seems so strange, after being used to having them so regularly.[32]

*

On 6 April, Good Friday, two months after Germany embarked on its policy of unrestricted submarine warfare, the USA declared war. American interests had been threatened directly, and President Wilson's peaceful stance had become untenable. It would take a long time for the effects of American involvement to be felt in the conflict so far from its shores. But the news was nonetheless welcome to the beleaguered Allies.

The weather was chilly that Good Friday. **Kate Parry Collins** and her mother wrapped up warm to walk to church. In these strained times, Kate found the service more than usually affecting:

> Mother and I went to the 3 hours service at Wooburn Church. It was conducted by the Vicar of Aylesbury and was a most beautiful service. It was most wonderfully impressive and this year while my heart is so attuned to sadness and anxiety it seems to have taken a deeper hold than ever. I prayed very earnestly for John and that he may be spared. I fear he is in the midst of it all and though I have had a letter most days lately he speaks of awful things doing which may not be mentioned. Oh dear oh dear!!![33]

John had probably written of the preparations for the forthcoming offensive at Arras, which were now in their final stages. On Easter Sunday, Kate made the journey to the village church once more, praying that next Easter she and John would be together again.[34] That would depend on the course of events over the next few days. The opposing armies now faced each other over the eastern edge of the Artois plateau. The battle was scheduled to commence the following morning.[35]

On the morning of 9 April, Easter Monday, British troops launched an attack on Arras in parallel with a Canadian assault on Vimy Ridge. The initial successes were remarkable: in less than an hour, almost the whole of the German frontline trench system had been breached, and within two hours troops reached the second line. 5,600 Germans were taken prisoner. At Vimy, the Canadians too had made considerable progress and taken 4,000 prisoners.[36]

James Butlin and the 6th Dorsets were in reserve. They were to follow the cavalry corps in the army of pursuit. But the third German lines – better fortified than any before – proved more difficult to penetrate, and the day passed and the 6th Dorsets were not called upon.[37] But James knew it was only a matter of time before they too were thrown into the battle – thinking of his new lover in Rouen he wrote a hasty note to Basil:

> A brief line to let you know I am still on the earth. Letters from France and from England are tremendously delayed nowadays. By the time you get this you will hear of great events and probably long before you get this. If I am killed in this battle, would you do me a great favour, please? i.e. write to Juliette and tell her. Of course if I come through alive you won't need to do anything, as I devoutly hope may happen.[38]

That night, snow fell on the forward troops who had little to protect them against it.[39] By the third day, the snow began to fall more heavily, and the initial British optimism began to waver as the advance became bogged down. That night, James and the 6th Dorsets were ordered to relieve the 44th Brigade in the trenches. They finally made it through the darkness and heavy snow to take up position shortly before dawn.[40]

The following day, 12 April, the 9th Division were attacking and orders were given for the 17th Division, including the 8th Dorsets, to attack in support. There was insufficient time to prepare, orders were confused, and the accompanying artillery barrage was wild and scattered. They were met with heavy shelling and machine-gun fire. James was one of the lucky ones who made it to the enemy outposts. It was for nothing, however, as a withdrawal was ordered at 11 p.m. since the position was too exposed to hold.[41]

The 6th Dorsets had suffered huge casualties. The next day's task was reclaiming the wounded and the dead.[42] James was lucky to be alive, and he knew it as he wrote to Basil:

> We have just come out of action: you will have read by this time pages and pages about the battle of Arras. We went into the show about the 2nd day, I think: I am not very clear about dates or days. The cold was awful and some of the nights spent in the open amidst snow and mud and shell fire are among the worst in my experience.
>
> When we went over the top we came up against a terrific shell and machine-gun fire: it was perfect hell. A company was very lucky, however, and no officer was hit. C company lost all its officers, D had one left. B company was kept in reserve. We gained our objective and the general was greatly braced with us.

A letter from Rouen has at least arrived. I wouldn't mind being back there again now. Will try to write again later on: at present I am a bit nervy and want all the rest I can get.[43]

It was only a brief respite.

The first phase of the Battle of Arras came to a close on 15 April. Terrible losses were suffered on both sides, but the Allies made advances of up to four miles and succeeded in diverting German troops from the river Aisne. There, the following day, the French launched their partner attack, the Nivelle Offensive (named after their new Commander-in-Chief, who had replaced General Joffre in December 1916). It was a disaster. In spite of territorial gains, the offensive was brought to a standstill after just a few days. 10,000 casualties had been predicted; 100,000 were incurred. French morale was at an all-time low and her men were mutinying. There was no let-up in sight for the exhausted British armies.[44]

Kate Parry Collins was trying to distract herself. She was sorting through a trunk of clothes that she'd put into storage in 1915. It was not only something to keep her busy; it was an attempt to economise in these lean times:

Found a place for everything, repacked coloured dresses etc. and tidied up. Agnes and I are still going about in a sort of half mourning – greys, blacks and mauves. I don't feel I can go into colours while the war lasts and besides it would mean an extravagant stock of new clothes to blend – and besides being unpatriotic I have not the wish now for finery. But I am horribly shabby.[45]

It was hard to keep going:

Saturday 21 April 1917: Nothing from John. They seem long days when I do not hear.[46]

That same day, **James Butlin** was still in reserve, awaiting the next assault with dread. He had written to Basil a few days earlier:

I am writing this from the depths of an old German dug-out; about 40 ft below the earth and accordingly pretty bomb proof. We have gone up the line again and are now in reserve about 2 miles from the line. Exactly what is coming off I can't say because I don't know. The weather is vile still, raining continually but not quite so cold. We have been living lately on iron rations more or less, in fact I haven't tasted bread since last Sunday week, 11 days ago. I have just heard that a loaf has arrived with the rations tonight so you can imagine my state of jubilation. Try living on bully beef and biscuits for a week and you will soon get enjoyment out of quite small things. I have had plenty of rum lately which has kept me going: you need a nerve-steadier pretty often on this game.

Lately we have seen an awful lot of air fighting. Some of these Hun pilots are the very devil: they seem to be able to out manoeuvre our blokes owing to the superiority of their machines. One of our fellows was attacked by a German plane, who fired on him till the English plane caught fire and fell headlong to the ground. It must have been an awful death. He fell to the ground just a streak of flame, one of the most unforgettable sights of a life-time.[47]

The Royal Flying Corps called this month 'bloody April' – they lost a third of their force in France. It was awful for the infantry too; in the renewed attacks at Arras, twice as many British as German soldiers would be killed.[48]

Kate Parry Collins had found another task to occupy her: spring cleaning. But at the end of a busy day, she finally got what she was longing for: word from John. Indeed, she got more than that:

I wasn't up very early but then settled down to work and worked all the afternoon. Then to the shops on the Green.

When we got up, about 7 o'clock, there was a parcel for me – 'One German helmet' from John. It was very exciting opening it – and it is a wonderful specimen of the Dolly Varden shape. John told me he had found one on the battlefield and would try and send it. There was a note inside it – and also a letter written some days later. I couldn't quite bear the helmet, it seemed so haunted by the dear German who wore it. I assume he is dead.[49]

Having finished writing her diary, she went to bed. She did not sleep
soundly:

> Last night I had a horrible night dreaming of the German who owned
> the helmet. I am sure his spirit was near.[50]

The Battle of Arras was finally brought to a close in the middle of
May. The British had made their greatest advances for two and half
years. Sixty-one square miles of territory and more than 20,000 prisoners
of war had been taken, in what had been by and large a well-planned
and well-executed campaign.

But the price paid had been very high. There had been almost 85,000
British casualties in just over a month of fighting. Since the beginning
of 1917, over 40,000 British men had been killed.[51]

In April, **Emily Chitticks** finally got word from the front. Her last
five letters to Will were returned to her. They were unopened. Along
with them came a letter from one of Will's comrades:

> Dear Miss Chitticks,
>   Being a personal friend of William Martin, who has been with me
> since we left England, and also aware that he was engaged to you, I
> thought it would be my duty to inform you, which I greatly deplore
> doing, that he has been killed in action. He suffered no pain. He is
> greatly missed by all in our platoon and we condole with you at your
> loss. This is my address just to let me know if you receive this or not.
> I.S. Huxley 40628 5 Platoon B Company B.E.F.
>   I remain yours sincerely
>   I.S Huxley[52]

The next day, she received a letter from Will's officer confirming the news:

> Dear Miss Chitticks,
>   I regret deeply to have to inform you that Pte. W. J. Martin was
> killed on the afternoon of Tuesday, March 27th while in the performance
> of his duty in the front line. He was hit in the head by a sniper's bullet
> and never recovered consciousness before he died. I am returning to you
> one or two small things which I found in his pocket which you might
> care to keep in memory of him.

Believe me, I am extremely sorry to have to give you such painful news, and I deplore his loss, just as do all his comrades in the platoon. Please accept my deepest sympathy for your loss and believe me to be

Sincerely Yours

C. Caleb[53]

The dreams of a future together that Emily and Will had cherished were over.

On 5 May, Lt. **James Butlin**'s name was published in the casualty lists, as injured. The truth was rather more complicated. Invalided back to Britain for the second time in the war, he wrote to Basil in buoyant mood, from Scotland:

My dear old Basil,

We left Kings X by the 10 o'clock express and got to Waverley Station, Edinburgh, without mishap. A motor met us at the station and took us out to this place. The inhabitants gazed at us in a peculiar manner, for which I afterwards discovered a reason.

After a ride of some 3 miles we fetched up here, had dinner and started to explore. It is a magnificent hydro standing in palatial grounds fitted with all the comforts that man's ingenuity can contrive. Swimming baths, billiards, gardening, bowls, tennis, etc., are some of the hobbies one is expected to take up. Personally I am thinking of writing a book: provided one is in by six o'clock and conforms to a few simple rules, life is a complete and glorious lark.

The inhabitants have two theories concerning us and as we are the only military hospital in Scotland and are compelled to wear blue bands at all times, there may be a little justification for what they believe. Their first theory is that we are lunatics under careful surveyance but none the less dangerous. The second that we are victims of venereal disease and confined here as a punishment. From the looks of the population I gather that the second theory is most strongly held. I am sending for my tennis things as I can see I shall go mad with nothing to do. I haven't had a drink for a fortnight which is highly creditable.

My name is in the casualty list today. Cheer oho, Yours ever, James[54]

James was writing from Craiglockhart Hospital: one of the first medical institutions for the treatment of 'shell shock'.

Kate Parry Collins was one of the few people who got good news in the aftermath of the Battle of Arras:

> The postman was very late – 9.50 instead of 9.30 – I always do wait breath-lessly for letters. Kathleen brought me up two – both from John. The first one I opened, I went hot all over and my breath gave out with excitement – he was called before the General and told he had been awarded the Military Cross. He does not say how, why, or when, but that is like him. Only that 'it's not his fault' and that he thought what he had done was of 'no consequence'. It's no use saying what I feel, but I am so proud and so thankful. But oh I do want him to keep on earth whatever happens.[55]

The details soon emerged. Not only had he done his own work, on fixing communications for the artillery – in the midst of the battle he had also helped the infantry advance:

> A letter from John telling me somewhat of why he has been decorated. It was at the Battle of Arras – he crossed 200 yds of No Man's Land, laid a telephone, located the barbed wire and smashed it up with his guns.[56]

At the back of her diary for 1917, Kate transcribed the citation of John's MC that was printed in *The Times* later that year:

> The King has been pleased to confer the Military Cross on the following Officers in recognition of their gallantry and devotion to duty in the Field:
>
>   Capt (Acting Major) John Robert Collins R.G.A.
>
>   For conspicuous gallantry and devotion to duty in observing for his battery and carrying out an effective report from a completely exposed position in advance of our outpost line. He and his two telephonists were under hostile shell fire and within close range of the enemy advanced posts, and were in great danger of being cut off; but they maintained communication throughout with great coolness and determination.[57]

*

Emily Chitticks had kept all the letters that Will had sent to her during their seven-month romance, and many of those she had written to him too. They would be her personal memorial to him. He was buried far away, in a hastily dug grave she could not visit, and there was no funeral service for her to attend. She wrote her simple final message to her fiancé on the back cover of her Bible, her most treasured possession besides their correspondence:

> In loving remembrance of my dearly loved and loving fiancé 'Will' who made the supreme sacrifice on March 29th 1917.
>
> 'Greater love have no man than this in that he lay down his life for his friend.'
>
> Until we meet again before God's throne dearest, its only 'goodnight.' Emily.[58]

In the midst of her grief, Emily had nonetheless politely replied to the two correspondents who had notified her of Will's death. But within a few weeks, both of the letters she had written were returned to her, unopened. Will's comrades had both since been killed in the Battle of Arras.

Another spring of intense fighting had come to an end. The snow had melted away; the bitter cold of nights spent in the open was waning; the hedgerows alongside the much-trodden roads and churned-up battlefields of France were starting to smell like summer. Conditions were improving; but the war was as greedy as ever. Whilst the corpses and debris were still being cleared from the battlefields near Arras, new bodies were still being shipped over the Channel to take their place.

19

IN FLANDERS FIELDS

May–December 1917

Oh Heavens: that first dead soldier is a sight that is practically photographed on my brain. On the sloping side of the crater lay somebody's son.
Arthur Roberts, 14 June 1917

On 19 May 1917, **Arthur Roberts** boarded the *Princess Victoria* at Folkestone for transport to Boulogne. He knew all about ships from his time at the Harland and Wolff shipyard in Glasgow. But that was his former life; now he was a soldier, in the uniform of the King's Own Scottish Border Regiment. As a black man he must have stood out from his comrades, but that was the only thing that distinguished him from the rest – he was a soldier bound for war, like any other.

Once they arrived in France, Arthur and the rest of his draft marched to a training camp at Étaples. On the first night there, he wrote in a small diary he had brought over with him. He had to do so cautiously, as it was strongly discouraged for a private soldier to keep such a diary:

I rose fine and fit this morning and prepared for breakfast of bully beef and dog biscuits and tea, after which the dreaded march was to commence. The draft started about 8 a.m. and after a gruelling march, which I shall never forget, it arrived in Etaples about 3.45 p.m. in a nearly exhausted condition, for the weather was terribly hot. After a good night's rest the remainder of our training will be resumed.[1]

Arthur had arrived in France at a crisis moment in the war. On the Eastern Front, Russia was still fighting, and the Provisional Government was committed to the war. But on the ground support was rushing away, and the armed forces were increasingly divided and rebellious.

And, on the Western Front, the French army too was in chaos: from late April, mutinies began; by June, 40,000 troops had been involved. Desertion rates were soaring.[2]

The onus, increasingly, was on Britain. But even in Britain, support for the war was not as enthusiastic as it once had been. The pacifist movement was growing – as were government anxieties over civilian morale. The pressures being put on the population by German submarine warfare was building. Civilian endurance was being tested as never before.[3]

Discipline in the British army was remarkably strong, but the situation facing it was grave. The commander-in-chief, Haig, was determined that the only way forward was to continue with yet another huge offensive on the Western Front that summer, this time in Flanders in Belgium. The French were no longer in a position to play their part as planned, but Haig was determined the offensive would go on; that the enemy must not have the time to recover after the offensive at Arras. In fact, he insisted, the attack was even more urgent now, to prevent the Germans exploiting the very real weakness on the French front.

The American army was not yet able to provide any real support. The French could now do no more than hold the line. The British army would have to fight alone.[4]

Duff Cooper had been exempt from service because of his job at the Foreign Office. He was one of the very few amongst his friends who had not joined up – and, because of that, he was one of the few who had so far survived the war. But in May 1917, the bar to his enlistment was lifted. Despite the endless losses he'd felt first-hand, Duff felt the choice for him was clear:

> The government want more men for the army and we in the foreign office are all to be medically examined and I think they will have to let some of us go. If anyone is allowed to go I shall be as I am the youngest of the permanent staff, unmarried and, I should think, perfectly fit.
>
> The thought fills me with exhilaration. I dare say that I shall very soon heartily wish myself back. But I am eager for a change. I always wished to go to the war, though less now than I did at first. I envy the experience and adventure that everyone else has had. I am not afraid of

death though I love life and would hate to lose it. The only drawback
is the terrible blow it would be to Mother. I don't know how I should
dare tell her. I think Diana, too, would mind.[5]

Just two days later he had his medical exam, and passed. That night,
Duff went away with a group of friends, including Diana. In the dead
of night, Duff crept into Diana's room:

Diana said she would come to me but at half past three I gave up hope
and went to her. It was perhaps the loveliest of all nights. We lay quietly
for a long time and talked. I confessed to her that I was really glad to
join the army which made her cry – she was so white and darling and
pathetic. I explained to her that it was no nonsense about dying for my
country or beating the Germans that made me glad to join, but simply
the feeling I have had for so long that I am missing something, the
vague regret that one feels when not invited to a ball even though it be
a ball that one hardly would have hoped to enjoy.[6]

Arthur Roberts was at the infantry base camp at Étaples, which was
notorious for its terrible conditions – specifically the harsh training
ground set amid the sand dunes known as the 'Bull Ring'. Arthur got
a painful introduction to it:

Our crowd was at the 'Bull Ring' today – and what a day. No wonder they
call it the 'Bull Ring'. It is only three miles from camp but I never had
such a tramp in my life. The sun blazed and there was hardly a breeze. We
were through all kinds of gases and what with nearly suffocating us, gassing
us and then marching us back again, with the blazing sun making our steel
helmets like red hot pudding basins, we were just about dead on arriving
about 5 p.m. being away since 8 a.m. Oh what a day![7]

Arthur and his comrades were back there numerous times over the
next week, training in everything from how to deal with gas attacks to
the art of guarding latrines. All this whilst getting used to carrying
their packs under the searing summer sun:

We again went to the 'Bull Ring' today. I thought the first day was bad
but today was worse. The heat was something terrific. When we had

covered a mile or more a fellow dropped in a fit through the heat. Throughout the whole day fellows were fainting for want of water. The water has been cut off for three days so that there was none even to wash ourselves with. While returning a motor ran over a fellow's leg. This has been a day of accidents. Fags were dished out today.[8]

Étaples was so unpleasant that Arthur couldn't wait to leave it behind – even if that meant going up to the front lines.

There had been no major action around Ypres since the epic defensive battles of 1914 and early 1915, but the fighting there never seemed to stop. The British front line that bulged around the rubble of the ancient town was virtually surrounded by the German army. Along this salient, skirmishes were constant, but it was a stalemate situation, with both armies on the defensive.[9]

The objective of the planned summer offensive was to secure the Belgian coastline. It was Belgium's ports that housed the German destroyers and submarines that were wreaking such havoc on Britain.[10] Haig planned two phases: an attack on Messines Ridge in early June – to neaten out part of the bulge in the front line – and the main thrust, the 'Northern Operation' to secure the Belgian coastline some weeks later. Haig was convinced that the Germans had been weakened by the spring actions and victory was possible for the Allies in 1917. The War Cabinet was not so optimistic and, by June, it had still refused to sanction the 'Northern Operation'.[11]

The preparations for it continued regardless. By now Arthur Roberts had left the regiment with which he had trained, and had been attached to the Royal Scots Fusiliers. On 4 June he arrived in Poperinghe, the main hub in Flanders:

This morning we marched to our special train of horse boxes. The train started about 8.15 a.m. on its slow lumbering journey. The comic events which took place during the journey are too numerous to mention but I laughed myself sore. Arguments were varied and plentiful but on coming within sound of the guns the arguments ceased and opinions ran in unison. The rest camp was reached about 11.45 p.m. but we were so interested in the flashes and noise of distant artillery that for a time we forgot bed. However drowsiness soon asserted itself and we remembered.[12]

A few days later, 7 June, the first phase of Haig's planned offensive began: an attack on Messines Ridge, in the southern sector of the Flanders line. Nineteen mines containing nearly a million pounds of high explosives were detonated under the German front line, in shafts that had been constructed over six months. Ten thousand German soldiers were killed outright. A terrific artillery bombardment followed, and an infantry assault by 80,000 men. The German army withdrew to a new line further east; the Allies had captured the vantage point of the ridge and smoothed out their front line. The casualties were high on the British side too, but the operation was a success.[13]

The main offensive was still to be given the go-ahead. But everything was in motion. The troops continued to pour into Poperinghe. The sun still shone.

British troops laying a new railway line as part of the preparations for the Third Battle of Ypres.

In June, **Duff Cooper** was given formal permission to join the army. He quickly secured the promise of a commission in the Grenadier Guards, the most senior regiment in the infantry. His desk job became a thing of the past:

> Today I left the foreign office without a single regret. I went there in the morning but did not return after lunch. I love to think of the dreary files of papers that I shall not see again. Even if I survive the war I

doubt whether I shall go back to the foreign office. I should hate to face that monotonous routine again.[14]

He was imagining a summer in the sunshine with like-minded companions, getting fresh air and becoming fit.

Arthur Roberts was a few miles down the line from the assault on Messines, having been sent on to Ypres. The front line was to the east of the town, at the bottom of a series of ridges held by the Germans, leading up to the Passchendaele Ridge about 5 miles away. In the dying light of a summer's day, he set off to the frontline trenches for the first time:

> We set off in a single file, up the trench. On we went round corners, and corners, and still more corners, while the verey lights gave us glimpses now and then of our very confined surroundings. The pace was just an ordinary walking pace, so we had time to pick our way when necessary.
>
> Through time we entered the front line. I was told off for first watch, and I must say my first look across no man's land was very disappointing to me. I expected to see corpses lying here, and these with an occasional gun lying on its side, and perhaps a horse or two. I looked in vain for the horrors of war. All I saw was a barren stretch of well-churned earth, disappearing into the gloom, and sparsely dotted with the distorted remains of the tree-trunks.
>
> Suddenly a couple of verey lights shot into the air, coming down in a big green blaze. Within the radius of the blaze I discerned running across my front many tangled lengths of barbed wire. The wire was about twenty yards out. I was greatly amused by the fire-works, and I think the relieving chaps saw this, and I was left to enjoy the spectacle all night. I don't know what I should have done if the Gerrys had come over, because I was not even thinking of them.[15]

It was in fact some time before Arthur became acquainted with the harsh reality of war. They were shelled pretty regularly over the following days and nights in the trenches, but it was only on his fifth day that it really hit home what was at stake for each and every one of them:

The day dawned with the usual chilly mist. What a lovely day it was, and how quiet everything was. I meandered along watching the H.E. bursting like masses of cotton wool high up in the sky. On I moved, mechanically following the twists and turns of the trench, and turning a corner, my absent minded gaze alighted on:

Oh Heavens: that first dead soldier is a sight that is practically photographed on my brain. The shell had burst right in the middle of the trench, so that now for several yards there was no trench. On the sloping side of the crater lay somebody's son. To me the poor corpse lay like a rag doll with all the stuffing out of it. The uniform was almost one big brownish red stain. The reason was only too apparent. The whole of the victim's back had been almost blown out. The head lay near the edge of the crater and half buried in the loose earth, one arm was also buried in the earth.

I turned and blindly staggered round a friendly corner.[16]

In early July, **Duff Cooper** began his training to become an officer in the illustrious Grenadier Guards. The system of granting commissions had become more sophisticated; since early 1916, all potential officers had to go through four and a half months of training, in an officer cadet unit. Duff was sent to Bushey, in Hertfordshire for his – and his dreams of a fun summer swiftly evaporated:

After lunching with Lady Essex I hired a motor and came down to Bushey, arriving soon after four. The men here are not only men who are applying for commissions in the Guards as I thought but for all regiments – and a great many, indeed the majority of them, have risen from the ranks. I was shown my sleeping quarters at which my heart sank. A room with 11 beds in it. Plain iron bedsteads – a mattress in three parts piled on top of one another – and four blankets on top of that – a wooden box at the end of each bed, a plain wooden floor and not another stick of furniture in the room.

Then our kit was distributed – a common private's uniform with terrible boots – and with some difficulty I found a man willing to black my boots and brighten my buttons for me. Dinner only increased my depression. There were others in the room with me – nearly all men risen from the ranks. They smoke sickening cigarettes and some of them slept in their shirts.[17]

The rigid, Edwardian class system had so far kept Duff away from men who lived so differently to him – at school, at work, in the social circles he mixed in. Of course, he had always had servants working for him, but they had been largely invisible and he had certainly never been expected to work and live alongside anybody from an ordinary background. When he awoke the next morning in his dorm room, Duff was feeling pretty desperate:[18]

> This morning I had a telegram from Diana saying 'Be brave darling, already I feel derelict'. I had indeed need of her exhortation. Never have I felt so miserable as this morning. The strangeness, roughness and degradation of it all appalled me. The worst of all was to think that these lovely summer months which I ought to be spending with her are being wasted.[19]

But there was no backing out now.

In early July, **Arthur Roberts** and his brigade were moved to the Tournehem training area, to practise for the coming attack, should it be authorised.[20] Elsewhere in Flanders, thousands of other men were doing the same. The training for the battle was thorough and well-organised. Scale models of the attack area were constructed in corps training areas, and infantry brigades endlessly rehearsed exactly what they had ahead of them. Arthur, however, was feeling ill and struggling to keep up in the July heat:[21]

Tuesday 10 July 1917:
After dinner today I bought some cherries and now I have both diarrhoea and headache. We are going over the top soon.

Wednesday 11 July 1917:
I have a touch of dysentery now and I can't eat. We were practising for the attack today. It was warm work.

Thursday 12 July 1917:
We were practising again today. I'm feeling worse. I've eaten nothing since dinner on Tuesday when I ate the cherries. I'll go to the doctor tomorrow.

<u>Monday 16 July 1917:</u>
The attack was practised again today. As we are leaving tomorrow we
are having a singsong tonight.

That day, the preliminary bombardment for the Northern Operations
was commenced. Arthur must have felt the ground shudder as 3,000
heavy guns opened up on the German lines. Gas operations and infantry
raids also began in the middle of July. The War Cabinet had still not
given the go-ahead. The date of Zero Day had been pushed back to
28 July – less than two weeks away.[22]

Duff Cooper had had enough of the army life. After two days of it,
he'd decided he needed a break, and broke the rules to get one:

> I had arranged the night before to have a motor here at 12:30. I said I
> was going to motor straight to Tadworth, as the one thing they object
> to here is one's going to or either passing through London. Once in the
> car, however, and within three quarters of an hour from St. James's Street,
> I could not resist the temptation. My delight to find myself once more
> in London was quite childish and I honestly felt as though I have been
> away for years. That I was here the day before yesterday seemed utterly
> incredible.
>
> I went to my flat, changed my shameful uniform for comfortable
> clothes, telephoned to Diana who had alas left for Rowsley (where her
> family took a house for the summer) and caught the 3:12 from Charing
> Cross for Tadworth. I felt as happy all the time as an escaped prisoner.[23]

On 20 July, Haig was authorised by the War Cabinet to carry out the
Flanders offensive, but on the condition that it would be called off if
the progress did not meet the high expectations they had been encouraged to have for it. The plan was ambitious: a 15 mile advance North-
East by the Fifth Army, timed to link up with a coastal operation by
the Fourth Army. Haig emphasised the need to continue attacking the
Germans even if they weren't gaining ground, to encourage the French
to keep on fighting. On 25 July, three days before Zero Day, the War
Cabinet telegraphed its wholehearted support to Haig. The final preparations were set in motion.[24]

On 27 July, Zero Day was pushed back again by a reluctant Haig, because the French were not yet ready. The following day, **Arthur Roberts** and the 2nd Royal Scots Fusiliers, along with hundreds of other infantry battalions, finally got the order they had been expecting. All the assaulting brigades were to be moved forward to the advanced assembly areas.[25] That day, the good weather came to an abrupt halt. Arthur arrived behind the front line south of Hooge in darkness. He wrote his diary the following morning:

We shifted yesterday but on arrival it was too dark to write the diary. The walking was so hot that our clothes and even equipment were wet with sweat. The rain came down mercilessly in the afternoon completely soaking us. We had to lie down in these wet things. To sleep was impossible. The guns and shells were banging and whizzing wholesale. Jerry sent over gas so we were up all night with our gas helmets on. We shift again tonight.[26]

They waited, in the rain, for further orders:

The ground, being low lying, soon became a mass of mud and slime. The small bivouac tents were poor shelters from the drenching downpour. We squatted under our low tents, wet, and miserable, so that when orders came to prepare to move we were glad to have something to do.

The roads were calf deep with mud, while the rest of the country was half lake, half quagmire. Frequently the enemy shells would land in the vicinity with sudden slaps and mud showers, so that we had a mud bath every now and then. Dead animals and disabled wagons lay scattered in profusion. In many cases these objects were almost buried in the boggy terrain. We made for some tree trunks that ran across our front about a couple of hundred yards away. On reaching our landmark, we saw that the trunks were followed by a communication trench and into this trench we filed.

Any duckboards that had not been blown away were either so badly broken as to be a danger to unwary feet, or had sunk so far in the muddy bottom as to be absolutely out of commission. The sides of the trench were of such shifting nature that frames of wire netting were required to hold them up. Anyhow, we all continued to follow the leader. Each man seemed busy with his own thoughts of home and the morrow. As another dreary day dawned, the drizzle was replaced by a very damp, unpleasant mist.[27]

They had arrived in the reserve trenches of the front line running between Zillebeke Lake and Sanctuary Wood. The rations were delivered; they gulped down tots of rum, and waited to move forward for the last time, to the frontline trenches from where they would go over the top:

> My thoughts are mixed and unsettled at present and I can't say I'm feeling too brave but it has to be done, so the sooner the better as this shelling is getting on my nerves. I think I'll come through all right – at least, I'll try to return for my parcel from home. These trenches are knee deep in mud and a drizzly rain has been on all day so it's pretty miserable. The rum came round this evening. My supply fairly warmed me up and it put new life into me. We move up tonight and over at dawn so here's luck.[28]

All along the front that night, the troops detailed to take part in the first assault cautiously moved into the final forward positions. Tank brigades moved forward simultaneously. Zero Hour was 3.50 a.m.: sunrise. The men waited for the whistle that would signal the hour had come. Arthur waited.[29]

The morning was misty, with low clouds overhead. It was still mostly dark when, at 3.50 a.m., a barrage of 18-pounder shrapnel exploded onto the German lines. A second later, the first men climbed out of the British trenches and started the scramble across no-man's-land. Amongst them was a young black man from Glasgow, fighting for a country that officially denied him the privilege of doing so. The German guns started firing.[30] So began the Third Battle of Ypres.

The day was a partial success. The first objectives were reached along much of the line, and in places troops had advanced much further. But the German second and third lines were much more heavily defended than anticipated. Arthur survived the first day of the third battle of Ypres; thousands did not. The worst casualties had been around Glencorse Wood, where Arthur had been fighting.[31] He had seen hell; but he didn't want to write about it:

> We were over this morning and I saw sights that I never saw before or wish to see again. It was terrible yet it was wonderful. I will not attempt to describe the sights, sounds and feelings that I saw, heard and felt because it would be impossible. I got through without a scratch.[32]

The next day was to be spent consolidating hard-won new positions. After a night largely spent in the open, Arthur was put on stretcher-bearer duty, risking the guns and shells to collect those who had survived the night – 'pretty rotten for one of my temperament.'[33]

Somehow – perhaps stuck in the mud trying to get to the wounded – Arthur was left behind when the relief came and his regiment moved back. He spent a second night of terror, in the open on the battlefield, amongst the bodies, in torrential rain. He had now not eaten, nor properly slept, since the night of the 30th. It was not until the following morning that he managed to find his regiment, now camped behind the lines:

> I came staggering into camp today covered with mud and soaked to the skin. I received a good rum issue, however, as I was just about done, not having had food for a couple of days. Shortly after the post corporal gave me a parcel and a letter from home. I immediately attacked the parcel after which I slept some hours. The weather is rotten and the roads ankle deep in mud.[34]

Stretcher-bearers struggle to carry a wounded man through knee-deep mud during the battle of Pilckem Ridge, 1 August 1917.

The next day, they were moved further back to a proper camp, and given a hot dinner. The first phase of the battle, The Battle of Pilckem Ridge, was over. In total, the Fifth Army had suffered 27,000 casualties.[35] Although the British army had made advances on much of the battlefront, a tactically vital plateau was still in German hands.

The next day was the beginning of the bank holiday weekend, and the 3rd anniversary of Britain's entry into the war. The headlines at home were naturally dominated by news of the battle raging in Flanders – celebrated so far as a British success. In London, crowds braved dreadful weather to go to Queen's Hall in Westminster to hear Lloyd George and the Archbishop of Canterbury address a great patriotic meeting. The National Anthem was sung by the thousands crammed into the hall as the rain splashed outside.[36]

On 7 August, as Britain went back to work, the French premier was in London for an Inter-Allied War Conference. Despite the best efforts of the official communiqués to make successes out of what were, at best, partial successes, the War Cabinet was not convinced. Lloyd George made it known that he believed they had taken the wrong course of action. Word got back to Haig. Even Haig's own generals were also starting to express their doubts. But Haig was convinced – the strategy was sound. The battle would go on.[37]

After a period of rest in France, **Arthur Roberts** was back in Belgium, in a different section of the front line.[38] They were under constant observation, and could do little more than sit tight in the dugouts and listen to the rattle of German shellfire at varying distances from where they sat. Compared to the hell they had been through at the Battle of Pilckem Ridge, it was a holiday camp – as Arthur put it: 'the cushiest trenches it has ever been my lot to live in.'[39] The danger came at night, when they would be sent out into the open to work.[40]

In early September, the 2nd Royal Scots Fusiliers were detailed to dig a new communication trench. The platoons took it in turns each night to do their bit. One moonlit night it was Arthur's turn:

> As the party 'fell in' on the parapet, the full moon was suspended like
> an enormous arc lamp. Not a breath of wind stirred the atmosphere.

Having called the roll, we moved off across the field through which the trenches ran, and struck the light railway up which we travelled. We were travelling light only having skeleton equipment, box helmet, and rifle, and bayonet, so our walk was fairly comfortable. Bye and bye, we came to a place where a road cut the track. Now as this road ran towards the front line, Jerry had it well taped, and casualties were many here abouts, so it had been decided that a communication trench should be made for use instead of the road, that was to be our job.

When the order was given to 'fall out', being in a moody frame of mind, I stood where I had halted. I did not feel inclined to talk, so remained gazing at the moon. Only an infrequent crack of a rifle, or still more infrequent stutter of a machine gun, indicated that the war was still on. How long we waited I know not, but I was gently pulled back to earth by the quietly spoken command of the officer to 'fall in.' No sooner had we formed up, then Boom! Bang! Crash! Crash! Whizzzz! Boom! A German battery was registering on the road with every shot. Verily the friends of Hell let loose in the form of 5-9 shells.

At the outset the officer came running down the line shouting 'Steady Boys'. He was among the first to be hit. We hesitated a few moments, but the deadly precision with which the shells landed, was too much for us. The fire swept down towards us like a hurricane, in fact it was a typhoon of splinters and death. To run was as bad as to stand, there was literally nothing but to fling ourselves into the ditches.

As I took an occasional peep over the top of the ditch, I could see the road clearly in the bright moonlight. Ah! What a change in a few moments. Oh my God what a sight. Bodies lay dotted along it. Big shell holes gaped here and there, but worse than all, the moans and shrieks of the unfortunate men. Some struggled madly, thoroughly un-nerved, but with their wounds, unable to much more than crawl. The others worked their limbs feebly, like sleepy children, while their blood dyed their khaki with big black stains.[41]

Arthur and the other survivors waited for the shelling to subside and then clambered out of the ditches to collect the wounded. There happened to be a truck at the roadside, and they loaded the injured men into it and pushed it as quickly as humanly possible to the nearest dressing station. The dead they had to leave behind. Once again, Arthur could not believe he was not amongst them. The next day the diminished regiment was moved forward again, back to Kemmel. Arthur wrote his diary that evening:

> What a night last night. I had a very narrow shave. One fellow in front of me had his head blew off. The chap beside him was severely wounded. The chap next to me was wounded and one of the chaps behind me was killed and the fellow beside him was wounded. I completely escaped. Everyone round me were either killed or wounded.[42]

Meanwhile, Haig had reported to the War Cabinet that, despite its limited success so far, the offensive must continue. Lloyd George was doubtful, but approval was given.

Kate Parry Collins had a lot to worry about. John had remained in the Arras area in France after the great battle of the spring. But now John received orders to move across the border to Belgium.

Kate's days now revolved around the postman's visits. She seemed to constantly be waiting for him, praying for a letter – and dreading the arrival of a telegram. In fact, in the second week of September, she got some good news. In a relatively quiet period on the Flanders front, whilst positions were consolidated before the attack was renewed, men were being given rest and leave. John was optimistic he'd be coming home soon:[43]

> A letter from John saying he was expecting the return of the Major who has been on leave and then he is to put in for leave. I wonder – I wonder. He seems to think Ypres pretty awful – can't dig proper dugouts because they so soon come to water and the smells are awful. He says they have to take more risks. I have been feeling it and do hate to think of him being there. He is seldom out of my thoughts.[44]

Kate's health had been poor for the past year, and now she was feeling pretty rotten and spent much of her time reading in bed. As the days passed, she half hoped his leave would be delayed until she was feeling better – but only half hoped it:

> No news from John – either letter or the telegram which I listen for all day. But if only he does come some time it is better really it should not

be while I am like this. Only all one's common sense about such a matter in the world does not prevent one wanting him. Now – now – this minute.

I should think they are very busy with the guns at Ypres. There really isn't much in the papers.[45]

She was right: the guns were very busy. Another big push was planned for 20 September. Winter was approaching, and the date originally set for the seaborne attack had long since passed. But Haig was still optimistic of a breakthrough.[46]

The first significant crack in the discipline of the British Army had appeared. A mutiny took place at the notorious base camp at Étaples. The town was fiercely segregated into areas for officers and the other ranks and on 9 September, a soldier from New Zealand was arrested for attempting to use a bridge that was reserved for officers. This provoked a furious reaction amongst the tens of thousands of soldiers stationed at the camp and the army was forced to call in reinforcements and set up pickets to contain angry demonstrations. The mutiny was short-lived but it showed that the dissatisfaction and disillusionment from three years of bloody war was not limited to Russian and French troops.

On 20 September, the next British assault, known as The Battle of the Menin Road, began in Ypres. The solidity of the defences behind the German front lines – concrete pillboxes and machine-gun nests – had been learnt the hard way, and this time the artillery's task was to destroy them. **Kate Parry Collins** was anxiously following the news that filtered back to Britain:

21 September 1917: There was great news in the paper about an advance on the British Front at Ypres – it began the early hours of Thursday morning after an extensive Bombardment. I guessed something must be going to happen there though John has not said anything, but I suppose it accounts for my intense anxiety these last few days.[47]

The opening days of the battle were a success, with the British advancing by as much as a mile in some places. But it was still not the dramatic breakthrough Haig needed, and on 23 September, he was forced to cancel the planned amphibious attack on the coast. On the ground, the troops pressed on.

By a week into the battle, Kate had not heard anything from John about his supposedly impending leave. In fact, she had not heard anything from him at all.

In early October, the heavens split open above the Western Front yet again. **Arthur Roberts** had been stationed out of the fighting, ten miles west of Ypres, in brigade reserve at Dranoutre. He was part of a hut-building detachment, and given painting duties. Their work was stopped by the torrential rain.[48] Arthur found himself with some leisure time, even if conditions made it difficult to really enjoy it:

> Today cleared up a bit, but only till evening when it started to rain as if making up for lost time. However a few fellows and myself resolved to visit the town even if we had to swim back. Between us we nearly cleared one shop of P.C.s. On our road back it was so dark that we only knew if we were together by the glow from our fags. We were drenched on arriving at the camp.[49]

The following day, perhaps because of his soaking wet tramp home the night before, Arthur experienced problems with his leg, possibly trench foot. He saw the doctor, who excused him from duty. A few days later, on 13 October, when the 2nd Royal Scots Fusiliers went back into action, Arthur remained behind at the field hospital.[50] He wrote guiltily from his comfortable bed:

> This place is fine. The food is excellent. The beds are grand. I've had the best bath I've had since landing in France. The rain came down in buckets last night and I couldn't help but think of the lads in the line. They must have been up to the waist at least.[51]

Arthur was right – conditions for the men were terrible. The work that had been done so diligently by troops and engineers during the lull in the fighting – laying duckboards and reinforcing trenches and roads

– was quickly undone. The guns jammed into the mud; shells had to be cleaned of slime before they could be used; both horses and men drowned; it was impossible to retrieve the dead from the morass.

On the 15th, Arthur attended a medical board. He then had to wait to hear its verdict, which would determine whether he would be going out into the hell of that battlefield, or if he was safe for a while longer.[52] Haig, meanwhile, remained as committed as ever to the strategy of exhausting the Germans on the Western Front, even if it meant exhausting his own men too. He was determined to see the offensive through to the bitter end.[53]

At the end of October, **Duff Cooper** sat the exam that determined whether or not he would be put forward for a commission as an officer in the Grenadier Guards. After four months of training, arguably the hardest of his life so far, a lot was at stake for him. The day after the exam he discovered the result:

> I got up early feeling nervous and depressed. At nine we assembled and waited three sickening quarters of an hour before the commandant arrived. At last he came and proceeded to read out, very slowly and deliberately, and in no order, the names of those whom he would recommend for commissions. It was a slow and agonising torture. Twenty seven names were read out and then came mine. The relief and delight were unspeakable. Oh the relief that Bushey is over. If I wake up for a moment in the night I remember it and go to sleep smiling. I wonder how I could ever have borne it.[54]

Duff was transferred to Wellington Barracks to start his training ready for deployment to France. He was overjoyed to be back in London, at least for now.

The rain continued over the jagged ruins of Ypres and the miles of devastated land around it. Four divisions of the Canadian Corps had been sent to Flanders, tasked with finally claiming the small village of Passchendaele and the ridge it sat upon. On the morning of 26 October their attack began, in the lashing rain and wind.[55]

Arthur Roberts was with his battalion again, who had come back into reserve after ten days in the trenches. That evening, on returning from a concert put on for his division, Arthur was informed he was to be leaving them for good. Because of the problem with his leg, which was not getting any better, he was being sent to the base at Étaples – back over the border, away from the carnage. After a last hurrah with his mates, who would soon be returning to the line, he left them for a new phase in his army career:

> What a night I spent, and what cash I spent last night. I went to a concert to pass the time and on returning to billets I immediately got down to it. I couldn't sleep for cold. About 7 am I went for some coffee, then I started for the train. A big crowd of German prisoners came on the same train. It was some train. More like a horse bus. On changing trains I managed to get a first class carriage. This train took the usual French time to travel a few miles but after great sufferance we arrived at our destination safely.[56]

The mutinous moment that had gripped Étaples a few months earlier had passed. Arthur was quite happy to be there:

> This is grand after being up yonder. I was in front of the adjutant this morning and he took down my complaint and effects. I was then put to work in the dining hall. It is fine, plenty to eat and no remarks passed. There was a Hallowe'en party this evening when the boys ducked apples, scrambled for nuts and apples, ate treacle scones, and played all the children's games. It was comical.[57]

Arthur was safe. He settled into the routine of work in the dining hall, fatigues and occasional night work.

The following evening, the Wooburn postman walked up the steep hill in the cold and dark to **Kate Parry Collins**'s home:

> A telegram arrived just about 7. I said as I opened it 'good news or bad' and then I saw John's name. He had got leave, was in London and arriving Wooburn at 6.43. We got up and began to prepare – soon after 7 he was here. Looking well, but much thinner – he has been very queer and that got him his leave at last. I couldn't believe, it is nearly 11 months

and yet it seemed like another life come back. Such a joy to have him really here.[58]

Kate was so overjoyed to see John again that her health problems seemed to have been forgotten:

It was lovely to have my dear old party with me. He is like a ray of sunshine. Seems in good spirits and as usual sees the humour of everything and there is so much to tell. I am so thankful he has so little sense of fear.[59]

Whilst John was home on leave, the Third Battle of Ypres limped to a close. On 10 November, the heights of the Passchendaele Ridge – so desired by the Allies, and which would give the battle its name – had finally been secured. Kate could be thankful that he did not belong to the casualty statistics that shocked Britain yet again: 250,000 men killed, wounded, and missing in three months of fighting. It was thought that the Germans had suffered similarly. The bodies of 42,000 Allied soldiers were never recovered, lost forever to the mud.[60]

In early November a letter arrived for **Andrew Clark** with the morning post from Charles Ward, now back in France. Andrew stuck it into his diary, as 'typical of a village lad's letter'. His comment belied the truth; that he was terribly fond of Chas and glad to hear from him:

Dear Sir,
I now take the pleasure in writing a few lines to you trusting you are getting on alright and keeping well. I was so glad to see you all. I am afraid you have been working very hard since I left. I expect you are having some cold weather at home now. It is very cold out here, one or two mornings of white frost – it is getting quite winter now and it will be a blessing when we can all get back for good. The time soon flies past – it can't last for ever.[61]

But it was beginning to seem as if it would. Another monumental effort had failed to win the war, and now another winter loomed. Allied troops were being moved from Flanders to help repel a surprise German attack on the Italian front, despite Haig's protestations that all efforts should remain focused on the Western Front.[62] On 16 November, Charles Henry Ward and the 14th Brigade Royal Horse Artillery were departing France for Italy.

As Charles stepped into the carriage of the train pulling out of Seurre station, the step came away. He fell beneath the train and was killed instantly. He was 25. His body was left with the local doctor, who saw to it that this boy from Great Leighs was given a good Christian burial, far from the fields of home. His comrades travelled on.[63]

Although Haig was convinced that the Western Front remained the only theatre in which the war could be won, the War Cabinet in London was no longer in agreement, and refused to abandon the Italian front. Haig did some calculations based on figures given to him by the War Office in early November. He believed that the German army would fight back on the Western Front in the spring, and he estimated that the British army would be dangerously short of infantrymen by the end of March – a quarter of a million men short, to be precise. The picture he painted was alarming.[64]

One more man was swelling the army's ranks, at least: **Duff Cooper**.

> Today I was gazetted and so am at last a full blown officer in the Grenadiers, which seems strange and improbable.[65]

The very next day Duff got a horrible reminder of what he was now facing – news of one of his last surviving friends, who had gone into battle at Cambrai on 20 November. Cambrai had been a new kind of assault: a surprise attack, supported by tanks and aeroplanes. The initial success was great; but it had failed to break through the German's defensive Hindenburg Line:

> In the afternoon I went home with Sydney to Montagu Square where we played bridge. We had settled down to a game of skip when Sybil came in and said she wanted to speak to me for a minute. I left the room feeling rather annoyed at her mysterious ways. On the landing she said 'Edward has been killed and Diana is waiting for you outside.' I went down and found Diana standing by the area railing crying. We got into a taxi and drove away. I haven't cried so much since John was killed nor have I felt anything so deeply.

After we had driven for some time we went back to her room in Arlington Street where we sat by the firelight talking a little and crying a lot. Edward meant so much in our lives. I loved no man better. His high courage and fine independence has so splendidly resisted the effects of the war that already he had begun to seem a glorious relic of the glorious past. By his death our little society loses one of the last assets that gave it distinction. And I think we have paid more than our share. Only Patrick and I remain. We can make no new friends worthy of the old ones. I begin to feel that the dance is already over and that it is time to go. I dined alone at the Junior Carlton. I drank the best champagne – Pommery 1906 – because I felt that Edward would have wished it and would have done so had I been killed first.[66]

And so began Duff's military career, as the fourth year of war ground to a miserable end.

20

ON BRITISH SOIL
May–December 1917

I only seemed to see the ghosts of the past gay days. We all tried to pretend
we were the same people; but in our hearts we knew we were not.

Hallie Miles's diary, summer 1917

Craiglockhart Hydropathic Institution dominated the small village of
Slateford. Its well-kept lawns swept up to an imposing stone building,
modelled on the spa resorts of Italy. The bustle of the city of Edinburgh
was a few miles away. The paying guests and spa treatments were long
gone, but the ample grounds were being put to good use: Craiglockhart
was now a treatment centre for shell-shocked officers.

'Shell-shock' had been recognised by doctors in 1915. The stresses
of trench warfare had started to cause strange symptoms amongst
some of its protagonists, such as mutism, paralysis and nervous exhaus-
tion. After the Battle of the Somme, the Army had been forced to
admit the causes were psychological, and began the attempt to fix up
the men broken by war – in order to send them back to it.[1]
Craiglockhart was requisitioned by the War Office and turned into
a hospital.

James Butlin had arrived at Craiglockhart in May, fresh from
Arras, and was now undergoing treatment The cognitive therapy
offered by the doctors was complemented by 'ergotherapy': work
and activity to help the patient re-establish links with the environ-
ment from which they'd become detached.[2] James did not take to it
immediately:

I have been interviewed by the Doctor: he is a clever man, a bit of a
philosopher, an eminent nerve specialist and somewhat of a crank. He

extracts from you your life history with such questions as: 'Is there any nervous trouble in your family?' 'Have you been ill as a boy?' 'Where were you at school?' 'Do you smoke much?' etc. etc.

His great idea, as I have been previously warned, is to get you to take up a hobby. He asked me what hobbies I had. I said that I played tennis and bridge. He said the 1st was all right but that the latter tended to keep you too much in the house. I then admitted that I had been playing bridge all day but that I liked literature. The latter was rather a false step, as he then asked me to join the staff of the 'Hydra', a fortnightly magazine published by the officers here. However I have so far escaped fairly lightly. By the way, there are some 150 officers in this place drawn from all sorts and conditions of life, among whom there are editors litterateurs.

At times I feel damnably bored: hence the length of this effusion and the fervent outpourings of a discontented soul. Why the devil they can't send me home for a couple of months, but there you are. Can you imagine me, my dear Basil, getting up and taking a swim before breakfast? Doing a little gardening and poultry farming before breakfast? Fretwork and photography after lunch? Viewing natural scenery after tea? Reading and writing after dinner and then to bed?[3]

After the screeching trauma of war, normality and gentle recreation felt alarming to twenty-one year-old James.

Helen Bentwich also found herself struggling to adjust to a quiet life after the din of the arsenal. The life of comfort and ease – a life without work – just didn't seem to fit her any more. Despondent, she wrote to her husband Norman, who was still serving in Egypt:

You can't imagine the depths of boredom to which one can sink if one has no work for even a few days, in these times, when everybody else is too busy to come and play. I think I'll be reduced to taking myself to a music hall this afternoon on my own.

Yesterday I was putting in order all the letters I've had from you since I've been back here. It's so damnable – nearly a year apart. And I've done nothing to justify it, except to make a howling mess of myself and everything else and show what a darned fool I am. And often I get queer sort of qualms about what you'll think of me when you see me again. You see, a year at this stage of my life can mean a lot and supposing I've changed

so as you won't want to have me as a wife any more? I've had a lot of
experiences that must have left some mark on me – do you ever think
that perhaps you won't love me so much when you see me again?[4]

Helen had hoped to return to work at the arsenal, but was told that
she wouldn't be welcome back because of her 'Bolshevik tendencies'.[5]
But her wartime experiences were not yet at an end. With three million
men serving in the army, there were plenty of jobs that needed doing
– even for those with increasingly socialist tendencies.

By the summer of 1917, one of the most pressing matters was ensuring
that British agriculture did all it could to feed the population at home.
As German submarines stopped more and more food coming in, the need
was urgent. The Women's Land Army was set up in February 1917 to
address this need, and Helen started to hope she might have found her
next calling.[6]

A recruitment poster for the Women's Land Army, 1917.

*

At the end of May, as the food situation grew increasingly bleak, the Admiralty agreed to use some of its warships to protect merchant shipping. A convoy system was introduced, which resulted in a noticeable decline in the huge losses at sea.[7] But the problem did not go away, and a plethora of initiatives to try to control the limited food supply were foisted upon the British public in the summer of 1917. One Sunday in May, for example, an announcement was read in every church, chapel, synagogue and Salvation Army barracks, calling on those present to eat less bread to help win the war.[8]

Andrew Clark no doubt followed his instructions and read the notice out from the pulpit of St Mary's. But for the villagers of Great Leighs, limiting consumption of food was not so much an act of patriotism as one of unwelcome necessity, as Andrew well knew. The government's efforts to exhort them to moderation irritated him. A few weeks later, he received a government circular in the post urging people to wear a purple ribbon to show their adherence to the campaign to eat less bread. As he recorded this in his diary, Andrew's normally restrained tone disappeared:

> Waste of paper; useless expenditure of clerks' time and of postman's time as though everyone had not heard the whole story over and over again or had any trust in a government officer, especially in one which has so discredited itself.[9]

The real issue for the locals was that food prices were continuing to rise as supplies became scarcer. In May even the local dairy had cause to put its prices up. As another summer of austerity began, the mood in the rectory – indeed in Great Leighs – was not buoyant.[10] At the end of May, Andrew wrote to a friend of the depression that had descended on the village:

> The Parish is very empty. The young men being on military service, and the young women at munition work. I cannot give a good account of my own health. I have gone steadily downhill for quite a year. I have lost 8 stone in weight, and am now lighter and thinner than when I went up to Oxford, a lad of 19, in 1874.[11]

Hardship was not, of course, limited to Great Leighs. Across Britain, unrest was building at the additional hardships that were being imposed on the workers by increased food prices, and strikes were becoming more common. In May, the Miners' Federation threatened to step up industrial action unless food prices were fixed.[12]

Hallie and Eustace Miles continued trying to do their bit to help. Eustace had been instrumental in the introduction of 'National Kitchens' by the Ministry of Food. These were community restaurants that would provide nutritious food cheaply to the masses. The economies of scale involved would, it was hoped, help to limit waste. The first such restaurant was opened in Westminster in May.[13] Hallie and Eustace were, of course, there to celebrate:

> Eustace has been in more request than ever lately at the Ministry of Food. He has been appointed as one of the Executive Committee of the new 'kitchen-for-all' [Public Kitchen] which was opened the other day by Queen Mary. We were both invited to the opening ceremony. It was most interesting to be right in the whole thing. The kitchen is in quite a poor part, out of the Vauxhall Bridge Road, so the crowd was mostly very poor. It was thrilling when we heard the distant cheering begin, swelling louder and louder, and coming nearer and nearer, until the Royal carriages drew up at our kitchen door.
>
> The Food Controller, Lord Devonport, and the chief kitchen ladies received the Queen. All the lady cooks wore chef caps and large white aprons, and looked so charming. First of all the Queen was shown all over the kitchen and introduced to the chief people. To my surprise I was fetched and introduced to the Queen. She smiled so kindly and said, 'Yours and your husband's names are well known to me.'[14]

Unfortunately, despite its illustrious start, the scheme did not turn out to be quite the hit with working people that it was intended to be, which must have been a disappointment to Hallie. Public dissatisfaction was building, and with it pressure on the government. The Food Controller, Lord Devonport, resigned in May.[15]

Helen Bentwich had been taken on by the Land Army as a group leader. Her job would see her visiting farmers to persuade them to take on women workers, recruiting workers to fill those jobs, and being on

hand to lead them in their work if needed. She was sent to a farm in
Berkshire for training. Whilst there, she had to try her hand at the
kinds of work she'd be supervising – and she fell in love with the horses:

> I've got awfully keen on horse-work, and I want to try for a carter's job,
> instead of a government one to ground-lead. If I don't go as a carter, I
> shall always be jealous of the girls I meet who are, because it's such much
> nicer work. Miss Mitchell, the instructress here, says I could do quite well
> at it; and the men who teach me ploughing and harrowing and all that
> say so, too. I can ride quite easily now on the farm horses without falling
> off. I've never liked anything so much before as being with these horses
> and learning this work – even in the rain and thunderstorms.[16]

The prospect of Helen – an upper-class, married woman – working as
a carter on a farm was an alarming one for her mother. She clearly did
not approve, and tried encouraging her daughter to stick to the skilled
work suitable to someone of her background. Helen was having none
of it, however:

> You know, you are all mistaken about group-leading. When anybody is very
> unfit for carting and work with horses, they are offered to go as leaders of
> groups and that sort of thing, because that is all unskilled work; and all
> that is wanted is someone to be tactful between the women and the employer
> – which wasn't my strong point in my last job! And carting is very skilled.
> There aren't many here fitted for it – physically, as well as having the skill,
> and not be afraid of horses. And don't think me conceited when I say that
> I have got on at it very well, and am given quite difficult bits of ploughing
> to do, and that, by doing carting, I'd be releasing a man for the army directly,
> and doing work which quite few women are able to do.[17]

It wasn't just Helen's mother who was shocked by the prospect of a
well-to-do woman – indeed, any woman at all – working the land.
Many farmers were reluctant to employ Land Army girls, and rural
populations were unsure how to react to the sight of women wearing
trousers and hefting farm tools. But they'd have to get used to it: by
the end of the year, there were over 100,000 British women wearing
the uniform of the Land Girls.[18]

*

The residents of Great Leighs were slowly getting used to seeing women working the fields around the village. **Andrew Clark** clearly thought it remained something noteworthy, however, and made sure he recorded any sightings of farming women in his war diary:

> Thursday 7 June: Mrs 'Alix' Alefounder is doing farm-work today, and was working in the field with Mrs Everett, wife of a farm-hand at Long's. Mrs. A. A. helps in the canteen. She wears gloves when at out-of-door work, so as not to have brown hands when serving in the canteen.
> Saturday 9 June: Today two Girton girls arrived at 'Valentines'. They are to work on Lyons Hall land for six or seven weeks.[19]

Such sights would have been absolutely unthinkable before the war, but now new and unthinkable things were foisted on Britons daily. On 25 May, one of the most shocking sights of all occurred – two German aeroplanes arrived in the skies above Britain in broad daylight. The five bombs dropped by the Gotha planes caused more damage than any Zeppelin raid. Three weeks later, a fleet of such planes were headed for London. Andrew heard them passing 12,000 feet above Great Leighs on their way to the capital:

> This forenoon (10.45 a.m. as I remember) we heard an unusual drumming noise in the E and SE. It went on for a considerable time. My daughter heard it about 11.15 a.m. I thought it was drums in Terling Camp, or a regiment on a route march on the road beyond that. My daughter thought it was an aeroplane, but out of order. It now appears as if it had been a squadron of German aeroplanes.
> 8.30 p.m. Edith Caldwell came. She brought a hastily written note from her father in which he had jotted down what he himself had seen. Her father was in his office at the time of the raid. It was in the very centre of the damage, being within five minutes walk of Liverpool Street Station. He wanted to get out to see the aircraft, but this was impossible because shrapnel was flying about everywhere. The street fronts of several of these buildings were crashing down. The women all went mad, shrieking and yelling.[20]

The reports that reached Great Leighs had not been exaggerated. More than 100 bombs had been dropped, 72 within a mile radius of Liverpool

Street Station; 162 civilians had been killed, including 18 children at Upper North Street School in East London. Another 432 people were wounded.[21] Britain was outraged, and Londoners like **Hallie Miles** were understandably terrified by this new development in German tactics:

> We have just had the most terrible aeroplane raid over London in broad daylight. They came over in such perfect formation that everyone thought they were ours. The Zeppelin raids at night were bad enough, but these day-light raids are even worse, when the streets and houses and shops are full of busy people; the deaths and mutilations have been too dreadful.
>
> The first bombs began to crash to earth, and the guns had to thunder forth, about 11am. Of course we all had to hurry down to the basement. Some of our clerks joined us there, white and shaken, many of them crying. And all the time the sun was shining and the sky an azure blue! As soon as I could, I hurried off to the Restaurant to hear how they had all fared, and found that some of our customers had come in to lunch, straight from the City, where they had the most wonderful escapes and had seen the most awful sights. A train in Liverpool Street Station was blown to pieces, and heaps of people have been killed. The number of children killed was too dreadful.[22]

In Westminster, the government began to worry that civilian morale – already under such pressure because of the food situation – was starting to crack.

Even **Helen Bentwich** – usually so hard to rattle – was shocked by the news of the raid when it reached her girls in Berkshire:

> Everyone was very spent by the raid, which is certainly the worst there's been. It's all too horrible and terrible to think of. That school in Poplar where the bomb dropped in the class room and another that fell on a crowd waiting for a bus – things such as those make one sick to think of. I was glad to come back to work the next day – work seems the only way not to dwell on these horrors.[23]

Helen's dream of becoming a carter had not materialised. No doubt to her family's relief, she'd become a gang-leader after all. Now she was at work out in the fields with a team of women, picking thistles. It was back-breaking; she felt that finally she could again brag to her husband Norman of how hard she was working:

> Gee, but it's hot. Worse than anything out your way, I'll be bound and anyoldhow, you don't have to stand for 7 hours a day in a field without an atom of shade, chipping off the damned heads of any blasted thistle in the vicinity. There, I feel better now. You'd do a grin if you saw me, in my khaki smock and breeches, with an excessively picturesque blue sunbonnet to keep me cool, followed by my gang. We are 9 or 10 strong now, all perfectly sane and in our right minds and it's all going on quite well. But I so wish it'd get cooler.[24]

Helen had spent the war years chipping away at the vision of Edwardian femininity that had long restricted upper-class girls like her. And now it wasn't only her uniform that might cause shock to those who had known her before her wartime adventures began: she'd bought herself a motorbike. Wearing her khaki trousers and smock, Helen roared up the country lanes to work:

> The bike is a dear. It's a bit lazy at times and sits down and sulks on the hills and I have a hard job making it up. But it's because I don't quite understand the throttle, I think, giving it enough petrol. It's exhausting pushing it up. If no kind of person is about to give me a shove, I take it down again and have another try. The starting it is the worst difficulty, as I have to run with my legs straddled across it to make it start and doing this uphill is tiring. But I'm strong and will soon get used to it tho' at present I'm fairly bruised in parts. But still, nearly 60 miles isn't bad considering that 4 days ago I'd never been on one.
>
> Mother seemed fairly reconciled to it. She begged me to be very careful and I said I would and I've sent her a cable to say I got here safe, so as she won't be worried. And I really am awfully bucked with it – and life is quite fairly tolerable.[25]

In June, **James Butlin** was still at Craiglockhart Hospital and trying his best to enjoy the summer too. He had not yet answered his doctor's calls to become involved in the literary pursuits that were on offer. A new patient arrived at the hospital that month who would embrace

Helen Bentwich on her motorcycle, c. 1917.

these distractions more enthusiastically: a young poet called Wilfred
Owen. Owen would go on to write some of the most famous poetry
about the conflict during his time at Craiglockhart.

James had decided to stick with his perennial hobby: chasing girls.
He had met a young woman locally called May, though his attempts
to woo her were not being made easy by the hospital's rules, as he
explained to Basil:

> Truly fortune is a fickle jade at times: my luck has been dead out lately.
> Misfortune rained upon misfortune but I have weathered the storm and
> have emerged a sadder and wiser man.
>
> One misfortune I will relate to you and leave you an impartial judge
> of how trivial an offence may be magnified so as to appear a crime of
> unparalleled enormity. I went to St Giles' Church on Sunday evening
> with my beloved May and afterwards she came back to the hydro with
> me and we sat on a seat in an out-of-the-way path in the grounds of
> the asylum, where I thought we were unobserved and far from the
> madding crowd. We were, I admit, perhaps sitting closer than the warmth
> of the evening necessitated and in the passion of love I implanted a few
> kisses on the cheek of my inamorata. At that critical and epoch-making
> moment the CO (of the hospital) and my doctor appeared in full view
> round the corner. Next morning my presence was requested by the CO

and he asked me what I meant by breaking hospital rules – visitors are not allowed except between 3 and 5 pm – to which I pleaded ignorance and apologised for all and any sins I had committed.

I learned shortly afterwards that a few minutes before he found me, he came upon an officer who had brought up some harlot from Edinboro and was in the act of copulation with her, which fact (or the knowledge of which fact) would naturally prejudice me in his eyes. I was and am perfectly innocent of any offence which he may have thought that I was contemplating. The incident which I have related above is not known to my people so I should suggest your burning this letter as soon as possible.[26]

As summer came to Great Leighs, **Andrew Clark**'s diary became dominated by the alarming food supply situation:

Thursday 21 June: Mr F. Chapping of Mr Jas. Bowtell's grocery-business, Braintree, came at 1.30 p.m. He said that applicants for sugar will receive only a third of what they asked to preserve their own fruits.
Friday 3 August: The 'government cheese', officially supplied to Mr H J Hicks, Supply Stores, Great Leighs, to be sold in the village at 1s,4d a lb, is New Zealand cheese, badly made and rank-tasted. Mr Hicks also has on sale Canadian cheese at 1s.8d a lb, also badly made, rank-tasted and over-salted. Mrs Hicks says she has sold hardly any margarine these last weeks. The village women have made much money pea-picking and at present will buy nothing but butter at 2s a lb.[27]

Over the summer, major changes had been taking place in the Ministry of Food under the new Food Controller, Lord Rhondda. Three thousand new staff had been employed, and increased powers had been assigned to the ministry under the Defence of the Realm Act, giving it complete control over imports and food prices. But dissatisfaction and anger at what they were being asked to endure was still growing amongst ordinary Britons.[28] Andrew's own fury at the government's efforts had not abated. In August, it was sparked off by a seemingly rather random new regulation:

If open imbecility could win a war we are on the sure road to victory. To justify their high salaries, the unspeakable fools who are government officials have 'thought' out a new device for beating the Germans: the prohibition of pictures in packets of cigarettes. One would have thought that many of these (Raemaker's cartoons, e.g) were silly enough to have appealed strongly to these feeble minded officials, as 'work' like their own.[29]

Andrew spent some time sticking thirty-two examples of such pictures into the diary. He was smoking heavily.

On 30 July, a declaration written by a decorated officer named Siegfried Sassoon was read out in Parliament. In it, he explained that he would not be returning to duty after a period of leave:

> I am making this statement as an act of wilful defiance of military authority because I believe that the war is being deliberately prolonged by those who have the power to end it. I am a soldier, convinced that I am acting on behalf of soldiers. I have seen and endured the sufferings of the troops and I can no longer be a party to prolong these sufferings for ends which I believe to be evil and unjust. I am not protesting against the conduct of the war, but against the political errors and insincerities for which the fighting men are being sacrificed.[30]

Sassoon was spared a court martial. He was diagnosed with shell shock, and put on the train to Craiglockhart War Hospital. There, whilst James Butlin was passing the summer unhappily, Sassoon would help foster the talent of the young Wilfred Owen, with whom he struck up a close friendship.

Helen Bentwich had moved to a different farm. She was now just outside Tring in Hertfordshire, having travelled up there on her motor-bike, which she had by now named 'Lewis'. Her work at Tring was no less back-breaking than at the previous farm: she was pulling up docks with her bare hands. She wrote with relish to Norman of the people she now found herself among:

> I do wish you could see my gang. Two very respectable young married women, one quite old one, who comes from Devon, and used to be a servant in London, she's very tall and lean. Then there's a slovenly, dirty,

low-caste girl of about 17. And the prize of the lot – a hugely fat, swarthy old woman, known as Mrs Smith or 'Smithie' who wears a hat with an ostrich feather and earrings and is a regular gypsy type. She told me that when she was young, from April to November her mother and her four sisters and sometimes her brother wandered round the country, through Middlesex and Kent, potato setting, hay making and harvesting, fruit picking and hopping and coming home again for the winter. Just like a person in a book, isn't it!

When we've done his fields, we're going to another farm nearby. I went to see the farmer after work yesterday and it was rather amusing. They were just going to have tea and made me have it with them in the kitchen with the farmer and his wife and two children and the servant girl and two friends. The farmer's daughter and servant both worked on the farm and appeared (like me) in breeches. They couldn't place me anyhow. So I tell the farmers my father has a small farm the other side of the hills we see in the distance and they treat me as one of themselves and talk to me as they never would if they thought I came from London and were the wife of a legal pundit! Do you mind a small farmer's daughter for a wife? [31]

As the national mood grew understandably darker, **Hallie Miles** tried to forget about all the troubles and enjoy a day out. But she could not escape her own depression:

I very seldom go out to any festivity nowadays, but today for a wonder I went out to tea at the Criterion with some friends, as in the days of the old. How changed everything was since I was last there! All the young men were in khaki: the orchestra played as usual, but it seemed so sad. After tea we went and sat in the park; and this was the saddest part of all. It would naturally have been the height of the season, but nearly every chair was empty; most of the men were in bath-chairs or on crutches and the carriages and motor-cars were full of wounded soldiers.

It was like a new and tragic world and I wished I had not gone there. I only seemed to see the ghosts of the past gay days, when I used to join the gay season crowds. We all tried to pretend we were the same people; but in our hearts we knew we were not. I could not bear it any longer, and so I left them. [32]

German air raids continued. In July and August more daylight bombing raids had been carried out, including one on Southend on a Sunday when people were there enjoying a day out by the seaside. A summer's afternoon turned into a nightmare. But the worst came at the beginning of September. The Gothas came at night this time. No warnings were given, and the bombs rained down, first on the naval base at Chatham and then on London. Hallie and the EM Restaurant had another narrow escape:

> A friend who joined us had come back from his office by tube; he told us that the sights in the Tubes were the most extraordinary imaginable. People were there in all sorts of queer clothes. Some had rushed from their beds to the nearest Tubes, carrying their wraps and even their boots in their hands; and the poor sleepy little children were wrapped up in the blankets off their beds, and were sleeping peacefully through it all. Women were dressing on the platforms, and taking their hair out of curling-pins; some were pulling on their stockings. Babies were being given their bottles, and mothers were nursing them. The staircases and platforms of the Tube Station were like a huge bedroom and 'night-nursery' on that awful night. These strange Tube scenes take place whenever there is a raid.
>
> Everyone is so war-weary! That first wonderful spirit of Patriotism seems to have died down. In some ways it is nearly gone; this is largely owing to the terrible blunders and heart-breaking mistakes that have been made by 'those in power'.

Even Hallie was now beginning to question the actions of government.

The Ministry of Food was trying numerous measures to promote the equitable supply of food. A scheme to subsidise bread – a staple of the working-class diet – was introduced, maximum prices were set for key foodstuffs, and the rationing of sugar began. But many of these controls had the undesired effect of disrupting distribution.[33]

It was not uncommon for queues to form outside shops before dawn in some areas. Some of these were truly gigantic; on one occasion it was reported that 3,000 customers waited outside a shop in southeast London in order to buy margarine. People were, naturally, getting sick of this state of affairs. The press began to pick up on and fan the simmering discontent. In November, the *Herald* ran an article, 'How They Starve at the Ritz' about lavish, six-course dinners the rich were still enjoying. This was reprinted in pamphlet form and distributed outside factory gates – feelings of class discrimination were growing.[34]

Helen Bentwich was fired up by it all. Before the war she would have thought nothing of a six-course dinner, but now she knew what it was like for the workers and she was outraged at what they were going through. She regularly sent the *Herald* to Norman out in Egypt; no doubt he received a copy of the article on the Ritz from her. She was optimistic on one point at least: she felt that things had got so bad, they might be about to change for good:

> I'm glad you are getting the revolutionary papers allright. I'm going to continue sending you the Herald, despite your protests, 'cos it's so jolly interesting. I'm more of a seething revolutionary than ever now. Their articles are a jolly good antidote to Lloyd George and Northcliffe, and they do make you see that it takes two to make a strike, and that the day of the workers is coming and the day of the capitalist is over.
>
> I feel it's getting more and more of a nightmare – there <u>must</u> be a revolution. It's the only way out. Why <u>can't</u> they see what it's all coming to. The hatred of royalty, the bitterness of the class against class, has never been as it is now. After all, the poor man probably doesn't grudge the rich one his motor or his 2 or 3 country houses – but he <u>does</u> grudge him his food and his lavish hotel dinners, while his own children are <u>literally</u> starving for milk or sugar, and his wife spends her whole day waiting in vain in food queues. Boy dear, you'd feel the same if you were here – but it makes me wild and rebellious as can be to see it all, and I wish ever so often that I weren't born a 'lady', but were the same as these people, and could really be their equal, instead of just playing at it as when I join a union or work in a factory.
>
> I'm ashamed of my 'class' - and the talk of my father and all his set (and the majority of people of the kind) makes me sick.[35]

As the fourth winter of the war descended on Europe, there was certainly a nip of revolutionary feeling in the air. The British elite were becoming concerned at the growing industrial unrest. *The Times* ran a series of articles under the provocative headline 'The Ferment of Revolution', questioning the loyalty of trades unions to the war effort. These fears must have intensified when, in November, the spectre of genuine revolution raised its head in Russia, when the Bolsheviks led by Lenin secured power in Petrograd and threw out the Provincial Government.[36]

Such a revolution at home was not a likely prospect, whatever the press might have pedalled. But the discontent was real, and growing: that month, one million working days were lost through strike action.[37] Many ordinary Britons were feeling increasingly depressed, and some of them were getting desperate.

In December, **Andrew Clark** became the victim of one person's desperation. He awoke in the darkness before sunrise one morning, lit a candle and struggled out of bed. Having dressed in warm clothes he slowly, deliberately, made his way downstairs. He was surprised to see the flicker of candlelight coming from the study doorway, and felt an icy draught blowing down the corridor:

> There was a burglar in this house early. How he got in, I do not know. I seem to have disturbed him by my early rising. He had lit one of the candles in the brass candlesticks in the study; opened the shutters of one of the study windows; threw up the sash and went out that way. I have missed nothing, except possibly half-a-crown from the study. He seems also to have been in the store-room.[38]

Given the privations they were suffering, it was hardly surprising that some people were resorting to crime. And now Britons were facing the most frugal Christmas many of them had ever known.

As 1917 came to a cold, joyless end for most Britons, **Hallie Miles** tried to look with equanimity upon these endless-seeming days of war:

> I am writing these records at the close of this sad year of 1917. One cannot help praying that 1918 might be a happier year! Oh! That it may. We are all feeling that our powers of endurance must be tested still further before things can get better. When one realises what our soldiers and air-men and sailors are going through, it seems only right that we should also take our share of danger, and be as calm and brave as they are.[39]

That year, Britain's soldiers and sailors had endured some of the most terrible ordeals of the war so far. Despite the new government in Westminster under Lloyd George, and despite the optimism that the commander-in-chief, Haig, had exuded for much of 1917, the war was not won. Passchendaele had stumbled to a close, without securing the Belgian ports or the ruin of the German army. The battle would go down in history as – indeed, it already was – a byword for the futility and horror of war.

The toll of three years of trench warfare on the men who were fighting it was now undeniable. In December, the senior doctor at Craiglockhart released a research paper. In it, he argued that the psychological damage he'd seen was unsurprising: the men 'have had to face strains such as have never previously been known in the history of mankind. Small wonder that the failures of adaptation should have been so numerous and so severe.'[40]

A cabinet document compiled by the Minister for National Service at the close of the year reported an increase amongst the fighting forces of desertion and drunkenness, as well as psychological disorders. There was an undeniable link between the dissatisfaction at home and that at the front – strengthened by the constant flow of soldiers and sailors between them.[41]

As 1917 came to its conclusion, people were beginning to wonder: how much more could Britons be expected to endure?

THE LAST PUSH

21

THE WORLD
IS CHANGING

Spring–Summer 1918

*It felt like someone's birthday – but in truth it was the birthday of a great
new era.*

Kate Parry Collins's diary, February 1918

Duff Cooper was at home in London, having returned from a few
days away in Berkshire with friends. He was writing to Diana. A fire
crackled in the grate of his living room at 88 St James's Street. Outside,
it was bitterly cold. The city was quiet. Only the occasional pedestrian
passed by the grand stone building on the corner of Pall Mall. Few
motorcars broke the stillness of New Year's Day. Even the post-
Christmas sales had got off to a disappointing start. *The Times* blamed
it on the high numbers of women who were now too busy working to
go bargain hunting.[1]

Like the majority of people, Duff had had a miserable time of late.
His diary, next to him on the desk, had concluded 1917 on a low note:

So ends 1917 – which has been, I think, the least happy year that I have
lived. The one thing which is important in my life and becomes increasingly so is my love for Diana and hers for me.[2]

However, 1918 seemed unlikely to be any less dire. The New Year's Day
message from the prime minister to the people of Britain printed in
The Times that day seemed to confirm this. Lloyd George told Britons
to prepare themselves for further sacrifices:

The sacrifices which the men are making at the front we all know. Despite all that they have gone through, they are still facing frost and mud, privation and suffering, wounds and death.

So long as they are called upon to endure these things let us see to it that we do not take our ease at the price of their sacrifice. To every civilian I would say: 'Your firing line is the works or the office in which you do your bit; the shop or the kitchen in which you spend or save. The road of duty and patriotism is clear before you; follow it, and it will lead ere long to safety for our people and victory for our cause.'[3]

Duff would not be amongst the civilians for much longer; 1918 must bring his departure for the front. There, he would face the 'frost and mud, privation and suffering' of war that he had eluded for so long.

Fifty miles away, in the rectory in Great Leighs, **Andrew Clark** had taken Lloyd George's message to heart and was thinking about the burdens of war. It was late on a cold January evening, and the reverend was sitting by the fire with his friend Major Caldwell. As well as discussing the scarcities of food and fuel, now a standard topic of conversation, they were also thinking further ahead, worrying about what might happen when the war was over, whenever that might be:

Major Caldwell has been told by West-End army men that the Government apprehends great disquiet after the war. Munition work will stop, and wages will fall, and there will be a bad time of unrest. The government are therefore encouraging the enrolment of as many special constables and volunteers as possible, to have a large force of partly trained men to preserve order.[4]

Unrest was not just a future concern. In the dark days between Christmas and the New Year, a conference had taken place in Westminster, attended by over 900 delegates from trade unions and the young Labour Party. Their message was clear: more strikes would follow in 1918 if the authorities did not act to control the privations being suffered by working people. A general strike was not ruled out.[5]

*

Duff Cooper's festive break was over. That morning, he had risen in darkness and left his flat before dawn to walk across St James's Park to his barracks. By late afternoon he was back at home once more and dressed for dinner. He was off to a bachelor party at the Ritz but found time to scribble a note to Diana before he left. However, the evening did not turn out to be the celebration he had expected:

> I arrived first, then Michael. We had to wait some time for William Rawle. He came at last and said, 'I'm sorry I'm late. Patrick Shaw-Stewart has been killed.' I felt stunned. This is the last blow. Lionel, Michael and William were all sad but none of them could have felt what I did. I courted forgetfulness in champagne but didn't get much comfort.[6]

Patrick had been Duff's last surviving close friend from the Oxford coterie. Going round and round his head when he arrived back in his rooms in the middle of the night were lines from *Anthony and Cleopatra*:

> *O, wither'd is the garland of the war,*
> *The soldier's pole is fall'n! Young boys and girls*
> *Are level now with men. The odds is gone,*
> *And there is nothing left remarkable*
> *Beneath the visiting moon.*[7]

Duff was due to go to Taplow Castle the following afternoon to stay with friends. Before he left London, he wrote his now-daily letter to Diana, in a deep depression:

> My darling – I am thinking so much about you and wondering how you feel. The anxiety for you helps me to forget my own misery. I am very tired and in no mood to find words for my sorrow. I wish we were together. To talk to you now would be better than tears.
>
> Do you remember that quotation from Swift – to the effect that he was of the opinion that there was no greater folly than to form a too great or intimate friendship which must leave the survivor miserable. I feel that in my bitterer moments but I know it isn't true. For what should I do now if I had not you – oh my love, my love. Duff.[8]

Diana's reply came the following day:

That two months should rob us of both Edward and Patrick should be enough to finish me, so any energy or interest that is left to me – were it not for you, my darling, who keeps every part of me alive.

　'As flies to wanton boys are we to the Gods
　They kill us for their sport'
　Darling – I love you. D[9]

Over the coming weeks, Duff couldn't shake his unhappiness. This last of the relentless series of losses he'd experienced seemed to hit him particularly hard. Perhaps because now he was pretty much the last man of their set standing, and he knew that this year he would face the gauntlet of war himself:

> I think at times that I am going to be ill. The extraordinary lethargy and lack of interest that I feel all the time may be due to some physical causes beside the cloud of sadness that darkens all my days. I have felt more keenly wretched but never more unutterably sad.[10]

If the food shortages were causing misery for the majority, they were still bringing success to **Hallie and Eustace Miles.** Business had never been better:

> Eustace and I are consulted every day by the government or organisations, or heads of big business, about meat-substitutes. Our meat-substitute food counter is nearly as crowded as the butchers' shops! It is so wonderful to look around now and see the fulfilment of Eustace's dreams and teachings and the fruits of all his past hard work in teaching thousands of people how to live without meat in the days of peace and plenty. I think the chief thing that keeps us going is our happiness in being able to help in this great food crisis.[11]

But Hallie was not so heartless that she didn't realise that what brought them success brought suffering for ordinary people. She saw for herself the queues outside the shops, and she saw for herself the hunger in the faces of those who passed by her restaurant, who could not afford to step in:

The food shortage is becoming very dreadful, especially for the working classes, with a lot of children to be fed; and for the munition and other war-workers. They get so hungry. It is strange to see the queues at the butchers' shops and at the shops for margarine and butter. We hope that with rationing, things will be better and foods more evenly distributed.[12]

As food shortages in Britain grew ever more serious, queues outside food shops such as this, in Reading, became an increasingly common sight.

Compulsory rationing was now seen as the only means of ensuring a fair distribution of diminishing supplies and easing the unrest, and it was on the way. At the end of December, the Food Controller had given local authorities the power to enforce food control in their districts. The nationwide rationing of sugar had come into effect on 1 January, and the compulsory rationing of bread, flour, meats and fats would follow.[13]

Andrew Clark received his first correspondence about the scheme in late January, when an application form for ration cards was delivered to the rectory. Andrew's reaction was lukewarm at best – the seriousness of the problem certainly had not gone away yet, and trouble persisted in the district:

<u>Friday 25 January:</u> 10 a.m. Morning's post brought an application-form for cards for butter or margarine. The Food Controller is accused of making an artificial famine of butter and eggs by prohibiting imports from Iceland.[14]

<u>Saturday 26 January:</u> FR Lewin says the agitation among the food queues in Braintree yesterday amounted almost to a riot, and the police were at their wit's end. Similar disturbance is looked for at Chelmsford today.[15]

The government was desperately trying to appease the masses. Union leaders and workers' representatives were courted by the creation of a Consumers' Council on which their leaders were invited to sit. Lord Rhondda, the Food Controller, went on a PR offensive, urging Britons to stick together and not to turn against each other, pointing out that things were much worse in Germany, and asking them to embrace the compulsory rationing system which would iron out any iniquities.[16]

But there was valid concern about the new regulations: what provision was there to check the consumption of rationed food in restaurants and clubs? Because conspicuous consumption by the wealthy seemed to be going on as ever it had.[17]

The Food Controller did *try* to impose restrictions on restaurant diners, by enforcing meatless days in public eating places, two days a week, from the end of January.[18] Added to the rationing of meat that followed in February, it seemed that **Hallie Miles**'s wildest vegetarian dreams had come true:

We have had the first official Meatless Day, and from 12 noon the E.M Restaurant was absolutely packed.

It was so strange registering at a butcher's for the small amount of meat we get for the servants. We now have to have meat and poultry cards and butter and margarine cards. The lady butcher who served me was so interested when she heard who I was that she at once sent an order for my book 'Health without Meat!'[19]

*

February 1918 was not only the month that saw the introduction of compulsory rationing, it was also the month that a far more enduring step towards making Britain a fairer society was taken. On 7 February, the Representation of the People Act was passed in Parliament. For the first time in history, all British men over 21 would have the vote. It was a move to prevent the terrible injustice, and inevitable outcry, that would occur if men who had fought for their country were not allowed to participate in an election on their return. The change to the political structure of Britain was huge: the electoral register for 1914 numbered 8 million voters; in 1918 that number was more than doubled.[20]

Many conservatives saw this as a necessary means of stymieing the socialist movement in Britain, particularly worrying in the wake of the Russian Revolution. But the socialists themselves were optimistic too. At a Labour Conference after the passing of the act, the party celebrated the fact that the next election would mark the birth of industrial democracy in Britain, as it would include workers in the political process for the first time.[21]

And it wasn't only working-class men who were invited in. Women over 30 who met certain property qualifications were given the vote for the first time too. **Kate Parry Collins** read of the passing of the act in the newspaper delivered to her cottage. A cold February morning was suddenly brightened into a day she would remember forever. It was indeed a watershed moment for British women – though they would have to wait until 1928 for full voting equality:

> A day of excitement. It felt like someone's birthday, a personal affair – but in truth it was the birthday of a great new era. The Daily Telegraph unusually early, with the announcement of the passing into law of the Franchise Bill and 'Votes for Women'. I had to do something to celebrate so I wrote as gracefully as I could to Mrs Cecil Chapman acknowledging her share in the movement and her leadership of the NCS.[22]

As male politicians in Westminster took the first leap towards creating political equality for womankind, **Helen Bentwich** was still in Essex with the Women's Land Army, another expression of the changing times for women. She and her comrades really were doing vital war work, just like the soldiers at the front – a fact that the Land Army

Handbook, issued to Helen and all of her fellow workers, took pains to point out:

> You are now in the Women's Land Army; serving your Country just like the Soldiers and Sailors. You have to grow food for them and for the whole country and your work is quite as important as theirs.[23]

But their employers rather desperately advised them that this didn't mean they should disregard their femininity altogether:

> You are doing a man's work and so you are dressed rather like a man; but remember that just because you wear a smock and breeches you should take care to behave like an English girl who expects chivalry and respect from everyone she meets.[24]

Whatever the moral imperative to resist change, the truth was that change had happened. Helen's life had already been transformed; now she was overjoyed at the partial enfranchisement of women that reflected this new reality, even though she would have to wait five years before she qualified to vote herself. She wrote to Norman of the good news:

> We have at last realized that woman is an animal with two legs, what don't come to any harm if they are exposed as such instead of pretending she's a sort of head on a pedestal. So we wear breeches openly and unashamedly, a smock or a coat to just above our knees – and we have a vote too if we're over 30.
>
> So you see, it's you men what are the back-numbers now.[25]

Increasing equality did not, of course, make her day-to-day life any easier. As another ordinary, hungry worker living amongst the people of Essex, she was struggling like the rest of them, albeit temporarily:

> The people at the Inn refused to give me supper. They were as rude as could be – and there was a rat in my bedroom. I'm finding it more and more difficult to get meals. I've been to see the Food Controller here, because I can never get any meat, even with coupons. But he only said: 'My dear young lady, next time complain in writing. You certainly don't look starved.'[26]

*

James Butlin had had a difficult start to the year. He had suffered another breakdown. He had finished his treatment at Craiglockhart Hospital at the end of the summer, and had been sent back to Wyke Regis to serve as a gas officer at the camp. In January, however, he had been admitted to hospital once more. He was subsequently given notice to report for a medical board at Wareham on 1 March. Its verdict was severe. Upon his return home to Weymouth afterwards, James wrote to his friend Basil, now working at the Foreign Office:

Yesterday I was sent off to Wareham to attend a special neurasthenic board. Strictly between ourselves I feel that a crisis was bound to occur sooner or later. I have felt and do feel extraordinary at times and I am beginning to reap the fruits of my two trips to France. To continue on home service is impossible nowadays and my prospects of general service are faint in the extreme. Whenever I do anything strenuous I am brought up against a dizzy and faint feeling in the head. I have been living a complete teetotaller etc. for months now and I still get no better.

Last medical board I got six months light service and was altogether surprised when a few days ago I received notification that I was to attend a special board yesterday. I entered in fear and trembling before the board and maintained that I was fit and well. They examined me and overhauled me generally and then sent me away. After about 20 minutes' consultation I was called in again and told that I was 'permanently unfit for further military service'. I protested slightly but they pointed out that were I to break down again as I did in January I should be months instead of weeks recovering.

Certain circumstances, however, impel me to make a fight against this decision. To begin with the army have taken all the best out of me and now wish to turn me out with an inadequate pension. Secondly I am just as likely to break down in civil life where I shall have to work harder than I do now. I think my case is being taken up and with any luck I may remain in the service. If however the rest board (which will be in about 3 weeks' time) confirms the decision of yesterday's board things will become a bit complicated. In fact I may really have to clear out, in which case can you suggest anything? Any chance of a job at the FO for instance? Write and let me know.

For all the bravado he had shown during their correspondence, James was not a well man. He had just turned 22 and should have felt as though his life was just beginning; instead he seemed to feel it was over.

On a beautiful early spring day in March, **Duff Cooper** was making the most of London while he still could, visiting his favourite haunts – as well as discovering some delicious new ones:

> Lunched with Goonie at the Café Royal. I had settled to meet Diana at 2.30 but I thought the arrangement only vague and weakly allowed myself to linger with Goonie til past three. Then Diana had left Arlington Street and it was not till four that I found her at my flat. She was angry with me and justly so. It was the most beautiful afternoon imaginable – as warm as summer. She had thought that we would go somewhere away from London and in her vexation and disappointment she cried like a child.
>
> I was terribly touched and torn with remorse. However, I comforted her at last and off we went in a taxi with a volume of Keats, first to buy cakes and preserved pears and then to the Serpentine. There we hired a boat and went for a row. I have never been in a boat on the Serpentine before in my life. It was all most lovely and the weather incredibly delightful. After we had gone a little way we let the boat drift and sitting side by side in the stern we read Isabella verse by verse – a most memorable afternoon.[27]

Sunlight danced on the water. The sounds of the park floated over the lake: the occasional shriek of a child, the call of those selling their wares to the sparse crowds who had turned out to enjoy the sunshine. But for those precious minutes, the privileged pair were in a world of their own; a world far from war and death.

Fifty miles east was the sea. **Helen Bentwich** could see it from where she was working in Essex that day, and the intoxicating sunshine and the first warm breath of summer in the country air almost made her forget the distant war too. Almost, but not quite:

Two young ladies boating on the Serpentine in London during the heatwave of 1914.

> There has never been such a spring as this: the country is gay with fruit blossom, hyacinths and daffodils. There are distant views of the sea over far-stretching marshes, and the water and sky merge in one great blue pattern. I can forget the war and the killing, until I get right down to the seashore, as I did today, and was stopped by a soldier with a fixed bayonet, forbidden to go any further.[28]

Despite the glorious weather, Helen was not having an easy day. Her motorbike, Lewis, had broken down again, so she was on a pushbike. She'd cycled to a small village called Tillingham, arriving late in the afternoon. Having visited the farmer she was scheduled to see, she set about finding herself a place to stay the night. As darkness began to fall, she found herself in a tricky spot:

> I went to the local registrar, who was supposed to find me a billet, but she wasn't helpful; so about 6.30 p.m. I decided to find one myself. I cycled to Bradwell-juxta-Mare, because I was fascinated by the name, and called at the 'Green Man' on the side of the Quay. A disagreeable old man there said he couldn't have me 'cos there aren't no womenfolk about.' I

went to another pub, where they couldn't take me, as they'd just had a baby, and there wasn't any room. I tried a number of cottages, but everywhere was told they hadn't any beds aired. I think it was partly due to my kit, as they'd never seen a Land Girl before, and my breeches put them off.

It was getting dark, and I felt miserable, and decided to sleep under a hedge. But it was cold, and a rat ran out nearby, so I went back to Bradwell, and happened to meet the village policeman. Fortunately, there was a full moon. He was a dear, and knocked up a lot more people, but they all refused. So he sent me to the Rectory, and the rector and his wife were perfectly charming, and I spent a very happy and comfortable night there. In the morning I went to family prayers, and the rector read the passage out of Matthew about the birds of the fields having their nests to go to, but the Son of Man having no place whereon to lay his head.[29]

Helen was Jewish; but she appreciated the thought.

A few days later, in another Essex rectory, **Andrew Clark** was sitting at his desk late on a Sunday afternoon. He'd earlier led the much-reduced village congregation in the annual Palm Sunday service. The chatter amongst the churchgoers afterwards had been dominated by two important topics. Firstly, the fact that the clocks were supposed to have been put forward that morning (the villagers were still dead against it). And secondly, the bad news that had travelled across the Channel from France:

Sunday 24 March: ('Palm' Sunday) 2 a.m., natural time became 3 a.m. artificial time which will henceforth be used in these notes. On Lyons Hall farms they are still keeping the old time and will do so for a fort-night longer. Some farmers (e.g. Richard Arnold) kept by the old time all last year, and will do so this year also.

Recognizing the general anxiety as to the Western front, the War Office had a bulletin— the first for a very long time.[30]

Three days earlier, the German army had unleashed a massive offensive against the British on the Western Front. In the aftermath of Passchendaele, and with the redeployment of troops to Italy at the end of 1917, the British armies there were reduced in strength. They had known an attack must come, but no one had anticipated the full fury that came at them on 21 March, when 76 German divisions and more than 1 million men, with around 10,000 guns and trench mortars, attacked 50 miles of the British front in France. They fired more than 1 million shells in just five hours – not many fewer than the Allies had fired in a whole week in their great assault on the Somme.[31]

The official war news, stuck by Andrew into his diary, tried to strike a positive note, but the alarming reality was all too apparent:

SUMMARY OF SATURDAY'S OFFICIAL WAR NEWS. 24 March.
The Battle is continuing with the greatest intensity on the whole front south of the Scarpe River. South and West of St Quentin our Troops have taken up their new positions and are heavily engaged with the enemy.

On the northern portion of the Battle Front the enemy's attacks have been pressed with the utmost determination and regardless of losses. Our Troops have maintained their positions on the greater part of this Front after a fierce and prolonged struggle. Great gallantry has been shown by the Troops engaged in the fighting in this area and to the South of it.

The enemy's attacks continue with great violence.[32]

The Germans had broken through the British lines, and taken almost one hundred square miles of territory in the first day alone. After three years of trench warfare, no one seemed to remember how to cope with such a dramatic onslaught. The Allies were in chaos.[33] In Germany, the Kaiser had declared that Sunday to be a national holiday, in celebration of the imminent victory.

Helen Bentwich had left the Essex rectory behind. In need of some proper rest, she'd gone home for the weekend to her family's West London townhouse. Her father always got *The Times*, and that weekend the news marking its pages was bleak:

Everyone here is feeling frightfully anxious today – I believe it's really rather touch and go whether we can keep them from breaking through our lines now, or will have to give in. Anyway, the slaughter is terrific, and even in Essex we could hear the incessant guns. Still, it's no use writing, because by the time you get this, it'll all be over, either way – this great battle that is raging now.[34]

It really did seem as if – quite suddenly – the war might soon be over. Could Great Britain really be on the verge of the unthinkable: a defeat?

Duff Cooper felt his hour had surely come:

> I begin a new volume of my diary – I wonder if I shall finish it. I am glad to have done with the last one. It was an ugly book and it recorded my four bad months at Bushey followed by the deaths of Edward and Patrick. I hope that this may be a luckier volume. It will probably deal with France.[35]

He braced himself to receive orders for France. But he received none.[36] Another week, and still he was a free man in his own city. Out with Diana, the moments they had left together seemed to be rushing away. A foreshadowing of Duff's now imminent departure brought it all home, to her at least:

> We dined at Claridge's. Afterwards I went for a little drive with Diana. We were going round St. James's Park and were ecstatically happy when we passed a body of men marching down the Mall. Diana saw that they were Grenadiers and were going to France. Immediately she burst into such a passion of tears and sobs as I have never heard from her. She cried that she could not bear me to go. I felt so sad and so proud. The moment was most beautiful and most dramatic. I had known there was a draft to parade at Chelsea at midnight but had forgotten it. Odd that we should meet them. When she left me she told me to read the sonnet beginning 'Thy bosom is endeared with all hearts' before I went to sleep. I did so and saw her meaning.[37]

Shakespeare's 'Sonnet 31' lingered in his mind as he closed his eyes, and he must have thought of all his friends, all those suitors of Diana's, who lay buried in the foreign fields he was destined for:

Thou art the grave where buried love doth live,
Hung with the trophies of my lovers gone,
Who all their parts of me to thee did give;
That due of many now is thine alone.
Their images I loved I view in thee,
And thou, all they, hast all the all of me.

In spite of the German advance, **James Butlin** was worrying about
what he could do with himself. The decision of the medical board had
been upheld and while he might get a small army pension, it wouldn't
be enough to make a life on. He wrote rather desperately to Basil, who
was still working at the Foreign Office. James's bragging letters, lording
his status as an officer over his 'shirking' friend, belonged to another
lifetime:

> If you have studied the gazette closely you will have read last Tuesday
> that 'Lt J.M. Butlin is placed on the retired list on account of ill health
> caused by wounds'. On Wednesday I went over to Cosham for a special
> medical board on the following day. Next morning I had a board before
> two civilian doctors who I believe assessed my pension but who have
> given me no indication of the amount at which they arrived. I came
> back to Weymouth later on that day and am now of course out of
> uniform.
>
> Now what the hell am I to do for a living? Can you tell me the
> answer to that question? Seriously though, I must get work soon or I
> shall be broke. Is there any chance of a job similar to what you are doing
> at the FO? I don't necessarily mean in your department but anywhere
> in town or practically anywhere. I don't fancy going back to Oxford, for
> pecuniary as well as other reasons. I can't afford to do nothing for two
> years, which is what going back to Oxford means. I have written to the
> Warden and asked him what work, how long etc it would be before I
> could get a degree.
>
> What of France, old cock? I don't think I ever gave you much hope
> of great and smashing victory, except on the Hun side. The will of the
> people may be all right, but the brains of the army aren't in the right
> place. We've been out-generalled.[38]

*

Despite the desperate situation abroad, at home the work went on as normal. One Saturday in April, **Helen Bentwich** was among two hundred Land Girls who assembled outside the Food Production Department in Victoria Street for a great recruiting rally. At the head of the procession, a six-foot-tall 'tractor woman' in breeches carried a Union Jack, and the music of a brass band heralded the unusual delegation as they made their way through the city. Helen wrote to Norman the next day, still full of the excitement of it all:[39]

> Yesterday was the great recruiting stunt. I took Cubby [Helen's dog] along, as a sheep-dog, and there were lambs and ducks and rabbits with us too, and the two inevitable farm-wagons. I had to recruit all along the side of the procession – that meant running by the side, in between the crowd and the procession, distributing pamphlets and magazines, and urging all likely girls to join up.
>
> It was great fun – we started in Victoria Street, and went up Whitehall, Haymarket, Regent Street, Oxford Street, and Tottenham Court Road, where we had lunch at the Y.M.C.A. hostel. I went into all the big shops, and talked to the girls and got rid of papers and jumped on and off the buses while they were going, and threw things in the taxis. It all probably sounds very puerile, but while you're doing it you get quite carried away, and forget everything else except the recruiting.
>
> After lunch I had to lead a horse, as the other girl was tired, and it nearly pulled my arms out. We went to Hyde Park, and there were meetings and recruitings again till 4, and then we collected the girls to go home. It was a rag, and we got heaps and heaps of girls. Only mother said I oughtn't to do it on a Saturday! I can't see it a bit, and I don't believe you will either. Things are so awfully serious and big these days, that 'you mustn't do it on the Sabbath' seems such a very feeble excuse. Men die and fight all days of the week; girls work on the land with their animals all days.[40]

The restrictions that had been imposed on Helen all her life by her Jewish religion, just like the other moral codes she'd been brought up with, suddenly seemed open to challenge:

> I wonder if I'll ever get over that tremendous sense of freedom and broken fetters I get when I realise that it is possible to do things on Saturday without the world coming to an end, or without becoming a

Christian altogether. I've absolutely no religious sense these days I'm afraid. You'll have to teach it to me when we settle down and get civilized once again.[41]

Duff Cooper had received the news he'd long been expecting: he was in the next draft for France. The time for goodbyes had finally come. Duff tackled them in typical style with a lunch, followed by a trip to the theatre, followed by tea, followed by a fine dinner:

I met Mother. We lunched at the Berkeley and it was a trying meal. Poor darling mother could hardly speak. She said she didn't want me to go and to see me in the evening – this was in fact to be our last meeting. As we left the restaurant she said to me very quickly that she wouldn't come out of the cloakroom till I had gone. She was looking very white and was on the verge of breaking down and so she left me.

I then met Diana and we went to a play called *Nothing But the Truth* which made us laugh a good deal. We had a box and there were tears between the acts. Even I shed a few at one moment holding her in my arms and feeling her body shaken with sobs. But it was all beautiful. Then we went and bought strawberries and she got sugar and cream from Arlington Street and we took them to St James' Street and ate them. We read some Browning and kissed a lot and cried a little and parted to dress – she for dinner and I for travelling. She came to pick me up as usual and drove me to Bleuie's where we were dining. She was looking very lovely but fighting all the time with tears. The atmosphere was a little strained at first but under the influence of wine it all went well enough, I thought . . .[42]

[Diana] dropped me at Chelsea. It was very dark on the square. The draft was already formed up. Teddie, the adjutant, was there and only laughed at my being late. Monty Bertie who is in charge of the draft had arrived but was too drunk to march to Waterloo and so had gone away again and was coming by taxi. I took charge and marched off the men, leading them with the drums in front. The band played nearly all the way from Chelsea to Waterloo and I felt proud, romantic, and exalted.[43]

Diana had clung to him, sobbed, kissed him, and then watched him go. The music and footsteps throbbed loud, and faded. Silence. She was left on an empty square, in the middle of the night.[44]

Duff wrote to her as soon as he possibly could, scribbling his final goodbye:

> Darling my darling
> How I loved you last night – how dreadfully I loved you. I couldn't think that I was going to the war, I could only think that I was leaving you. Will you love me as much when I come back? Please do.
> Goodbye, my little love, my heart and soul, my brains and blood and marrow. I adore you. Duff.[45]

After three and a half years of spectating the war from London, feeling its blows from afar, Duff was finally going to live it for himself. And the Allies' struggle was now desperate.

22

WITH OUR BACKS
AGAINST THE WALL
May–August 1918

I was glad to find that I was no more frightened than other people and I really think rather less so – especially, I must confess – after dinner.

Duff Cooper, diary entry for 21 May 1918

Duff Cooper disembarked at Boulogne on a cool spring day, a Sunday. The first thing he'd done upon arrival was to locate the British Officers' Club in order to have some lunch. It was housed in a series of huts behind the Louvre Hotel, and was crowded, as always. Duff tucked into omelette, fried potatoes and bread and butter and was well satisfied. Thus fortified, he made his way to the railway station, to board the train to Étaples. His day went downhill from there:

A dreary journey to Etaples, where we arrived after 8. A miserable march in rain and darkness to the camp. I felt for the first time a little depressed and could not but remember how a week ago I was sitting down to dinner at Wilton by the side of Diana. Monty and I set out in search of food and drink but after a long and very tiring walk we returned hungry and thirsty having found that everything was shut as it was past 10. We shared a wretched tent with a sandy floor. However I made myself fairly comfortable in my sleeping bag and slept well.[1]

So ended Duff's first day at war, and it was a war that suddenly wasn't going well at all. The German spring offensive had begun over a month ago and it had blown apart the hard-won and hard-held British line. The first phase of the assault, Operation Michael, had forced a retreat from the Somme, and caused 212,000 Allied casualties plus another 90,000 soldiers taken prisoner. The Germans had called it off in early April, without achieving the general breakthrough they'd hoped for, but it left the Allies more vulnerable than they'd been since 1914.[2]

They had only a few days to recover before the Germans struck again; this time in the Lys Valley. Now it was land in the Ypres Salient that was lost. The Passchendaele Ridge, won at such a terrible price just five months earlier, fell back into German hands. The Allies had been forced back to the gates of the city. As Duff slept in his tent in Étaples, British and French soldiers were fighting bitterly to hold on.[3] Douglas Haig had issued a desperate call to arms to the men: 'There is no other course open to us but to fight it out ... With our backs to the wall and believing in the justice of our cause each one of us must fight on to the end.'[4]

The bad news filled the papers at home. Kemmel Hill, a key strategic high point to the southwest of Ypres, had fallen. The Germans were inching closer and closer to Ypres. Over the weekend that Duff made his way to France, **Kate Parry Collins** devoured the terrifying reports that reached her little cottage:

> Friday 26 April: Read the daily paper and the evening paper – had 2 letters from John in the morning. The news is not good but might be worse. I don't see how we can save Ypres.
>
> Monday 29 April: I suffer terribly in these anxious days, the one thought above and beyond everything – is John safe?

That day, the headlines were particularly worrying: 'Battle Nearing Ypres' screamed *The Times*; 'each day the fighting has been closer to Ypres', 'Menace to the Ypres Salient'.[5] But the papers had left the printing presses in London early that morning – in fact the German offensive had been called off. The advancing army had not reached their final objectives, but it had cost the Allies dearly to hold them off, and they were left worryingly exposed in Flanders.[6]

Yet, for now, the worst danger was over. Kate could relax. The following morning the newspaper delivered to her cottage brought her better news: 'Great Allied Defence: Enemy Onslaughts Repulsed', 'Big German Defeat: Splendid Work by British Troops'.[7] There was now a pause, whilst the Germans readied their next move – and the Allies desperately tried to prepare themselves to meet it.

Diana Manners did not want to wait around at home worrying about Duff. She determined to leave the relative comfort of the family's own officers' hospital and lose herself in the austerity of Guy's Hospital again. Her mother, the duchess, was dead against it, of course. Diana poured out her troubles to Duff, who had been blamed for this seemingly rash decision:

> Darling Duff, It all went off far worse than I hoped. When Her Grace came in I started bravely enough with 'Now, darling, about Guy's' and then God! Hands up, shrieks, gasps for restoratives, so I withdraw . . .
>
> I long to know how much she connects this intolerance, this great remonstrance and inability to be even civil, with love or sorrow for you. But now this morning the continuance of scenes and ravings make me waver, yet if I waver now I shall always waver so I must try: my determination I find greatly strengthened by your absence, darling. It's rather sad but so understandable – so much was tolerable with you to dally and philander secretly with, so much I was content to forfeit in sops. Now it seems any single straw will break my back.
>
> 11 p.m. I have had it out with Mother. She was pathetic, tamed, and bleated of the loneliness of her life but I didn't waver and shall probably leave next week. She thinks it is a penance; for what? Too much life, or too much love, or too much suffering.[8]

Like all newly arrived infantry in France, **Duff Cooper** had travelled on from Étaples to his base depot for further training, before he went on to join his battalion. In early May he was at the Guards Depot just outside Le Havre. Although another German hammer blow was expected any moment, thus far the war was not exactly challenging him:

> Two letters from Diana this morning and two from mother. I dined in camp and had an extraordinarily good dinner. I always drink a pint of champagne – but the champagne they have here – called Dry Royal – is not good. Played bridge after dinner.[9]

Diana was having a less pleasant time. She had started back at Guy's and it was a massive shock to find herself on her feet all day, working the ward again. She'd been assigned to a women's surgical ward – and the patients were a world away from the officers she'd attended to in the ballroom wards of her own home[10]:

> My darling, I have endured great physical pain today, hip and thigh, calf and foot. Wards claim one from 7.30 a.m. to 8 p.m., and with the exception of ¾ for lunch and ½ for tea, during which I hung my legs in cold water just to calm them, one is not off one's feet. I don't remember it being so torturing last time – do you? Perhaps novelty and patriotism stiffened my sinews. It was one of our spring days – but one must lead the leisured life to appreciate weather, I'm glad to say; once busy it matters little except to one's general spirits. The poor don't notice it at all.[11]

Ted Poole had just had his eighteenth birthday. His call-up papers were delivered to his home in Shacklewell, a working-class district of northeast London, shortly afterwards. In May 1918, Ted walked out of the front door to join the 3rd London Regiment in training at Aldershot. It was the second time a Poole boy had left home to join the army. Ted's older brother Thomas had joined up voluntarily in 1915. He had been killed on the first day of the Battle of Passchendaele in 1917.[12]

Ted left behind his father Thomas, his sister Dolly, his brother Frank, and Tiger the cat. They were a close family, and Ted wrote to them regularly from his new home in 'B' Block of Albuhera Barracks, one of many blocks in the sprawling military camp at Aldershot. Two years into conscription, the other new recruits he now lived alongside were mainly teenagers too, only just eligible to fight.[13]

Ted wrote to his little sister Dolly about his initial experiences:

> I had my first day at P.T. (Physical Training) today and it was cold, as you have to do it with your jacket off, shirt open at the neck and sleeves tucked right up. I don't get much time to myself as I am parading and drilling all day, and after tea when I have got the time to myself I have got so many things to clean that am not finished til nearly bed-time. I must now close, so goodbye for the present, hoping you are in good health as this leaves me. From your loving brother Ted xxxxxxxxxxx
>
> p.s. Love to father, Frank and Tiger.[14]

It was Dolly's birthday soon afterwards, and he sent her his regimental badge as a present.[15] Ted might have been taking things calmly enough; but his father was deeply anxious – he'd already lost one boy to this war. His letters questioned Ted minutely about the training he was getting – and Ted dutifully answered him:

> Just a few lines in answer to your letter, which I received today. Yes I have got used to the putties, as they have got shaped to my legs by now. And I am getting used to my other things now, as I have been dished out with a rifle and bayonet, and now when I go on parade I have got to wear my belt, bayonet and cartridge pouch and also take the rifle. They have been teaching us bayonet fighting today and I can tell you it makes your arms ache when you make a point, that is, when you lunge out at some imaginary enemy, with the rifle at arm's length. I think with this hard training, they will either make a man of me, or kill me.
>
> You ought to see me in my shrapnel helmet, and gas mask, it WOULD make you laugh, especially as the helmet wobbles from side to side, every time I walk. Yes I get my food alright, and you can have supper if you like to go to it. I am taking your advice and eating all I can.
> Well, I think I will have to close now as I haven't got anything more to say just at present. Hoping you are quite well. From your loving son, Ted xxxxxxx[16]

Duff Cooper's training was over. He was going to join his battalion at the front line for the first time. Seemingly calmed by poetry, he wrote to Diana before he set off:

> One word, darling love, before I go into battle. I am starting in a few minutes and am going to ride there. I had always imagined a long exhausting march to the trenches, but it is pleasant and romantic to be able to ride there comfortably after tea. I had a thirst for poetry this morning, having brought none with me. I found a volume of Rupert Brooke. Far the loveliest and the one which I tried to learn by heart this morning and have already forgotten begins – 'These hearts were woven of human joys and cares'. Read it and tell me what you think.[17]

The 3rd battalion of the Grenadier Guards, which Duff was joining, had gone into the front line a few days earlier at St-Amand, near

Arras.[18] Towards the end of a beautifully sunny afternoon, Duff set off to join them. After reporting to battalion HQ, Duff travelled on to the trenches to join his company:

> We walked over green fields while the sun set beautifully and except for many shell holes the country looked peaceful enough. At last I reached my destination and in a dugout I found my company commander. He is a quiet fellow. We immediately had dinner. I was rather agreeably surprised with the food – on this evening we had soup, hot fish, cold beef with potatoes, peas and pickles, prunes and cheese. I drank whiskey and soda and port. Immediately afterwards I had to go on to relieve Clifton Brown who was in the frontline slits waiting for dinner. He went back and left me there feeling astonished to find myself at last in charge of a portion of the front line with nothing between myself and the German army.[19]

It was relatively quiet, but the killing went on. By the time the battalion was relieved on 24 May, two men of the battalion had been killed and twenty-five wounded, after just four days in the front line.[20] The next battle of the German spring offensive hadn't yet begun – but it was about to.

As Duff was relieved from the front line, **Diana Manners** was heading for a much-needed rest after a horrible day at the hospital. She was lonely, and desperately worried about Duff.[21] His letter to her, written as he went 'into battle,' had arrived for her that day. Once she reached the comfort of Arlington Street, she immediately wrote in reply:

> My dearest, I have had my worst day. It is cold and dark. I changed my ward and was sent to one in the pent of the roof. There was bed after bed of burnt children of three and four, on whom I was made to prac-tise the new treatment of very hot melted wax poured on their raw surfaces; the pain is excessive, and they scream like tortured not babyish things. They are held down while it is done. The few remaining beds were occupied by four little girls each with such virulent gonorrhea that gloves are worn to tuck them up.
>
> All afternoon I felt sick and fighting with a wish to ask for removal, knowing that it was terribly bad to give under. At the tea half hour, feeling terribly weak, I found in its pigeon hole a letter from you and for the first time in years I cried and cried with joy. And then my darling

its news, when other petty woes had done their worst, overthrew me and I collapsed with the misery of you in the battle, and that I must not drag on not hearing from you for days, and that the torture of mind must go on indefinitely.

Keep warm baby. Diana.[22]

Kate Parry Collins had also had a letter from France that day. Its contents, however, were rather more humdrum. John had written of the latest news concerning Trotsky. Not the Russian Marxist Leon Trotsky, head of the Red Army and currently fighting a Civil War to maintain the Bolsheviks' hold on power. No, this Trotsky was a stray dog that John's battery had taken on:

Friday 24 May 1918: A letter from John saying he is very busy and that Trotsky the dog seems better.[23]

Clearly John was not giving Kate enough war news, because she continued to devour the papers. John was currently stationed near Béthune, which was twenty-five miles from Ypres. Severe fighting had broken out in April, when the advancing German army got within five miles of the town. Now, in May, they had commenced a terrific bombardment on that sector of the line:

Saturday 25 May 1918: I went to the post and to get the evening papers. 'Heavy shelling in the Bethune sector' was the headline. It makes me very miserable. John writes that he is still near B but further north and west.[24]

But the real might of the German army was unleashed further south a few days later. Its numbers were still growing on the Western Front, as more divisions moved over from the east. The German commanders were desperate to exploit the advantage before the Americans tipped the balance back against them. On 27 May, they attacked just north of the River Aisne, from where Paris became accessible. They swiped resistance away and advanced thirteen miles in a matter of hours. Within three days they'd reached the River Marne. It was another shocking reversal of Allied fortunes.[25] The outlook was suddenly very, very worrying.

Following a short period of rest, **Duff Cooper** was back in the front line and under fire:

> The usual night of restlessness, though I did manage a few hours' sleep, then a beautiful red dawn which was accompanied by a terrific bombardment which funnily enough hurt nobody. All this morning enemy aeroplanes are buzzing around exactly like mosquitoes. We fire at them, they go away, we never hit them – and a quarter of an hour later back they come again humming triumphantly, and the same thing happens again and again.
>
> A most beautiful black and white butterfly has just settled here. I have never seen one like it. It is very modern – or perhaps just a little démodé. It reminds me of a dress you used to have – I can't describe it – one evening that you wore it was an evening that we danced at the St James' Palace Hotel and we quarrelled because I didn't want you to drive home with Michael, and I gave you scent the next day. Good bye, Baby. Duff.[26]

The shelling resumed that night with equal ferocity. Duff, however, always found the terrors of trench warfare easier to bear after a good meal:

> I was glad to find that I was no more frightened than other people and I really think rather less so – especially, I must confess – after dinner. On the whole the line was not as bad as I expected – the dirt is the chief inconvenience and the difficulty of washing.[27]

A few nights later, Duff and his comrades were woken by a bombardment of 'blue cross' gas shells. These released a fine dust which could penetrate a gas mask and irritate the wearer sufficiently to make him remove it. A lethal gas attack would follow:

> My darling – there was another letter from you last night. You are the best and bravest, most beautiful and perfect mistress in the world.
>
> I was rudely awakened at three this morning by a gas attack. Fumbling for my gas mask in the darkness and trying to hold my breath the while I got a whiff or two but am none the worse. It was not the very deadly kind I think but the kind which produces symptoms like a cold in the

head, sometimes bronchitis or at the very worst pneumonia. Perhaps it's
a pity I didn't get more of it.[28]

Duff was now thinking of Diana almost constantly. As their separation
continued, both were realising that – despite all the game-playing of
the last few years – they were deeply, truly in love.[29] Now Duff just
had to survive long enough to get back to her.

By 3 June, the German Army had advanced to within forty miles
of Paris. Fifty thousand prisoners had been taken and the main Paris–
Nancy railway line had been broken. One million Parisians fled in fear.
In London, the British cabinet discussed the previously unthinkable:
the possible evacuation of the BEF.[30] Duff might be coming back to
Britain after all. But it would not be the triumphant homecoming he'd
imagined. The Germans were on the brink of victory.

Most British people did not realise how close the Allies were to defeat.
In training at Aldershot, **Ted Poole** certainly seemed unconcerned. He
was worrying about whether his father was receiving his pay on his
behalf, and he was pleased with the news that his brother Frank had
been promoted at work. Ted was working hard himself, and was keen
to report his latest endeavours to his father, who he knew would be
glad to hear of all the specialist training he was getting:

> We have had some rotten weather down here lately. It has been raining
> on and off for the last 3 or 4 days now. We had another route march
> today of about 7 miles and you can guess, I felt a bit tired when I got
> back as it was all up and down hills and also I had to carry a rifle, gas
> mask and cartridge pouch, which was more than I had when I went on
> the last route march.
>
> And they had something new as well today. After we had been
> marching about 1¼ hours our Officer suddenly threw down a smoke
> bomb and called out gas. We at once had to halt and put our gas masks
> on as quick as possible and then we had to march about ½ mile in the
> gas mask. Perhaps this doesn't sound very much but I can tell you that
> you sweat like hell when you have got a gas mask on for only a few
> minutes on a hot day, so you can guess what it was like after walking
> for ½ mile. In fact, the sweat was running down my chin and dripping

from the mask on to my coat, and the eyepieces of the mask were so misty that I couldn't see where I was going and I kept kicking the boy's heels in front of me.

Well I don't think I have got any more news just at present, hoping you are as well as this leaves me. From your loving son, Ted xxxxx

p.s. I am glad to hear that Tiger is getting on all right.[31]

Diana Manners was leaving Guy's Hospital, this time for good. She'd been there a month and that had been more than enough for her, given the difficulties of some of the tasks she'd had to face. She would go back to work at the family hospital on Arlington Street. On the ward for the last time, she was thinking of Duff in France:

My darling one. Today, my last day, I am rather glad to find myself so very popular with the nurses and the patients. They bring me bunches of very tired flowers when they have their half holiday and rush home to Peckham – and the young girl patients wink at me to wash them, and lie to get me. It is nice.

I'm glad I'm going tomorrow – though there will be many disadvantages and I have been, as it were, left very much with you in this ordered place, and once out of it, they will be buzzing and questioning and no regular time for my duties to you. A lovely letter from you tonight – terrifying – my darling. Good night, keep warm, baby. Diana.[32]

The situation in France was slowly improving for the Allies. The German advance on the Marne, which had begun with such ferocity, was now slowing. And Diana could let some of her anxiety subside since **Duff Cooper** was going into rest once more. He left the front line on the evening of 7 June, and arrived at a large farm in La Bazèque, southwest of Arras.[33] Duff was pleased with his new home:

Remember the largest farm you have ever seen and then imagine one just twice as big. A perfect rectangle with a great pool in the middle. In front is a gentleman's house – or at least a gentleman farmer's house – with two large rooms downstairs and a multitude of little bedrooms above. It must have been so lovely when it worked.

We are supposed to be here for a month's rest though I doubt there

Dorothy Lloyd, Alan Lloyd's widow,
with their son David.

Will Martin in civilian clothes, prior to his deployment to the Western Front.

One of a series of posters issued towards the end of 1916, suggesting ways in which the British public could help alleviate the increasingly severe shortage of coal.

Xmas Day.

Dearest,

This Xmas I hope you are having a peaceful time, don't ask me how I am spending mine, that there exists such places as Sutton, Codford, Wooburn, I cannot imagine, even the men who have been out 3 times have never seen anything like this, Xmas will have more memories for me than I can say.

My last told you that I was going up to my position but it did not tell you that my guns & stores were handed over to someone else & that I had to take over an old position complete, but that is so, poor Euphorbia however the horseshoe was missing which means that the luck it was to have brought still goes with us & not with those who have taken the gun over.

A letter from John Collins to his wife, Kate, written on Christmas Day, 1916.

Arthur Roberts in uniform as a soldier in
the Royal Scots Fusiliers.

British infantry moving up in artillery formation during
the Battle of Arras, 9 April 1917.

'The Underworld' by Walter Bayes, showing Londoners sheltering
in Elephant and Castle tube station during an air raid, 1918.

Ruins of the Cloth Hall (Lakenhalle), Ypres, with remains of gun carts and horses caught by shell fire in the foreground, 29 September 1918.

London's Paddington station, deserted during the rail strikes of October 1918.

A British field gun firing in the dawn barrage during the battle of the Canal du Nord, 27 September 1918.

Joyful scenes on the streets of Birmingham as the news breaks that the Armistice has been signed, 11 November 1918.

Crowds gather at the base of the Cenotaph during
the Peace Day celebrations of 19 July 1919.

being much rest about it. We shall be training all the morning and playing compulsory games in the afternoon. Added to which the Commanding Officer has just informed me that he wants me to give a lecture to the Battalion on the working of the Foreign Office. Oh darling – how do you think I shall do it? However, a bottle of brandy fifty years old has just arrived, and that may help me through. Don't worry, beloved, about my drinking too much. For one thing there is not so very much to drink, and for another the effect of this open air life is to make one's head like a rock, on which one could build a house or found a church.[34]

The following day, 9 June, the German Army launched their next blow. It was intended to draw British troops out of Belgium and secure a good German defensive line in advance of an attack in the north. A massive artillery bombardment was launched along the River Matz, held by the French. The German army advanced six and a half miles behind it into Allied territory. But Allied confidence was building; they were learning how to cope with this new style of German attack, so different from the trench warfare of the past three years. Two days later, the French counter-attacked. The Germans were surprised, and, weakened after months on the offensive, had to call off their advance in the middle of June.[35]

Since March, the Germans had gained a staggering ten times more territory than the Allies had done in 1917. But they had suffered almost 1 million casualties in the process; and though Allied losses were also enormous, American troops were beginning to arrive and bolster their numbers. To add to the German losses, up to half a million German soldiers went down with flu in June. The Allies dared to hope that this was the moment the tide would turn.[36]

Duff's mind, perhaps spurred on by the danger and uncertainty of his present circumstances, had turned to the future of his relationship with Diana. He had asked her to marry him before, but money – his relative lack of it – had always been the sticking point for both her and her aristocratic parents. In these grim and desperate days, such concerns seemed so superficial. In early July, just as his latest stint in rest was coming to an end, he received a letter from a friend in London, telling him how miserable Diana was without him.[37] He decided to try his luck again:

You surely, darling, have never doubted how madly proud and wildly happy I should always have been and always will be to marry you under any conceivable conditions, how little I should mind poverty, how gladly I should renounce all my extravagances and vices, break my champagne glasses, throw away my cigars, tear up my cards, sell all my books, the first editions first, study the habits of buses and the intricacies of tubes to obtain that inconceivable honour. You don't believe this – you shake your lovely head, your pale eyes look reproaches for past transgressions and too recent ones but, oh my best, you can surely see how different it would all be then. Believe me, believe me how gladly I would spurn the delights and live laborious days – and indeed what could it matter then how the days were spent.

But what would Her Grace say, and His Grace too? Though two old people with three legs in the grave between them should never be allowed to hinder us. So I propose to you again. It is just five years since I did so first – by letter in fun, do you remember. I can still remember your answer. I wonder what it will be this time. Whatever it is, my life, it cannot make me love you more. Duff.[38]

Two days later, Duff boarded a bus heading for the front line.[39]

American soldiers arrive in France, 8 July 1918.

As Duff wrote to Diana, **Ted Poole** was trudging through the countryside near his camp in Aldershot, laden down with 60 pounds of equipment. The training was intensifying, as the men's departure for the front got closer. It was a roasting July day, and they'd been on the go since 9.45 a.m., only allowed to rest for a few minutes at a time. Now, by late afternoon, men were dropping like flies. Ted kept at it, lying down in the grass whenever they were allowed to stop but keeping up as they marched. They got back to camp just before 7 p.m.

Ted's father had clearly been as solicitous and concerned as ever, sending him lots of instruction and encouragement from London. The day after the march, Ted found time to answer his most recent letter:

Dear Father,

Yes, I know that the gas mask is one of my best friends, in fact it is next to my rifle and bayonet but it is a hateful thing to wear, all the same. I know all about the terrible mustard gas too, as we have lessons on gas and gas drill 3 or 4 times a week and do you know that it is counted as a crime in France now if you are gassed, as they say you must have been slow in putting your gas mask on. I expect to go through my gas test here shortly, and I am going to take everything out of my pockets before-hand, because I have been told that it turns your buttons and everything you have got on you blue.[40]

As July went on, the weather changed. The fine hot weather of the beginning of the month disappeared and stormy, wet weather took its place. It presented difficulties for Ted in training – and for his father at home:

So, it has been raining in London has it? Well I think we have had enough rain down here to lay the dust for a little while. It has been raining on and off since last Wednesday week, it did come down at awkward times. We would be getting on with our physical training just nicely when it would come, and we would have to tear across the parade ground for our hats, coats and things and you can bet I said a few choice words to myself.

I am sorry to hear about the fowl house falling down. I know it has been shakey for a long time and it has been a wonder to me how it has managed to keep up so long.

I think I told you in my last letter about going on my first course on the ranges. Well since then I have been on a 3 days course of bombing. Then on the Saturday we went over to a special piece of waste ground to throw two live bombs each. You see we are behind a parapet made of sand bags, about 5 foot high, and you have to throw at a post fixed in the ground with a bag on the top. I felt a bit nervous when I threw the first one but after that I liked it and I wanted to throw more than 2 but there weren't any bombs left after all the boys had thrown.[41]

Ted's father was hoping that he might get leave soon, but Ted told him he thought it unlikely. He had now been in the army for almost three months.

In mid-July, **Duff Cooper** was in Divisional Reserve after a stint in the front line at Ransart, near Arras. He got a letter that would change his life – Diana's reply to his proposal:

My beloved angel, such a wonderful letter this morning about our marrying. It was my cure, my wings, my darling Duff with me. I feel it may be so. I know I cannot be as happy without you. In a sense the world shapes to hide our possible squalor, no one shall have motors since we cannot, there shall be fewer servants all round, and food is not to be bought, but wine shall flow which our guests' other hosts lock up and so they'll love us best, and never pity our poverty.

My darling, you know that I would marry you and love you for years, and that I would fly to you with the jubilance and excitement of a child – but so far, for you and me there is no betrothing, no nothing – only stolen days and nights and perfect as they are, young in our love as they have kept us, one day we will boast to the world instead. Your letter gave me many castles to build all day. I do not dare allow them – they will tempt this Fortune who will whirl you out of life and my sight in revenge for my forgetting her.

I love you, love you. Diana.[42]

Not only did she feel as he did, but she dared to hope that the war – which had changed the world around them so much – might have made marriage a real possibility now.

It was exactly what he wanted to hear. There were still obstacles in their way: it would not be an easy battle to persuade the Duke and

Duchess of Rutland that the 'poor', playboy Duff was any match for their daughter. But finally Diana wanted what he did: to become his wife. The main challenge now was staying alive long enough to make it happen. They were going back into the front line tomorrow – until then, Duff was making the most of his last day in rest:

> Warned to go up the line the next day. Carroll Carstairs discovered a place in the village where one can get champagne. He and I went there before dinner and had two bottles and returned after dinner and had two more. It was very pleasant, sitting in a garden, talking about poetry and women and getting drunk.[43]

The German army had begun yet another offensive a few days previously, to the south near Rheims. But the Allies – French troops supported by Americans – were much better prepared this time. Though west of Rheims the Germans had crossed the Marne, east of Rheims the advance was halted. Then on 18 July, as Duff and the 3rd Grenadier Guards moved forward, the French mounted a furious counter-attack. The German commanders ordered a retreat, though the fighting persisted.[44] Duff arrived at company HQ behind the forward trenches, but still well within the firing line. Eventually his turn came to lead a platoon to the front line under cover of darkness:

> There was a lot of shelling all night and this morning the whole place smelt of gas and explosives and corpses. There are a lot of graves all round us which haven't been dug deep enough. I left about midnight for the front line. I was glad to leave.[45]

Each morning the men stationed in the forward trenches would observe 'stand to arms' for the hour before dawn. At 3 a.m. Duff oversaw his men, rifles loaded, bayonets fixed, waiting to repel any attack that might come at them. None came, and he returned safe to the company HQ that afternoon, where he found two bottles of port waiting for him – and wrote to Diana:

> Darling – I should be justified in not writing today as I have so little time for sleep but I can't sleep happy until I have written. My feet are cold and wet and my legs are muddy but my hands are clean and my

face is smooth, clean enough to touch your hands, smooth enough to kiss your face. Duff.[46]

Nearby, the shells continued to fall.

It was the fragrant, warm dusk that followed a summer's day. **Ted Poole** and his fellow conscripts were assembled in readiness for their first ever night operation. The air was cooling as the light ebbed from the sky above them; restless feet crunched the dirt. When they set off it was almost dark; the rattle of bullets began.

Ted thoroughly enjoyed himself, as he wrote to his little sister a few days later:

> What do you think Dolly, we went on night operations last Tuesday (30th July) and it was fine fun. We started out at 8.45 p.m. in gas masks and had to keep them on all the time until we came back, which was 2 hours later, I can tell you it <u>was</u> a game, what with blank cartridges, gas bombs (not real ones, but made of gunpowder and paper), verey lights, parachute lights, red and green signal lights, and mines exploding, there was <u>some</u> noise as you can guess. I wouldn't mind another night like that.[47]

It could not be much longer before he would get one. As his father well knew, his time in training must soon be up:

> Dear Father,
>
> Yes I <u>am</u> practically a trained soldier now. I am on another course now, which we call the SOS and which stands for Senior Officers School. The officers in this school are men who have come back from France and have forgotten their training. Well we are taken out to a large plain (about 2½ miles from Aldershot) and there we are set out into platoons and sections. You see we are supposed to be troops in France about to advance on to a German position and capture it. I can tell you it is pretty hard work, and there is plenty of running in it, especially when you do the last 30 yards with fixed bayonets.
>
> No father, a hand grenade does not go off 5 seconds after you take the pin out, but five seconds after it leaves your hand. But still, I will do as you say and be careful, although I don't suppose I shall throw any more until I get to France.[48]

Ted's father was desperate to see him, and kept asking about leave. Ted kept telling him not to expect him home any time soon.

Duff Cooper and the 3rd Grenadier Guards were relieved and moved back into the support trenches. Twelve men had been wounded and one killed in their latest stint in the front line. The weather was terrible, the trenches were in a very poor condition, and the men had to work constantly to keep them from collapsing. As an officer, Duff Cooper was allocated a decent dugout, but he was feeling the effects of ten days in the front line with little sleep and in constant danger. He wrote to Diana on his first day back in support, haunted by the distance between them.[49] The rain poured down:

> I felt ill last night and couldn't sleep – nor have since – although I have been looking forward to sleep for so long. And I thought of you and worked myself into a fever – a real fever – of jealousy. I thought of other people's arms round you and others' awful ghastly mouths – a waking nightmare – and I wondered and like a flagellant tortured myself with the speculation how much you would tell me of any folly that wine and melancholy and loneliness might induce you to . . .
>
> Understand that I am a little tired and a little feverish – that I want to know always everything you do, who drives you home, who tries to kiss you, who succeeds, to whom in your more wretched and too, too few moments of passing ecstasy you yield a little and perhaps shut your eyes and think – oh, my conceit – of me.
>
> I begin to rave. Know only this that you are everything and the only thing I care for in my world and whenever I am in danger or think of death, I shudder to think of making you unhappy and of not seeing you again. Love me, trust me, think of me as much, as utterly, as always, as I love, trust and think of you. Duff.[50]

That day, 100 American soldiers were attached to Duff's battalion.[51] Similar bolstering of numbers by American troops was happening up and down the line. By now a million American troops had arrived in France. Allied confidence was growing as the ranks swelled, knowing their opponents had exhausted their own reserves.[52]

That very day, as Duff fought insomnia, the British, French and American commanders in chief met just outside Paris, at the HQ of the new commander in chief of all Allied armies, Marshal Foch. Having successfully managed the latest German offensive, and recognising their own growing strength and their enemy's declining fortunes and morale, they decided that it was now the moment to go on the offensive themselves. Emulating the latest tactics the Germans had unleashed on them, they would now deliver rapid surprise attacks on limited objectives. Haig had already been planning an attack of his own, and he submitted it to his peers at the conference. Now believing Flanders to be safe, he suggested an Allied attack east and southeast of Amiens.

Two days later, Marshall Foch gave Haig's proposal his approval. After four months of fighting 'backs to the wall' to stay in the war, the British army had now to prepare to go on the attack. And to begin as soon as possible.[53]

The same day, since the weather had cleared up a bit, Duff had walked up the hill from his dugout, taking his binoculars with him. Through them he could see the ruins of Arras Cathedral, a monument to the war. The war that had claimed so many of his friends, and which he had finally experienced for himself. And yet, for all its misery and horror, there was still something about it that stirred him:

> It is so pleasant here – more like one's old-fashioned idea of war – standing on the top of a hill and seeing the battle fields all round you. We can see miles of the country held by the enemy which looks much closer from here than it does from the front line.
>
> These new poets – all that I have read – seem to me especially bad about the war. They can't see anything in it but lice and dirty feet and putrid corpses and syphilis. God knows that nobody living loathes the war more than I do or realizes more fully the waste and folly and universal unrelieved unnecessary harm it does. But there is romance in it. Nothing so big can be without it – and there is beauty too – I have seen plenty from our parting at Waterloo until today. And those poets ought to see it and reproduce it instead of going on whining and jibing. And the ones that don't whine say it is all so glorious because we're fighting for liberty and the world set free and to hell with the Hohenzollerns and the Yanks are coming. This attitude of course is even more tiresome than the other.[54]

A view over Arras with the ruins of the cathedral visible in the background, June 1918.

In early August, the German commanders were ordered to adopt strategic defensive positions. Their shattering series of offensives was over – now they would have to try to hold on whilst their opponents had their turn. Foch issued the directive for the forthcoming attack by the French First Army and British Fourth Army, commanded by Haig: the objective was to disengage Amiens and the Paris–Amiens railway.[55] Whilst the men in France prepared for yet more bloodshed, at home Britons waited in uncertainty. Seemingly against the odds, the war had not been lost. But neither had it yet been won, and the descent into a fifth winter was on its way.

Kate Parry Collins was enjoying the warm weather while it lasted. It was a proper summer's evening, and she was sitting outside her cottage on the hill, when she got the surprise of her life:

> I sat out the front of the house with Agnes and 4 small children who would not leave the precincts. I at last invited them into the porch and read them poetry and had just embarked on a fairy story when I noticed a 'fly' coming up the road. I went on til the fly drew up – and there was John. So our fairy story ended abruptly, the children were scattered and another fairy story began. John on leave for 14 days! John and I came

upstairs and I couldn't believe it, but he was pleased. He looked so well. He's brought his valise and a German rifle in it!!![56]

Unlike millions of other Britons, Kate would be spared the desperate, unknowing worry when, a few days later, news of a great battle began to fill the papers.

23

ALMOST OVER

August–October 1918

It does really seem that all my friends are marked out for death.
                                    Duff Cooper's diary, October 1918

It was 4 August 1918. Four years ago to the day, the people of Great Leighs had gone back to work after the bank holiday, most of them blissfully unaware that Britain would be embroiled in a European war by the time night fell. Even those who had understood the gravity of the events unfolding on the Continent, like the Rev. **Andrew Clark**, could never have imagined that Britain would still be at war now.

This year, 4 August fell on a Sunday. Andrew had done his work for the day and was back at the rectory. He was no doubt thinking of all that the war had done to the little community; of the thirteen village men sacrificed so far, whose families he had helped to grieve. Particularly of Charles Ward, who had died almost a year ago. His mother had called in at the rectory only a few days earlier, to show Andrew the few things Charles had had with him when he died; they had just been returned to her. Andrew faithfully recorded the simple list:

His fountain-pen, his purse with three farthings in it, a ring given him by his sister's husband, and a few letters from home.[1]

The fourth anniversary of the outbreak of the war had been a national day of remembrance, marked by special intercession services in churches up and down the country. The squire had provided the order of service with the appropriate forms of prayer for the one Andrew had led in

St Mary's earlier.[2] The mood amongst the congregation had been fairly buoyant, considering all they'd been through; the next day was the Bank Holiday Monday, and they were looking forward to a day off. More than that, many of them believed that the end of the war might be approaching:

> Sunday 4 August: The villagers have got a singular idea of Lloyd George's much advertised stagey pronouncement tomorrow. At 9.30 p.m. on Monday 5 Aug L-G is to announce the conclusion of peace, all public houses are to be closed at 9 p.m. to prevent people getting too festive.

They would have to wait. Lloyd George's address the following day was in fact a plea to the nation and empire to hold on a little longer. But the note was one of optimism: the end was, he promised, in sight. One final, mammoth effort was needed to reach it:

> I say 'hold fast' because our prospects of victory have never been so bright as they are today. But the battle is not yet won. Having set our hands to the task, we must see it through till a just and lasting settlement is achieved. In no other way can we ensure a world set free from war. Hold fast![3]

In France and Belgium, the 4th anniversary of the war had also been marked by services of intercession and remembrance, though the preparations for the forthcoming offensive went on. The following day, Haig met his commanders in chief at Fourth Army HQ, and on 6 August the final orders for the next battle were issued. Zero Hour was fixed: the Fourth Army would strike east of Amiens at 4.20 a.m. on Thursday 8 August.[4]

Duff Cooper was in the Third Army, and stationed north of the battle area, nearer to Arras. He awoke on 8 August to a dawn buried in fog and the explosive boom of guns less than 20 miles away. They began at the same time as the infantry assault – there had been no preliminary bombardment in order to preserve the element of surprise.

Duff's work would not start until that evening. Meanwhile, as the battle raged on, Duff had time on his hands:

Spent the day reading The Corsican – an interesting collection of
Napoleon's writings arranged into an autobiography. It has stirred up in
me a little more enthusiasm for my present profession which is a good
thing. I am going out on patrol tonight and feel elated and excited – and
perhaps a little bit frightened – but I'm not sure. I should be very disappointed if I were told now that I was not to go.[5]

As night fell, Duff was restless, waiting to head out. News had reached
them of the staggering successes of the battle further south. By mid-
afternoon the Allies had advanced up to eight miles, capturing over
12,000 prisoners and 400 guns. German General Ludendorff called it
a 'Black Day' for his army. Duff wanted a piece of the action himself.
The patrol he joined, to reconnoitre the German positions in front of
them, was a paltry second best:

It didn't after all prove very exciting. I went out with the HQ patrol
men – none of whom I knew and I had to allow myself more or less
to be guided by them. We went out to observation trench when I went
on with two men to within about 40 yards of a German machine gun
post. We came in about 3.[6]

Over the coming nights, as the battle in the south continued, Duff and
the 3rd Grenadier Guards went out on patrol. On 10 August, a night
raid took place on a supposed machine-gun post. The officer who led
it found neither Germans nor a machine gun there.[7] Duff was getting
impatient. On the afternoon of the 11th, he went to fetch a gas mask
left on the previous night's raid – and decided to see if he couldn't find
some action:

This afternoon I crawled out to Observation Trench to get de Geijer's
respirator which he had dropped there. I found it and crawled into the
Sunken Road where I found a skeleton stretching a gloved hand out of
the earth. I went on to No.10 post which I got into without being seen
by the sentry. It was rather a foolish thing to do but it showed how
insecure No.10 post is.[8]

That day, the Battle of Amiens was brought to a close. The Allied troops
were facing increased German resistance and the decision was taken
to stop whilst they were still ahead. Twenty-two thousand British and

French casualties had already been suffered; but there would be no further inexorable grinding on and on, as there had been in the great, tragic Battle of the Somme that had taken place on much the same ground in 1916.[9]

That day, **Andrew Clark**'s daughter Mildred was in London. It was sunny and warm and she was in Hyde Park. On the corner near Marble Arch, a shrine had been unveiled the week before, on the fourth anniversary of the outbreak of war. It was a memorial to all those men who were now serving, and all those who would never return home. Some 200,000 flowers were left there within ten days. The war was not yet over, but the need for Britons to remember was too powerful to resist – to remember all they'd been through, all they'd lost, and all that was still at stake:[10]

> Notes from my younger daughter: On Sunday 11th Aug Mildred saw a great crowd collected round a temporary war-shrine in Hyde Park near the Marble Arch, but was unable to get near it. It seemed to be a white pillar, draped with red, white and blue at the base. Lying at the foot of it were a great many flowers, probably wreaths. All the big motors and all the officers' cars in London are now driven by women.[11]

Back in Great Leighs, the mood amongst the parishioners was pretty low. The end of the war had not come as they'd expected, and the hardships they were enduring had not gone away. The most recent deprivation they'd had to suffer was a shortage of alcohol: at the latest market in Braintree, there had been no beer or port wine at all for sale.[12] But at least a notice stuck up in the post office window gave them reason to be optimistic:

> *SUMMARY OF OFFICIAL WAR NEWS (10th Aug)*
> British attack launched yesterday by the right of the French first Army South of Montdidier was developed by our allies this morning with complete success. Montdidier fell to the French before midday. South of Lihons British Troops have overcome Enemy's resistance and made substantial progress. Number of prisoners increasing. No further news to hand.

*

The Battle of Amiens had been a great moral success. The German army had, it seemed, stopped believing in the inevitability of their own victory, and the Allied commanders wanted to capitalise on the ascendency they had suddenly gained. Foch planned to extend the wings of the previous attack, with the French Tenth Army attacking to the south of the previous battleground, the British Third Army to the north.[13] **Duff Cooper**'s moment had come.

The British attack was fixed for 21 August, with the objective of taking the line of the Albert–Arras railway. It was to be a smaller operation than the previous one, with only one third the number of tanks. The battleground lay between that of the Somme in 1916 and Arras in 1917, which had been devastated by the German retreat to the Hindenburg Line. Many of Duff's peers had already fought and died in these miles of muddy French earth, which was cut up by valleys and spurs from the Somme and the Scarpe. At 9 a.m. on the 20th, the battle orders were distributed. The 3rd Grenadier Guards were to start in reserve, and follow up the initial advance once the first objectives were achieved.[14]

Duff was ready. He wrote to Diana before going up the line to his first ever battle. He was confident, but aware of the huge danger he faced the following day:

> Darling, my darling – one line in haste to tell you that I love you more today than ever in my life before. You have intensified all colours, heightened all beauty, deepened all delight. I love you more than my life, my beauty, my wonder. Duff.[15]

In the early evening they had 'a sort of high tea', and then motor lorries escorted them to 'somewhere near Hendecourt', southeast of Arras. From there they marched on to where they were to spend the night. As the men walked in silence in the gentle dark of a moonlit summer's night, a mist began to blur the countryside around them. They were cheerful; the mood was optimistic.[16]

Duff and the other officers and men of the 3rd Grenadier Guards snatched what sleep they could; then breakfasted in the dark of the very early morning. Duff led his platoon into position. Zero Hour was 4.53 a.m. The mist of the following evening had turned into a dense fog, and the tanks that were supposed to accompany the infantry troops had been held up. But the barrage began on time, and twenty minutes

later the men were given the signal to proceed. So began Duff's first
battle: [17]

> The barrage was terrific – I had never heard anything to touch it. The
> mist was so thick you could only see about 20 yards. My platoon was
> on the left – but we never succeeded in getting into touch with the rest
> of the company. [I] set out in what I hoped was the right direction. We
> met an officer in the Coldstream with a platoon. He said the Scots
> Guards had failed to get to their objective – that everyone was lost and
> that the trench we were then in was full of Germans. I said I would
> work down the trench, which I thought was our first objective.
>
> After this I pressed on alone with my platoon, guiding myself roughly
> by the sound of our guns behind us. We were occasionally held up by
> machine-gun fire and we met one or two stray parties of Guards without
> officers. Finally we met a fairly large party of the Shropshires who I
> knew should be on our right. The officer with them did not know where
> he was but we agreed to go on together. We ran into a small party of
> enemy of whom we shot six and took two prisoners. [18]

The fog was causing severe problems for the attack. Bullets came from
unseen enemy machine gunners. Allied troops occasionally turned on
their own men in their confusion. Map reading by compass was difficult in normal conditions; in the fog it was nigh on impossible. [19] But
Duff pressed on:

> We had gone a good deal too far to the right. I tried to get back by
> going up a road to the left but could not get on owing to a machine
> gun firing straight down the road. There were several dead men lying
> about this road, one particularly unpleasant one with his face shot away.
> These were the first sights of the kind that I had seen and I was glad
> to find that they did not affect me at all. I had often feared they might
> have some physical effect on me as in ordinary life I hate and always
> avoid disgusting sights.
>
> I went back to the beginning of the road where I found a tank which
> like everyone else had lost its way in the mist. It consented to go up
> the road in front of us and we were not troubled further by the machine
> gun. I got on to another road which led straight up to the Halte on the
> Arras to Albert railway. This was to the right of the final objective of
> my Company. There was a ruined building there from which a few shots

were fired. We lay down and returned the fire with rifles and Lewis guns. Six Germans ran out with their hands up. We took them prisoner. There was a steep bank on the edge of the railway along which I told the men to dig themselves fire positions.

So we obtained our objective. Not only were we the first to do so but we were the only platoon in the Company who succeeded in doing so at all. I sent a report to the Commanding Officer and later in the day I got his reply, only two words 'Well Done'.[20]

It was only 9 a.m.; the day was far from over. The fog soon began to lift; it was now hot. Duff was sent assistance, and he and Captain Fryer of the platoon that had joined him went to reconnoitre the railway to the north. They ran into German machine-gun fire from the other side of the railway – and decided to try to stop it:

Fryer told me to take a Lewis gun and a couple of sections and capture or knock out the machine gun. It was rather an alarming thing to be told to do. However I got my Lewis gun up to within about 50 yards of it by creeping along the hedge. The Lewis gun fired away. When it stopped I rushed forward. Looking back I saw that I was not being followed. I learnt afterwards that the first two men behind me had been wounded and the third killed. The rest had not come on.

One or two machine guns from the other side of the railway were firing at us. I dropped a few yards from the gun I was going for and crawled up to it. At first I saw no one there. Looking down I saw one man running away up the other side of the cutting. I had a shot at him with my revolver. Presently I saw two men moving cautiously below me. I called to them in what German I could at the moment remember to surrender and throw up their hands. They did so immediately. They obviously did not realize that I was alone. They came up the cutting with hands up – followed to my surprise by others. There were 18 or 19 in all. If they had rushed me they would have been perfectly safe for I can never hit haystack with a revolver and my own men were 80 yards away. However they came back with me like lambs.[21]

It was an audacious act of bravery from Duff. He found a dugout and snatched a few hours' sleep. He had been awake for the best part of thirty-six hours, and had only consumed an orange, a few biscuits, whiskey and water. After dark, he led his men to rejoin the company, in a steep bank some way back, where rations and water awaited them. Twelve hours behind schedule, the battalion had met its objectives for the day. On the whole front, a considerable amount of ground had been gained. And Duff specifically came in for great praise.[22]

Still, he did not get much rest. The advance was to continue the following day, both on their front and that of the Fourth Army to the south. Duff was on duty again at 2 a.m., and before dawn a German bombardment exploded on their section of the line:

> We had several casualties. Two men were killed close to me and a small piece of shrapnel from the shell that killed one of them hit me in the face drawing a little blood and remaining in my cheek. At last it stopped and we had breakfast. There were some eggs which they cooked for us and very glad we were of them. All that day, which was a very hot one, we sat in a shallow bank – and from 4.30 till 7 we were shelled continuously. We expected to be relieved that evening – had been told we were to be and lived on the hope.[23]

The 22nd brought further success: the Fourth Army gained their objectives on the Somme and the Third Army advanced a further 2,000–4,000 yards. At a conference at 2 p.m., Haig ordered that the advance must go on, and VI Corps, including the 3rd Grenadiers, were to capture Gomiécourt. Their longed-for rest did not come. There was very little time to prepare, and the men had hardly slept. Duff's platoon had suffered many casualties in the day's shelling, and his sergeant was too drunk to be of any use. At 4 a.m. on 23 August, the guns opened up once again and Duff led his ten men forward:[24]

> The attack itself was beautiful and thrilling – one of the most memorable moments of my life. The barrage came down at 4 a.m. A creeping barrage – we advanced behind it. We kept direction by means of a star and a huge moon shone on our right. I felt wild with excitement and glory and knew no fear. When we reached our objective, the enemy's trench, I could hardly believe it, so quickly had the time passed it seemed like one moment. We found a lot of Germans dead there. The living surrendered.
>
> Later, at about 9.30, Tuffy told me to go with a few men as far down on the right as possible to try to deal with machine guns which were firing at us both from in front and behind. I never liked an order less.

Courage is half a matter of health and energy and I was feeling worn out and not at all brave.

We went down the trench pretty slowly as we had to run and jump and crawl half the way. At 11 o'clock we had reached the furthest point we had set out for when suddenly our guns behind put down a barrage not very far in front of us. Soon afterwards we saw our own men pouring over the ridge behind. It was a fine sight to see them come on in perfect formation as on a field day. Our only fear was lest they should mistake us for the enemy. We waited until they were close and then all stood up together and waved our hats and cheered. When they were in line with us we advanced with them for a few hundred yards. Germans were giving themselves up on all sides.[25]

It had been another day of huge gains. Duff and his men were finally relieved at nightfall. Duff's first battle of the war was over, and he had covered himself in glory. He went into rest, and revelled in the praise that came his way.

Troops of the 3rd Grenadier Guards attending a wounded soldier during the Battle of Albert, 21 August 1918.

Duff wasn't the only one who had just come out of his first battle. Fifty per cent of the thirteen divisions of the Third Army who had taken part in the Battle of Albert were young men new to war.[26] Eighteen-year-old **Ted Poole** had arrived in France, but not in time to see action in the tide-turning battles of August. He was still in training, at the Infantry Base Depot. Even that was quite overwhelming for a young lad from London, who probably had never left the city before he was conscripted:

> Dear Father,
>
> Just a few lines to tell you I have arrived at the base safely. Well Father, I have slept in some different places since I have been in the army, but it is quite a novel experience to have to ride and sleep in a cattle truck, which I have had to do since I landed here Wednesday.
>
> Well, I can't say that I like tents very much. When you get 14 of you and your equipment in one tent it is a bit crowded! And what is worse is that if it is a wet day like it has been today, you are going to bring about a ton of mud in on your boots, and deposit it all over the floor where you are going to sleep at night. I'm sure I shall never get on with this French money. I get messed up every time I go to buy anything.
>
> Well father, I don't think I have anything else to tell you just at present. Hoping you are quite well. From your loving son, Ted.[27]

The good news about the progress of the Allied campaign filtering back to Britain must have helped to reassure Ted's father, at least.

Two days after the conclusion of the battle, the official news bulletin was up in the post office window in Great Leighs, belatedly reporting its initial success. It had been a busy few weeks in the village too: it was harvest time.

Now most of the wheat was in and threshed; the farmers were waiting until it was cooler to thresh the oats. The weather had been fine and the harvest was good. The labourers who had brought it in this year were happy: their wages had soared due to the scarcity of able workers.[28] And it wasn't just farm workers who were enjoying new-found wealth and status, as Andrew noted in early September:

A munition girl came into Aldiss' shop, the draper's, Braintree, to buy a hat. She was shown one at 12s 11d. That, she said, was not nearly good enough for her. Aldiss said he had no better but could trim one up for her. She said she would call in and see it in the evening. He took the flower out; put another in; and priced it at 18s 11d. She was entirely pleased with it.

A nephew of Miss Truelove [Mrs Tritton's maid] spent last night at Lyons Hall. He is twenty-one years old. Before the war he was a clerk in an accountant's office. He enlisted at the age of eighteen. This spring he was offered a commission and sent for training to Pembroke College, Cambridge. There he has had the time of his life. He feels that, after the war, he ought to be able to get a much better post than he previously had, because he is now better educated and is more 'widely informed' than he was three years ago.[29]

And yet for most of the villagers, the same worries remained: food and fuel. In September, forms were issued for the rationing of coal in the coming winter, causing much confusion and anxiety:

Mrs Jennings who supplies a good many of the villagers with coal, says that the coal forms are no end of worry. The villagers have made a horrid mess of the forms. They did not fill in the number of rooms, or filled them in wrong, putting 10 for 2 or 3. Her man says he didn't know there were so many palaces in Great Leighs.[30]

The shortages and the accompanying restrictions were affecting even relatively well-off Britons. The dismal chill of the approaching winter reached **Hallie Miles**, in her tastefully decorated flat in central London:

We are now all being rationed in lighting and heating, and are already beginning to feel it. For instance, today there is a biting N-E wind, and it is pouring with icy rain, and yet I dare not have my gas-fire on. We have applied for extra allowance on account of my health. If we exceed our rations we shall have all our gas and electric light cut off, until we have made up what we have exceeded![31]

Yet despite the deprivations she herself was feeling, Hallie had little sympathy for those who tried to do something to improve their lot:

the workers who now felt they were entitled to better conditions. Trade union activity had expanded dramatically over the course of the war, with one in three workers now unionised. And as summer drew to a close, they increasingly employed their greatest tool in the struggle for better rights: strikes. They were becoming a feature of daily life for Londoners, and Hallie was not impressed with such 'unpatriotic' activity:

> They 'strike' at the heart of everything. I shall never forget the scenes during the 'bus strikes, and the tube-strikes. If only the strikers had to suffer, one would not mind so much; but, as usual, the innocent suffered for the guilty. One felt so sorry for the old and weak, who could not struggle into whatever vehicles or trains were still running, and who had to crawl home as best they could! I am thankful to say things are normal now as regards 'buses and tubes. But there has been another big railway strike; and also a miners strike: and, worst of all, there is a strike of ship-builders on the Clyde.[32]

The workers of Britain had played a huge role in getting Britain to this point in the war. But now, after four long years, the strain was beginning to show.

By mid-September, it was getting cold in France too. The Allied advance continued, whilst the weather allowed it. The Germans had been pushed back almost as far as the Hindenburg Line, from which they had launched the spring offensive that had come close to winning them the war. **Ted Poole** was now nearing the front. He had been transferred to the 1/2nd Battalion, City of London Regiment (Royal Fusiliers), who were in divisional reserve in Vis en Artois, southeast of Arras.[33] He wrote to his father, reassuring him that he was getting used to life in France now, despite its hardships:

> Just a few lines in answer to your letter which I received safely Monday, and to tell you I am getting on alright. No, Father, I have left the base, yes, I am getting on alright with French money now. I am not in a tent now, but in a home-made sort of dugout. Yes, you will want the home fires burning soon, now the winter is coming on. I know it's jolly cold of a night time out here. I woke up the other night with my feet nearly frozen, and the cramp all up one leg, so now I put two pairs of socks

on, and bandage my feet up in my puttees, which keeps them nice and warm.

Well Father, I am getting on, I have done two guards since I have been here. The other night I was on guard over one of our boys, who was doing 14 days field punishment for stealing apples and last night I was on from 9 o'clock til 12.10 as a gas guard, in case Jerry sent over any gas shells. But still, I am off parade today, so I don't mind.

Well father, I don't think I have any more news to tell you just at present, hoping this will find you in the pink. I remain, your loving son, Ted.[34]

Ted and the 1/2nd London Regiment were to move up the line the following day. They were to participate in a 'grand offensive' on the Hindenburg Line, a triple assault by French, British and American forces that Foch believed would finally end the war.

In mid-September, **Duff Cooper** was in reserve at Lagnicourt, just a few miles south of Ted and the 1/2nd City of London regiment.[35] His division had been busy in early September; they had attacked again, advancing as far as the Canal du Nord. This time, they had met with very little resistance: the Germans had retreated.[36] Now Duff was enjoying a bit of a break and making the most of the privileges afforded to an officer:

Bombing in the morning. A glorious dinner with Nos 1 and 2 Companies in the evening. There were six of us. The menu was – caviar, turtle soup, lobster rissoles, roast chicken, chocolate pudding, foie gras. There was also plenty to drink and we had a very cheerful evening.[37]

They too would take part in the Anglo-American-French offensive at the end of September: they were to attack east and west of the Canal du Nord. A piece of ground was found that resembled the attack area, and the enemy's trenches and other salient features were reconstructed on it. Over the next few days, the men practised over and over on this mock battleground. Then, on the evening of the 23rd, they moved up into the front line. It was quiet initially, but on the second day the Germans attempted a raid, accompanied by a severe bombardment.[38] Duff was impatient for the real battle to begin:

A terrific enemy bombardment began at about 9 a.m. I had to go up to the front line in the midst of it. My runner was wounded on the way. I found out that at one post we had had three men, including a sergeant killed. They were terribly knocked about. Stayed on duty till 1.30 when I came back and had a good lunch — wrote to Mother and Diana, from both of whom I heard last night. We hear the attack will not be until the day after tomorrow which is a bore. The sooner the better.[39]

The next day the officers were given their final orders for the battle, which was scheduled for the following day.[40] Duff was ready for it:

I felt unexpectedly calm, cheerful and confident, although during the last week I had several times felt fear. The nearer we came to the battle the less uneasy I felt.[41]

On 26 September, the great Triple Offensive began in France. The American First Army and the French Fourth Army struck between the Meuse and Rheims. Other attacks would follow over the next three days: by the British First and Third Armies in the Cambrai sector on the 27th; by the British Second Army and the Belgian Army in Flanders on the 28th; and by the British Fourth Army and French First Army on the Hindenburg Line in the region of the St-Quentin canal on the 29th. Twelve armies attacking over one long fighting front. It was hoped it would be more than the Germans could stand.[42]

Ted Poole and the 1/2nd London Regiment were to take part in the push towards Cambrai, around the Canal du Nord, one of the German Army's last defensive systems. The Canadian Corps was to force a crossing of the formidable obstacle of the canal; the 56th Division, including Ted, was to advance over the crossing and proceed along the line of the canal.[43]

The morning of 27 September broke wet and misty. **Duff Cooper** and the 3rd Grenadier Guards were also waiting to go into action on the Canal du Nord. They'd arrived in their assembly positions at 1.15 a.m., and been issued with extra rations of sugar and tea to keep them warm and ready. They were to attack at right angles to the main attack, to take out a pocket of German resistance between their battalion and the canal.[44] Duff had breakfast and a stiff drink before getting his men into the attack position, ready for Zero Hour at 5.20 a.m.:

I drank some port and had a mouthful of rum. It had been raining hard in the night but had stopped when we left the dugout at about 4am. It was very dark. Zero was at 5.20am and we went over the top simultaneously with the beginning of the barrage. I was just scrambling up the parapet when two of our own trench mortars fell almost among us, wounding two men. The rest scrambled back into the trench. I waited half a minute and then went on again.

We attacked in three parties. I was leading the centre platoon. Nearly all the enemy we came in contact with surrendered at once. I soon got right down to the Canal du Nord. Here I was very nearly hit by a bomb which a small party of Germans threw before running away. It landed just behind me and hit my runner. It was light by now and a beautiful morning. We were soon in touch with the company who were attacking on our left. The Germans tried to counter-attack on the left and three times they advanced over the ridge but there was no heart in it and a little Lewis gun fire sent them back each time. Machine guns continued to fire in front for some time but before midday all was quiet and the battle had rolled away from us.[45]

Allied troops file forward during the battle of the Canal du Nord, 27 September 1918.

Ted Poole did not advance until later in the morning. As Duff pushed forward, the Canadian Corps to the north had met stiff resistance while trying to build a bridge over the canal. Ted and his fellow conscripts had to wait for this to be completed before they could proceed – it was a nerve-wracking time for the untested young men. Finally, at noon, they got the signal to proceed. They crossed the assault bridge to the village of Sauchy Lestree. They captured the village, and pushed on, encountering little resistance.[46]

Duff Cooper's battle had, meanwhile, come to a halt. He spent the afternoon watching the action further up the line and waiting to be relieved:

> We lunched in a German dugout and spent the afternoon watching from the slag-heap the distant battle and the large batches of German prisoners coming in. In the evening we were relieved and marched back to near Dorignies. We found a good hot meal awaiting us and although we were very crowded we made ourselves pretty comfortable and had a good night's sleep.[47]

Ted Poole and his comrades pushed on until 3 a.m., when they achieved their final objectives. It was one of the most successful operations the battalion had taken part in over the entire war. Casualties were relatively light: 6 men had been killed, 4 officers and 61 other ranks wounded. Ted's first battle was over – and he'd survived.[48]

On 28 September, as Ted finally got some sleep back in the village of Sauchy-Lestrée, the attack on Flanders began. The American army group in Flanders gained more ground in one day than had been taken in the whole of the Passchendaele offensive a year earlier. The same day, the biggest bombardment of the war to date was opened in advance of the British assault on the Hindenburg Line. The news also broke that Germany's ally, Bulgaria, had requested an Armistice with the Allies. The German commander General Ludendorff, said to have suffered a nervous breakdown, concluded that the time had come for peace negotiations to begin.[49]

Duff Cooper was in more familiar territory: he was on leave in Paris, a city he knew and loved. He'd left his battalion in reserve, training for another attack.[50] Duff awoke in the comfort of the Mirabeau Hotel

in excellent spirits. Not only was he still alive, he'd just learnt that he
had been awarded the Distinguished Service Order:

> It was a great joy to get up this morning in Paris. A hot bath of water
> clearer than we have been accustomed to drink, a delicious saunter
> through the sunny streets, two letters from Diana at the Ritz and an
> excellent lunch there completed my delight.
>
> In the afternoon I went to 18 Rue Pasquier – an establishment I
> knew before the war and which apparently has if anything improved
> since. There I was satisfied by a tall fair thin girl. I dined with Healy
> and Carroll at the Ambassadeurs. We saw there another Grenadier –
> Drummond in the 2nd Battalion and asked him to join us which he
> did.[51]

While Duff was engaged in rather questionable liaisons, Paris was also
hosting a more serious rendezvous. Lloyd George and the French
premier, Clemenceau, had arrived in the city. They were there to discuss
the implications of the Bulgarian Armistice. But the agenda was torn
up when the news reached them that, on the night of 4 October, the
German chancellor had sent a note to US President Wilson requesting
that arrangements be made for an immediate armistice and peace
negotiations. The Americans were not present at the conference, and
it angered the European allies that they had been side-lined. However,
they realised that this news heralded the beginning of the end of the
Great War, and began to consider what terms they might be prepared
to accept from Germany.[52]

Over the next few weeks of October, a public exchange of messages
took place between Washington and Berlin, whilst the European Allies
could do little more than look on. Look on, and fight on. The fact that
peace might suddenly be in sight did not mean that the war was ended.
Both sides wanted to strengthen their hand in any forthcoming negotiations.[53] The great Allied assault was steaming forwards again; the
Hindenburg Line, the Germans' last prepared line of defence, had been
well and truly breached.

As if to underline the fact that – while peace might be on the horizon –
the war was still going on, the first weeks of October brought the worst
possible news to a number of families in Great Leighs. **Andrew Clark**

could only try to provide comfort to the women and children left behind, and note the details in his diary:

> Thursday 3 October: News was received this morning that 'Ernie' Wright has been killed. He leaves six quite young children, and a wife who is not always quite in her right mind. Mrs. Louis Wright, High Road, has not heard from her husband for a long time.
> Sunday 6 October: News came today that Chas. Digby jnr has been killed; was married; and has three quite little children. He had been a soldier and had served his time before the war. His younger brother, Ernest Digby, was wounded and is a prisoner of war.
> Thursday 10 October: Fred Mansfield was killed on 29 Sept.[54]

On Sunday evening, while he was having a well-deserved rest, Andrew's friend Major Caldwell called by for one of their customary chats about the latest war news. It wasn't just Great Leighs that had suffered some serious blows in the recent struggles:

> Sunday 12 October: 7.30 p.m.: Major Jas Caldwell called. He said our losses in killed and wounded, in the recent fighting, are said to have been tremendous. They are sending very young, untrained soldiers at once into the fighting line – the need for men being so great.[55]

At just 18, **Ted Poole** was one such young soldier, and was in the midst of the fighting again. Cambrai had fallen on 9 October, and the German army continued their retreat. Two days later the village of Fressies on the south bank of the Sensée Canal was captured. On 12 October, it was decided that a presence on the northern bank of the canal should be established forthwith. The 1/2nd London Regiment was given the task of going across and taking the village of Aubigny-au-Bac the following day.

Before the attack could begin, the Royal Engineers had to first build an assault bridge, all original bridges spanning the seventy-foot-wide canal having been destroyed. The 1/2nd Londons were in the forward positions ready to go once it was completed, which it finally was at 3 a.m. The night was pitch black, and it was raining like hell. It was impossible to fully assess the conditions on the far bank without delaying the attack. The first men went over.

Before dawn the whole of the advance company had made their way across to the northern bank. Zero Hour was 5.15 a.m. They waited, cold and wet, for the barrage to begin. As soon as it did, they stormed the unsuspecting village of Aubigny-au-Bac, taking 160 prisoners. Meanwhile, further platoons made their way across in support. As they made their way to the assembly point, some platoons came under fire from enemy artillery and suffered heavy casualties, but at Brigade HQ the mood remained buoyant – the colonel played tunes from *The Mikado* on the piano.

On the northern side of the canal, attempts were now being made to extend the advance to the next village, and to establish new posts by the railway station. But the enemy barrage was becoming intense. German troops followed in its wake and forced their way into Aubigny-au-Bac. The 1/2nd Londons – those who had not been badly hit – withdrew, back to the northern bank of the canal. They stood firm as long as they could, with their backs to the water, but the resistance they faced was fierce and they were eventually forced back over their bridge. That evening and the following morning, attempts were made to re-establish a footing on the northern bank, but they failed.

Six men of the 1/2nd Londons had been killed and fifty-one were wounded. Fifty-six were missing – captured, injured or dying on the other side of the canal.[56]

As Ted and the 1/2nd Londons battled it out in the rain, in London, **Hallie Miles** was awoken by paper boys shouting beneath her window. It was news worth getting out of her comfy bed for – if, indeed, it was true:

I shall never forget last Sunday; all the week such great things were happening; it seemed as if the Germans really were going to surrender, and on Sunday morning, when the early papers were being called in the street, I was awakened by the boys shouting 'The War is Over! The War is Over!'

It was only a result of rumours, but it gave one a foretaste of what it will feel like when those wonderful words really do come true. It is a sort of comfort to have had even this glimpse of what peace will mean to each one of us, individually. I did not feel a bit hilarious, not even a bit like 'mafficking' [celebrating]! I just felt as if Heaven had suddenly

drawn nearer to us, instead of the Powers of Darkness that have seemed
to be let loose amongst us in these awful days.[57]

It might have been a false rumour, but further steps towards peace had
been taken – Wilson had replied to the German appeal for an Armistice
on 8 October, and the Germans responded on the 12th. But the end
was still a way off. The same day that Germany sent their second note
to Wilson, a German U-boat torpedoed a British liner, killing over 450
people.[58]

The next day Wilson sent his second note to Berlin, stipulating some
conditions for the ceasefire: political change in Germany and the
recognition of Allied military superiority. The German Cabinet met to
review the situation a few days later. General Ludendorff believed that
if the German army could hold out for just a few weeks longer, the
winter would slow the Allied advance. But the new government was
losing faith in him. The negotiations would go on.[59]

As the Allies prepared for another conference in Paris, **Duff Cooper**'s
holiday there came to an end. On 20 October he rejoined his battalion,
who were briefly in rest. In his absence, his comrades had fought in
the advance from the Sensée River; and they were exhausted. They had
been engaged in the attack on the River Selle, the next line of German
defence after the Hindenburg Line, which had now also been successfully breached, though at the cost of many casualties:[60]

> The first news which greeted me on my return to the Battalion was that
> Peter Adderley had just died of wounds. It does really seem that all my
> friends are marked out for death. A succession of calamities has left me
> callous – I was really fond of Peter and yet I felt that I could not feel
> his death.[61]

The end seemed close enough to taste. Good news of Allied victories
poured across the Channel. In mid-October, German troops began to
abandon the Belgian coastline – territory so desired by the Allies and
so firmly held by their enemies for so long – and by 19 October the
main ports were in Allied hands. **Hallie Miles**, like most Britons, waited
anxiously to hear news – genuine news – of an end to hostilities:

It is like a miracle that the Belgian Coast is now clear of the Germans; that Lille is free; that Ostend is free; and that perhaps, before many weeks are over, King Albert will have once more entered Brussels with his heroic Army. The German retreat has been so masterly, so well organised, that one wonders what they are up to. One feels so fearful that they have some terrible plans in the background; for they do not appear to have any idea of being conquered yet.[62]

Berlin replied to the latest note from the U.S. on 20 October. They promised to stop attacks on passenger ships and accepted that the Allies would decide the military ceasefire terms. Wilson replied a few days later: he now agreed to forward the Armistice request to his European Allies.[63]

The end, when it came, could hardly be called a victory. The mammoth cost in human flesh and blood that had been paid to get Britain to this point was all too evident. Hallie had been reminded of this as the last blows of the war were exchanged, through her work with her patriotic choir:

> We have been in such request for our hospital concerts that all my time has been taken up. And what tragedies we come across at them! Oh! The courage and patience of these wounded men! It makes one want to weep to see our London streets so full of one-legged and one-armed men.
>
> The whole outlook is new – the whole world seems new, since the war. When we speak of pre-war days, it seems like a hundred years ago. And yet one has become used to it. There is the great comradeship of sorrow existing between us all; it seems like invisible chains linking us all together so that we work, and if needs be, suffer together.[64]

On 26 October, the German military commander General Ludendorff was dismissed. A few days later the Allies met again in Paris to settle the ceasefire terms they were willing to offer Germany. Turkey made peace with the Allies on 30 October, and the Austro-Hungarian Empire, which had also approached Wilson for an armistice, was officially dissolved the next day. The Germans were left to fight alone, as the Allied advance stormed onwards.[65]

If the end of the war came in the first weeks of November, as it now promised to do, **Duff Cooper** would not be there to see it. On the last day of October, he was on his way home; he had been allocated leave, home leave this time. Six months after leaving Diana in a dark square to the music of a brass band, he was on his way to see her again:

> A wet morning. Left Boulogne in a very fast motor about 10. We had a smooth crossing and managed to get seats in the Pullman at Folkestone. We had lunch on the train. Somewhat to my surprise I was met at Victoria by Mother, Sibbie and Sidney. Mother was very excited but not too overcome. She drove back with me to 88 St. James's St where I found the flat all prepared and looking delightful. A fire burning and the room full of flowers. As I walked into it the telephone rang. It was Diana. I arranged for her to come when Mother had gone. Mother and I sat and talked for some time and then I went out to the hairdresser. I came back to the flat and waited for Diana, walking up and down the room and wondering whether it were all true. She came – and all that I had hoped of happiness for the last six months came true. We had so much to say and were so happy.[66]

Unlike so many of her lovers and friends, Duff had come back home to her unharmed.

In the final days of war, as the newspapers were filled with the good news of the imminent victory, a letter was received by Thomas Poole of Wellington Road, London. **Ted Poole**'s father had already lost his oldest son at Passchendaele. He recognised the envelope of an official letter, but dared to hope it might not be the message he'd dreaded ever since Ted had left home in May. Its opening words drained any such hope:

> It is my painful duty to inform you that a report has been received from the War Office notifying the death of 245814 Private Ted Poole 1st/2nd Battalion London Regiment (Royal Fusiliers) which occurred in France on the 13th of October 1918. The report is to the effect that he was killed in action.[67]

More than half a million soldiers were killed or wounded during the weeks spent haggling over the terms of the ceasefire. Most of them fell on the Western Front. Eighteen-year-old Ted had not survived that wet, terrible day of fighting on the Sensée Canal. [68]

His father requested that the inscription on his son's gravestone, in a field in a foreign country, should read: 'From the stress of the doing, into the peace of the done.'[69]

Britain waited for peace.

24

ARMISTICE

November 1918

The last few days we have been living in History.
                        Hallie Miles's diary, November 1918

It was the ninety-fourth day of the fifth year of the war, and Guy Fawkes Night. But there was no wood piled high in readiness for bonfires this year – that hadn't been allowed since 1914. What made that fifth of November special was not the crackle of roaring fires. It was the sense of expectation hanging in the air. People everywhere dared to talk about something they had long hoped for, but had begun to fear would never come: the end of the war.

Helen Bentwich's father read *The Times* that morning as he did on every other. Helen might have flicked through it herself that day; she was staying with her family in London, having been terribly ill with the flu. An epidemic had gripped the country over recent weeks, and Helen was one of the lucky ones who had survived it. The newspaper that day reported that in the past twenty-four hours on the London streets alone, fifty-six people had been stricken with sudden illness.[1]

Apart from the news of the epidemic, the paper was, on the whole, cheering reading. The articles all looked forward to the end of the war. The Allied advance continued virtually unchecked. Europe was being redrawn in the wake of the collapse of the Austro-Hungarian Empire. The terms of the Armistice the Allies were preparing to offer Germany any day now had already been agreed in the grand surrounds of the Hotel Trianon in Versailles.[2]

Helen was not only thinking about the future of Europe. Inevitably she was looking back to Guy Fawkes Day four years earlier when Norman had proposed to her. They hadn't seen each other for over two years now, since he had joined Camel Transport Corps in Egypt. In fact, the war in the Middle East had already come to an end with the Armistice with Turkey on 31 October, but Norman was busy in occupied Palestine, where he was serving in the legal system of the military administration. Helen might join him there at some point soon, but for now she wrote:

> My dearest old man,
>
> Guy Fawkes day has come round once again, and it is four years since you and I dined at the Carlton – and the war, which was very new and thrilling then, is at its last gasp now. And you, who were a humble civvy lecturer, are now a Major and an attorney general; and me, who was an aspiring V.A.D., is an aspiring land worker instead. Of all these things, I believe the most incredulous would have been if someone had told us that I was to wear breeches and be as natural in them as a skirt, it would have seemed the strangest. It's a queer world.
>
> The war news is as overwhelming as ever – what difference will it make to you, Turkey being out of it! I suppose all the campaigns your way will come to an end, and the C.T.C. all be disbanded. And you yourself will be just as busy trying bad prisoners as ever.[3]

The men and women of Great Leighs were also thinking about the end of the war. The prospect was not entirely rosy, as **Andrew Clark** recorded:

> Tuesday 5 November: 8.15 p.m.: Miss Eliza Vaughan called: Crittalls have told their work people that when the war ends, it will end suddenly, and the firm will not know what to do. There will be no work for the people.[4]

Being without the well-paid factory work which many, particularly women, had enjoyed for some years now was a worrying prospect.

And the end was getting closer every day. Allied forces had that day advanced to within ten miles of Mons, the symbolic starting point of their retreat in August 1914. Mutinies on the enemy side, which had begun amongst sailors at Kiel, were spreading like wildfire across Germany. By 7 November, many cities were in open revolt, under the control of hastily established soldiers' and workers' councils. Their leaders were demanding the abdication of the Kaiser. The German army had run out of options and Chief of Staff Hindenburg telegraphed Allied Supreme Commander Foch, asking to begin negotiations for an Armistice.[5]

Rumours about the end of the war were rife in Essex, though there was also the more immediate concern of the flu epidemic, from which the area had not been spared:

> <u>Friday 8 November:</u> Braintree was agitated yesterday by a rumour that the war was over. Fresh cases of influenza still occur. Though some attacks have been severe, there had been no death in this parish from it, directly or indirectly. Chelmsford today (market day) was full of rumour that Germany had laid down arms.[6]

In fact, the market-folk of Chelmsford were not far off the truth that day. Early on the morning of 8 November, the German delegation had crossed the front line and arrived at Marshall Foch's HQ at Senlis. They were taken to his personal train, standing in a gun siding in the heart of the Compiègne forest, where they were presented with the Armistice terms and told they had seventy-two hours to consider them. The countdown to the end had begun.[7]

Duff Cooper and **Diana Manners** did not have to be content with only letters any more. Duff was back in England on leave, safe and well. The day that the Armistice negotiations began across the Channel, Duff and Diana travelled to Norfolk, where friends of theirs had recently bought a beautiful Elizabethan manor house. They'd spent the night together. The following morning broke fine and cold – the perfect weather for shooting, of the good old-fashioned kind:

> The most perfect, frosty, sunny morning imaginable. Edwin and I started out shooting at 10. The country was looking most beautiful and I contrasted it with the stricken fields of France I had left. We had capital sport but I shot badly. I was glad to get back to the warm fire. They greeted us with the news of the Kaiser's abdication. I never felt so tired.[8]

The German chancellor had announced the Kaiser's abdication in a desperate attempt to stave off the revolution. This had failed – the chancellor himself had been ousted later that day and a republic had been proclaimed in Berlin. But the mechanics of war and politics were of little concern in comparison with the simple joy Duff felt in being reunited with Diana:

> I had a bath and a sleep before dinner. This night Diana and I were as happy as the night before but more peaceful and slept deeply in each other's arms.[9]

Helen Bentwich was still recovering from her illness. Her tendencies were, of course, rather more left wing than Duff's – in no little part thanks to her war experiences – and she shared her excitement at events in Germany with Norman:

> I think the German Revolution is rather a fine thing, don't you! It seems the only way to prevent it all happening over again. And it doesn't make us have such an overwhelming victory as we would ordinarily – we can't defeat a disintegrated nation. I should think it's partly got up on purpose, to avoid an indemnity.
>
> It's quite thrilling about the armistice, too. It's all so very nearly over.[10]

The seventy-two hours allowed for the consideration of the Armistice terms were indeed fast slipping into the past; thirty-six hours had already passed. But the war wasn't over, and meanwhile, the fighting continued. In France and Belgium, men continued to die.

Hallie Miles wanted to be ready for the victory celebrations, whenever they came. She had been out shopping so that she would have everything to hand when the moment arrived. Like everyone else in the country, she was following the news intently:

> Yesterday I was buying flags for Peace Day; when it comes. And whilst I was choosing our empire flags and the flags of the allied nations, and as they lay in a glorious riot of colour on the counter, I thought of those

who have lost their dear ones, and who cannot share the joy of peace with us; whose flags are half-mast high.

We waited all yesterday for the news, but it came not! The last few days we have been living in History. We have been reading of kings and kingdoms falling like nine-pins; only the Kaiser left – and his Kingdom dropping to pieces around him, with anarchy simply running wild at his very doors. And then came the wonderful news that he had abdicated; and we knew that the end was in sight.[11]

Late on Sunday afternoon, **Andrew Clark** stopped to take note of the official war bulletin pinned up in the post office window. Its news was, as always, already a little out of date:

SUMMARY OF SATURDAY'S OFFICIAL WAR NEWS
British: On our right, Fourth and Third Armies are advancing along Sambre towards Belgian frontier meeting with little organized resistance. In centre First Army progressing rapidly astride Mons-Condé canal.

The German chancellor announces that 'the KAISER and his SON decided to renounce the THRONE.'[12]

That day, 10 November, the Kaiser fled to Holland. The German negotiators in France were shown newspaper reports of his flight, to speed their acceptance of the terms. The British Army reached Mons. Everyone now knew that the war was as good as over. In churches all across Britain that day, special services were being held, in thanksgiving for the vindication of the cause of the Allies.[13]

Andrew was on his way to St Mary's, to lead the village in theirs. He preferred to think of it as a 'memorial service', a chance to remember all the men of Great Leighs who would not be there to see the victory they'd helped secure. Only that day, Andrew had learned of the death of yet another: Ernest Digby had died in a prisoner of war camp in Germany. That meant that sixteen men from Great Leighs had fallen:[14]

6.30 p.m.: Memorial Service for Great Leighs men who have died in the war. Full choir. Good congregation. Service lasted exactly one hour. Collection for St Dunstan's blinded soldiers.[15]

The bugler of the Chelmsford cadets played the 'Last Post' at the service. The villagers donated generously as they filed out into the cold air. They knew that there would be a frost that night. What they didn't know was that by the time they awoke to see it, in a railway carriage 250 miles away, the war would have been ended. At 5 a.m. Paris time, the German negotiators finally put their signatures to the Armistice terms.

Andrew didn't sleep well that night, and was awake before dawn – though, after that, the day seemed to begin normally enough:

> Monday 11 November: 3.30 a.m.: Dark morning. Sky all clouded over. White fog. No rain as yet. 9 a.m.: Sky gloomy with cloud-drift S.W. to N.E. F. Fuller, Cole farm, has offered Mrs Arnold 7d. for every egg she can let him have. I do not know at what figure he re-sells them, but he has to drive them into Braintree or Chelmsford and make his profit.[16]

Two hours later, the guns on the Western Front would fall silent. The war would end on the eleventh hour, of the eleventh day, of the eleventh month.

At 10.45 a.m., most Britons were oblivious to what had happened. Even in the capital city, the news of the imminent end to over four years of war had not yet broken. On the Mall, those who weren't at work on this Monday morning wandered as normal. Some stopped to look at the array of captured German guns on display; others stood at the gates of Buckingham Palace to watch the changing of the guard. The Royal Standard flew in the breeze, the only flag to be seen. But at a few minutes before 11 a.m., a ripple of excitement passed through the people, a rumour. A police officer at the palace gates confirmed it: yes, the war was over.

Meanwhile, a small crowd had gathered on Downing Street. They waited quietly. They hoped what they'd heard was true, but there had been so many rumours before. A few minutes before 11 a.m., Lloyd George appeared outside the door of Number Ten. A huge cheer went up. He addressed the crowd: 'At eleven o'clock this morning the war will be over. We have won a great victory.' The crowd cheered again. 'You are entitled to rejoice. You have all had a share in it.'

A typewritten copy of the prime minister's announcement of the cessation of hostilities was posted outside the railings of Buckingham Palace. The police officer ushered wounded soldiers and officers from amongst the crowd inside the gates of the palace. The crowd was swelling. Suddenly, as eleven o'clock at last arrived, maroon rocket signals exploded in the air above the city.

Hallie Miles, in her restaurant near Trafalgar Square, was at first startled:

> Today at 11 a.m. suddenly the maroons went off. At first I thought it was a daylight raid, for the guns began to fire too, just like a raid. Suddenly there came something so beautiful – the Bugler passed down the streets sounding the ALL CLEAR SIGNAL. When we looked out of the windows, people were rushing wildly to and fro, children were hurrahing; then, as if by a fairy wand, flags appeared everywhere, the air resounded with victory sounds, and we realised it meant peace at last!
>
> I quite broke down – how could I help it, for sometimes joy is harder to bear than sorrow; we have grown so used to sorrow that joy is like putting on a new, strange garment; it seemed so unfamiliar to be joyful again.[17]

As the crowds filled the streets all around and the sounds of cheering poured up to her window, Hallie pulled herself together. She was well prepared for this moment, after all:

> We had a big Union Jack flag waving from the flagstaff outside the EM Restaurant . . . How thankful I was I had bought the flags so early, for the price of flags to-day is simply awful, and hardly any were to be had. Of course amidst all these scenes of rejoicing I have noticed many sad and tearful faces too. For instance, whilst we were hanging out the flags from our windows, we saw a woman sobbing at her window opposite.[18]

Men and women poured along the Mall and through Green Park. Horses galloped past them, bearing their riders towards the palace. Taxis and motorcars filled the streets and people jumped on their roofs. Within just ten minutes, some 5,000 people had assembled outside the gates and began to call for the king. At 11.15 a.m. the royal family stepped out onto the balcony; the National Anthem was struck up by the band and the din of cheers turned to that of thousands of voices united in song. Hallie might well have heard their chorus from her restaurant.[19]

A happy crowd celebrate the signing of the Armistice, London,
11 November 1918.

As always, Great Leighs received the news a little late. **Andrew Clark**
recorded the detail of the unfolding of this momentous occasion:

> News of the signing of the armistice by Germany reached Chelmsford
> soon after 11 a.m. The works there immediately went on holiday. 'Jim'
> Carpenter, who works at the Marconi Works, Chelmsford, when he
> came back said that the workers were so excited that it would have been
> no use carrying on. The news reached Braintree about the same time.
> The news was passed on to Great Leighs post office from Chelmsford;
> spread rapidly and the cottagers were very excited.
>
> Mr Sam. Woodirvin, Great Waltham, who was at Great Leighs PO
> said he might now hope to have back undamaged his son who had been
> at the front in France for four years.

Kate Parry Collins was a little late getting the news too. In her little
cottage on Berghers Hill, the steep hill from Wooburn village, she was
alerted by the sound of guns firing, and went out to investigate what
it meant. Her immediate thoughts were of John, naturally enough:

I was thinking and wondering every inch of the morning, and could not settle to anything. Was cleaning a collection of shoes about 11.30 in my room, the windows were open – I sat up and listened. Boom-boom-boom – then a hooter and then I thought it time to bestir myself and went in to Agnes then downstairs to Kathleen and out to listen to the various sounds proclaiming that the Armistice has been signed.

And thank God for our many and great mercies. As soon as I could settle to anything I sat me down and wrote to John. Is he safe, and will he really be spared to come home to me?[20]

Helen Bentwich had now left London. She was staying with friends in Hertfordshire, trying to make herself useful in the fields, but she wasn't really quite up to it yet following her illness. As she struggled alongside the local Land Army girls pulling up root beets, the local church bells began to ring. It could only mean one thing. The women she was working with rushed off home to celebrate.

Helen lay under a hedge and wept. She couldn't stop thinking of all the innocent people who had been killed or maimed. She put it down to her illness, but she wasn't alone in feeling like that on this day of celebration.[21]

Duff Cooper and **Diana Manners** were fashionably late to the party. At 11 a.m., as the maroons went off in London, they were getting on a train at Norfolk – and it wasn't until a few stops later that they learnt the news:

We left by train at about 11. Two Flying Corps officers got in at Cambridge and said that they had received an official wireless to say that the armistice had been signed. As we got nearer London we saw flags flying and in some places cheering crowds. We had a motor to meet us at Liverpool Street.

All London was in uproar — singing, cheering, waving flags. In spite of real delight I couldn't resist a feeling of profound melancholy, looking at the crowds of silly cheering people and thinking of the dead.[22]

*

Hallie Miles had joined the crowds in the streets, and marvelled at the changed world – the bells that had been silenced for four years added to the noise:

> As I walked in the streets the sights I saw and the sounds I heard were unbelievable; the 'Bells of St Martins' and other bells were clanging and clashing; the buses and taxis had people riding anyhow and anywhere! Nearly everybody carried, or wore, flags, and waved them wildly as they walked along. Perfect strangers smiled to each other and said, 'Isn't it glorious?' and some even kissed each other in the street!
>
> The scenes in Trafalgar Square were extraordinary; and the Strand was simply a black mass of people, all with flags. The buses gave up their 'routes' and became quite mad too. They took people for 'joy-rides' through the City, and even the ambulances were filled with happy people.[23]

At Victoria station, a barrel organ competed with the noise of whistles and hooters; girls danced on the pavements alongside. A bus careered past, overloaded with exuberant passengers; 'Free to Berlin!' chalked on its side. Street vendors appeared, who furnished any revellers less organised than Hallie with flags of all sizes. Even a little dog was seen with

Londoners celebrate the end of the war, 11 November 1918.

the colours of the Union Jack tied to his tail. The war was over; the celebrations had well and truly begun. It began to rain, but that didn't matter, not today.[24]

The people of Great Leighs were celebrating too – and **Andrew Clark** was happy to help where he could:

> Major Wm. Brown gave his men a holiday. Mrs E. A. Hammond sent across from the church school to ask a half-holiday. The school flag was hoisted. (The Council School is closed because of influenza.) J. L. Palmer, Wakerings, sent one of his men to W. H. Dee, Church clerk, to ask if the church bells might be rung. The five ringers arranged to ring for half an hour at 5 p.m. When W. H. Dee came to the Rectory for the belfry key at 4.30 p.m. he said that the hooters had begun at Braintree and all about a little after 11 a.m. and went on for about an hour.[25]

At 5 p.m. the bells of St Mary's rang out loudly for the first time in years, and Andrew strolled around the village, recording how the residents had chosen to mark the occasion:

> There was a considerable display of flags along the Great Road today. Jesse S. Wright had an enormous Union Jack at his gate, near Deers Bridge. Mrs Jennings at 'the Victoria' (coffee-house), Mr A. G Port, shopkeeper; Mrs Humphreys, bicycle shop; Mrs H. Hicks, Supply Stores – all had flags out. St Anne's (public house) contented itself with a written notice in one of its windows 'Armistice signed. Hostilities cease today.'[26]

In London, the celebrations continued, in spite of the rain, as darkness began to fall. People were amazed to see lights on again – theatres ablaze with lights and streetlights unmasked for the first time in years. Searchlights swung in celebration in the skies overhead. The light in the tower of the Houses of Parliament was on again.[27] **Hallie Miles** was a bit taken aback by some of the more raucous revellers she passed on her way home:

On the night of Armistice Day, when I had to walk home alone through the surging crowds, I didn't feel a bit nervous, except at one moment when suddenly there was a roar of guns and no one could tell where it came from. I thought it was the Germans taking advantage of our sense of security, to have a raid! And then we heard the thunder of a gun being galloped through the streets, firing blank cartridges as it went, and it was a captured German gun manned by Tommies, on its way to Trafalgar Square, where they had fine doings, only far too rowdy![28]

Not only were the bells allowed to ring again, and the lights allowed to shine again, restrictions on restaurant and club serving times and opening times were also temporarily relaxed, to allow everyone to celebrate in style. **Duff Cooper** had never been stopped by such rules before. Tonight, however, he was not in the mood for fun:

Although I felt ill I thought I must go out this night. I dined at the Ritz. I sat between Diana and Olga. There was an enormous crowd, the intervals between the courses were interminable and the food when it came was cold and nasty. I could not enjoy myself and as soon as possible Diana and I slipped away and came back to St James's Street. The streets were full of wild enthusiasm. Diana shared the melancholy with which these filled me — and once she broke down and sobbed.[29]

Duff awoke the next morning, the first day of peace in 1,566 days, feeling terrible. He got up, had a bath, and then went back to bed. He had influenza. As he lay in bed with a soaring temperature, he thought what a cruel irony it would be to survive the war only to die from flu in his own London flat.[30]

Back in Great Leighs, as others celebrated the end of war, one woman still waited for news of two of her menfolk. Mrs. Wright's husband was serving in France, and their only son, Louis, was in hospital in Kent. Louis had contracted bronchitis in France, and then had fallen ill again when home on leave. On the night of wild celebrations across Britain, Mrs. Wright learnt that he had passed away that very afternoon. **Andrew Clark** added the news to his record of the day:

Young Louis Wright, 19, died in hospital at Sheerness today of double-pneumonia. His mother was told yesterday that on Sat. at 9 p.m. he was dangerously ill. Being herself ill and her daughter ill, with influenza, she was unable to go. His uncle, Ernest Wilsher Wright went (at 10.30 a.m.) this morning, but arrived at Sheerness only at 4 p.m., too late. Louis was the only son. They are bringing the body home for burial.[31]

A seventeenth boy from Great Leighs had not survived the war.

In spite of such tragedy, Great Leighs – like most places across Britain – didn't stop celebrating on 11 November. All the next day, the bells of Chelmsford Cathedral were clanging merrily and could be heard in the village eight miles away (so Andrew Clark was told; his hearing wasn't quite up to detecting it). As the light drained from the sky late that afternoon, the dim peals of bells floating over the fields died away, but celebratory searchlights took their place. Many villagers only went back to work on 13 November – and even then the party went on. In Braintree, the town band did a tour of all the factories, despite the protestations of the managements:[32]

It would be many months before all the soldiers would be home with their families again, but the process of demobilisation began immediately. Soldiers who had enlisted early in the war were given priority, as were those who worked in vital industries. The newest conscripts would have to wait the longest.

Just a few days after the Armistice, **Hallie Miles** saw the first soldiers returning home:

To-day I saw some 'returned' soldiers marching through the streets, carrying flags and wearing their war helmets on their backs. Next week the poor prisoners will be returning. It will be a very tragic home-coming for some.

Everything seems like a sort of Symbol of Peace; we can hardly believe that it really is Peace. It is so strange and significant to hear the boom of Big Ben wafted to us after the long silence; we now notice sounds that we used to hardly hear before the Great War. When I see lights burning brightly from uncurtained windows, I feel as if we ought to ring up the police station, as we used to in the Zeppelin days when

spies and traitors let their lights glare out upon the darkness if a raid
was expected.

There are still the notices, with fingers pointing to 'Air-Raid Shelters',
reminding us of the 'Terror by Night' which is now gone forever, we
hope and believe. I have cleared out all our basement air-raid 'comforts'
– the tea-service; the kettle; the oil stove; the rugs; the bandages and
plaster; the gas-masks; the little camp-stools; everything that could a
tale unfold of nights of horror, and perhaps sudden death! How merci-
fully we have been preserved through it all! I do not regret all it has
taught us of Courage and Endurance.[33]

Things were not simply 'going back to normal', however quickly Hallie
might have worked to eradicate the memory of the war from her own
home. Britons had been changed by what they had lived through; and
Britain had changed to reflect that. As Hallie made notes in her diary
that day, Parliament was being dissolved. The first election since 1910
had been called by Lloyd George, and it would be quite unlike any
that had gone before it. The franchise had been dramatically expanded
to include more working-class men – and some women. Hallie, as a
property-owner aged over 30, would have a vote for the first time in
her life:

And now the general election is going to add more excitement and more
crowds. Fancy us women having won the vote through the War![34]

Helen Bentwich was only 26, and she would have to wait another four
years to vote in an election – but that didn't stop her getting involved
this time. She was back in London on 14 November. She crammed
into the Royal Albert Hall with hundreds of other Labour supporters
that evening to kick off the campaign for this, the first election in
which working-class men could participate equally. Helen perhaps heard
what she wanted to hear: the message of sensible socialism. Other
reports of the meeting mention speakers calling for a red flag over
Buckingham Palace:[35]

The meeting at the Albert Hall on Thursday was awfully inspiring. The
Albert Hall was packed, and there were over 2,000 people outside. There

were hundreds of well-educated modern girls there – the constitutional suffrage crowd has mostly gone over to Labour en masse – and a large number of educated men, and older men and women, besides of course crowds of manual workers. And very many older men to whom this time is the culmination of all they have striven for. First they gave the Labour songs to the organ – the Red Flag, and lots of others, and it was jolly inspiring.

Then they had speeches. Adamson, the head of the Labour Party in the House spoke first, and was a wash-out – he kept alluding to the great and glorious victory, and he was hooted down, and they all sang the Red Flag to drown him; and yelled 'are we Bolshevists', and some answered yes and some no, and 'Where is John Maclean' – the man who got 5 years for inciting the Clyde workers and things like that. But Lansbury appealed for the right of free speech, and they subsided.

Lansbury [said] what we had to do now was to run the world on love and not on hate. It was interesting to hear leaders who were trying to hold back and restrain their following, instead of leading them on to more advanced things. It made me long to chuck up the L.A. for these last few weeks, and go whole-heartedly into the Labour campaign for the election. I'd love to be able to speak, me, about socialism and Labour and sometimes I believe I could. I'm dead set on politics at the moment.[36]

She could, for the first time, entertain a career in mainstream politics. Thanks to a bill passed in the last days of the war, women would not only be allowed to vote in the next election, they would be able to stand as parliamentary candidates.

On Sunday 17 November, less than a week after the cessation of hostilities on the Western Front, Britons up and down the country were wrapping up warm to go to church for thanksgiving services. **Kate Parry Collins** was amongst them:

A fine day, though cold. Woke up at 7 and went off to Church as a beginning to my day of Thanksgiving. I did wish I could have had a letter from John but I tried to give a whole-hearted thanksgiving for our many and great mercies.

When I got in, the Postie has just been bringing me a letter from

John, written on the 11th. Oh I was thankful and feel indeed to have a
grateful heart! He is safe and well and of course very, very pleased and
looking forward to coming home.

Now she really could give thanks – her husband was safe. John was in
the artillery, which was statistically safer than the infantry. Nonetheless,
as an officer who had served in France and Flanders for almost two
years, he was lucky to have come through alive, and Kate knew it. That
afternoon in the crowded church in Wooburn, she might have sung a
little more loudly than she had that morning:

> Mother, Agnes and I off to the special service of Thanksgiving at 3
> o'clock. The church was just packed, every one there including Sir John
> and Lady Thomas. Such singing and the reading of that wonderful and
> extraordinary lesson from Isaiah – a nice sermon from the vicar and the
> singing by him more or less of 'Land of Hope and Glory'.[37]

Later, writing her diary by the fire back at home, she reflected on how
much she'd been through; on how much everyone had been through.

> What a world of change – so much doing that I don't believe I have
> even remarked on the passing of the Bill to enable women to sit as
> Members of Parliament. What a change indeed.[38]

Andrew Clark was in the midst of a very busy Sunday. He'd done the
usual morning service, but still had two special services to perform in
St Mary's. The first was not one he relished: Louis Wright's funeral.
To make matters worse, Louis' father, serving in France, had not replied
to the messages sent to him informing him of his son's death. Andrew
made his way to the Wrights' home, from where the funeral procession
was to depart. Because Louis was a soldier, he was to be given a military send-off:

> Louis Wright, the father, did not arrive last night. He has not been
> heard from for about three weeks. Mrs. Louis Wright is very anxious
> about him. The rumour in the district is that there were heavy casualties
> (yet unpublished) in the last days of fighting. Telegrams to him about
> his son's funeral have brought no answer.

Louis Wright was a short lad, but his coffin was 6ft 2in. Geo Taylor, the undertaker in Great Leighs says that at hospitals and other places where there have been many deaths they do not measure for coffins. They stock the coffins in two sizes – one for men, one for women and fill up any vacant space with cotton wool.

The party of soldiers was half an hour late at the Wrights' House. The military party seemed to be Royal Fusiliers and consisted of six bearers; a firing party of fourteen; a bugler; and the sergeant in charge. The firing party stood in two ranks. They fired three volleys in the air. I had never seen a firing party before, and did not think it at all a solemn proceeding. There was too much hoarse shouting of orders by the sergeant. After the volleys had been fired, the bugler sounded the 'Last Post.' Order was then given to fix bayonets; shoulder rifles; to march off two abreast. The bearers fell in behind the others. The funeral was to have been at 3 p.m. but the cortege did not reach the church gate till 3.45 p.m. There was a very large crowd of young people waiting all the time at the gate.[39]

Louis had been just 18. The evening service that followed the funeral was the prescribed thanksgiving for the Armistice, but it was a sombre occasion. Andrew got home that night with a heavy heart, and looked through the post that had arrived that day:

Today's post brought circulars as to the approaching election of members of parliament. Politicians are greatly exercised as to the unknown issues of 'the leap in the dark' taken by the enlarged franchise.[40]

The war was over; but it didn't feel as if the world was getting back to normal.

Duff Cooper was still alive. He had survived the war that had killed most of his friends, and now he'd defied flu too. Diana had been to see him twice a day, every day for the past week. And their resolve had been hardened: they would marry. Life, they knew – better than any twenty-somethings in the previous generation had known – was frighteningly short. They wanted to begin their future without delay. They arranged for the news of their intentions to be broken to Diana's parents:

Viola broke to the Duchess that Diana and I wanted to marry. Terrible scenes appear to have taken place at Arlington Street – the Duchess in a great state. Matters have been rather precipitated but it is a good thing to have got it out.[41]

They hoped that the suffering they'd survived, that Britain had survived, had shaped the world enough that their dreams might be possible now. They hoped, and they waited.

25

THE FUTURE BEGINS

November 1918–July 1919

One was feeling too much to realize all one was feeling, but the top note of it all was the thankfulness – the deep thankfulness for our mercies.
Kate Parry Collins's diary, January 1919

Now that peace had come, the immediate hope of most Britons was that things would get back to 'normal'. They'd endured fifty-two months of separation, toil, trauma and death, which had cost the Allies three and a half million of their people and 130 billion dollars.[1] The war had changed the Western world, and it had changed the people who had worked for it or fought in it. Things were not going to get back to 'normal' overnight; the first task was to work out what 'normal' now was.

Duff Cooper hoped that for him it would mean finally being able to settle down with the woman he loved. But to have any hope of that he had to make sure he was around to argue his cause. He couldn't do that if he was in France and he began negotiations with the War Office to let him stay in London. His leave was extended while he awaited the arrival of definite instructions. He didn't know if he would be sent back out to rejoin his regiment, so he and Diana wasted no time in pressing on with their campaign to persuade her parents to consent to their engagement. The negotiations did not get off to a good start:

> I met Diana just as I was leaving the Ritz. She had had a terrible morning with her mother and was still tearful. The Duchess says that she had rather Diana had had cancer than was married to me.[2]

The duchess, clearly, did not think the war had changed much at all, certainly not as far as Duff was concerned. It had changed him, though;

he was determined – he hadn't survived the horrors of the trenches just to give up now.

But the blows didn't stop coming. In early December his sister Steffie contracted pneumonia, having been suffering with flu herself. Duff and Diana had been invited to spend the weekend with the press baron, Lord Beaverbrook. It was a relationship they needed to cultivate: they desperately needed to raise some money for a married life together, and both thought they might be able to write for him. Duff didn't want to leave his sister, but he went. He returned to London the following Monday to very bad news:

> In Dover Street I met Neil Arnott the doctor who told me that Steffie had died not many minutes ago. Her temperature had gone down last night and she had seemed better, but they now knew that her lungs were full of poison and the case was hopeless. I went upstairs and found mother in the drawing room. Mother was standing in the window looking out. We didn't speak for a long time. Tolly and Mother were both calm. These last few years have so inured me to death that I can no longer feel it very deeply.[3]

Duff's experiences had changed him irrevocably. He was granted one small mercy amid the family's pain at the loss of Steffie – he was told his return to his regiment in France was cancelled and he was to receive orders to resume work at the Foreign Office.[4]

Andrew Clark was watching the general election campaign with some alarm, and he was not the only person. For a start, it was highly xeno-phobic; not, in fact, fought on grand hopes for peace, but on the more immediate and less noble issue of how to punish the Germans with the peace settlement that was now being negotiated.[5] But this was not the greatest concern amongst the more conservative elements of society – including, one might surmise, a country vicar in his sixties. The electorate had been massively expanded; those who feared the onward march of socialism worried how the working classes were going to use their new power. In early December, Andrew noted down the rumours he'd heard about local workers' intentions:

> The workers at Hoffmann's are said to be all going to vote for the 'labour' candidate.[6]

In fact, Andrew and many of his peers were rather concerned at the workers' behaviour in general during the first weeks of peace. One night in December, less than a month after the conclusion of the Armistice, Andrew and Major Caldwell were sitting in the rectory. Over the years, the latest news of the war had dominated their conversations. Now they were worrying about the world left behind in its wake – concerned that the changes it had wrought might, in fact, be permanent:

> 7.30 p.m. Major Jas. Caldwell called: Cubitt's works in London have been employing a great many women in the making of gasmasks. As these are no longer needed, this work has come to an end, and the women have been paid off. This week Major Caldwell saw a procession of about 1,000 of them, with a big flag, and singing, marching to Downing Street, to interview the Prime Minister and demand continuance of employment and high wages.
>
> The women who have been discharged from various government offices are receiving, temporarily, weekly pay. A friend this week saw a crowd of them outside a pay-office, waiting for their pay. They were very showily dressed (fur coats; jewellery), and looked for all the world like flash barmaids.[7]

As women around Britain fought what would – for most of them – be a losing battle to keep the jobs they'd taken on in the war, Andrew had plenty to keep him busy in Great Leighs.[8] December saw the first of many visitors to the rectory, requesting Andrew's help in filling out forms for pensions for the dead, or writing letters of petition to get the living home.[9] At least there were some positive changes to report:

> <u>Friday 13 December:</u> morning's post brought a slip intimating discontinuance of rationing for tea.[10]

The following day was the general election. **Kate Parry Collins** did not go out to vote, despite everything she'd done for the cause. She met the age qualification (she was over 30) and the property qualifications (she was married to the tenant of a property of more than the required value), but the seat in her constituency was uncontested, so she had no chance to exercise her hard-won democratic right.[11] She

celebrated the occasion nonetheless, and liked to think her own
campaign work had played some part in it:

> It is simply splendid to read in the accounts of yesterday's polling that
> the women turned out most splendidly – and voted early. Some waited
> an hour for the stations to open. At Dover they polled 10 women to 1
> man in the morning. I wonder if I had a hand in that.[12]

The first general election in the post-war world was a symbol of the
dawn of a new Britain. But the results, at the end of December, showed
that for now people wanted continuity above anything else. Lloyd George
was celebrated as the man who had won the war, and the wartime coalition Conservative and Liberal candidates won an easy victory. However,
the Labour Party did become the main opposition party for the first
time in history, beating Asquith's Liberal Party into third place.

A Labour election poster of 1918, with the tagline: 'You could not make War
without us, you cannot make Peace without us!'

Day-to-day life for Kate – as for most people – had not been suddenly transformed with the onset of peace. With John still away in France, she continued to live a rather frugal, lonely life in the cottage on the hill with her mother and sister. John had initially thought he was going to be amongst the troops sent to occupy the Rhineland. But then plans changed. On 30 December Kate got a wonderful surprise: John arrived home on leave and they were able to celebrate the New Year together:

> And what a New Year to let in! We heard the bells and sweet indeed they sounded – one was feeling too much to realize all one was feeling, but the top note of it all was the thankfulness – the deep thankfulness for our mercies. We had another gramophone number as being fitting to salute the new born year with sweet sounds and thought the most suitable to be Beethoven's 'Coriolan' by the Queens Hall Orchestra. Then we went upstairs to climb as high as we could, then John went out of the back door and we let him in the front after 3 raps and then we went to bed. But it was a long time before I slept. A glorious night, all starry and clear.[13]

John and Kate could – for the first time since they'd been married – actually start to plan their future. In early January, they went up to London to look for a flat of their own, which was what Kate had been dreaming of for years. Accommodation was very hard to come by, but they finally found a little three-room flat, in Notting Hill.[14]

They were just about to move in, when John fell ill and was rushed to hospital with influenza and double pneumonia. By a cruel twist of fate, the hospital was in the hotel they'd spent their very happy wedding night in four years earlier.

In early January, **Andrew Clark** and Major Caldwell were once again chewing the fat. On this Saturday night – the day after there had been mutinies at various British ports – the topic was demobilisation:

> Saturday 4 January: 7.30 p.m. Major Jas Caldwell called: Major C. thinks there will be no rapid progress with demobilization. The authorities are weeding out the inefficient as fast as they can and sending them away. But efficient men will be kept under arms, until there is better prospect of the ferment in Europe settling down.[15]

It wasn't just in Europe that British troops were being held back: they were also wanted to keep order in Palestine, German East Africa, Mesopotamia and Egypt. Many Great Leighs lads were still far from home in early 1919 and it wasn't only a question of when the British army could spare the men to come home; some of them had been in the hands of the German army. Ernest Suckling was a private in the Royal Garrison Artillery in 1914. He had been captured and had spent most of the war as a prisoner. In mid-January he arrived home, emaciated and traumatised after more than three years in a German prison camp:

> Friday 17 January: From Mrs F. Mann, wife of the baker, Little Leighs: Her husband has seen Ernest Suckling. He is in a terribly nervous state, and cannot realise that he is free. He is on the jump the whole time, constantly looking round expecting people behind him.[16]

Many of the boys who did come home to Great Leighs in early 1919 were not able to simply pick up where they left off. Not Ernest Suckling, nor Reggie Ketley, who was suffering from the effects of being gassed and could not go back to full-time labouring. And many of the boys did not *want* to pick up where they had left off, for that matter. They weren't the same people any more; their old lives didn't quite seem to fit. A number of them actually took up the army's offer to re-enlist, to get away again:

> Saturday 8 March: Albert Smith has re-joined the army. Jack Taylor has also re-joined. Charlie Collins is already grumbling at the dullness of farm work. He says 'it is like being taken from among a thousand men and put in a coal hole.'[17]

It wasn't just in Great Leighs that soldiers who had fought so hard to come home found it not quite the utopia they'd envisaged for all those years. Many war workers were disillusioned too – they were losing well-paid, secure jobs now that peace had ended the need for munitions. Riots broke out in Glasgow at the end of January. They were so intense that the government feared a socialist revolution, and sent in English troops to control them. The workers won a ten-hour reduction in their working week. But that was far from the end of it: over 1919, industrial conflict and protest was rife, especially amongst serving troops.

Britons who had been through so much simply weren't prepared to put up with all they had done before.[18]

Kate Parry Collins did not spend most of the first months of 1919 in her new home alongside John, as she should have done. She spent it at his hospital bedside wondering if – after surviving the war – he was now going to die in front of her. After two months battling for his life, he was finally discharged in April. He was lucky to have survived the influenza spreading all across the globe. It would claim three times as many lives as the war had done. When he was properly recovered, they moved into the flat in Notting Hill.

Now began the next challenge: they had to adjust to peacetime living again, and moreover, to living as a couple. The first step for John was going without uniform after all this time. Kate had always like him in khaki:

> It is very wonderful to be home in our dear little flat and with John practically well again.
>
> John prepared to depart out. Nothing looked right at first – one didn't know if the clothes were too big or too small, or what; but I suppose we shall get used to him in a day or two. He went to Hill Bros for a fitting of his suit.[19]

Kate was now 41, and it was highly unlikely that she'd ever have children. Whether Kate could have got pregnant if she and John had not been parted by war is impossible to say – but it is estimated that almost three-quarters of a million babies were never conceived because their fathers were mobilised.[20] But even without a family to support, they needed an income. At the end of April, John was demobilised and back in civvies full time, and started trying to pick up his acting career again. In May, he got a three-week job with a theatre company in Plymouth. Kate, meanwhile, busied herself writing a play. It was called *Cease Fire*, and was about the end of the war – which now, finally, felt real for her.[21]

Duff Cooper could hardly believe it. Diana's parents, the Duke and Duchess of Rutland, had consented to their marriage. It had happened quite suddenly at the end of April. Now here he was, surrounded by newspapers emblazoned with reports of his own engagement and photos of his beautiful, well-known fiancée. It had captured the nation's imagination – everyone wanted a story with a happy ending just now:

> The *Daily Express* and the *Daily Sketch* came out with the announcement of our engagement. The whole front page of the latter was taken up with pictures of Diana. Ever since, events have moved so fast and the days have been so full that I cannot hope to chronicle them. The evening papers were full of our engagement – especially the Evening Standard. I went to see Mother before dinner. She is delighted. I had a letter from the Duchess – a silly letter – still protesting that all her opposition had been because she doubted Diana's love for me – and that Diana never tried to convince her.[22]

However, the problems that had prevented their engagement in the past had not miraculously gone away. Diana was used to a life of luxury – of townhouses and country estates and endless wealth – and Duff could not provide it for her on a very limited Foreign Office salary. Diana did not want to be poor, but she did not mind being modern and sharing the problem with Duff. As their wedding approached, she and Duff were hatching plans for how they might make money, as his diary records:

> We dined at the Ritz with a new rich American called Mrs Cooper-Hewitt. I sat next to her and found her terrible. She looks like a tart and is full of pseudointellectual nonsense and crude snobbery. Diana has been offered 75,000 dollars to go to America for 3 months and act cinema. The Americans at dinner swore she could get four or five times that amount. I doubt it. For a huge sum it would be worth doing – but not for a small one.[23]

It might not be the aristocratic life of ease that Diana's parents had hoped for their daughter, but the future was opening out ahead of the newly engaged couple towards a vast, sun-kissed horizon.

On 2 June 1919, hundreds of people gathered in Westminster to witness the society wedding of the year. A mere Foreign Office clerk had returned from the war a hero, and had won the hand of the beautiful Lady Diana. Londoners wanted to see the fairytale ending for themselves. Duff had had a bit of a stressful morning thanks to a tailors' strike that meant his wedding wardrobe was not properly finished. However, soothed by some cocktails and champagne over lunch, he arrived at St Margaret's Church feeling ready for what was to come:

> There was a great crowd outside St Margaret's – an incredible crowd. I felt no tinge of nervousness. I felt only pride and love. I held Diana's hand through most of the service and we whispered to one another now and then. I was conscious of all the love I feel for her. I was very happy and I enjoyed every moment of the ceremony. On leaving the church we were greeted by many small lightly clad grandchildren of Sir Herbert Tree who scattered rose leaves before us – also by a thousand cameras and cinematographs. The enthusiasm of the crowd was most remarkable. It was not for me but I enjoyed it thoroughly. When we reached Arlington Street we found a further crowd assembled there.
>
> The reception seemed to pass very quickly and was not unpleasant. My only sorrow and shame was the appearance of my sister Hermione who looked like a mad tart of the year 2000AD. There were fortunately no tears shed by either mother and all went as merry as possible.
> About five we started off in a motor. There was a tremendous crowd waiting in Arlington Street to see us off, who positively clambered on the car. We had a pleasant drive down to Philip's house at Lympne. The country was looking beautiful but it was not a pretty day as I should have wished – no sun – or at least no sunset. Philip's house we found charming – almost ideal for a honeymoon.
>
> Our night, like so many of the main incidents in our love story was very old fashioned and conventional. There were tears, cries, bloodshed and great joy. The only unintended and slightly farcical incident was when I, meaning to turn on the light, rang by mistake the bell and Miss Wade came swiftly but most unwelcome to the assistance of her poor little mistress. We sent her away swearing we hadn't rung. There must have been a story and a laugh in the servants' hall.[24]

Duff and Diana's happy ending struck a chord with many Britons. But for some, the photos that filled their newspapers of the glamorous, fortunate couple must have caused a degree of pain. The war had stolen such a happy ending from many, many people.

Duff and Diana Cooper leaving the church on the day of their wedding.

At the start of 1919, **Emily Chitticks** was just 21 and was still working as a servant in the farmhouse near her family home. It was not the life she'd dreamed of with Will. Two years after his death she still had not been informed of where her fiancé was buried, and continued to chase the War Office to find out.

The task of recovering and identifying the thousands and thousands of corpses left behind on the battlefields of Europe was an enormous one, though efforts were already underway. The Imperial War Graves Commission had been established in 1917, to painstakingly sift through mass and unmarked graves, and to dig up battlefields in search of corpses that had never been buried at all. The British government had decided to bury those bodies they could identify near to where they had fallen. It was a blow for many Britons who wanted their loved ones near them. At least there was some equity between those who were found and marked with a gravestone, and those others, like Will

Martin, who lay undiscovered in the French countryside.[25] Judging from the latest letter Emily received from the War Graves Commission, that was how he was destined to remain:

> Madam,
>
> In reply to your letter of the 16th ultimo, I regret to say that it has not yet been possible for the officers of the Graves Registration Unit to verify the reported location of the grave of Private W.J. Martin which was sent to you on the 19th May 1917. A thorough search is now being made in all areas for the graves of the fallen and should that of your husband be located you will be informed at once.
>
> I am to add that it is the intention of the commission to erect memorials to those officers and men whose graves cannot be found, in the most suitable British Cemetery near the place where they are supposed to have fallen. The precise form which this memorial will take is not yet decided, but you may rest assured that the dead who have no known grave will be honoured equally with the others.[26]

Emily underlined Will's name and 'your husband' in her own hand, and added at the bottom of the letter: 'A man gave his life and they could not even be bothered to check the letter. His name should have told them that we were not married.' She had dearly wanted to be Will's wife, and to have it assumed that she was, when she would now never be, was salt on the wound.[27]

On Saturday 28 June, exactly five years after the assassination of Archduke Franz Ferdinand and the descent into world war, the Treaty of Versailles was signed between Germany and 'the Principal Allied and Associated Powers'. After months of tense negotiation at the peace conference in Paris, the deal had finally been done. The map of Europe was redrawn; Germany lost her overseas territories and was forced to take both financial and moral responsibility for the conflict.[28] The Allied victory was complete. It was another moment for celebration – or perhaps for contemplation, as **Kate Parry Collins** found:

> Peace Day. News came in the afternoon that Peace had been signed and I heard the guns – even saw the flashes about 6 o'clock. And I stood at

the window and wept. Not for joy – a real sorrow – for the remembrance of those millions of sacrificed lives, and what has it all been for – unless this can be the last of such terrors.[29]

Almost one million men from the British Empire had perished in the conflict. Over half a million of them had fallen on the Western Front. In all, ten million men of different nations had been killed. Even for the lucky ones like Kate, whose loved ones had returned, it was hard to find reason to celebrate.[30]

If there was no appetite for celebration, there was a deeply felt need for commemoration. **Andrew Clark** had begun this process in his own way when he started his war diary years before. Now, with the conclusion of peace, he felt his work was done.

Saturday 28 June: 7.30 p.m.: Dull evening: Evening paper (The Star) intimated signing of Peace Treaty: 'Versailles, Saturday. The German Plenipotentiaries signed the Peace Treaty at 3:12pm this afternoon.'
Sunday 29 June: 8.30 p.m. high, westerly wind: much cloud-drift W. to E., but no present promise of much-needed rain.

Andrew Clark, 29 June 1919: This diary in its present form is discontinued.[31]

The completed war diary ran to an epic ninety-two volumes and three million words.[32] He had first offered it to the Bodleian Library in 1915, and now sent the final volumes to join the rest.[33] The war experience of the people of Great Leighs would not be forgotten.

And the residents of Great Leighs themselves wanted to ensure that the men they had lost were suitably commemorated. Discussions over the form a memorial might take were begun. Communities across Britain were doing the same. The practice of installing memorials to the local men who had fallen had actually started in East End communities during the war. Now it exploded – eventually around 54,000 memorials were built in the British Isles.[34]

The nineteenth of July was 'Peace Day': the official day of celebration at the conclusion of the Treaty of Versailles and the Allied victory.

Thousands of Allied soldiers and the war leaders paraded through the streets of London. Their route took them past a series of national war memorials, which had been hastily thrown up to meet the need for focal points for people's grief. One of these temporary wooden structures was the Cenotaph – Greek for 'empty tomb' – erected on Whitehall. Within an hour of its unveiling, it was almost lost behind the thousands of bunches of flowers placed around it.

It is unlikely **Emily Chitticks** made the trip to London that day. Perhaps she braved a local celebration in Essex, or perhaps she found such occasions too hard to bear.

Not far away, in Great Leighs, the villagers went to a sports day and children's tea. **Andrew Clark** enjoyed himself at the evening party in the Council School, but, traditional as always, was cross that a number of children failed to attend lessons on Monday, having decided they were due a day's holiday.[35]

Kate Parry Collins was not in London to see the celebrations either. She was in Stratford-upon-Avon, where John was in a play. It poured with rain, and she couldn't help thinking this was appropriate, repeating Shakespeare to herself: 'the sun for sorrow will not show his head.'[36]

Duff and Diana Cooper, however, did not miss out on the party. They watched the colourful procession of soldiers and their commanders and then battled the crowds to travel across London – rather daringly, by tube – to a dinner party. Duff knew Diana was desperate to see the fireworks that had been promised that evening:

> There was a rumour that the fireworks had begun. They all dashed upstairs – Diana of course went first – I lingering over a glass of port came last. We climbed to the top floor whence there were steps up to the roof. I was at the bottom of these – just about to go up. I heard suddenly a crash of breaking glass – then after what seemed minutes the terrible thud of a falling body.[37]

Diana had fallen through the skylight. She was remarkably lucky yet again and only broke a leg.

Perhaps life was getting back to normal, after all.

Epilogue

Andrew Clark did not finish his diary in July. He filled two more volumes, depositing the last of them with the Bodleian Library along with the rest in December 1919. In January 1920, he finally found someone to take on the work in the rectory grounds that he'd struggled with since Chas Ward had left him in 1916, though his health continued to deteriorate. In December 1920, he led the residents of Great Leighs in the dedication of a memorial tablet to their war dead, placed in the church boundary wall.

After his daughter Mildred graduated from medical school and emigrated to South Africa his health got rapidly worse, and he died in March 1922, aged 65. He was buried alongside his wife Mary, and a plaque was installed in St. Mary's church in memory of his 28 years as the parish priest. The squire, Mr Tritton, died the following year. It was around this time the first motor plough arrived in the village; Great Leighs was changing.[1]

After his stint in the convalescent camp in Shoreham **Reg Evans** went on to a desk job at the Brigade HQ of the Bedfordshire Regiment. Though his wounds were healed his face was heavily scarred and his false teeth never quite fitted him. Despite what he'd been through and the ongoing discomfort he suffered, he was not content to be out of the action. In summer 1918 he volunteered for service in 'an unknown destination' with the 11th Royal Sussex Regiment. It was sent to North-West Russia to support the anti-Bolshevik forces in the Civil War, arriving in Murmansk in September. Reg was there for the Armistice, and for two Arctic winters, finally arriving home in 1920. He moved to Armitage with his mother, but sadly she only lived for a few months after their reunion. Reg was unable to settle without her, and moved around the country, trying his hand at various jobs and toying with moving to Australia, though he couldn't raise the fare.

In 1923 he returned to Armitage to stay with his brother and met Eva Walker, the eldest daughter of the stationmaster, who determined to make him her own. They were married in June 1924, and rented a grocery shop in Westbourne Grove in London. The city did not suit him, however, and his health fluctuated (Reg had to take medication for the rest of his life because of his injury.) They returned to Armitage in 1930, with a son Bill and a daughter Mary, and ran the village newsagents. They had two further children: a son who died as a baby and a daughter, Pam. Reg was an active and popular member of the community: he reported for the Staffordshire Press, was Parish clerk, secretary of the British Legion and served on the Home Guard in the Second World War. He died in 1943 from cancer. The family could not afford a gravestone for him until some years later.[2]

Duff and Diana Cooper set up what was a very humble home by the standards of their set, in Bloomsbury, with just a few servants. Duff continued to make slow progress at the Foreign Office. In 1922, Diana was paid a substantial amount of money to star in two Hollywood films, before taking on the part of the Madonna in *The Miracle* on Broadway. It made them enough money for Duff to give up his salary and launch himself on a political career. He was elected Conservative MP for Oldham in 1924 and became a junior minister.

In a subsequent brief spell out of parliament he launched a career as a non-fiction writer with a biography of the French diplomat Talleyrand and though he soon resumed his political career he continued to write. He was one of the fiercest critics of the British policy of appeasement of Nazi Germany in the 1930s, and resigned his post as First Lord of the Admiralty when Neville Chamberlain signed the Munich Agreement with Hitler in 1938. He had various roles in Churchill's cabinet during the Second World War, before becoming the British Ambassador to Paris in 1944. He left office in 1947 and was knighted, becoming Lord Norwich.

Duff and Diana had one son in 1929, John Julius, and remained happily married – despite Duff's numerous infidelities – until his death in 1954. Diana lived until she was 93, and died in 1986.

Emily Chitticks never married. She continued her efforts to find Will's grave, but was told in 1922 that it was unlikely to ever be located. In 1932 a memorial to the missing who had fallen in the Arras area was unveiled, designed by Lutyens. Emily cut out and kept an article on it, adding it to her collection of the correspondence between her and Will. She continued to live in Essex, and died in 1973, alone, in a council flat. She was buried in an unmarked grave.

The council worker who cleared out her flat after her death found the letters, and the note she had written requesting they be buried with her. Too late to do as she'd wished, he deposited them with the Imperial War Museum. Joanna Lumley later included some extracts of the correspondence in a book she wrote about Forces Sweethearts, and arranged for a copy of the letters to be buried next to Emily's grave.

John and Kate Parry Collins kept a London flat for much of the 1920s, and John worked in the theatre as an actor and stage manager, though he did not enjoy great success. Kate had persistent difficulties with her health. She acted in her final play in the early 1930s, touring with John in a production of *The Miracle*. In the early 1920s, Kate and John bought a couple of little properties from relatives in Berghers Hill, the Buckinghamshire hamlet she had lived in for the latter part of the First World War. Their home was initially very basic and, although they gradually improved it, life was difficult and isolated. Kate continued to write plays, but the only ones ever performed were topical sketches she wrote during the Second World War for performance in their own, tiny 'Woodman's Hut Theatre'. John developed dementia in the 1950s and Kate nursed him at home for several years before, unable to cope and without the funds for a nursing home, she was forced to admit him to a Mental Hospital. She survived him by little more than six months, dying at the age of 81 in a Buckinghamshire nursing home in 1959.[3]

Kate had written a diary from the age of nine until a few months before her death. They were her main bequest in her will, bundled together with a vast archive of photographs and ephemera collected over her long life. Separated from anyone who knew her, the diaries ended up languishing in a damp basement, until they were purchased by suffrage historian and collector Elizabeth Crawford in 2009.

Helen Bentwich moved to Palestine in 1919, to be reunited with Norman who had been appointed Attorney-General under the British Mandate. She got involved in various welfare projects during the decade she spent there, setting up nursery schools and arts and crafts centres, and she sat on the Palestine Council of Jewish Women. It was on her return to London with her husband in 1931 that she finally realised her political ambitions. She joined the Labour Party and stood as a labour candidate in the general elections of 1932 and 1935, though she failed to be elected as an MP. She found her calling in the London County Council Educational Committee, which she sat on from the mid 1930s, becoming chairperson of the council in the 1950s. She was made a CBE in 1965. She died in 1972, a year after Norman. They had no children.

Dorothy Lloyd maintained a correspondence with many of Alan's fellow officers for the rest of the war. One of them was Lieutenant Charles Marshall. He was promoted to Captain and survived the war. When he returned to Britain he and Dorothy became close and they were engaged in summer 1919.[4] They married and had another child, a daughter Audrey, in 1922. Dorothy died in 1936, aged just 51. Her son David Alan Lloyd was married two years later, in 1938. When the war broke out David's wife was terrified that history would repeat itself – David fought in the artillery like his father. He survived, however, and afterwards worked as a barrister. David and his wife Norah had two children, Vivien and Jonathan Alan.

On 4 August 1956, the 50th anniversary of Alan's death on the Somme, David placed an announcement in *The Times*: 'Lloyd: in proud and loving memory of Lieutenant Alan Scrivener Lloyd MC, killed on the Somme near Longueval on August 4th, 1916. "He died as he lived, brave and fearless".'[5]

Hallie and Eustace Miles continued to run the EM Restaurant on Chandos Street after the war, and expanded the business to include a second restaurant in Chelsea, a vegetarian guesthouse in Surrey, and health food shops across London. It did not make them rich, however, and the business shrank rapidly in the 1930s. They died in relative poverty, within a year of each other, just after the Second World War.

Arthur Roberts spent the rest of the war at Le Havre, out of front line service, though he did do some time as an aircraft gunner here as well as working with engineering companies as a fitter. He was demobilised in December 1919 and returned to his apprenticeship at Harland and Wolff. He missed the fierce race riots that gripped Glasgow in the summer of 1919, which saw violence perpetrated against ethnic minorities, but did suffer from racial prejudice himself in later life, due to his relationship with a white woman. In 1935 he set up home with Jessie Motherwell, whom he finally married in Blackpool in 1956, shortly before her death. They had no children. He worked in shipbuilding and heavy engineering until his retirement, and died in a care home in the 1980s, with no known relatives.

He had added to his diaries over his lifetime, writing reminiscences and painting pictures of the battlefields from memory. He carefully packaged these up before his death, and they were found in the loft of a house in the Mount Vernon area of Glasgow by the young couple that moved in.

James Butlin returned to Oxford after the war and gained a double first in Classics. He married Norah Ransome-Jones from Monmouthshire in 1924, and they had two children, Anne and Thomas, with whom they lived in Barnes. James had a successful career as a teacher and in educational publishing. He served as a reservist in the Second World War, and then worked for the Allied Control Council administering Allied management of the defeated Germany. In later life he worked as a private tutor from his home in Barnes, and enjoyed gardening and travelling.

Norah died in 1976, James in 1982. Their daughter found his First World War letters when he moved out of his home into sheltered accommodation, and donated them to the Imperial War Museum.

Notes

Chapter 1

1 http://www.metoffice.gov.uk/media/pdf/k/c/Mar1914.pdf
2 *The Times*, March 1914.
3 Gertrude Lloyd, 'Biography of Alan Scrivener Lloyd', Lady Cockcroft's Private Collection (cited hereafter as LCPC).
4 Ibid.
5 The 1901 census states that the Lloyd household had six servants.
6 Lloyd (LCPC), 'Alan Scrivener Lloyd'; Private papers of Lieutenant A. S. Lloyd MC, Documents.20535, The Imperial War Museum (cited hereafter as 20535 IWM), letter from Alan Lloyd to Dorothy Hewetson, 24 August 1915; See also: Dr Judy Lloyd, PhD thesis: 'The Lloyds of Birmingham: Quaker Culture and Identity 1850–1914' (University of London, 2006).
7 Lloyd (LCPC), 'Alan Scrivener Lloyd'.
8 Letters from Lloyd to Hewetson (20535 IWM), 18 and 27 March 1914.
9 *The Times*, Monday 30 March 1914, 14.
10 *The Times*, Tuesday 31 March 1914, 5: '*A well dressed young man was charged before Mr. Mead at Marlborough Street Police Court yesterday with behaving in a disorderly manner. A constable said on Saturday night he saw the prisoner in the neighbourhood of Piccadilly riding with a number of other young men on the top of a taxi cab. Mr Mead – People don't ride on the roofs of taxi cabs?*
   The constable – Yes they do on Boat Race night (laughter.)'
11 Indenture papers, 1905, Kent and Sons; Pamela Armitage Campbell's private collection.
12 'A Call to Juniors' by Reg Evans, West Herts Conservative and Unionist Association newsletter, April 1912.
13 Andrew Rosen, *Rise Up Women! The Militant Campaign of the Women's Social and Political Union 1903–1914* (Routledge and Kegan Paul, 1974), 229–30.
14 Ibid., 232–3.

15 Diary of Kate Parry Frye, Elizabeth Crawford's Private Collection (cited hereafter as ECPC), entry for 7 July 1914.

16 Frye (ECPC), entry for 21 May 1914.

17 *Brisbane Courier*, 23 May 1914, 5; Rosen, *Rise Up Women!*, 232–3.

18 *Luton Times and Advertiser*, 30 March 1906.

19 1911 census.

20 Hallie Killick, 'Life's Scenery' in *Life's Orchestra* (1st edn. 1904) (London: Eustace Miles, 1923).

21 Hallie Eustace Killick Miles, preface, *The Ideal Home and Its Problems* (London: Methuen, 1911).

22 Nathaniel Newnham-Davis, *The Gourmet's Guide to London* (New York: Brentano's, 1914), 75–6.

23 Ibid.

24 Letter from Lloyd to Hewetson (20535 IWM), 18 June 1914.

25 Letter from Lloyd to Hewetson (20535 IWM), 29 June 1914.

26 Frye (ECPC), entry for 29 August 1914.

27 Frye (ECPC), entry for 10 July 1914.

Chapter 2

1 Frye (ECPC), entry for 25 July 1914.

2 Letter from Lloyd to Hewetson (20535 IWM), 28 July 1914.

3 Frye (ECPC), entry for 30 July 1914.

4 *Worthing Gazette*, 29 July 1914, 4.

5 Ibid., 5 August 1914, 3; Frye (ECPC), entry for 1 August 1914.

6 Hallie Killick, *Life's Orchestra* (1st edn. 1904) (London: Eustace Miles, 1923), 134–5.

7 *Thanet Times*, 31 July 1914, 5.

8 Hallie Miles, *Untold Tales of Wartime London: A Personal Diary by Hallie Eustace Miles* (London:Cecil Palmer, 1930), entry for 1 August 1914.

9 Ibid.

10 Letter from Lloyd to Hewetson (20535 IWM), 2 August 1914.

11 *The Times*, 1 and 2 August 1914.

12 Frye (ECPC), entry for 2 August 1914.

13 Introduction to *Echoes of the Great War: The Diary of the Reverend Andrew Clark, 1914–19*, ed. James Munson (Oxford: Oxford University Press, 1985).

14 Clark, entry for 2 August 1914, quoted in *Echoes of the Great War*, 5.

15 Ibid.

16 *The Times*, Monday 3 August 1914, 4.

17 *The Times*, Tuesday 4 August 1914, 4.

18 Frye (ECPC), entry for 3 August 1914.

19 *Worthing Gazette*, 5 August 1914, 3.

20   Frye (ECPC), entry for 3 August 1914.

21   *Hemel Hempstead Gazette and West Herts Advertiser*, 8 August 1914.

22   Frye (ECPC), entry for 4 August 1914.

23   *Worthing Gazette*, 5 August 1914, 5.

24   *The Times*, 5 August, 5, 9.

25   *The Times*, 5 August, 6.

26   Winston Churchill, *The World Crisis, 1911–1918, vol I* (1st edn. 1923) (London: Oldhams Press, 1939), 186.

27   *The Times*, 5 August, 5, 9.

28   *Worthing Gazette*, 5 Aug 1914, 5.

29   Frye (ECPC), entry for 4 August 1914.

30   Miles, *Untold Tales of Wartime London*, entry for 4 August 1914.

31   Killick, 'Hope' in *Life's Orchestra*.

Chapter 3

1   'The Declaration of War', *The Times*, 5 August 1914, 7.

2   Introduction to *Echoes of the Great War: The Diary of the Reverend Andrew Clark, 1914–19*, ed. James Munson (Oxford: Oxford University Press, 1985).

3   Clark's introduction to his war diary, August 1914, quoted in *Echoes of the Great War*, 3.

4   *Hemel Hempstead Gazette and West Herts Advertiser*, 8 August 1914, 5.

5   Ibid. Without a national health service, the health of the working classes was largely left to fate and many would-be soldiers up and down the country were deemed unfit for service, principally on account of defective teeth and eyes.

6   David Stevenson, *1914–18: The History of the First World War* (Harmondsworth: Penguin, 2004), 198–203.

7   *The Times*, 6 August 1914, 4.

8   Gertrude Lloyd, 'Biography of Alan Scrivener Lloyd', Lady Cockcroft's Private Collection (cited hereafter as LCPC).

9   Private papers of Lieutenant A. S. Lloyd MC, Documents.20535, The Imperial War Museum (cited hereafter as 20535 IWM), letter from Alan Lloyd to Dorothy Hewetson, 6 August 1914.

10   Letter from Hewetson to Lloyd (20535 IWM), undated but c. 6/7 August 1914.

11   Hallie Miles, *Untold Tales of Wartime London: A Personal Diary by Hallie Eustace Miles* (London: Cecil Palmer, 1930), entry for August 1914.

12   Ibid.

13   Diary of Kate Parry Frye, Elizabeth Crawford's Private Collection (cited hereafter as ECPC), entry for 8 August 1914.

14   Ibid.

15   Ibid.

16   'The Herts territorials: How They Are Faring' in the *Hemel Hempstead Gazette and West Herts Advertiser*, 15 August 1914, 5.

17   Letter from Reg Evans to Frances Evans, Liddle Collection, Leeds University Special Collections, LIDDLE/WW1/GS/1816 (cited hereafter as LC), 9 August 1914.

18   Ibid.

19   Letter from Reg Evans to Frances Evans (LC), 11 August 1914.

20   Clark, entry for 18 August 1914, quoted in *Echoes of the Great War*, 7–8.

21   Clark, entry for 16 August 1914, quoted in *Echoes of the Great War*, 7.

22   Speech by J. Herbert Tritton, 6 September 1914, quoted in *Echoes of the Great War*, 13.

23   Clark, entry for 8 September, quoted in *Echoes of the Great War*, 16.

24   Letter from Hewetson to Lloyd (20535 IWM), 11 August 1914.

25   Letter from Lloyd to Hewetson (20535 IWM), 11 August 1914.

26   Letter from Lloyd to Hewetson (20535 IWM), 18 August 1914.

27   Peter Simkins, *Kitchener's Army: The Raising of the New Armies 1914–1916* (Manchester: Manchester University Press, 1988).

28   Frye (ECPC), entry for 28 August 1914.

29   Frye (ECPC), entry for 30 August 1914.

30   Frye (ECPC), entry for 6 September 1914.

31   Wedding announcement in *Boston Spa News*, 4 September 1914.

32   Letter from Dorothy Lloyd to Mrs Lloyd (20535 IWM), 2 September 1914.

33   Letter from Alan Lloyd to his father John Henry Lloyd (20535 IWM), 3 September 1914.

34   Letter from Reg Evans to Frances Evans (LC), 2 September 1914.

35   Ibid.

36   Telegram to Alan Lloyd (20535 IWM), 3 October 1914; Lloyd (LCPC), 'Scrivener Lloyd'.

37   Letter from Alan Lloyd to John Henry Lloyd (20535 IWM), 6 October 1914.

38   Miles, *Untold Tales of Wartime London*, undated entry but September/October 1914.

Chapter 4

1   This is where the terms a 'mention in despatches' or being 'gazetted' derived from.

2   *London Gazette*, 14 August 1914, issue number 28870:
     http://www.london-gazette.co.uk/issues/28870/pages/6387,
     http://www.london-gazette.co.uk/issues/28870/pages/6388

http://www.london-gazette.co.uk/issues/28870/pages/6389

3   *Hemel Hempstead Gazette and West Herts Advertiser*, 22 August 1914, 7.

4   *Hemel Hempstead Gazette and West Herts Advertiser*, 15 August 1914, 5 and 22 August 1914, 5.

5   Hallie Miles, *Untold Tales of Wartime London: A Personal Diary by Hallie Eustace Miles* (London: Cecil Palmer, 1930), undated entry but September/ October 1914.

6   Ibid.

7   1911 census.

8   Miles, *Untold Tales of Wartime London*, undated entry but September/ October 1914.

9   *The Times*, 15 August 1914, 7.

10 'How to be Useful in Wartime': Series of articles in *The Times*, August 1914.

11 Letter from Helen Franklin to Norman Bentwich, The Women's Library, LSE, 7HBE (cited hereafter as TWL), August 1914.

12 Letter from Franklin to Bentwich (TWL), 8 September 1914.

13 For impact on employment see: Jon Lawrence, 'The Transition to War in 1914', in *Capital Cities at War*, ed. Jay Winter and John-Louis Robert (Cambridge: Cambridge University Press, 1997).

14 Official letter from Mrs Chapman, President of the New Constitutional Society for Women's Suffrage, 12 August 1914, Elizabeth Crawford's Private Collection.

15 Diary of Kate Parry Frye, Elizabeth Crawford's Private Collection (cited hereafter as ECPC), entry for Friday 28 August 1914.

16 Introduction to *Echoes of the Great War: The Diary of the Reverend Andrew Clark, 1914–19*, ed. James Munson (Oxford, New York: Oxford University Press, 1985).

17 Clark, entry for 11 August 1914, quoted in *Echoes of the Great War*, 6.

18 Clark, entry for 21 August 1914, quoted in *Echoes of the Great War*, 9.

19 Clark, entry for 31 August 1914, quoted in *Echoes of the Great War*, 11.

20 Miles, *Untold Tales of Wartime London*, undated but c. October 1914.

21 Ibid., entry for 26 September 1914.

22 *Thanet Times*, 7 August 1914, 5.

23 *Thanet Times*, 25 September 1914, 3.

24 Clark, entry for 14 September 1914, quoted in *Echoes of the Great War*, 17–18.

25 Clark, entry for 26 September 1914, quoted in *Echoes of the Great War*, 19–20.

26 Clark, entry for 29 September 1914, quoted in *Echoes of the Great War*, 20–21.

27 Frye (ECPC), entries for 31 August, 1 and 10 September 1914; NCSS workroom pricelist.

28   Frye (ECPC), entry for 4 September 1914.

29   Frye (ECPC), entry for 2 September 1914.

30   Marian McKenna, 'The Development of Air Raid Precautions in World War 1', in *Men at War: Politics, Technology and Innovation in the Twentieth Century*, ed. Timothy Travers and Christon Archer (first ed. 1982) (New Jersey: Transaction Publishers, 2011), 179.

31   Miles, *Untold Tales of Wartime London*, undated entry, October 1914.

32   Ibid.

33   McKenna, 'The Development of Air Raid Precautions', 179.

34   Clark, entry for 17 October 1914, quoted in *Echoes of the Great War*, 23.

35   Ibid.

36   Clark, entries for 29 and 30 October 1914, quoted in *Echoes of the Great War*, 23.

37   Clark, entry for 3 November 1914, quoted in *Echoes of the Great War*, 27.

38   Letter from Franklin to Bentwich (TWL), 26 November 1914.

39   Helen Bentwich, *If I Forget Thee: Some Chapters of an Autobiography* (London: Elek, 1973), 33.

40   Letter from Franklin to Bentwich (TWL), 26 November 1914.

41   Frye (ECPC), entry for 8 October 1914.

42   Frye (ECPC), entry for 17 October 1914.

43   Frye (ECPC), entry for 18 October 1914.

44   Ibid.

45   Miles, *Untold Tales of Wartime London*, undated entry but November 1914.

Chapter 5

1   Met Office monthly report, October 1914.

2   Introduction to *Echoes of the Great War: The Diary of the Reverend Andrew Clark, 1914–19*, ed. James Munson (Oxford, New York: Oxford University Press, 1985).

3   Clark, entry for 27 October 1914, quoted in *Echoes of the Great War*, 25.

4   Clark, entry for 14 October 1914, quoted in *Echoes of the Great War*, 22–3.

5   *Hemel Hempstead Gazette and West Herts Advertiser*, 31 October 1914, 5.

6   1st Battalion Hertfordshire Regiment, war diary 1914–1918, November 1914.

7   Letter from Reg Evans to Frances Evans, Liddell Collection, Leeds University Special Collections, LIDDLE/WW1/GS/1816 (cited hereafter as LC), 4 November 1914.

8   Letter from Reg Evans to Frances Evans (LC), 6 November 1914.

9   *Hemel Hempstead Gazette and West Herts Advertiser*, 5 December 1914, 3; Letter from Reg Evans to Will Evans, 25 November 1914 (published in the *Hemel Hempstead Gazette and West Herts Advertiser*, 5 December 1914).

10   Private papers of Lieutenant A. S. Lloyd MC, Documents.20535, The Imperial War Museum (cited hereafter as 20535 IWM), letter from Dorothy Lloyd to Mr Lloyd, 18 October 1914.

11   Letter from Alan Lloyd to Mr Lloyd (20535 IWM), 29 October 1914.

12   Letter from Dorothy Lloyd to Gertrude Lloyd (20535 IWM), 11 November 1914.

13   David Stevenson, *1914–1918: The History of the First World War* (Harmondsworth: Penguin, 2004) 76; Liddell-Hart, *A History of the World War 1914–18*, [London: Cassell, 1970], 174.

14   BG J. E. Edmonds, *History of the Great War: Military Operations France and Belgium 1914, vol II* (London: Committee of Imperial Defence, 1925), 446.

15   Ibid.

16   1st Battalion Hertfordshire Regiment, war diary, November 1914; *Hertfordshire Gazette*, 5 December 1914, 3; Letter from Reg Evans to Will Evans (LC), 25 November 1914.

17   Edmonds, *Ops France and Belgium 1914*, vol. II, 448.

18   Letter from Reg Evans to Frances Evans (LC), 12 November 1914.

19   Letter from Will Evans to Frances Evans, LC.] 19 November 1914.

20   1st Battalion Hertfordshire Regiment, war diary, November 1914.

21   Clark, entry for 17 November 1914, quoted in *Echoes of the Great War*, 31–32.

22   Clark, entry for 21 November 1914, quoted in *Echoes of the Great War*, 32–33.

23   1st Battalion Hertfordshire Regiment, war diary, November 1914; Edmonds, *Ops France and Belgium 1914*, vol. II, 448.

24   1st Battalion Hertfordshire Regiment, war diary, November 1914; and *Hemel Hempstead Gazette and West Herts Advertiser*, 28 November and 5 November 1914.

25   A Jack Johnson was a German shell that released lots of black smoke – so named after the boxer Jack Johnson, the first black American world heavyweight champion.

26   Letter from Reg Evans to Frances Evans (LC), 2 December 1914.

27   1st Battalion Hertfordshire Regiment, war diary, November 1914.

28   Letter from Reg Evans to Will Evans (LC), 25 November 1914.

29   Letter from Reg Evans to Frances Evans (LC), 22 November 1914.

30   Letter from Mrs Tritton to Mildred Clark, 25 November 1914, quoted in *Echoes of the Great War*, 35.

31   Stevenson, *1914–1918*, 76.

32   Stevenson, *1914–1918*, 179.

33   Letter from Dorothy Lloyd to Mrs Lloyd (20535 IWM), 26 November 1914.

34   Edmonds, *Ops France and Belgium 1915* vol. I, 4; Stevenson, *1914–1918*, 179.

35   Letter from Reg Evans to Frances Evans (LC), 2 December 1914.

Chapter 6

1   Selfridges and Co. advert, December 1914.
2   Met Office weather report for December 1914.
3   Diary of Kate Parry Frye, Elizabeth Crawford's Private Collection (cited hereafter as ECPC), entry for 4 December 1914.
4   Frye (ECPC), entry for 7 December 1914.
5   Frye (ECPC), entry for 10 December 1914.
6   Hallie Miles, *Untold Tales of Wartime London: A Personal Diary by Hallie Eustace Miles* (London: Cecil Palmer, 1930), undated entry but November–December 1914.
7   Ibid., undated entry but December 1914–January 1915.
8   Ibid., entry for 5 December 1914.
9   *Hertfordshire Gazette*, Saturday 5 December, 3; Saturday 12 December, 5.
10 Letter from Reg Evans to Frances Evans, Liddle Collection, Leeds University Special Collections, LIDDLE/WW1/GS/1816 (cited hereafter as LC), 9 December 1914; other duties may well have included trench digging: at this point the British were working on their back lines; J. E. Edmonds, *History of the Great War: Military Operations France and Belgium 1915* (London: Committee of Imperial Defence, 1925) (cited hereafter as Edmonds, *Ops France and Belgium 1915*), vol. I, 5.
11 Letter from Reg Evans to Frances Evans (LC), 2 December 1914.
12 Letters from Reg Evans to Frances Evans (LC), 2 and 9 December 1914.
13 Andrew Clark, entry for 15 December 1914, quoted in *Echoes of the Great War: The Diary of the Reverend Andrew Clark, 1914–19*, ed. James Munson (Oxford, New York: Oxford University Press, 1985), 38.
14 Robert Massie, *Castles of Steel: Britain, Germany and the Winning of the Great War at Sea* (London: Jonathan Cape, 2004), 324–5.
15 Clark, entry for 16 December 1914, quoted in *Echoes of the Great War*, 38.
16 When the news did get into the papers there was outrage: 'This is not warfare, it is murder' ran the *Independent*.
17 Clark, entry for 22 December 1914, quoted in *Echoes of the Great War*, 39.
18 Frye (ECPC), entry for 25 December 1914.
19 Frye (ECPC), entry for 23 December 1914.
20 Ibid.
21 J. M. Winter, *The Great War and the British People* (first ed. 1985) (Hampshire, New York: Palgrave Macmillan, 2003), 251.
22 Sir John Ross of Bladensburg, *The Coldstream Guards 1914–18* (Oxford: Oxford University Press, 1928), vol. I, 293.
23 Edmonds, *Ops France and Belgium 1915*, vol. I, 17–20.
24 1st Battalion Hertfordshire Regiment, war diary 1914–1918, December 1914; Edmonds, *Ops France and Belgium 1915*, vol. I, 22.

25   Ibid., 23.

26   Letter from Reg Evans to Frances Evans (LC), 3 January 1915.

27   1st Battalion Hertfordshire Regiment, war diary, December 1914.

28   Met Office monthly weather report, December 1914.

29   Clark, entry for 28 December, 1914, quoted in *Echoes of the Great War*, 40.

30   Clark, entry for 30 December 1914, quoted in *Echoes of the Great War*, 40.

31   Clark, entry for 2 January 1915, quoted in *Echoes of the Great War*, 41.

32   Introduction to *Echoes of the Great War*.

Chapter 7

1   Met Office monthly weather report, January 1915.

2   Telegram from Miss Elizabeth Tritton to the Rev. Andrew Clark, 2
      January 1915, quoted in *Echoes of the Great War: The Diary of the Reverend
      Andrew Clark, 1914–19*, ed. James Munson (Oxford, New York: Oxford
      University Press, 1985), 41.

3   Martin Gilbert, *The First World War* (London: Weidenfeld & Nicolson,
      1994), 124.

4   Clark, entry for 4 January, 1915, quoted in *Echoes of the Great War*, 41.

5   Imperial War Museum, statistic used in the 'In Memoriam' exhibition,
      2008–09.

6   See BG J. E. Edmonds, *History of the Great War: Military Operations
      France and Belgium 1915* (London: Committee of Imperial Defence, 1925)
      (cited hereafter as Edmonds, *Ops France and Belgium 1915*), and David
      Stevenson, *1914–1918: The History of the First World War* (Harmondsworth:
      Penguin, 2004).

7   Private papers of Lieutenant J. H. Butlin, Documents.7915, Imperial War
      Museum (cited hereafter as 7915 IWM), letter from James Butlin to Basil
      Burnett Hall, 13 December 1914.

8   See *C. H. Dudley Ward, The History of the Dorsetshire Regiment 1914–19*
      (Dorsetshire: Ling, 1932).

9   Letter from Butlin to Burnett Hall (7915 IWM), 1 March 1915.

10   Gertrude Lloyd, 'Biography of Alan Scrivener Lloyd', Lady Cockcroft's
      Private Collection (cited hereafter as LCPC).

11   Stevenson, *1914–18*, 156–7.

12   Private papers of Lieutenant A. S. Lloyd MC, Documents.20535, Imperial
      War Museum (cited hereafter as 20535 IWM), letter from Alan Lloyd
      to John Henry Lloyd, 12 January 1915.

13   In the First Army, the average casualty rate for the first weeks of 1915
      was 2,144 officers and men daily. See *Edmonds, Ops France and Belgium
      1915*, vol. I, 27–8.

14   1st Battalion Hertfordshire Regiment, war diary 1914–1918, January 1915.

15 Letters from Reg Evans to Frances Evans, Liddle Collection, Leeds University Special Collections, LIDDLE/WW1/GS/1816 (cited hereafter as LC), 14 and 23 January 1915.

16 Edmonds, *Ops France and Belgium 1915*, vol. I, 29–30.

17 1st Battalion Hertfordshire Regiment, war diary 1914–1918, January 1915, and Edmonds, *Ops France and Belgium 1915*, vol. I, 29–30.

18 Letter from Reg Evans to Frances Evans (LC), 21 February 1915.

19 The offensive was abandoned after a matter of days due to shortage of men, supplies and poor communication. See Edmonds, *Ops France and Belgium 1915*, vol. I, 149–153.

20 Letter from Butlin to Burnett Hall (7915 IWM), 3 April 1915.

21 See Col. H. C. Wylly, *The Green Howards in the Great War, March/April 1915* (Yorkshire: Privately printed, 1926).

22 Letter from Butlin to Burnett Hall (7915 IWM), 9 April 1915.

23 Letters from Butlin to Burnett Hall (7915 IWM), 3 and 9 April 1915.

24 Letter from Reg Evans to Frances Evans (LC), 26 March 1915.

25 Edmonds, *Ops France and Belgium 1915*, vol. I, 155–6.

26 Ibid., 166–78.

27 Letter from Butlin to Burnett Hall (7915 IWM), 30 April 1915.

28 Letter from Alan Lloyd to Mr Lloyd (20535 IWM), undated but April 1915.

29 Letter from Dorothy Lloyd to Mrs Lloyd (20535 IWM), 8 April 1915.

30 Edmonds, *Ops France and Belgium 1915*, vol. II, 6–32; 1st Battalion Hertfordshire Regiment, war diary 1914–1918, May 1915; Wylly, *The Green Howards*, 59.

31 Edmonds, *Ops France and Belgium 1915*, vol. II., 11–37.

32 Letter from Butlin to Burnett Hall (7915 IWM), 22 May 1915.

33 Edmonds, *Ops France and Belgium 1915*, vol. II, 67, and Wylly, *The Green Howards*, May 1915, 59–60.

34 Letter from Butlin to Burnett Hall (7915 IWM), 22 May 1915.

35 Edmonds, *Ops France and Belgium 1915*, vol. II, 59–73; 1st Battalion Hertfordshire Regiment, war diary 1914–1918, May 1915.

36 Letter from Reg Evans to Frances Evans (LC), 26 May 1915.

37 1st Battalion Hertfordshire Regiment, war diary 1914–1918, 19 May 1915.

38 Letter from Reg Evans to Frances Evans (LC), 26 May 1915.

39 Letter from Reg Evans to Frances Evans (LC), 1 June 1915.

40 *The Times*, 14 May 1915, 8.

41 Letter from Reg Evans to Frances Evans (LC), 26 May 1915.

42 Letter from Butlin to Burnett Hall (7915 IWM), 3 June 1915.

43 Edmonds, *Ops France and Belgium 1915*, vol. II., 93–95.

44 Letter from Butlin to Burnett Hall (7915 IWM), 18 June 1915.

45 'The Second Action of Givenchy' on 'The Long, Long Trail: The British Army in the Great War 1914–18' http://www.1914-1918.net/bat12.htm

46   Letter from Butlin to Burnett Hall (7915 IWM), 23 June 1915.

47   Letter from Reg Evans to Frances Evans (LC), 15 June 1915.

48   Letter from Alan Lloyd to Dorothy Lloyd (20535 IWM), 17 July 1915.

49   Lloyd (LCPC), 'Alan Scrivener Lloyd'.

Chapter 8

1   Hallie Miles, *Untold Tales of Wartime London: A Personal Diary by Hallie Eustace Miles* (London: Cecil Palmer, 1930), entry for 5 March 1915.

2   Kate Parry Collins, Unpublished Diaries, Elizabeth Crawford's Private Collection (cited hereafter as ECPC), entry for 9 January 1915.

3   Collins (ECPC), entry for 9 January 1915.

4   Letter from Helen Franklin to Norman Bentwich, The Women's Library, LSE, 7HBE (cited hereafter as TWL), 16 December 1914.

5   Letter from Franklin to Bentwich (TWL), 30 December 1914.

6   See Chapter 6 in Diana Cooper, *The Rainbow Comes and Goes* (London: Century, 1984).

7   Duff's starting salary was £200 a year at the FO: Duff Cooper, *Old Men Forget* (London, Hart-Davis, 1953), 38.

8   Cooper, *The Rainbow*, 99; Letter from Duff Cooper to Diana Manners, 19 April 1913, quoted in *A Durable Fire: The Letters of Duff and Diana Cooper 1913–50*, ed. Artemis Cooper, (1st edn. 1983) (London, Hamish Hamilton 1985), 4–5.

9   See chapter 6 in Cooper, *The Rainbow*.

10   Cooper, *The Rainbow*, 117–130; Philip Ziegler, *Diana Cooper* (Harmondsworth: Penguin, 1983), 63–5.

11   Letters from Cooper to Manners, 18 October and 3 November 1914, quoted in Cooper, *A Durable Fire*, 18–19.

12   Letter from Franklin to Bentwich (TWL), 29 January 1915.

13   Ibid.

14   Cooper, *The Rainbow*, 117–130; Ziegler, *Diana Cooper*, 63–5.

15   Cooper, *Old Men Forget*, 44–51.

16   Letter from Manners to Cooper, February 1915, 19.

17   Letter from Cooper to Manners, February 1915.

18   Cooper, *The Rainbow*, 133; Ziegler, *Diana Cooper*, 65–6.

19   Letter from Franklin to Bentwich (TWL), 10 March 1915.

20   Helen Bentwich, *If I Forget Thee: Some Chapters of an Autobiography*, (London: Elek, 1973), 39.

21   Collins, entry for 1 January 1915.

22   Collins, entries for 1 and 3 February 1915.

23   Letter from Franklin to Bentwich (TWL), 29 April 1915.

24   Ibid.

25 Andrew Clark, entry for 1 May 1915, quoted in *Echoes of the Great War: The Diary of the Reverend Andrew Clark, 1914–19*, ed. James Munson (Oxford, New York: Oxford University Press, 1985), 58–9.

26 Clark, entry for 2 May 1915, quoted in *Echoes of the Great War*, 59.

27 Clark, entry for 16 May 1915, quoted in *Echoes of the Great War*, 62–3.

28 UK Parliamentary Papers, 1921 [Cmd. 1193] *General annual reports on the British Army (including the Territorial Force) for the period from 1st October, 1913, to 30th September, 1919.*

29 Duff Cooper's diary, entry for 15 May 1915, quoted in *The Duff Cooper Diaries*, ed. John Julius Norwich (1st ed 2005) (London: Phoenix, 2006), 10.

30 Cooper, *The Rainbow*, 133.

31 Quoted in Ziegler, *Diana Cooper*, 68.

32 Cooper, *The Rainbow*, 133.

33 Letter from Franklin to Bentwich (TWL), 7 and 10 May 1915.

34 See Ziegler, *Diana Cooper*, 65–7; Cooper, *The Rainbow*, 136.

35 Collins (ECPC), entry for 19 May 1915.

36 Collins (ECPC), entry for 17 July 1915.

37 *Brisbane Courier*, Monday 9 July 1915, 7.

Chapter 9

1 Hallie Miles, *Untold Tales of Wartime London: A Personal Diary by Hallie Eustace Miles* (London: Cecil Palmer, 1930), entry for 26 January 1915.

2 Martin Gilbert, *The First World War* (London: Weidenfeld & Nicolson, 1994), 125.

3 John H. Morrow Jnr, 'War in the Air', in *The Oxford Illustrated History of the First World War*, ed. Hew Strachan (Oxford: Oxford University Press, 2000), 265–7.

4 Miles, *Untold Tales of Wartime London*, undated entry but February 1915.

5 Letter from Helen Franklin to Norman Bentwich, The Women's Library, LSE, 7HBE (cited hereafter as TWL), 27 May 1915.

6 Letter from Franklin to Bentwich (TWL), 27 May 1915.

7 Gilbert, *The First World War*, 127–8.

8 Miles, *Untold Tales of Wartime London*, undated entry but spring 1915.

9 Miles, *Untold Tales of Wartime London*, undated entry but early May 1915.

10 Gilbert, *The First World War*, 156–7.

11 Bentwich, *If I Forget Thee: Some Chapters of an Autobiography* (London: Elek, 1973), 39.

12 Letter from Franklin to Bentwich (TWL), 14 May 1915.

13 Cooper, entry for 7 May 1915, quoted in *The Duff Cooper Diaries*, 8.

14 Cooper, entry for 12 May, 1915, quoted in *The Duff Cooper Diaries*, 8–9.

15 Cooper, entry for 13 May, 1915, quoted in *The Duff Cooper Diaries*, 9.

16 Cooper, entry for 11 June 1915, quoted in *The Duff Cooper* Diaries, 12.

17 Cooper, entry for 16 April 1915, quoted in *The Duff Cooper Diaries*, 3–4.

18 Diana Cooper, *The Rainbow Comes and Goes* (London: Century, 1984), 136; Philip Ziegler, *Diana Cooper* (Harmondsworth: Penguin, 1983), 69.

19 Cooper, *The Rainbow*, 143–4; Ziegler, *Diana Cooper*, 80–81.

20 See Duff Cooper's diary entry for 31 May 1915, quoted in *The Duff Cooper Diaries*, 11, he had been trying to woo Bulgaria but problems with Serbia; diary of Kate Parry Collins, Elizabeth Crawford's Private Collection (cited hereafter as ECPC), entries for May–1 June 1915; letters from Franklin to Bentwich (TWL), 29 May and 1 June.

21 Saul David, *100 Days to Victory* (London: Hodder & Stoughton, 2013), 143.

22 Gilbert, *The First World War*, 165.

23 Collins (ECPC), entry for 1 June 1915.

24 Letter from Franklin to Bentwich (TWL), 1 June 1915.

25 Letter from Franklin to Bentwich (TWL), 3 June 1915.

26 Gilbert, *The First World War*, 165.

27 Miles, *Untold Tales of Wartime London*, undated entry but early June 1915.

28 Letters from Franklin to Bentwich (TWL), 20 June and undated June 1915.

29 Collins (ECPC), entry for 20 August 1915.

30 Collins (ECPC), entry for 25 August 1915.

31 Collins (ECPC), entry for 27 August 1915.

32 Collins (ECPC), entry for 28 August 1915.

33 Cooper, *The Rainbow*, 138–141.

34 Cooper, entry for 27 August 1915, quoted in *The Duff Cooper Diaries, 14–15*.

35 Letter from Duff Cooper to Diana Manners, 30 August 1915, quoted in *A Durable Fire: The Letters of Duff and Diana Cooper 1913–50*, ed. Artemis Cooper (first ed. 1983) (London: Hamish Hamilton, 1985), 24.

36 Cooper, *The Rainbow*, 141.

37 Captain Joseph Morris, *The German Air Raids on Great Britain 1914–18* (1st edn 1925) (Stroud: Nonsuch Publishing, 2007), 53.

38 Miles, *Untold Tales of Wartime London*, entry for 28 September 1915.

39 Gilbert, *The First World War*, 93; Morris, *The German Air Raids*, 54.

40 Miles, *Untold Tales of Wartime London*, undated entry but September 1915.

41 Miles, *Untold Tales of Wartime London*, undated entry but October 1915.

42 Bentwich, *If I Forget Thee*, 43.

43 Letter from Helen Bentwich to her mother (TWL), 8 September 1915.

44 Letter from Helen Bentwich to her mother (TWL), 29 and 30 September 1915.

Chapter 10

1   J. E. Edmonds, *History of the Great War Based on Official Documents: Military Operations France and Belgium 1915* (London: Committee of Imperial Defence, 1925) (cited hereafter as Edmonds, *Ops France and Belgium 1915*), vol. II, 83–6.

2   NB: though Germans referred to conflict as *Weltkrieg*, the English term 'world war' did not come into common usage until the 1930s. Before then, it was known as 'the great war'.

3   David Stevenson, 1914–1918: *The History of the First World War* (Harmondsworth: Penguin, 2004), 107–119; Gilbert, *The First World War*, 146.

4   It was estimated that Germany and Austria were turning out 250,000 rounds of gun ammunition per day compared to Britain's 22,000. Edmonds, *Ops France and Belgium 1915*, vol. II, 116.

5   Ibid., vol. II, 115–116.

6   1st Battalion Hertfordshire Regiment, war diary 1914–1918, June 1915.

7   Letter from Reg Evans to Frances Evans, Liddle Collection, Leeds University Special Collections, LIDDLE/WW1/GS/1816 (cited hereafter as LC), 21 June 1915.

8   Second Division order number 2170, from Major General Commanding Second Division, 20 October 1915, Pamela Campbell's Private Collection.

9   1st Battalion Hertfordshire Regiment, war diary 1914–1918, July 1915.

10 Letter from Reg Evans to Frances Evans (LC), 9 and 27 July 1915.

11 Letter from James Butlin to Basil Burnett Hall, Private papers of Lieutenant J. H. Butlin, Documents.7915, Imperial War Museum (cited hereafter as 7915 IWM), 27 July 1915.

12 Letter from Butlin to Burnett Hall (7915 IWM), 27 July 1915.

13 Letter from Alan Lloyd to Dorothy Lloyd, Private papers of Lieutenant A. S. Lloyd MC, Documents.20535, Imperial War Museum (cited hereafter as 20535 IWM), 15 July 1915.

14 Edmonds, *Ops France and Belgium 1915*, vol. II, 97–105; 78th Bge RFA, 17th Division, war diary, Nat Archives WO 95/1991/3, July 1915.

15 Letter from Alan Lloyd to Dorothy Lloyd (20535 IWM), 21 July 1915.

16 Letter from Alan Lloyd to Dorothy Lloyd (20535 IWM), 21 July 1915.

17 Letter from Alan Lloyd to Dorothy Lloyd (20535 IWM), 27 July and undated, but end July 1915.

18 Edmonds, *Ops France and Belgium 1915*, vol. II, 103–5; 78th Bge RFA, 17th Division, war diary, July–August 1915.

19 Letter from Alan Lloyd to Dorothy Lloyd (20535 IWM), 30 July 1915 and 1 August 1915.

20 Edmonds, *Ops France and Belgium 1915*, vol. II, 90–1.

21   Letter from Butlin to Burnett Hall (7915 IWM), 31 July 1915.

22   C. H. Dudley Ward, *History of the Dorsetshire Regiment 1914–19*, August 1915. (Dorsetshire: Ling, 1932).

23   Letter from Butlin to Burnett Hall (7915 IWM), 27 August 1915.

24   Edmonds, *Ops France and Belgium 1915*, vol. II, 125–9.

25   Letter from Alan Lloyd to Dorothy Lloyd (20535 IWM), undated but mid-August 1915.

26   Edmonds, *Ops France and Belgium 1915*, vol. II, 130.

27   Letter from Reg Evans to Frances Evans (LC), 31 August 1915.

28   Letter from Alan Lloyd to Dorothy Lloyd (20535 IWM), 2 September 1915.

29   Letter from Alan Lloyd to Dorothy Lloyd (20535 IWM), 6 September 1915.

30   Letters from Alan Lloyd to Dorothy Lloyd (20535 IWM), 6 and 9 September 1915.

31   1st Battalion Hertfordshire Regiment, war diary, September 1915; Reg Evans's unpublished account of September 1915, Pamela Campbell's Private Collection (cited hereafter as PCPC); Edmonds, *Ops France and Belgium 1915*, 163–4.

32   Letter from Reg Evans to Frances Evans (LC), 16 September 1915.

33   Edmonds, *Ops France and Belgium 1915*, 164.

34   Reg Evans's unpublished account of September 1915 (PCPC).

35   Reg Evans's unpublished account of September 1915 (PCPC).

36   Letter from A. C. Daly, Brig. General (LC), 23 September 1915.

37   Edmonds, *Ops France and Belgium 1915*, 168–70; Gilbert, *The First World War*, 197.

38   Edmonds, *Ops France and Belgium 1915*, 252–6; 1st Battalion Hertfordshire Regiment, war diary, September 1915.

39   Ibid.

40   Letter from Reg Evans to Frances Evans (LC), 29 September 1915.

41   Edmonds, *Ops France and Belgium 1915*, 259–64.

42   Letters from Alan Lloyd to Dorothy Lloyd (20535 IWM), 26 September, undated September, 22 September 1915.

43   78th Bge RFA, 17th Division, war diary, October 1915.

44   Letter from Alan Lloyd to Dorothy Lloyd (20535 IWM), 4 October 1915.

45   Letter from Reg Evans to Frances Evans (LC), 6 October 1915.

46   Gilbert, *The First World War*, 201; Edmonds, *Ops France and Belgium 1915*, 391–400.

47   Letter from Butlin to Burnett Hall (7915 IWM), 27 September 1915.

48   78th Bge RFA, 17th Division, war diary, October 1915; letter from Alan Lloyd to Dorothy Lloyd (20535 IWM), 7 October 1915.

49   Letter from Alan Lloyd to Dorothy Lloyd (20535 IWM), 8 October 1915.

Chapter 11

1   Text of Andrew Clark's speech on 28 September, 1915, quoted in *Echoes of the Great War: The Diary of the Reverend Andrew Clark, 1914–19*, ed. James Munson (Oxford, New York: Oxford University Press, 1985), 85–7.

2   Text of Clark's speech on 28 September 1915, quoted in *Echoes of the Great War*, 85–7.

3   Clark, entry for 1 October, quoted in *Echoes of the Great War*, 87-8.

4   Duff Cooper's diary, entry for 28 September 1915, quoted in *The Duff Cooper Diaries*, ed. John Julius Norwich (1st edn. 2005) (London: Phoenix, 2006), 16.

5   Cooper, entry for 1 October 1915, quoted in *The Duff Cooper Diaries*, 17.

6   Cooper, entry for 21 October 1915, quoted in *The Duff Cooper Diaries*, 18.

7   Edmonds, *History of the Great War: Military Operations France and Belgium 1915* (London: Committee of Imperial Defence, 1925) (cited hereafter as Edmonds, *Ops France and Belgium 1915*), vol. II, 391–2.

8   Letter from Reg Evans to Ernest Kent, 9 October 1915, Pamela Campbell's Private Collection.

9   Letter from Reg Evans to Frances Evans, Liddle Collection, Leeds University Special Collections, LIDDLE/WW1/GS/1816 (cited hereafter as LC), 25 and 31 October 1915.

10 Letter from Alan Lloyd to Dorothy Lloyd, Private Papers of Lieutenant A. S. Lloyd MC, Documents.20535, Imperial War Museum (cited hereafter as 20535 IWM), 31 October and 21 October, 1915.

11 Martin Gilbert, *The First World War* (London: Weidenfeld & Nicolson, 1994), 201.

12 C. H. Dudley Ward, *History of the Dorsetshire Regiment 1914–19* (Dorsetshire: Ling, 1932); Martin Gilbert, *Somme: The Heroism and Horror of War* (London: John Murray, 2006), 16, 29.

13 Letter from James Butlin to Basil Burnett Hall, Private papers of Lieutenant J. H. Butlin, Documents.7915, Imperial War Museum (cited hereafter as 7915 IWM), 14 October 1915.

14 David Stevenson, *1914–1918: The History of the First World War* (Harmondsworth: Penguin, 2004), 198–203.

15 Letters from Butlin to Burnett Hall (7915 IWM), 23 October and 1 November 1915.

16 Clark, entry for 11 October 1915, quoted in *Echoes of the Great War*, 90; Stevenson, *1914–18*, 203.

17 Clark, entry for 9 October 1915, quoted in *Echoes of the Great War*, 90.

18 Clark, entry for 25 October 1915, quoted in *Echoes of the Great War*, 92. Note: recruitment was lowest in southern English and Irish agricultural communities.

19   Clark, entry for 1 May 1915, quoted in *Echoes of the Great War*, 58–9.

20   Cooper, entry for 11 November 1915, quoted in *The Duff Cooper Diaries*, 19–20.

21   Cooper, entry for 21 November 1915, quoted in *The Duff Cooper Diaries*, 20–1.

22   Letter from Diana Manners to Duff Cooper, 20 November 1915, quoted in *A Durable Fire: The Letters of Duff and Diana Cooper 1913–50* (1st ed 1983) (London, Hamish Hamilton 1985), 26.

23   Stevenson, *1914–18*, 161.

24   Letter from Reg Evans to Frances Evans (LC), 25 November 1915.

25   1st Battalion Hertfordshire Regiment, war diary 1914–1918, November–December 1915.

26   Letters from Reg Evans to Frances Evans (LC), 25 November and 12 December 1915.

27   Letter from Ernest Kent to Reg Evans (Pamela Campbell's Private Collection), 26 November 1915.

28   Letters from Alan Lloyd to Dorothy Lloyd (20535 IWM), 18, 20 and 21 November, 1915.

29   Letters from Alan Lloyd to Dorothy Lloyd (20535 IWM), 3 and 5 December 1915.

30   Letter from Butlin to Burnett Hall (7915 IWM), 4 December 1915.

31   Letter from Butlin to Burnett Hall (7915 IWM), 9 December 1915.

32   Clark, entry for 6 December 1915, quoted in *Echoes of the Great War*, 98–9.

33   Clark, entry for 11 December 1915, quoted in *Echoes of the Great War*, 100.

34   78th Bge RFA, 17th Division, war diary, National Archives WO 95/1991/3, December 1915.

35   Martin Gilbert, *The First World War*, 223.

Chapter 12

1   Hallie Miles, *Untold Tales of Wartime London: A Personal Diary by Hallie Eustace Miles* (London: Cecil Palmer, 1930), entry for 1 January 1916; Duff Cooper, entry for 1 January 1916, quoted in *The Duff Cooper Diaries*, ed. John Julius Norwich (1st ed 2005) (London: Phoenix, 2006), 24; Andrew Clark, entry for 1 January 1916, quoted in *Echoes of the Great War: The Diary of the Reverend Andrew Clark, 1914–19*, ed. James Munson (Oxford, New York: Oxford University Press, 1985), 105.

2   Letter from James Butlin to Basil Burnett-Hall, Private papers of Lieutenant J. H. Butlin, Documents.7915, Imperial War Museum (cited hereafter as 7915 IWM), 1 January 1916.

3   Ward, *History of the Dorsetshire Regiment 1914–19;* Martin Gilbert, *The First World War* (London: Weidenfeld & Nicolson, 1994), 216, 224.

4   1st Battalion Hertfordshire Regiment, war diary 1914–1918, January 1916.

5   Letter from Reg Evans to Frances Evans, Liddle Collection, Leeds University Special Collections, LIDDLE/WW1/GS/1816 (cited hereafter as LC), 12 December 1915.

6   1st Battalion Hertfordshire Regiment, war diary 1914–1918, January 1916.

7   Letter from Reg Evans to Frances Evans (LC), 9 January 1916.

8   78th Bge RFA, 17th Division, war diary, January 1916.

9   Letter from Alan Lloyd to Dorothy Lloyd, Private papers of Lieutenant A. S. Lloyd MC, Documents.20535, The Imperial War Museum (cited hereafter as 20535 IWM), 8 February 1916.

10   Letter from Alan Lloyd to Dorothy Lloyd (20535 IWM), 3 and 4 February 1916.

11   Gilbert, *The First World War*, 230; David Stevenson, *1914–1918: The History of the First World War* (Harmondsworth: Penguin, 2004), 162.

12   Stevenson, *1914–18*, 166.

13   Clark, entry for 23 February 1916, quoted in *Echoes of the Great War*, 113.

14   Clark, entries for 23 and 26 February 1916, quoted in *Echoes of the Great War*, 113.

15   Clark, entry for 27 February 1916, quoted in *Echoes of the Great War*, 113.

16   Letter from Butlin to Burnett-Hall (7915 IWM), 15 February 1916.

17   Gilbert, *The First World War*, 230.

18   Letter from Reg Evans to Frances Evans (LC), February 1916.

19   1st Battalion Hertfordshire Regiment, war diary 1914–1918, February 1916; Letter from G. E. Whitfield to Frances Evans (LC), 16 February 1916.

20   J. E. Edmonds, *History of the Great War Based on Official Documents: Military Operations France and Belgium, 1916* (London: Committee of Imperial Defence, 1925) (cited hereafter as Edmonds, *Ops France and Belgium 1916*), vol. I, 164–6; 78th Bge RFA, 17th Division, war diary, Nat Archives WO 95/1991/3, February 1916.

21   Edmonds, *Ops France and Belgium 1916*, vol. I, 167; letter from Alan Lloyd to Dorothy Lloyd (20535 IWM), 3 March 1916.

22   Edmonds, *Ops France and Belgium 1916*, vol. I, 169–71; 78th Bge RFA, 17th Division, war diary, March 1916.

23   Letter from Alan Lloyd to Dorothy Lloyd (20535 IWM), 3 March 1916.

24   Edmonds, *Ops France and Belgium 1916*, vol. I, 171.

25   Gilbert, *The First World War*, 237.

26   Gilbert, *The First World War*, 231.

27   Dudley Ward, *History of the Dorsetshire Regiment 1914–19*.

28   Letter from Butlin to Burnett Hall (7915 IWM), 25 February 1916.

29   Edmonds, *Ops France and Belgium, 1916*, vol. I, 166.

30   See Munson's note, *Echoes of the Great War*, 116.

31   Clark, entry for 9 March 1916, quoted in *Echoes of the Great War*, 116.

32   Clark, entry for 19 March 1916, quoted in *Echoes of the Great War*, 116–17.

33   Clark, entry for 20 March 1916, quoted in *Echoes of the Great War*, 117.

34   Letter from Alan Lloyd to Dorothy Lloyd (20535 IWM), 9 March 1916.

35   Dudley Ward, *History of the Dorsetshire Regiment 1914–19.*

36   Letter from Butlin to Burnett-Hall (7915 IWM), 11 March 1916.

37   Letter from Reg Evans to Frances Evans (LC), 19 February 1916.

38   Letter from G. E. Whitfield to Frances Evans (LC), 16 February 1916.

Chapter 13

1   Letters from Reg Evans to Frances Evans, Liddle Collection, Leeds
      University Special Collections, LIDDLE/WW1/GS/1816 (cited hereafter
      as LC), 5 March 1916 and undated but March 1916.

2   Letter from James Butlin to Basil Burnett-Hall, Private papers of
      Lieutenant J. H. Butlin, Documents.7915, Imperial War Museum (cited
      hereafter as 7915 IWM), 19 March 1916.

3   Martin Gilbert, *The First World War* (London: Weidenfeld & Nicolson,
      1994), 237; Martin Gilbert, *Somme: The Heroism and Horror of War* (London:
      John Murray, 2006), 19.

4   Dr Judy Lloyd, PhD thesis: 'The Lloyds of Birmingham: Quaker Culture
      and Identity 1850–1914' (London: University of London, 2006), 216.

5   Letter from Alan Lloyd to Dorothy Lloyd, Private papers of Lieutenant
      A. S. Lloyd MC, Documents.20535, The Imperial War Museum (cited
      hereafter as 20535 IWM), 6 April 1916.

6   Captain Joseph Morris, *The German Air Raids on Great Britain 1914–18*
      (first edn 1925) (Stroud: Nonsuch Publishing, 2007), 69–70.

7   Hallie Miles, *Untold Tales of Wartime London: A Personal Diary by Hallie
      Eustace Miles* (London: Cecil Palmer, 1930), undated entry but March
      1916.

8   Andrew Clark, entry for 1 April 1916, quoted in *Echoes of the Great War:
      The Diary of the Reverend Andrew Clark, 1914–19*, ed. James Munson
      (Oxford, New York: Oxford University Press, 1985), 120–21.

9   Morris, *The German Air Raids on Great Britain*, 70–2.

10   Clark, entry for 1 April 1916, quoted in *Echoes of the Great War*, 121.

11   Morris, *The German Air Raids on Great Britain*, pp.72–3.

12   Letter from Helen Bentwich to Caroline Franklin, The Women's Library,
      LSE, 7HBE (cited hereafter as TWL), 3 January 1916.

13   Letter from Alan Lloyd to Dorothy Lloyd (20535 IWM), 24 and 29 April
      1916.

14   David Stevenson, *1914–1918: The History of the First World War*
      (Harmondsworth: Penguin, 2004), 169.

15   Clark, entry for 8 April 1916, quoted in *Echoes of the Great War*, 123.

16   Clark, entry for 21 April 1916, quoted in *Echoes of the Great War*, 125.

17   Gilbert, *The First World War*, 242.

18   Morris, T*he German Air Raids on Great Britain*, pp. 74–6; Reports in e.g. *The Times* on the 'insane rising' – see 'The Irish Disturbances' 26 April 1916, 7.

19   Clark, entry for 27 April 1916, quoted in *Echoes of the Great War*, 126–7.

20   Gilbert, *Somme*, 25.

21   Letter from Alan Lloyd to Dorothy Lloyd (20535 IWM), 1 May 1916.

22   Morris, *The German Air Raids on Great Britain*, 77.

23   Letters from Reg Evans to Frances Evans, Liddle Collection, Leeds University Special Collections, LIDDLE/WW1/GS/1816 (cited hereafter as LC), 4 and 9 April 1916.

24   Letter from Bentwich to Franklin (TWL), 11 April 1916.

25   Letter from Bentwich to Franklin (TWL), 31 May and 10 June 1916.

26   Gilbert, *The First World War*, 251–3.

27   Letter from Bentwich to Franklin (TWL), 10 June 1916.

28   Gilbert, *Somme*, 34.

29   Letters from Butlin to Burnett-Hall (7915 IWM), 30 May and 4 June 1916.

30   Clark, entry for 11 May 1916, quoted in *Echoes of the Great War*, 128.

31   Clark, entry for 23 June 1916, quoted in *Echoes of the Great War*, 136–7.

32   Letter from Helen Bentwich to Norman Bentwich (TWL), 29 June 1916.

33   Gilbert, *Somme*, 26.

34   Gilbert, *The First World War*, 238.

35   Letter from Helen Bentwich to Norman Bentwich (TWL), 7 September 1916.

36   Gilbert, *Somme*, 34.

Chapter 14

1   Martin Gilbert, *Somme: The Heroism and Horror of War* (London: John Murray, 2006), 19–22.

2   Ibid., 27.

3   Letters from Alan Lloyd to Dorothy Lloyd, Private papers of Lieutenant A. S. Lloyd MC, Documents.20535, The Imperial War Museum (cited hereafter as 20535 IWM), 3 and 7 June 1916.

4   Ibid., 8 and 9 June 1916.

5   Gilbert, *Somme*, 35.

6   Letter from Helen Bentwich to Norman Bentwich, The Women's Library, LSE, 7HBE (cited hereafter as TWL), 11 September 1916.

7   Letter from Helen Bentwich to Norman Bentwich (TWL), 11 September 1916.

8   78th Bge RFA, 17th Division, war diary, Nat Archives WO 95/1991/3, June 1916.

THE GREAT WAR

9   Letters from Alan Lloyd to Dorothy Lloyd (20535 IWM), 17 and 18 June 1916.

10   J. E. Edmonds, *History of the Great War Based on Official Documents: Military Operations France and Belgium 1916* (London: Committee of Imperial Defence, 1925) (cited hereafter as Edmonds, *Ops France and Belgium 1916*), vol. I, 299–302.

11   Letter from Alan Lloyd to Dorothy Lloyd (20535 IWM), 19 June 1916.

12   Gilbert, *Somme*, 36.

13   Robin Prior and Trevor Wilson, *The Somme* (New Haven, CT: Yale University Press, 2005).

14   Letter from Helen Bentwich to Norman Bentwich (TWL), 11 September 1916.

15   Gilbert, *Somme*, 37.

16   78th Bge RFA, 17th Division, war diary, June 1916.

17   Letter from Alan Lloyd to Dorothy Lloyd (20535 IWM), 23 June 1916.

18   David Stevenson, *1914–1918: The History of the First World War* (Harmondsworth: Penguin, 2004), 169; Edmonds, *Ops France and Belgium 1916*, vol. I, 300–2 and vol. II, 1.

19   Edmonds, *Ops France and Belgium 1916*, vol. I, 302–3.

20   Letters from Alan Lloyd to Dorothy Lloyd (20535 IWM), 25 and 26 June 1916.

21   Stevenson, *1914–1918*, 169; Edmonds, *Ops France and Belgium 1916*, vol. I, 304–6; Gilbert, *Somme*, 43.

22   Gilbert, *Somme*, 45–6.

23   Edmonds, *Ops France and Belgium 1916*, vol. I, 306–7.

24   William Philpott, *Bloody Victory: The Sacrifice on the Somme* (London: Little, Brown, 2009), 173–5; Martin Gilbert, *The First World War* (London: Weidenfeld & Nicolson, 1994), 258; Stevenson, *1914–18*, 169.

25   Gilbert, *Somme*, 51–4; Philpott, *Bloody Victory*, 175.

26   Andrew Clark, entry for 1 July 1916, quoted in *Echoes of the Great War: The Diary of the Reverend Andrew Clark, 1914–19*, ed. James Munson (Oxford, New York: Oxford University Press, 1985).

27   Stevenson, *1914–18*, 169–70.

28   Philpott, *Bloody Victory*, 175.

29   Letter from Arthur Burke to his brother Reg, July 1916, Private papers of A.P. Burke, Documents.1665, Imperial War Museum.

30   Saul David, *100 Days to Victory: How the Great War Was Fought and Won* (London: Hodder & Stoughton, 2013), 257; Edmonds, *Ops France and Belgium 1916*, vol. II, 1–2.

31   Clark, entry for 2 July 1916, quoted in *Echoes of the Great War*, 139.

32   Clark, entry for 2 July 1916, quoted in *Echoes of the Great War*, 140.

33   Hugo Charteris was killed in April 1916 at the Battle of Katia but confirmation of his death was not received until 3 July 1916.

34 Duff Cooper's diary, entry for 3 July 1916, quoted in *The Duff Cooper Diaries*, ed. John Julius Norwich (1st ed 2005) (London: Phoenix, 2006), 32–3.

35 Letter from Duff Cooper to Diana Manners, 3 July 1916, quoted in *A Durable Fire: The Letters of Duff and Diana Cooper 1913–50*, ed. Artemis Cooper (London: HarperCollins, 1983), 29.

36 Gilbert, *Somme*, 99.

37 Edmonds, *Ops France and Belgium* 1916, vol. II, 20–4; 78th Bge RFA, 17th Division, war diary, July 1916.

38 Letter from Alan Lloyd to Dorothy Lloyd (20535 IWM), 6 July 1916.

39 Gilbert, *Somme*, 101; Edmonds, *Ops France and Belgium* 1916, vol. II, 24; 78th Bge RFA, 17th Division, war diary, July 1916.

40 Gilbert, *Somme*, 103.

41 Letter from Alan Lloyd to Dorothy Lloyd (20535 IWM), 10 July 1916.

42 78th Bge RFA, 17th Division, war diary, 11 July 1916; Gilbert, *Somme*, 105.

43 Gilbert, *Somme*, 112.

44 Gilbert, *Somme*, 112; 78th Bge RFA, 17th Division, war diary, July 1916.

45 Letter from Alan Lloyd to Eric Lloyd (20535 IWM), 21 July 1916.

46 Philpott, *Bloody Victory*, 237; Gilbert, *Somme*, 113.

47 Letter from Alan Lloyd to Dorothy Lloyd (20535 IWM), 20 July 1916.

48 78th Bge RFA, 17th Division, war diary, July 1916.

49 Gilbert, *Somme*, 3, 18.

50 Letter from Helen Bentwich to Norman Bentwich (TWL), 24 July 1916.

51 Clark, entry for 26 July 1916, quoted in *Echoes of the Great War*, 144

52 Clark, entry for 19 July 1916, quoted in *Echoes of the Great War*, 143.

53 Notice of Military Cross (20535 IWM), 27 July 1916.

54 Letter from Alan Lloyd to Dorothy Lloyd (20535 IWM), 29 July 1916.

55 Letter from Alan Lloyd to Dorothy Lloyd (20535 IWM), 1 August 1916.

56 78th Bge RFA, 17th Division, war diary, 1 August 1916.

57 Letter from Alan Lloyd to Dorothy Lloyd (20535 IWM), 3 August 1916.

58 Cooper, entry for 23 August 1916, quoted in *The Duff Cooper Diaries*, 35.

59 Cooper, entry for 18 September 1916, quoted in *The Duff Cooper Diaries*, 37.

60 Letter from Diana Manners to Duff Cooper, 18 September 1916, quoted in *A Durable Fire*, 29–30.

61 Telegram from London War Office to Mrs Lloyd (20535 IWM) – 8 August 1916, received 9.21 a.m.

62 Telegram from Hexham Road to Mrs D. Lloyd (20535 IWM), 8 August, handed in 5.10 p.m., received Budleigh Salterton 6.57 p.m.

63 Letter from Arthur E. Impey to Dorothy Lloyd (20535 IWM), 5 August 1916.

Chapter 15

1　William Philpott, *Bloody Victory: The Sacrifice on the Somme* (London: Little, Brown, 2009), 600; David Stevenson, *1914–1918: The History of the First World War* (Harmondsworth: Penguin, 2004), 166.

2　Martin Gilbert, *The First World War* (London: Weidenfeld & Nicolson, 1994), 299.

3　Hallie Miles, *Untold Tales of Wartime London: A Personal Diary by Hallie Eustace Miles* (London, Cecil Palmer: 1930), undated entry but Autumn 1916.

4　http://www.sciencemuseum.org.uk/broughttolife/people/roehampton. aspx; Stevenson, 1914-1918, p. 551.

5　Letter from Harold Gillies to Dr Lyndon Peer, 14 May 1959, quoted in Reginald Pound, *Gillies, Surgeon Extraordinaire: A Biography* (London: Joseph, 1964), 33; Harold Gillies uncited source, quoted in Pound, *Gillies, Surgeon Extraordinaire*, 39.

6　Dr Andrew Bamji, *The Broken Faces of War* (unpublished draft, 2013), 54.

7　Harold Gillies uncited source, quoted in Pound, *Gillies, Surgeon Extraordinaire*, 38.

8　Pound, *Gillies, Surgeon Extraordinaire*, 36; Bamji, 'The Broken Faces of War', 46.

9　Letter from Reg Evans to Frances Evans, Liddle Collection, Leeds University Special Collections, LIDDLE/WW1/GS/1816 (cited hereafter as LC), 20 April 1916.

10　See Reg's case notes in Harold Gillies, *Plastic Surgery of the Face: Based on Selected Cases of War Injuries of the Face* (London: Frowde, 1920), 100.

11　Letters from Dorothy Lloyd to Gertrude Lloyd, Private papers of Lieutenant A. S. Lloyd MC, Documents.20535, The Imperial War Museum (cited hereafter as 20535 IWM), 25 August and 5 September 1916.

12　Letter from Helen Bentwich to Norman Bentwich, The Women's Library, LSE, 7HBE (cited hereafter as TWL), 15 October 1916.

13　Great Leighs War Memorial: http://www.geograph.org.uk/photo/1368867

14　See editor's note in *Echoes of the Great War: The Diary of the Reverend Andrew Clark, 1914–19*, ed. James Munson (London, New York: Oxford University Press, 1985), 164.

15　Clark, entry for 30 October 1916, quoted in *Echoes of the Great War*, 165.

16　Met Office weather for October 1916: http://www.metoffice.gov.uk/ media/pdf/h/m/Oct1916.pdf

17　Letter from Will Martin to Emily Chitticks in Private papers of W. J. Martin, Documents.2554, The Imperial War Museum (cited hereafter as 2554 IWM), 4 October 1916.

18 1911 Census.

19 Letter from Emily Chitticks to Will Martin (2554 IWM), 5 October 1916.

20 Gillies, *Plastic Surgery*, 82.

21 Letter from Reg Evans to Frances Evans (LC), 16 June 1916.

22 Letter from Helen Bentwich to Norman Bentwich (TWL), 18 October 1916.

23 Letters from Helen Bentwich to Norman Bentwich (TWL), 28 and 30 October 1916.

24 Letter from Reg Evans to Frances Evans (LC), 1 July 1916.

25 Ibid.

26 Reg's case notes in Gillies, *Plastic Surgery*, 100.

27 Letter from Emily Chitticks to Will Martin (2554 IWM), undated but October 1916.

28 Letters from Will Martin to Emily Chitticks (2554 IWM), undated but October 1916 and 11 October 1916.

29 Reg's case notes in Gillies, *Plastic Surgery*, 100.

30 Letter from B. K. Cunningham to Frances Evans (LC), 16 August 1916.

31 Letter from Reg Evans to Frances Evans (LC), 4 September, 1916.

32 Diary of Kate Parry Collins, Elizabeth Crawford's Private Collection (cited hereafter as ECPC), entry for 28 October 1916.

33 Letter from Nurse Oakes to Reg Evans (LC), 25 September, 1916.

34 Letter from Will Martin to Emily Chitticks (2554 IWM), 30 October 1916.

35 Letter from Emily Chitticks to Will Martin (2554 IWM), 31 October 1916.

36 Letters from Will Martin to Emily Chitticks (2554 IWM), undated but November 1916 and 10 November 1916.

37 Letter from Emily Chitticks to Will Martin (2554 IWM), undated but November 1916.

38 Reg Evans's patient notes, in the Archives of The Royal College of Surgeons.

39 Letter from Reg Evans to Frances Evans (LC), 28 October 1916.

40 Letter from Helen Bentwich to Norman Bentwich (TWL), 5 November 1916.

41 Letters from Dorothy Lloyd to Gertrude Lloyd (20535 IWM), 30 September and 4 October 1916.

42 Collins (ECPC), entry for 8 November 1916.

43 Collins (ECPC), entry for 12 November 1916.

44 Letters from Will Martin to Emily Chitticks (2554 IWM), undated but November 1916.

45 Letter from Emily Chitticks to Will Martin (2554 IWM), 11 November 1916.

46 Letter from Reg Evans to Frances Evans (LC), 10 November 1916.

47 Clark, entry for 13 November 1916, quoted in *Echoes of the Great War*, 167.

48 Clark, entry for 16 November 1916, quoted in *Echoes of the Great War*, 167.

49 Gilbert, *The Somme*, 243.

Chapter 16

1   Met Office: http://www.metoffice.gov.uk/media/pdf/7/d/Nov1916.pdf

2   Diary of Kate Parry Collins, Elizabeth Crawford's Private Collection (cited hereafter as ECPC), 19 November 1916.

3   Collins (ECPC), entry for 21 November 1916.

4   Collins (ECPC), entry for 26 November 1916.

5   Andrew Clark, entry for 21 November 1916, quoted in *Echoes of the Great War: The Diary of the Reverend Andrew Clark, 1914–19*, ed. James Munson (Oxford, New York: Oxford University Press, 1985), 169.

6   Clark, entry for 25 November 1916, quoted in *Echoes of the Great War*, 165.

7   W. Miles, *History of the Great War Based on Official Documents: Military Operations France and Belgium 1916* (London: Committee of Imperial Defence, 1925) (cited hereafter as Edmonds, *Ops France and Belgium 1916*), vol. II, 530–3, 553.

8   Edmonds, *Ops France and Belgium 1916*, vol. II, 533.

9   Emily Chitticks' note, Private papers of W. J. Martin, Documents.2554, The Imperial War Museum (cited hereafter as 2554 IWM).

10 Letter from Will Martin to Emily Chitticks (2554 IWM), 23 November 1916.

11 Telegram exchange between Will Martin and Emily Chitticks (2554 IWM), 2 December 1916.

12 Letter from Will Martin to Emily Chitticks (2554 IWM), 3 December 1916.

13 Collins (ECPC), entries for 27 and 30 November 1916.

14 Collins (ECPC), entry for 3 December 1916.

15 Duff Cooper's diary, entry for 3 December 1916, quoted in *The Duff Cooper Diaries*, ed. John Julius Norwich (1st ed 2005) (London: Phoenix, 2006), 40.

16 'Reconstruction: Prime Minister's Decision' in *The Times*, 4 December 1916, 9.

17 Quoted in 'H. H. Asquith and David Lloyd George,' in John Campbell, *Pistols at Dawn: 200 Years of Political Rivalry* (London, Vintage, 2010), 171.

18 Collins (ECPC), entries for 6 and 7 December 1916.

19 Letters from Will Martin to Emily Chitticks (2554 IWM), 7 and 10 December 1916.

20 Note from Commander-in-Chief to Head of Imperial General Staff, 21 November 1916, in Edmonds, *Ops France and Belgium 1916*, vol II., 536.

21 Collins (ECPC), entry for 10 December 1916.

22 Collins (ECPC), entry for 14 December 1916.

23 Clark, entry for 6 December 1916, quoted in *Echoes of the Great War*, 171.

24 Ibid., entry for 11 December 1916.

25 Ibid., entry for 10 December 1916.

26 Ibid., entry for 25 December 1916.

27 Letter from Miss L. P. Adams to Mildred Clark, received 25 December 1916, quoted in *Echoes of the Great War*, 172.

28 Collins (ECPC), entry for 25 December 1916.

29 Letter from John Collins to Kate Parry Collins (ECPC), 25 December 1916.

30 Letter from Will Martin to Emily Chitticks (2554 IWM), 25 December 1916.

31 Letter from Emily Chitticks to Will Martin (2554 IWM), 26 December 1916.

32 Letters from Will Martin to Emily Chitticks (2554 IWM), 28 and 31 December 1916.

Chapter 17

1 Cyril Falls, *History of the Great War Based on Official Documents: Military Operations France and Belgium 1917* (London: Committee of Imperial Defence, 1925) (cited hereafter as Falls, *Ops France and Belgium 1917*), vol. I, 23.

2 Ibid., xxxii.

3 Letter from Reg Evans to Frances Evans, Liddle Collection, Leeds University Special Collections, LIDDLE/WW1/GS/1816 (cited hereafter as LC), 3 January, 1917.

4 L. Margaret Barnett, *British Food Policy During the First World War* (London, Allen and Unwin, 1985), 69.

5 Ibid., 102.

6 Ibid., 105.

7 Andrew Clark, entry for 2 December 1916, quoted in *Echoes of the Great War: The Diary of the Reverend Andrew Clark, 1914–19*, ed. James Munson (Oxford, New York: Oxford University Press, 1985), 170.

8 Barnett, *British Food Policy*, 105.

9 Clark, entry for 20 January 1917, including letter from Mrs Harry Lewin, quoted in *Echoes of the Great War*, 177–8.

10 Barnett, *British Food Policy*, 116.

11 Barnett, *British Food Policy*, 85–6, 106.

12 Hallie Miles, *Untold Tales of Wartime London: A Personal Diary by Hallie Eustace Miles* (London: Cecil Palmer, 1930), entry for February 1917.

13 Miles, entry for February 1917, in *Untold Tales of Wartime London*.

14 Barnett, *British Food Policy*, 118.

15 Letters from Helen Bentwich to Norman Bentwich, The Women's Library, LSE, 7HBE (cited hereafter as TWL), 14 and 17 November 1916.

16 Duff Cooper, entry for 3 January 1917, quoted in *The Duff Cooper Diaries*, ed. John Julius Norwich (1st ed 2005) (London: Phoenix, 2006), 45.

17 Cooper, entry for 17 February 1917, quoted in *The Duff Cooper Diaries*, 48.

18 Ibid., entry for 27 February 1917.

19 Letter from Reg Evans to Frances Evans (LC), 19 January 1917.

20 Letter from Helen Bentwich to Norman Bentwich (TWL), 25 January 1917.

21 Letter from Helen Bentwich to Norman Bentwich (TWL), 5 February 1917.

22 Miles, *Untold Tales of Wartime London*, entry (misdated as) November 1916.

23 Martin Gilbert, *The First World War* (London: Weidenfeld & Nicolson, 1994), 345.

24 Falls, *Ops France and Belgium* 1917, vol. I, 30–1.

25 Ibid., xxxiii.

26 Barnett, *British Food Policy*, 103.

27 Clark, entry for 7 February, quoted in *Echoes of the Great War*, 180.

28 Ibid.

29 Barnett, *British Food Policy*, 116.

30 Leaflet: National Rations 1917 (N.A. MAF 60/52) in Barry Cinchen, *Food Economy, Food Control and Rationing, 1914–20, Compiled using copies of contemporary ephemeral material*, IWM, vol. I, 37.

31 Barnett, *British Food Policy*, 115.

32 Miles, *Untold Tales of Wartime London*, entry for April 1917.

33 Letters from Helen Bentwich to Norman Bentwich (TWL), 10 and 14 February 1917.

34 Letters from Helen Bentwich to Norman Bentwich (TWL), 10 February and 7 March 1917.

35 Clark, entries for 16 and 24 February, quoted in *Echoes of the Great War*, 182, 184.

36 Clark, entry for 16 February, quoted in *Echoes of the Great War*, 182–3.

37 Letter from Helen Bentwich to Norman Bentwich (TWL), 4 April 1917.

38 Reg Evans's patient notes, in the Archives of The Royal College of Surgeons and in Harold Gillies, *Plastic Surgery of the Face: Based on Selected Cases of War Injuries of the Face* (London: Frowde, 1920), 101.

39 Letter from Reg Evans to Frances Evans (LC), 12 March 1917.

40 Clark, entry for 21 April, quoted in *Echoes of the Great War*, 189–90.

41 Falls, *Ops France and Belgium* 1917, vol. I, xxxiv.

Chapter 18

1   Cyril Falls, *History of the Great War Based on Official Documents: Military Operations France and Belgium 1917* (London: Committee of Imperial Defence, 1925) (cited hereafter as Falls, *Ops France and Belgium 1917*), vol. I, 11.

2   Letters from Will Martin to Emily Chitticks, Private papers of W. J. Martin, Documents.2554, The Imperial War Museum (cited hereafter as 2554 IWM), 1 January 1917, undated January 1917 and 12 January 1917.

3   Falls, *Ops France and Belgium* 1917, vol. I, 65.

4   Letter from James Butlin to Basil Burnett-Hall, Private papers of Lieutenant J. H. Butlin, Documents.7915, Imperial War Museum (cited hereafter as 7915 IWM), 13 January 1917.

5   Letter from Will Martin to Emily Chitticks (2554 IWM), 14 January 1917.

6   8th Devonshire Regiment, war diary, WO 95/1655/2, January 1917; Falls, *Ops France and Belgium* 1917, vol. I, 234.

7   Huw Strachan, *The First World War* (London: Simon and Schuster, 2006), 243–4.

8   Falls, *Ops France and Belgium* 1917 vol. I, 66.

9   Letter from Will Martin to Emily Chitticks (2554 IWM), undated but January 1917.

10 8th Devonshire Regiment, war diary, January 1917; C. T. Atkinson, *The Devonshire Regiment, 1914–18* (Exeter: Eland Bros; London: Simpkin, Marshall and Co, 1926) 236; Letter from Will Martin to Emily Chitticks (2554 IWM), undated but January 1917.

11 Letter from Butlin to Burnett-Hall (7915 IWM), 18 February 1917.

12 Diary of Kate Parry Collins, Elizabeth Crawford's Private Collection (cited hereafter as ECPC), entry for 28 February 1917.

13 Letter from Will Martin to Emily Chitticks (2554 IWM), 6 February 1917.

14 8th Devonshire Regiment, war diary, February 1917.

15 Letters from Will Martin to Emily Chitticks (2554 IWM), 17 and 22 February 1917.

16 8th Devonshire Regiment, war diary, February 1917; Falls, *Ops France and Belgium* 1917 vol. I, 96–7.

17 8th Devonshire Regiment, war diary, February 1917; Falls, *Ops France and*

Belgium 1917, vol. I, 96–7; Martin Gilbert, *The First World War* (London: Weidenfeld & Nicolson, 1994), 308.

18   Falls, *Ops France and Belgium* 1917, vol. I, 97.

19   8th Devonshire Regiment, war diary, March 1917; Falls, *Ops France and Belgium* 1917 vol. I, 104.

20   Letters from Will Martin to Emily Chitticks (2554 IWM), 7 and 11 March 1917.

21   Letters from Emily Chitticks to Will Martin (2554 IWM), undated but March 1917.

22   Falls, *Ops France and Belgium* 1917, vol. I, xi.

23   Gilbert, *The First World War*, 314–16.

24   Letter from Butlin to Burnett-Hall (7915 IWM), 21 March 1917.

25   Cyril Falls, *History of the Great War Based on Official Documents: Military Operations France and Belgium* 1917 (vol. 1), pp.146-165; War diary of the 8th Devonshire Regiment, March 1917, WO 95/1655/2

26   Emily Chitticks, letter to Will Martin, 26th March 1917, (2554 IWM).

27   Falls, *Ops France and Belgium* 1917, vol. I, 15–17.

28   Ibid.

29   Jacqueline Jenkinson, 'All in the Same Uniform? The Participation of Black Colonial Residents in the British Armed Forces in the First World War', The Journal of Imperial and Commonwealth History, vol. 40, 2 (June 2012): 207–30.

30   Ibid.

31   Letter from Arthur Roberts to his aunt Lillah Armstrong, Morag Miller's Private Collection (cited hereafter as MMPC), March 1917.

32   Letter from Emily Chitticks to Will Martin (2554 IWM), 28 and 29 March 1917.

33   Collins (ECPC), entry for 6 April 1917.

34   Collins (ECPC), entry for 8 April 1917.

35   Falls, *Ops France and Belgium* 1917, vol. I, 174.

36   Gilbert, *The First World War*, 320.

37   C. H. Dudley Ward, *History of the Dorsetshire Regiment 1914–19* (Dorsetshire: Ling, 1932), 128.

38   Letter from Butlin to Burnett-Hall (7915 IWM), 9 April 1917.

39   Dudley Ward, *History of the Dorsetshire Regiment*, 128; Gilbert, *The First World War*, 320–1.

40   Gilbert, *The First World War*, 321–2; Dudley Ward, *History of the Dorsetshire Regiment*, 128; Falls, *Ops France and Belgium* 1917, vol. I, 268–9.

41   Dudley Ward, *History of the Dorsetshire Regiment*, 128–9; Falls, *Ops France and Belgium* 1917 vol. I, 282.

42   Dudley Ward, *History of the Dorsetshire Regiment*, 130.

43   Letter from Butlin to Burnett-Hall (7915 IWM), 16 April 1917.

44 Strachan, *The First World War*, 242; Gilbert, *The First World War*, 322–5; Falls, *Ops France and Belgium* 1917, vol. I, 20.
45 Collins (ECPC), entry for 20 April 1917.
46 Collins (ECPC), entry for 21 April 1917.
47 Letter from Butlin to Burnett-Hall (7915 IWM), 19 April 1917.
48 Gilbert, *The First World War*, 322–5.
49 Collins (ECPC), entry for 24 April 1917.
50 Collins (ECPC), entry for 25 April 1917.
51 Spencer C. Tucker (ed.), *World War One: Encyclopedia* (Santa Barbara: ABC-CLIO, 2005), vol. I, 131; The War Office, *Statistics of the Military Effort of the British Empire During the Great War* (London: HMSO, 1922).
52 Letter from I. S. Huxley to Emily Chitticks (2554 IWM), 30 March 1917.
53 Letter from C. Caleb to Emily Chitticks (2554 IWM), 30 March 1917.
54 Letter from Butlin to Burnett-Hall (7915 IWM), 5 May 1917.
55 Collins (ECPC), entry for 25 July 1917.
56 Collins (ECPC), entry for 23 July 1917.
57 Transcribed in Collins (ECPC), diary for 1917.
58 Copy of note in Emily Chitticks' Bible (2554 IWM).

Chapter 19

1 Diary of Arthur Roberts, Morag Miller's Private Collection (cited hereafter as MMPC), entry for 21 May 1917.
2 Martin Gilbert, *The First World War* (London: Weidenfeld & Nicolson, 1994), 326–33; Huw Strachan, *The First World War* (London: Simon and Schuster, 2006), 242.
3 Gilbert, *The First World War*, 333–5; Cyril Falls, *History of the Great War Based on Official Documents: Military Operations France and Belgium 1917* (London: Committee of Imperial Defence, 1925) (cited hereafter as Falls, *Ops France and Belgium 1917*), vol. II, viii.
4 Falls, *Ops France and Belgium* 1917, vol. II, viii; 21–2.
5 Duff Cooper's diary, entry for 17 May 1917, quoted in *The Duff Cooper Diaries*, ed. John Julius Norwich (1st ed 2005) (London: Phoenix, 2006), 53.
6 Cooper, entry for 20 May 1917, quoted in *The Duff Cooper Diaries*, 53.
7 Roberts (MMPC), entry for 23 May 1917.
8 Roberts (MMPC), entry for 1 June 1917.
9 Lyn Macdonald, *They Called It Passchendaele* (Harmondsworth: Penguin, 1993), 11.
10 Falls, *Ops France and Belgium 1917*, vol. II, 1–2.
11 Falls, *Ops France and Belgium 1917*, vol. II, 26, 99.

12   Roberts (MMPC), entry for 4 June 1917.

13   Gilbert, *The First World War*, 336; Falls, *Ops France and Belgium 1917*, vol. II, iii; Macdonald, *They Called It Passchendaele*, 33.

14   Cooper, entry for 22 June 1917, quoted in *The Duff Cooper Diaries*, 54.

15   Roberts (MMPC), description of the 9 June 1917, in his 'Reminiscences'.

16   Roberts (MMPC), description of 14 June 1917, in his 'Reminiscences'.

17   Cooper, entry for 5 July 1917, quoted in *The Duff Cooper Diaries*, 55.

18   Duff Cooper, *Old Men Forget* (London: Hart-Davis 1953), 63–64.

19   Cooper, entry for 6 July 1917, quoted in *The Duff Cooper Diaries*, 55.

20   *The 30th Division in France and Flanders*, Compiled from official sources by the Commonwealth War Graves Commission, July 1917.

21   Falls, *Ops France and Belgium 1917*, vol. II, 147.

22   Macdonald, *They Called It Passchendaele*, 88, 91; Falls, *Ops France and Belgium 1917*, vol. II, 104–5, 134–9.

23   Cooper, entry for 7 July 1917, quoted in *The Duff Cooper Diaries*, 56.

24   Falls, *Ops France and Belgium 1917*, vol. II, 124, 105–6, xiii; Macdonald, *They Called It Passchendaele*, 86.

25   Macdonald, *They Called It Passchendaele*, 97; Falls, *Ops France and Belgium 1917*, vol. II, 147.

26   Roberts (MMPC), entry for 28–9 July 1917.

27   Roberts (MMPC), description of 29–30 July 1917, in his 'Reminiscences'.

28   Roberts (MMPC), entry for 30 July 1917.

29   Falls, *Ops France and Belgium 1917*, vol. II, 148–9; Macdonald, *They Called It Passchendaele*, 101.

30   Falls, *Ops France and Belgium 1917*, vol. II, 149–50.

31   Macdonald, *They Called It Passchendaele*, 123–4.

32   Roberts (MMPC), entry for 31 July 1917.

33   Ibid., entry for 1 August 1917.

34   Ibid., entry for 2 August 1917.

35   Falls, *Ops France and Belgium 1917*, vol. II, 178.

36   Macdonald, *They Called It Passchendaele*, 133; see *The Times* 1–4 August 1917.

37   Macdonald, *They Called It Passchendaele*, 147–53

38   *The 30th Division in France and Flanders*, Compiled from official sources by the Commonwealth War Graves Commission, August 1917.

39   Roberts (MMPC), description of 1 September 1917 in his 'Reminiscences'.

40   Macdonald, *They Called It Passchendaele*, 173.

41   Roberts (MMPC), description of 1 September 1917 in his 'Reminiscences'.

42   Roberts (MMPC), entry for 2 September 1917.

43   Macdonald, *They Called It Passchendaele*, 173.

44   Diary of Kate Parry Collins, Elizabeth Crawford's Private Collection (cited hereafter as ECPC), entry for 12 September 1917.

45   Collins (ECPC), entries for 14 and 16 September 1917.

46 Macdonald, *They Called it Passchendaele*, 177, 180.

47 Collins (ECPC), entry for 21 September 1917.

48 *The 30th Division in France and Flanders*, Compiled from official sources by the Commonwealth War Graves Commission, September–October 1917; Roberts (MMPC), entries for 29 September–7 October 1917.

49 Roberts (MMPC), entry for 8 October 1917.

50 *The 30th Division in France and Flanders*, Compiled from official sources by the Commonwealth War Graves Commission, October 1917.

51 Roberts (MMPC), entry for 12 October 1917.

52 Roberts (MMPC), entry for 15 October 1917.

53 Haig memo of 8 October, and meeting with Pétain 18 October, cited in J. E. Edmonds, *History of the Great War Based on Official Documents: Military Operations France and Belgium 1918* (London: Committee of Imperial Defence, 1925)(cited hereafter as *Ops France and Belgium 1918*), vol. I, 12, 21–23.

54 Cooper, entry for 1 November 1917, quoted in *The Duff Cooper Diaries*, 60.

55 Macdonald, *They Called It Passchendaele*, 223–8.

56 Roberts (MMPC), entry for 28 October, 1917.

57 Roberts (MMPC), entries for 30 and 31 October 1917.

58 Collins (ECPC), entry for 7 November 1917.

59 Collins (ECPC), entry for 7 November 1917.

60 Macdonald, *They Called It Passchendaele*, 241.

61 Letter from Charles Ward to Andrew Clark, received 3 November, 1917, quoted in *Echoes of the Great War: The Diary of the Reverend Andrew Clark, 1914–19*, ed. James Munson (Oxford, New York: Oxford University Press, 1985), 217.

62 Edmonds, *Ops France and Belgium* 1918, vol. I, 24–6.

63 Letter from Major R.F. Adam, 30th November, 1917, in Andrew's Clark's papers.

64 Edmonds, *Ops France and Belgium* 1918, vol. I, 26–8.

65 Cooper, entry for 22 November 1917, quoted in *The Duff Cooper Diaries*, 60.

66 Cooper, entry for 23 November 1917, quoted in *The Duff Cooper Diaries*, 60–1.

Chapter 20

1 Eighty-seven per cent of British soldiers diagnosed with shell shock were back on frontline duties within a month. David Stevenson, *1914–1918: The History of the First World War* (Harmondsworth: Penguin, 2004), 209.

2 Edgar Jones, Adam Thomas and Stephen Ironside, 'Shell Shock: An

Outcome Study of a First World War "PIE" Unit', in *Psychological Medicine* 2007, 37.

3   Letter from James Butlin to Basil Burnett-Hall, Private papers of Lieutenant J. H. Butlin, Documents.7915, Imperial War Museum (cited hereafter as 7915 IWM), 11 May 1917.

4   Letter from Helen Bentwich to Norman Bentwich, The Women's Library, LSE, 7HBE (cited hereafter as TWL), 30 April 1917.

5   Helen Bentwich, *If I Forget Thee: Some Chapters of Autobiography 1912–1920* (London: Elek, 1973), 105.

6   http://www.iwm.org.uk/history/the-womens-land-army-in-pictures

7   Martin Gilbert, *The First World War* (London: Weidenfeld & Nicolson, 2004), 329.

8   Barry Cinchen, *Food Economy, Food Control and Rationing, 1914–20, Compiled using copies of contemporary ephemeral material*, IWM, vol. 1, 44; L. Margaret Barnett, *British Food Policy During the First World War* ((London, Allen and Unwin, 1985), 115.

9   Andrew Clark, entry for 28 May 1917, quoted in *Echoes of the Great War: The Diary of the Reverend Andrew Clark, 1914–19*, ed. James Munson (Oxford, New York: Oxford University Press, 1985), 194.

10   Clark, entry for 21 June 1917, quoted in *Echoes of the Great War*, 198.

11   Letter from Clark to William Redman, 21 May 1917, quoted in *Echoes of the Great War*, 192.

12   Barnett, *British Food Policy*, 129–30.

13   Barnett, *British Food Policy*, 151.

14   Hallie Miles, *Untold Tales of Wartime London: A Personal Diary by Hallie Eustace Miles* (London: Cecil Palmer, 1930), undated entry but must be May 1917.

15   Barnett, *British Food Policy*, 121, 151.

16   Letter from Helen Bentwich to Caroline Franklin (TWL), 16 May 1917.

17   Letter from Helen Bentwich to Caroline Franklin (TWL), 20 May 1917.

18   http://www.iwm.org.uk/history/the-womens-land-army-in-pictures

19   Clark, entries for 7 and 9 June 1917, quoted in *Echoes of the Great War*, 195, 196.

20   Clark, entry for 13 June 1917, quoted in *Echoes of the Great War*, 196–7.

21   Thomas Fegan, *The Baby Killers: German Air Raids on Britain in the First World War* (Barnsley: Pen and Sword Books, 2002), 51–2; Captain Joseph Morris *The German Air Raids on Great Britain 1914–18* (1st edn 1925) (Stroud: Nonsuch Publishing, 2007), 149; Cyril Falls, *History of the Great War Based on Official Documents: Military Operations France and Belgium 1917* (London: Committee of Imperial Defence, 1925) (cited hereafter as Falls, *Ops France and Belgium 1917*), vol. II, 134–5.

22   Miles, *Untold Tales of Wartime London*, entry for 24 June 1917.

23   Letter from Helen Bentwich to Norman Bentwich (TWL), 10 June 1917.

24   Ibid., 12 June, 1917.

25   Ibid., 3 June 1917.

26   Letter from Butlin to Burnett-Hall (7915 IWM), 26 June 1917.

27   Clark, entry for 21 June and 3 August 1917, quoted in *Echoes of the Great War*, 198, 205.

28   Barnett, *British Food Policy*, 126.

29   Clark, entry for 14 August 1917, quoted in *Echoes of the Great War*, 206.

30   Siegfried Sassoon, statement read out in parliament, 30 July 1917, http://en.wikisource.org/wiki/File:Sasssoon-againstwar-letter.jpg

31   Letter from Helen Bentwich to Norman Bentwich (TWL), 2 July 1917.

32   Miles, *Untold Tales of Wartime London*, undated but summer 1917.

33   Barnett, *British Food Policy*, 134–141.

34   Barnett, *British Food Policy*, 142.

35   Letter from Helen Bentwich to Norman Bentwich (TWL), 4 December 1917.

36   Barnett, *British Food Policy*, 143–4.

37   Ibid.

38   Clark, entry for 17 December 1917, quoted in *Echoes of the Great War*, 223.

39   Miles, *Untold Tales of Wartime London*, 29 December 1917.

40   W. H. Rivers, 'Repression of the War Experience', speech to the Royal Society of Medicine, 4 December 1917, published in *The Lancet* 2nd Feb 1918.

41   Barnett, *British Food Policy*, 144.

Chapter 21

1   *The Times*, 'First Day of the Sales: Fewer Buyers and More Money', 1 January 1918, 3; Duff Cooper's diary, entries for 29 December 1917 and 1 January 1918, quoted in *The Duff Cooper Diaries*, ed. John Julius Norwich (1st ed 2005) (London: Phoenix, 2006), 63.

2   Cooper, entry for 29 December 1917, quoted in *The Duff Cooper Diaries*, 63.

3   Asquith's New Year's Day message: 'A Message to the Nation', quoted in *The Times*, 1 January 1918, 7.

4   Andrew Clark, entry for 11 January 1918, quoted in *Echoes of the Great War: The Diary of the Reverend Andrew Clark, 1914–19*, ed. James Munson (Oxford, New York: Oxford University Press, 1985), 225.

5   Reuters Telegram, 29 December 1917, printed in *The Mail* (Adelaide), 29 December 1917, http://trove.nla.gov.au/ndp/del/article/64044765; L. Margaret Barnett, *British Food Policy During the First World War* (London, Allen and Unwin, 143, 146–7.

6   Cooper, entry for 3 January 1918, quoted in *The Duff Cooper Diaries*, 63.

7   Cooper, entry for 4 January 1918, quoted in *The Duff Cooper Diaries*, 63.

8   Letter from Duff Cooper to Diana Manners, 4 January 1918, quoted in *A Durable Fire: The Letters of Duff and Diana Cooper 1913–50*, ed. Artemis Cooper *(*1st ed 1983) (London, Hamish Hamilton 1985), 42–43.

9   Letter from Manners to Cooper, 5 January 1918, quoted in *A Durable Fire*, 43–44.

10 Cooper, entry for 8 January 1918, quoted in *The Duff Cooper Diaries*, 64.

11 Hallie Miles, *Untold Tales of Wartime London: A Personal Diary by Hallie Eustace Miles* (London: Cecil Palmer, 1930), entry for 27 January and undated but January/February, 1918.

12 Ibid.

13 Barnett, *British Food Policy*, 148.

14 Clark, entry for 25 January 1918, quoted in *Echoes of the Great War*, 225–6.

15 Clark, entry for 26 January 1918, quoted in *Echoes of the Great War*, 226.

16 Lord Rhondda, speech on 20 January 1918 at the Aldwych Club, quoted in *The West Australian*, 21 January 1918, http://trove.nla.gov.au/ndp/del/page/2807911

17 Barnett, *British Food Policy*, 151–3; See also *The Times*, 18 January 1918, 3.

18 Barry Cinchen, *Food Economy, Food Control and Rationing, 1914–20. Compiled using copies of contemporary ephemeral material, vol. I,* (Imperial War Museum), 88.

19 Miles, diary entry for 27 January and undated but January/February 1918.

20 Register for 1914: 8,000,000 parliamentary voters; new register: 18,300,000. Quoted in *The Times*, 11 February 1918, 3.

21 Ibid.

22 Diary of Kate Parry Collins, Elizabeth Crawford's Private Collection (cited hereafter as ECPC), entry for 7 February 1918.

23 Women's Land Army Documents, Documents.8783, Imperial War Museum (cited hereafter as 8783.IWM)

24 Women's Land Army Handbook, (8783.IWM.)

25 Letter from Helen Bentwich to Norman Bentwich, The Women's Library, LSE, 7HBE (cited hereafter as TWL), undated but summer 1918.

26 Letter from Helen Bentwich to Norman Bentwich (TWL), March 1918.

27 Cooper, entry for 22 March 1918, quoted in *The Duff Cooper Diaries*, 66–7.

28 Letter from Helen Bentwich to Norman Bentwich (TWL), 22 March 1918.

29 Ibid.

30 Clark, entry for 24 March 1918, quoted in *Echoes of the Great War*, 230.

31 David Stevenson, *1914–18: The History of the First World War* (Harmondsworth: Penguin, 2004), 408–9; J. E. Edmonds, *History of the Great War Based on Official Documents: Military Operations France and Belgium 1918* (London: Committee of Imperial Defence, 1925) (cited hereafter as Edmonds, *Ops France and Belgium 1918*), vol. II (March–April), 461, 471.

32   Official war news summary, 24 March 1918, stuck into Clark's diary, quoted in *Echoes of the Great War*, 230.

33   Stevenson, *1914–18*, 409.

34   Letter from Helen Bentwich to Norman Bentwich (TWL), 24 March 1918.

35   Cooper, entry for 26 March 1918, quoted in *The Duff Cooper Diaries*, 67.

36   Cooper, entry for 28 March 1918, quoted in *The Duff Cooper Diaries*, 67.

37   Cooper, entry for 6 April 1918, quoted in *The Duff Cooper Diaries*, 67.

38   Letter from James Butlin to Basil Burnett Hall, in Private papers of Lieutenant J. H. Butlin, Documents.7915, Imperial War Museum (cited hereafter as 7915 IWM), 29 March 1918.

39   'Women War Workers: Land Army Procession', *The Times*, 22 April 1918, 4.

40   Letter from Helen Bentwich to Norman Bentwich (TWL), 21 April 1918.

41   Ibid.

42   Cooper entry for 27 April 1918, quoted in *The Duff Cooper Diaries*, 69.

43   Ibid.

44   Diana Cooper, *The Rainbow Comes and Goes* (1st edn. 1958), (London: Century, 1984), 162.

45   Letter from Cooper to Manners, 28 April 1918, quoted in *A Durable Fire*.

Chapter 22

1   Duff Cooper's diary, entry for 28 April 1918, quoted in *The Duff Cooper Diaries*, ed. John Julius Norwich (London: Phoenix, 2006), 70.

2   David Stevenson, *1914–18: The History of the First World War* (Harmondsworth: Penguin, 2004), 409–12.

3   Ibid., 412–13.

4   Special Order of the Day, by Field Marshall Sir Douglas Haig, 11 April 1918.

5   *The Times*, Monday 29 April, 8, 9.

6   Stevenson, *1914–18*, 413–14.

7   *The Times*, Tuesday 30 April, 6.

8   Letter from Diana Manners to Duff Cooper, 30 April 1918, quoted in *A Durable Fire: The Letters of Duff and Diana Cooper 1913–50*, ed. Artemis Cooper (1st edn. 1983) (London, Hamish Hamilton 1985), 50-51.

9   Cooper, entry for 6 May 1918, quoted in *The Duff Cooper Diaries*, 70.

10   Diana Cooper, *The Rainbow Comes and Goes* (1st edn. 1958), (London: Century, 1984), 164.

11   Letter from Manners to Cooper, 9 May 1918, quoted in *A Durable Fire*.

12   Private papers T. C. Poole, Documents.4352, The Imperial War Museum.

13   See Malcolm Brown, *The Imperial War Museum Book of 1918: Year of Victory*

(London: Sidgwick & Jackson, 1998), xxv.

14   Private papers of E. J. Poole, Documents.4351, The Imperial War Museum (cited hereafter as 4351 IWM), letter from Ted Poole to Dolly Poole, 14 May 1918.

15   Letter from Ted Poole to Thomas Poole (4351 IWM), 28 May 1918.

16   Ibid.

17   Letter from Cooper to Manners, 21 May 1918, quoted in *A Durable Fire*.

18   3rd battalion Grenadier Guards, war diary, May 1918, WO 95/1219/1.

19   Cooper, entry for 21 May 1918, quoted in *The Duff Cooper Diaries*, 70–1.

20   3rd battalion Grenadier Guards, war diary, May 1918.

21   Letter from Manners to Cooper, 23 May 1918, quoted in *A Durable Fire*.

22   Letter from Manners to Cooper, 24 May 1918, quoted in *A Durable Fire*.

23   Diary of Kate Parry Collins, Elizabeth Crawford's Private Collection (cited hereafter as ECPC), entry for 24 May 1918.

24   Collins (ECPC), entry for 25 May 1918.

25   Stevenson, *1914–18*, 416–18.

26   Letter from Cooper to Manners, 28 May 1918, quoted in *A Durable Fire*.

27   Cooper, entry for 21 May 1918, quoted in *The Duff Cooper Diaries*, 70–1.

28   Letter from Cooper to Manners, 2 June 1918, quoted in *A Durable Fire*.

29   See Cooper, *The Rainbow*; Philip Ziegler, *Diana Cooper* (Harmondsworth:Penguin 1983).

30   Stevenson, *1914–18*, 418.

31   Letter from Ted Poole to Thomas Poole (4351 IWM), 18 June 1918.

32   Letter from Manners to Cooper, 3 June 1918, quoted in *A Durable Fire*.

33   3rd battalion Grenadier Guards, war diary, June 1918.

34   Letter from Cooper to Manners, 8 June 1918, quoted in *A Durable Fire*.

35   Stevenson, *1914–18*, 418–19; J. E. Edmonds, *History of the Great War Based on Official Documents: Military Operations France and Belgium 1918* (London: Committee of Imperial Defence, 1925) (cited hereafter as Edmonds, *Ops France and Belgium 1918*), vol. III (May–July), v.

36   Stevenson, *1914–18*, 418–420.

37   Cooper, entry for 4 July 1918, quoted in *The Duff Cooper Diaries*, 72.

38   Letter from Cooper to Manners, 4 July 1918, quoted in *A Durable Fire*, 79–81.

39   3rd battalion Grenadier Guards, war diary, July 1918.

40   Letter from Ted Poole to Thomas Poole (4351 IWM), 5 July 1918.

41   Letter from Ted Poole to Thomas Poole (4351 IWM), 18 July 1918.

42   Letter from Manners to Cooper, 8 July 1918, quoted in *A Durable Fire*, 81–82.

43   Cooper, entry for 17 July 1918, quoted in *The Duff Cooper Diaries*, 73.

44   Stevenson, *1914–18*, 423.

45   Cooper, entry for 20 July 1918, quoted in *The Duff Cooper Diaries*, 73.

46 Letter from Cooper to Manners, 21 July 1918, quoted in *A Durable Fire*, 89.

47 Letter from Ted Poole to Dolly Poole (4351 IWM), 6 August 1918.

48 Letter from Ted Poole to Thomas Poole (4351 IWM), 4 August 1918.

49 3rd battalion Grenadier Guards, war diary, July 1918.

50 Letter from Cooper to Manners, 23 July 1918, quoted in *A Durable Fire*, 89–90.

51 3rd battalion Grenadier Guards, war diary, July 1918.

52 Stevenson, *1914–18*, 418–19; Edmonds, *Ops France and Belgium* 1918, vol. III, 318; Ibid., vol. V, 577.

53 Ibid., vol. III (May–July), 313–19.

54 Letter from Cooper to Manners, 26 July 1918, quoted in *A Durable Fire*.

55 Stevenson, *1914–18*, 423–4; Edmonds, *Ops France and Belgium* 1918, vol. III (May–July), 320.

56 Collins (ECPC), entry for 11 August 1918.

Chapter 23

1 Andrew Clark, entry for 27 July 1918, quoted in *Echoes of the Great War: The Diary of the Reverend Andrew Clark, 1914–19*, ed. James Munson (Oxford, New York: Oxford University Press, 1985), 243.

2 Clark, entry for 20 July 1918, 243.

3 'Hold Fast: PM's Message to the Empire' quoted in *The Times*, 6 August 1918, 5.

4 J. E. Edmonds, *History of the Great War Based on Official Documents: Military Operations France and Belgium 1918* (London: Committee of Imperial Defence, 1925) (cited hereafter as Edmonds, *Ops France and Belgium 1918*), vol. IV, 30–1.

5 Duff Cooper, entry for 8 August 1918, quoted in *The Duff Cooper Diaries*, ed. John Julius Norwich (first edn. 2005) (London: Phoenix, 2006), 74–5.

6 Ibid.

7 Lt. Col. The Right Hon. Sir Frederick Ponsonby, *The Grenadier Guards in the Great War of 1914–18* (London: Macmillan, 1920), 94; 3rd battalion Grenadier Guards, war diary, August 1918, WO 95/1219/1; Cooper, entry for 10 August 1918, quoted in *The Duff Cooper Diaries*, 75.

8 Cooper, entry for 11 August 1918, quoted in *The Duff Cooper Diaries*, 75–77.

9 Edmonds, *Ops France and Belgium 1918*, vol. IV, 151–2.

10 Christopher Howse, 'Shrines Built While the First World War Still Went On', in *The Telegraph*, 19 June 2009.

11 Clark, entry for 17 August 1918, quoted in *Echoes of the Great War*, 245–6.

12 Clark, entry for 8 August 1918, quoted in *Echoes of the Great War*, 244–5.

13   David Stevenson, *1914–18: The History of the First World War* (Harmondsworth: Penguin, 2004), 427; Edmonds, *Ops France and Belgium 1918*, vol. IV, 153–73.

14   Stevenson, *1914–18*, 428; Edmonds, *Ops France and Belgium 1918*, vol. IV, 179–81; Ponsonby, *The Grenadier Guards*, 94–5.

15   Letter from Duff Cooper to Diana Manners, 20th Aug 1918 quoted in *A Durable Fire: The Letters of Duff and Diana Cooper 1913–50*, ed. Artemis Cooper, (1st edn. 1983) (London, Hamish Hamilton 1985), 99.

16   Cooper, entry for 20th Aug 1918, quoted in *The Duff Cooper Diaries*, 75.

17   Ponsonby, *The Grenadier Guards*, 95–6.

18   Cooper, entry for 20 August 1918, quoted in *The Duff Cooper Diaries*, 75–7.

19   Ponsonby, *The Grenadier Guards*, 96–7; Edmonds, *Ops France and Belgium 1918*, vol. IV, 575.

20   Cooper, entry for 20 August 1918, quoted in *The Duff Cooper Diaries*, 75–7.

21   Ibid.

22   Ponsonby, *The Grenadier Guards*, 100; Cooper, entry for 20 August 1918, quoted in *The Duff Cooper Diaries*, 75–7.

23   Cooper, entry for 22 August 1918, quoted in *The Duff Cooper Diaries*, 77–8.

24   Edmonds, *Ops France and Belgium 1918*, vol. IV, 211–22.

25   Cooper, entry for 22 August 1918, quoted in *The Duff Cooper Diaries*, 77–8.

26   Edmonds, *Ops France and Belgium 1918*, vol. IV, 181.

27   Private papers of E. J. Poole, Documents.4351, The Imperial War Museum (cited hereafter as 4351 IWM), letter from Ted Poole to Thomas Poole, 31 August 1918.

28   Met Office weather summary for August 1918: http://www.metoffice.gov.uk/media/pdf/g/o/Aug1918.pdf; Clark, entries for 8 and 25 August 1918, quoted in *Echoes of the Great War*, 244–5, 247.

29   Clark, entry for 12 September 1918, quoted in *Echoes of the Great War*, 248–9.

30   Clark, entry for 16 September 1918, quoted in *Echoes of the Great War*, 249.

31   Hallie Miles, *Untold Tales of Wartime London: A Personal Diary by Hallie Eustace Miles* (London: Cecil Palmer, 1930), undated diary entry but August/September 1918.

32   Miles, *Untold Tales of Wartime London*, undated diary entry but August/September 1918.

33   Major W.E. Grey, *The 2nd City of London Regiment (Royal Fusiliers) in the Great War* (1914–19) (London: Naval and Military Press, 1929), 381.

34   Letter from Ted Poole to Thomas Poole (4351 IWM), 25 September 1918.

35   3rd battalion Grenadier Guards, war diary, September 1918.

36   Edmonds, *Ops France and Belgium 1918*, vol. IV, 418–9.

37   Cooper, entry for 14 August 1918, quoted in *The Duff Cooper Diaries*, 80.

38   3rd battalion Grenadier Guards, war diary, September 1918; Ponsonby, *The Grenadier Guards*, 131.

39 Cooper, entry for 25 September 1918, quoted in *The Duff Cooper Diaries*, 80.

40 3rd battalion Grenadier Guards, war diary, September 1918; Ponsonby, *The Grenadier Guards*, 133–4.

41 Cooper, entry for 26 September 1918, quoted in *The Duff Cooper Diaries*, 81.

42 Malcolm Brown, *The Imperial War Museum Book of 1918: Year of Victory* (London: Sidgwick & Jackson, 1998), 251; Edmonds, *Ops France and Belgium 1918*, vol. V, viii–v.

43 Grey, *The 2nd City of London Regiment*, 381–4.

44 3rd battalion Grenadier Guards, war diary, September 1918; Ponsonby, *The Grenadier Guards*, 134.

45 Cooper, entry for 27 September 1918, quoted in *The Duff Cooper Diaries*, 81.

46 Grey, *The 2nd City of London Regiment*, 384–7.

47 Cooper, entry for 27 September 1918, quoted in *The Duff Cooper Diaries*, 81.

48 Grey, *The 2nd City of London Regiment*, 386–8.

49 Stevenson, *1914–18*, 468–9; Grey, *The 2nd City of London Regiment*, 390.

50 3rd battalion Grenadier Guards, war diary, October 1918.

51 Cooper, entry for 7 October 1918, quoted in *The Duff Cooper Diaries*, 82.

52 Stevenson, *1914–18*, 471–7.

53 Stevenson, *1914–18*, 472.

54 Clark, entries for 3, 6 and 10 October 1918, quoted in *Echoes of the Great War*, 251–2.

55 Clark, entry for 12 October 1918, quoted in *Echoes of the Great War*, 253.

56 Grey, *The 2nd City of London Regiment*, 388–90; Stevenson, *1914–18*, 390–7.

57 Miles, *Untold Tales of Wartime London*, entry for 20 October 1918.

58 Stevenson, *1914–18*, 472–3.

59 Stevenson, *1914–18*, 472–5.

60 3rd battalion Grenadier Guards, war diary, October 1918.

61 Cooper, entry for 22 October 1918, quoted in *The Duff Cooper Diaries*, 84.

62 Miles, *Untold Tales of Wartime London*, entry for 20 October 1918.

63 Stevenson, *1914–18*, 474.

64 Miles, *Untold Tales of Wartime London*, entry for 15 September 1918.

65 Stevenson, *1914–18*, 475–85.

66 Cooper, entry for 22 October 1918, quoted in *The Duff Cooper Diaries*, 85.

67 Private papers of E. J. Poole (4351 IWM).

68 Stevenson, *1914–18*, 481.

69 Private papers of E. J. Poole (4351 IWM).

Chapter 24

1   'Influenza Mystery' in *The Times*, 5 November 1918, 3; Helen Bentwich,
    If I Forget Thee: Some Chapters of Autobiography 1912–1920 (London: Elek,
    1973), 150–1.

2   *The Times*, 5 November 1918, 6, 7.

3   Letter from Helen Bentwich to Norman Bentwich, The Women's Library,
    LSE, 7HBE (cited hereafter as TWL), 5 November 1918.

4   Andrew Clark, entry for 5 November 1918, quoted in *Echoes of the Great
    War: The Diary of the Reverend Andrew Clark, 1914–19*, ed. James Munson
    (Oxford, New York: Oxford University Press), 256.

5   Malcolm Brown, *The Imperial War Museum Book of 1918: Year of Victory*
    (London: Sidgwick & Jackson, 1998), 284.

6   Clark, entry for 8 November 1918, quoted in *Echoes of the Great War*, 257.

7   Brown, *The Imperial War Museum Book of 1918*, 284.

8   Duff Cooper, entry for 9 November 1918, quoted in *The Duff Cooper
    Diaries*, ed. John Julius Norwich (1st ed 2005) (London: Phoenix, 2006),
    85.

9   Ibid.

10 Letter from Helen Bentwich to Norman Bentwich (TWL), 9 November
    1918.

11 Hallie Miles, *Untold Tales of Wartime London: A Personal Diary by Hallie
    Eustace Miles* (London: Cecil Palmer, 1930), undated entry but November
    1918.

12 Clark, entry for 10 November 1918, quoted in *Echoes of the Great War*, 257.

13 'Hush Before Dawn', *The Times*, 11 November 1918, 6.

14 Clark, entry for 10 November 1918, quoted in *Echoes of the Great War*, 257.

15 Ibid., 258.

16 Clark, entry for 11 November 1918, quoted in *Echoes of the Great War*, 258.

17 Miles, *Untold Tales of Wartime London*, entry for 11 November 1918.

18 Ibid.

19 *The Times*, 12 November 1918, 5, 9, 10.

20 Diary of Kate Parry Collins, Elizabeth Crawford's Private Collection
    (cited hereafter as ECPC), entry for 11 November 1918.

21 Helen Bentwich, *If I Forget Thee*, 150–1.

22 Cooper, entry for 11 November 1918, quoted in *The Duff Cooper Diaries*,
    85.

23 Miles, *Untold Tales of Wartime London*, entry for 11 November 1918.

24 *The Times*, 12 November 1918, 5, 9, 10.

25 Clark, entry for 11 November 1918, quoted in *Echoes of the Great War*,
    258–9.

26 Ibid.

27 *The Times*, 12 November 1918, 5, 9, 10.

28 Miles, *Untold Tales of Wartime London*, entry for 14 November 1918.

29 Cooper, entry for 11 November 1918, quoted in *The Duff Cooper Diaries*, 85.

30 Cooper, entry for 12 November 1918, quoted in *The Duff Cooper Diaries*, 86; Duff Cooper, *Old Men Forget* (London: Hart-Davis, 1953), 92.

31 Clark, entry for 11 November 1918, quoted in *Echoes of the Great War*, 258–9.

32 Clark, entries for 12 and 15 November 1918, quoted in *Echoes of the Great War*, 259–60, 262.

33 Miles, *Untold Tales of Wartime London*, entry for 14 November 1918.

34 Ibid.

35 Dennis Judd, *George VI* (London: I. B. Tauris, 2012), 72.

36 Letter from Helen Bentwich to Norman Bentwich (TWL), undated but November 1918.

37 Collins (ECPC), entry for 17 November 1918.

38 Collins (ECPC), entry for 22 November 1918.

39 Clark, entry for 17 November 1918, quoted in *Echoes of the Great War*, 262–3.

40 Clark, entry for 17 November 1918, quoted in *Echoes of the Great War*, 262–3.

41 Cooper, entry for 17 November 1918, quoted in *The Duff Cooper Diaries*, 86.

Chapter 25

1 David Stevenson, *1914–18: The History of the First World War* (Harmondsworth: Penguin, 2004), 504.

2 Duff Cooper, entry for 30 November 1918, quoted in *The Duff Cooper Diaries*, ed. John Julius Norwich (1st ed 2005) (London: Phoenix, 2006), 87.

3 Cooper, entry for 9 December 1918, 89.

4 Cooper, entry for 10 December 1918, quoted in *The Duff Cooper Diaries*, 89.

5 Stevenson, *1914–18*, 515.

6 Andrew Clark, entry for 6 December 1918, quoted in *Echoes of the Great War: The Diary of the Reverend Andrew Clark, 1914–19*, ed. James Munson (Oxford, New York: Oxford University Press, 1985), 266.

7 Ibid.

8 The extension of women's employment opportunities did not materialise as Andrew feared and many women hoped. White-collar employment and the professions did see a rise in female employment after the war,

THE GREAT WAR

but as a rule after 1918 women were bundled unceremoniously out of the labour market. By May 1919 three quarters of the unemployed were women (see Stevenson, 1914–18, 542–3).

9   Clark, entry for 13–30 December 1918, quoted in *Echoes of the Great War*, 267–70.

10 Clark, entry for 13 December 1918, quoted in *Echoes of the Great War*, 267.

11 Diary of Kate Parry Collins, Elizabeth Crawford's Private Collection (cited hereafter as ECPC), entry for 14 December 1918. See also: Elizabeth Crawford, *Campaigning for the Vote: Kate Parry Frye's Suffrage Diary* (London: Francis Boutle Publishers, 2013), 212.

12 Collins (ECPC), entry for 15 December 1918.

13 Collins (ECPC), entry for 1 January 1919.

14 See Crawford, *Campaigning for the Vote*, 17–18.

15 Clark, entry for 4 January 1919, quoted in *Echoes of the Great War*, 271.

16 Clark, entry for 17 January 1919, quoted in *Echoes of the Great War*, 274.

17 Clark, entry for 8 March 1919, quoted in *Echoes of the Great War*, 280.

18 Stevenson, *1914–18*, 552.

19 Collins (ECPC), entries for 14, 15 and 17 April 1919.

20 Stevenson, *1914–18*, 544.

21 Collins (ECPC), entries May–June 1919.

22 Cooper, entry for 2 May 1919, quoted in *The Duff Cooper Diaries*, 98.

23 Cooper, entry for 15 May 1919, quoted in *The Duff Cooper Diaries*, 99.

24 Cooper, entry for 2 June 1919, quoted in *The Duff Cooper Diaries*, 102–3.

25 Stevenson, *1914–18*, 546.

26 Letter from the Imperial War Graves Commission to Emily Chitticks, 11 February 1920, Private papers of W. J. Martin, Documents.2554, The Imperial War Museum (cited hereafter as 2554 IWM).

27 Note written by Emily Chitticks on the letter from the Imperial War Graves Commission, 11 February 1920 (2554 IWM).

28 Stevenson, *1914–18*, 504–30; Martin Gilbert, The First World War (London: Weidenfeld & Nicolson, 1994), 517–18.

29 Collins (ECPC), entries for 29 June 1919.

30 Stevenson, *1914–18*, 597.

31 Clark, entries for 28 and 29 June 1919, quoted in *Echoes of the Great War*, 286–7.

32 Introduction to *Echoes of the Great War* xx.

33 He actually continued to write and filled another two volumes.

34 Stevenson, *1914–18*, 547.

35 Clark, entry for 20 July 1919, quoted in *Echoes of the Great War*, 287.

36 Collins (ECPC), entry for 19 July 1919.

37 Cooper, entry for 19 July 1919, quoted in *The Duff Cooper Diaries*, 106.

Epilogue

1   *Echoes of the Great War: The Diary of the Reverend Andrew Clark, 1914–19*,
     ed. James Munson (Oxford, New York: Oxford University Press), 291–296.
2   Note by Reg's daughter, Pamela Armitage Campbell, 1997, Pamela
     Campbell's Private Collection.
3   See Elizabeth Crawford, *Campaigning for the Vote: Kate Parry Frye's
     Suffrage Diary* (London: Francis Boutle, 2013).
4   'Marriages', *The Times*, 12 July 1919, 15.
5   'Deaths', *The Times*, 4 August 1956, 2.

Picture Credits

Integrated Images

250: courtesy of IWM (Private Papers of W.J. Martin, Documents.2554)
263: © IWM (Q 5440)
275: © IWM (Art.IWM PST 13375)
279: © IWM (Q 15364)
288: © IWM (Q 4694)
291: © IWM (Q 1805)
308: © IWM (Q 35499)
315: © IWM (Q 5935)
328: © IWM (Art.IWM PST 5996)
335: by kind permission of Jenifer Glynn
349: © IWM (Q 56276)
355: Topical Press Agency/Hulton Archive/Getty Images
374: © IWM (Q 46445)
381: © IWM (Q 6731)
391: © IWM (Q 6966)
397: © IWM (Q 9326)
413: © IWM (Q 65858)
415: Topical Press Agency/Hulton Archive/Getty Images
427: © IWM (Art.IWM PST 12194)
433: Popperfoto/Getty Images

First Plate Section

Alan Lloyd, whilst at Cambridge: by kind permission of Vivien Cockroft
Dorothy Lloyd (née Hewetson): by kind permission of Vivien Cockroft
Kate Parry Collins (née Frye): by kind permission of Elizabeth Crawford
Queues outside Whitehall Recruiting Office: © IWM (Q 42033)
Reg Evans in uniform: by kind permission of Pamela Campbell
Letter from Reg to his mother, 9 August 1914: Pamela Campbell/Liddle Collection, Leeds University Special Collections (LIDDLE/WW1/GS/1816)
Wedding of Alan and Dorothy Lloyd: by kind permission of Alan Lloyd
James Butlin in uniform: by kind permission of Robert Butlin
Lady Diana Manners in VAD uniform: Topical Press Agency/Hulton Archive/Getty Images
Australian officer at Gueudecourt: © IWM (E(AUS) 572)
'On her their lives depend' poster: © IWM (Art.IWM PST 0402)
Telegram reporting Alan Lloyd's death: Vivien Cockroft/IWM (Private papers of Lieutenant A. S. Lloyd MC, Documents.20535)
Reg Evans's injury illustrations: Gillies, H. D., Plastic Surgery of the Face, (London: Frowde, 1920)

Second Plate Section

Dorothy and David Lloyd: by kind permission of Alan Lloyd

Will Martin in civilian clothes: courtesy of IWM (Private Papers of W.J. Martin, Documents.2554)

'Fewer hot baths – and save coal!' poster: © IWM (Art.IWM PST 13443)

Letter from John Collins to Kate, 25 December 1916: by kind permission of Elizabeth Crawford

Arthur Roberts in uniform: by kind permission of Morag Miller

British infantry during Battle of Arras: © IWM (Q 5117)

'The Underworld' by Walter Bayes: © IWM (Art.IWM ART 935)

Ruins of the Cloth Hall, Ypres, 29 September 1918: © IWM (Q 11759)

Paddington station, October 1918: A. R. Coster/Hulton Archive/Getty Images

The dawn barrage, battle of the Canal du Nord: © IWM (Q 9333)

Birmingham on Armistice Day, 11 November 1918: © IWM (Q 63690)

Crowds at the base of the Cenotaph, 19 July 1919: © IWM (Q 28762)

Index

Page numbers in *italics* indicate illustrations. Main entries are in **bold**.